AF599016

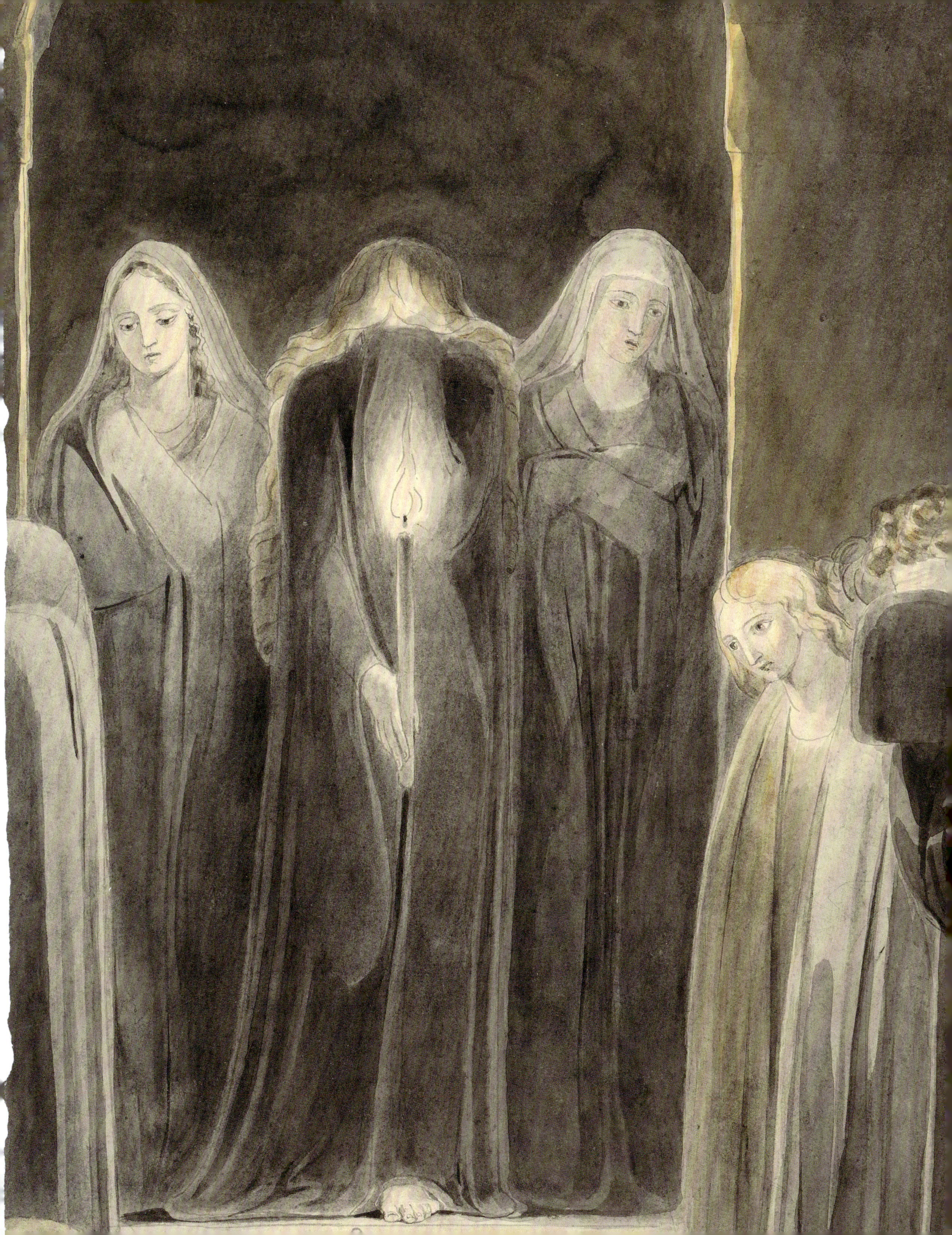

WILLIAM BLAKE

VISIONARY

EDINA ADAM with **JULIAN BROOKS**

and an essay by **MATTHEW HARGRAVES**

THE J. PAUL GETTY MUSEUM ◦ LOS ANGELES

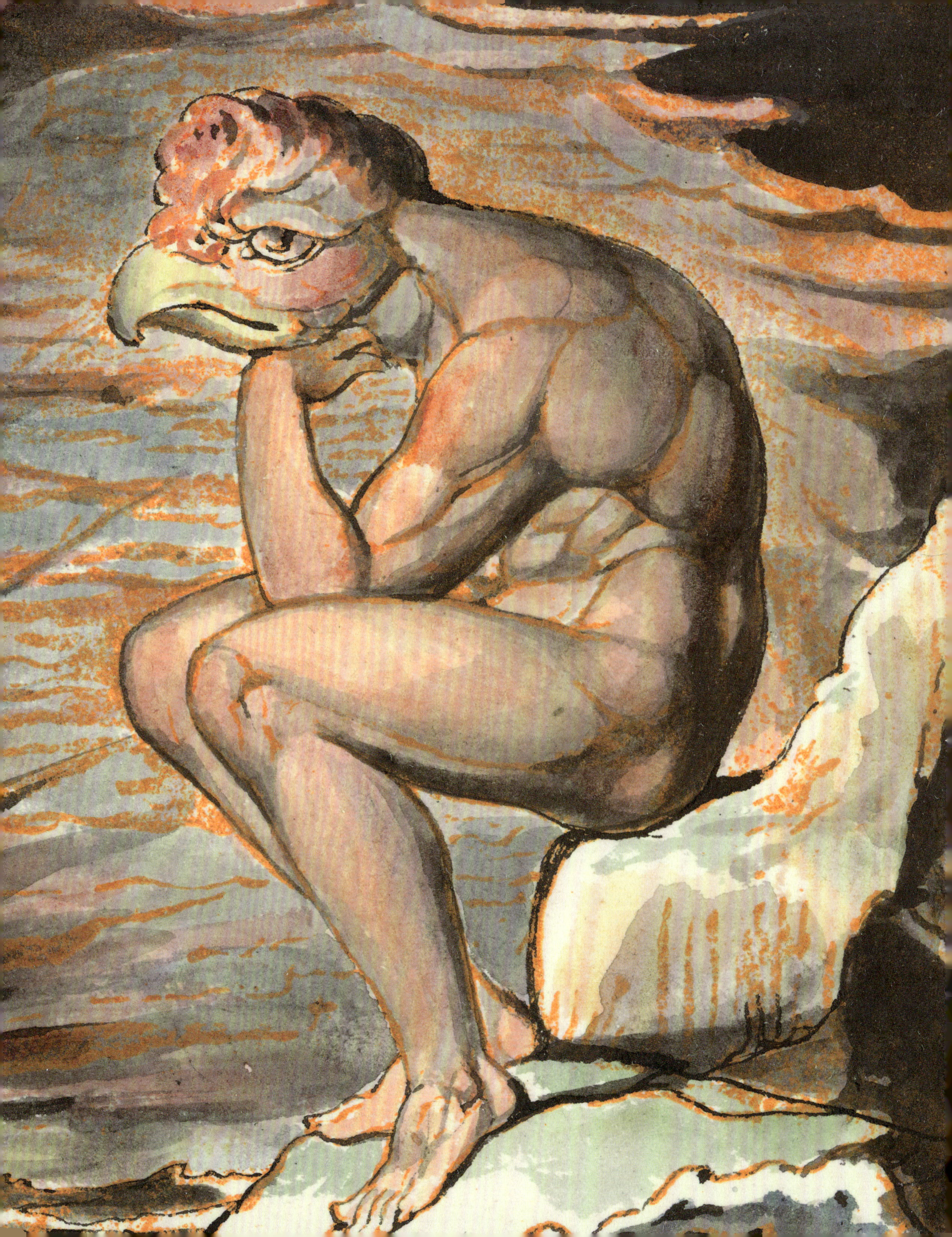

Contents

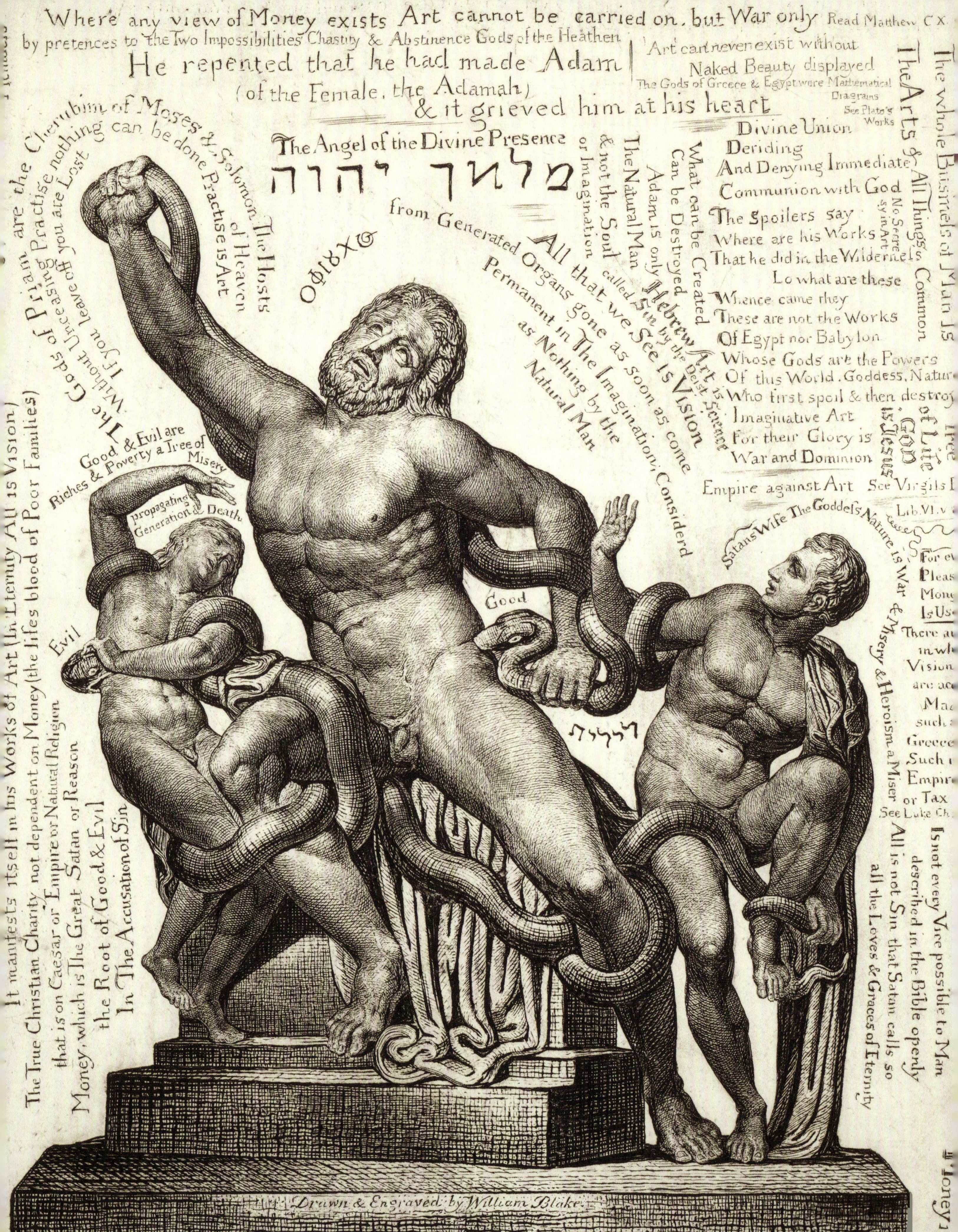

Where any view of Money exists Art cannot be carried on, but War only Read Matthew CX
by pretences to the Two Impossibilities Chastity & Abstinence Gods of the Heathen
He repented that he had made Adam
(of the Female, the Adamah)
& it grieved him at his heart
Art can never exist without Naked Beauty displayed
The Gods of Greece & Egypt were Mathematical Diagrams See Plato's Works
The Angel of the Divine Presence
מלאך יהוה
Οφιουχος
from Generated Organs gone as soon as come Permanent in The Imagination; Considerd as Nothing by the Natural Man
All that we See is Vision
Hebrew Art is called Sin by the Deist Science
Adam is only The Natural Man & not the Soul or Imagination
What can be Created Can be Destroyed
Divine Union Deriding And Denying Immediate Communion with God The Spoilers say Where are his Works That he did in the Wilderness Lo what are these Whence came they These are not the Works Of Egypt nor Babylon Whose Gods are the Powers Of this World. Goddess. Nature Who first spoil & then destroy Imaginative Art For their Glory is War and Dominion
No Secresy in Art
The whole Business of Man Is The Arts & All Things Common
Tree of Life God is Jesus
Empire against Art
Satans Wife The Goddess Nature is War & Misery & Heroism a Miser
The Gods of Priam are the Cherubim of Moses & Solomon The Hosts of Heaven
Without Unceasing Practise nothing can be done Practise is Art
If you leave off you are Lost
Good & Evil are Riches & Poverty a Tree of Misery
propagating Generation & Death
Evil
Good
לילית
It manifests itself in his Works of Art (In Eternity All is Vision)
The True Christian Charity not dependent on Money (the lifes blood of Poor Families)
that is on Caesar or Empire or Natural Religion
Money, which is The Great Satan or Reason
the Root of Good & Evil
In The Accusation of Sin
Is not every Vice possible to Man described in the Bible openly
All is not Sin that Satan calls so
all the Loves & Graces of Eternity
Drawn & Engraved by William Blake.

Foreword

The English artist, poet and religious visionary William Blake was one of the most remarkable cultural figures of the late eighteenth and early nineteenth centuries. During his lifetime and long after, however, recognition of Blake's achievement suffered from his reputation as an "English eccentric," a figure who did not conform to the Academy, and whose work transgressed the traditional boundary between the visual and literary realms. On the other hand, this is precisely the aspect of Blake's legacy that has appealed to artists and writers of the twentieth and twenty-first centuries, for whom "disruption," "counterculture," and "visionary" are badges worn with pride.

Remarkably, it is more than eighty years since a loan exhibition of Blake's work was last mounted on the West Coast of the United States. Organized in 1936 by the book dealer and advisor Alice Millard, in her Frank Lloyd Wright-designed house in Pasadena, that display was drawn largely from the collection of Lessing Rosenwald, which was later acquired by the National Gallery of Art, Washington. Since then the Huntington Library, Art Museum, and Botanical Gardens, too, has presented selections of Blake's work, both from their own holdings and from the collection of Blake scholar and collector Robert N. Essick.

The current exhibition is born of a collaboration with Tate Britain in London. This is the third Getty-Tate partnership in recent years, following projects on *J. M. W. Turner: Painting Set Free* and *London Calling: Bacon, Freud, Kossoff, Andrews, Auerbach, Kitaj*. Tate's unrivaled holdings of William Blake's work form the core of the exhibition, including the famous tempera *The Ghost of a Flea*, very rarely seen outside London, and a mesmerizing selection of large color prints and Dante watercolors. For enabling us to present a more rounded picture of Blake, we are also grateful to colleagues at the Yale Center for British Art, who have generously lent the entirety of *America a Prophecy* as well as ten plates from the finest hand-colored copy of *Jerusalem*, and their *Ancient Days*. The Huntington, too, has kindly supported the project, as has Robert N. Essick, from whose collection comes the intense *Self-Portrait*.

Edina Adam, assistant curator of drawings, and Julian Brooks, senior curator of drawings, are to be thanked and congratulated for bringing the exhibition to fruition and for writing this stimulating catalogue. The essays explore the sources and background of Blake's art as well as the love affair that American collectors have had with his work. I am confident that visitors and readers unfamiliar with the visionary world of William Blake will be astonished and captivated by the weird and wonderful originality of his creative imagination. No doubt this work will also continue to inspire contemporary artists, poets, musicians, and performers of a "romantic" or "visionary" perspective, as it has over the past century.

Timothy Potts
Director, J. Paul Getty Museum

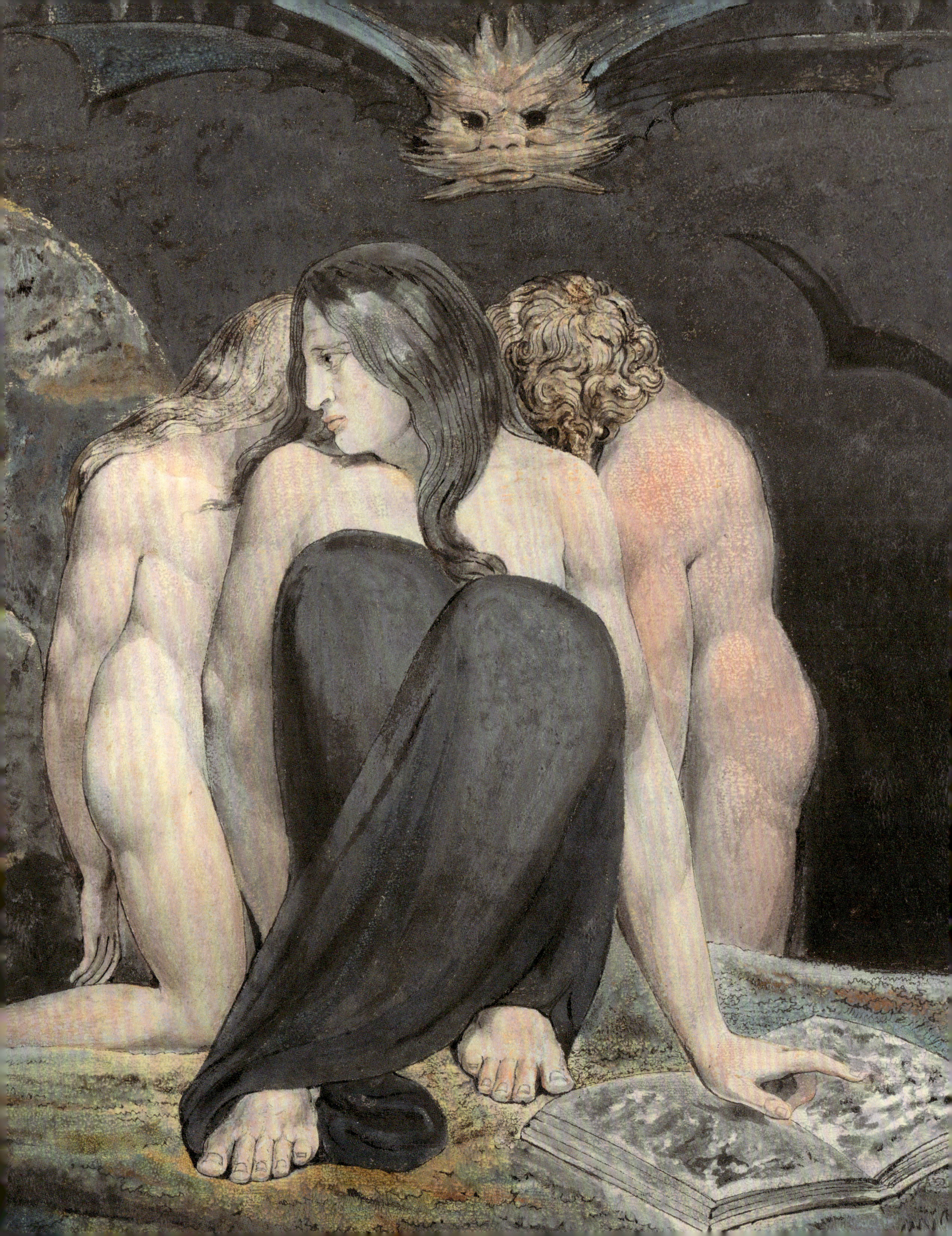

Acknowledgments

We dedicate this volume to the Blake scholar and collector Robert N. Essick. As we engaged with this material, his constant encouragement, expert knowledge, and generous support has been invaluable. He has made the navigation of the deep, dark, and often mysterious waters of William Blake study not just feasible but a great joy and a source of boundless, ongoing fascination. Bob's reassuring presence at the end of a telephone line—essentially a "Blake helpline"—with his consistent warm humor and profound yet unassuming expertise, is something for which we offer heartfelt gratitude.

Born of a collaboration with Tate Britain, this project relied not only on Tate's magnificent Blake collection but also on their staff's fulsome participation, and Martin Myrone, lead curator, British art to 1800; Amy Concannon, curator, British art 1790 to 1850; and James Finch, assistant curator, nineteenth-century British art, have been good colleagues. Kerryn Greenberg, head of international collection exhibitions, and Elizabeth Brooke, exhibitions project manager, steered the project.

We are very grateful to the additional lenders who have enabled us to show Blake at his best through their very generous loans, in particular our colleagues at the Yale Center for British Art: Courtney J. Martin, director; Amy Meyers, former director; and Matthew Hargraves, chief curator, whose essay on Blake and America further provides a valuable contribution to this catalogue. Robert N. Essick has likewise been a generous lender. At Huntington Art Museum we thank Christina Nielsen, Hannah and Russel Kully Director; Melinda McCurdy, associate curator; and Michele Ahern, registrar; at the Huntington Library: Sandra L. Brooke, Avery Director; Stephen Tabor, curator of rare books; and Jenny Werner, registrar. Our colleagues at the Getty Research Institute have likewise shared a number of works: we thank Mary Miller, director; Marit Coyman-Myklebust, registrar; Stephan Welch, associate conservator; and Kevin Young, senior mountmaker.

The exhibition and publication have relied extensively on the enthusiastic support and involvement of a huge team at the Getty Museum: Timothy Potts, director; Richard Rand, associate director, collections; Carolyn Marsden-Smith, associate director, exhibitions; Susan McGinty, senior exhibitions coordinator; John Giurini, assistant director of public affairs and museum communications; Maite Alvarez, associate interpretive content specialist; Sahar Tchaitchian, interpretive content specialist; Sheila M. Flaherty-Jones, editor; Laurel Kishi, head, public programs; Greg Sandoval, senior public programs specialist; Betsy Severance, chief registrar; Sandy Choi Beacom, associate registrar; Cherie Chen, senior registrar; Amanda Ramirez, senior designer; Alexandra Shanley, designer; Sudha Palepu, graduate intern; Michelle Sullivan, associate conservator; David McDaniel, senior mountmaker; Stephen Heer, senior mountmaker; Kevin Marshall, head of preparations; Michael Mitchell, lead preparator; and their team. We thank our colleagues in the Department of Drawings, in particular, Casey Lee, curatorial assistant, and Talitha Schepers, graduate intern.

The team at Getty Publications who produced this beautiful catalogue have been a pleasure to work with: Kara Kirk, publisher; Karen Levine, editor in chief; Ruth Evans Lane, editor; Kurt Hauser, senior graphic designer; Nina Damavandi, rights coordinator; and Suzanne Watson, senior production coordinator. We are also grateful to Mark Crosby, associate professor at Kansas State University, for his insightful comments.

We further extend our thanks to Joseph Viscomi, James G. Kenan Distinguished Professor at the University of North Carolina. This epic journey in Blakeland has been an immersive experience: Edina appreciates the support of her husband, Aaron, and her friends Sameer, Nate, and Jamie. Julian offers gratitude for his wife, Lena, and daughter, Phoebe, and cherishes the memory of his late brother, Andrew.

Edina Adam and Julian Brooks

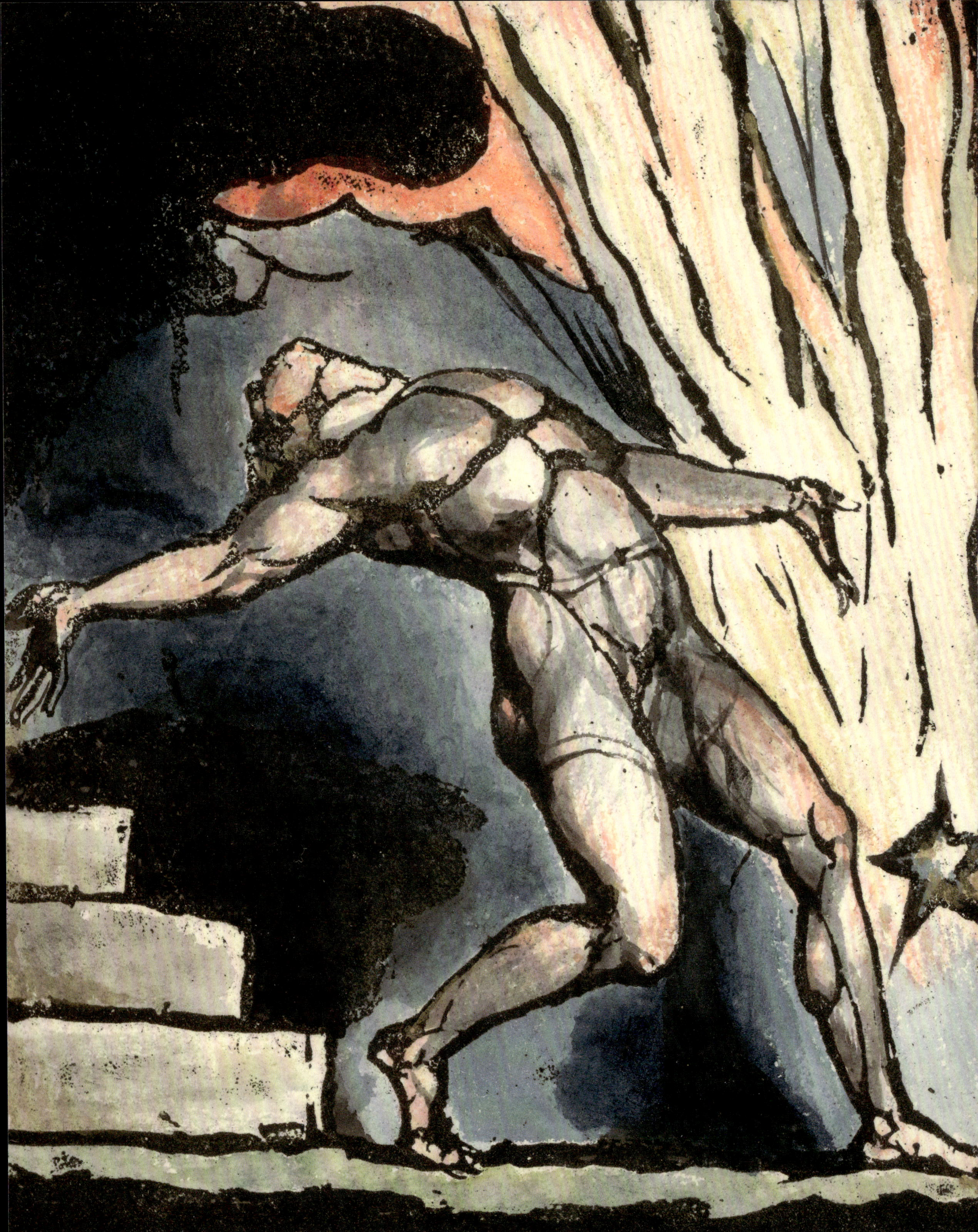

Introduction

EDINA ADAM and JULIAN BROOKS

William Blake (1757–1827) is an immensely complex character, as is evident from the huge body of literature dedicated to his life, poetry, and art.[1] The book you hold in your hands, and the related Getty exhibition, are modest contributions aimed at bringing the artist and his works to a wider US audience. The project is realized in collaboration with Tate in London following the museum's 2019 re-examination of Blake. Generous loans from the collections of the Yale Center for British Art, the Huntington Library, Art Museum, and Botanical Gardens, and the Blake scholar Robert N. Essick have made it possible to represent the breadth of his output while bringing together some of his most iconic works. In this book, the illustrations are arranged by theme to give a taste of the different facets of Blake's practice. These include glimpses of his activity as a professional printmaker (which over his career—only just—sustained him and his wife, Catherine), his role as a painter-illustrator (making works in tempera and watercolor representing scenes from the Bible, English literature, and history), Blake as a poet-painter (using the technique of relief etching to easily and directly combine verse and image on the same copper plate), a look at his artistic contemporaries, and finally his visionary prophetic books, including all eighteen plates of *America a Prophecy.* Two essays anchor the volume. The first studies aspects of Blake's distinctive vision and its origins, while the second is a timely exploration of American collectors' fascination with the artist, which has resulted in the United States being home to some of the richest holdings of his work.

The forceful nature of Blake's personality emerges from his self-portrait (plate 1), made in expressive monochrome washes at the age of about forty-five. The intense, hypnotic expression tallies with a description by a devotee, the artist Samuel Palmer (1805–1881): "His eye was the finest I ever saw: brilliant, but not roving, clear and intent, yet susceptible; it flashed with genius, or melted in tenderness. It could also be terrible. Cunning and falsehood quailed under it, but it was never busy with them. It pierced them, and turned away. Nor was the mouth less expressive; the lips flexible and quivering with feeling."[2]

It was into a restless world that William Blake was born in 1757. His lifetime overlapped with the reign of the inept, illness-compromised King George III (r. 1760–1820), during which Great Britain underwent significant political, economic, and social changes. The country engaged in three major military conflicts that ranged over five continents. The Seven Years' War (1756–63) and the Napoleonic Wars (1803–15) increased British colonial power, while the country's humiliating defeat in the American Revolution (1765–83) resulted in

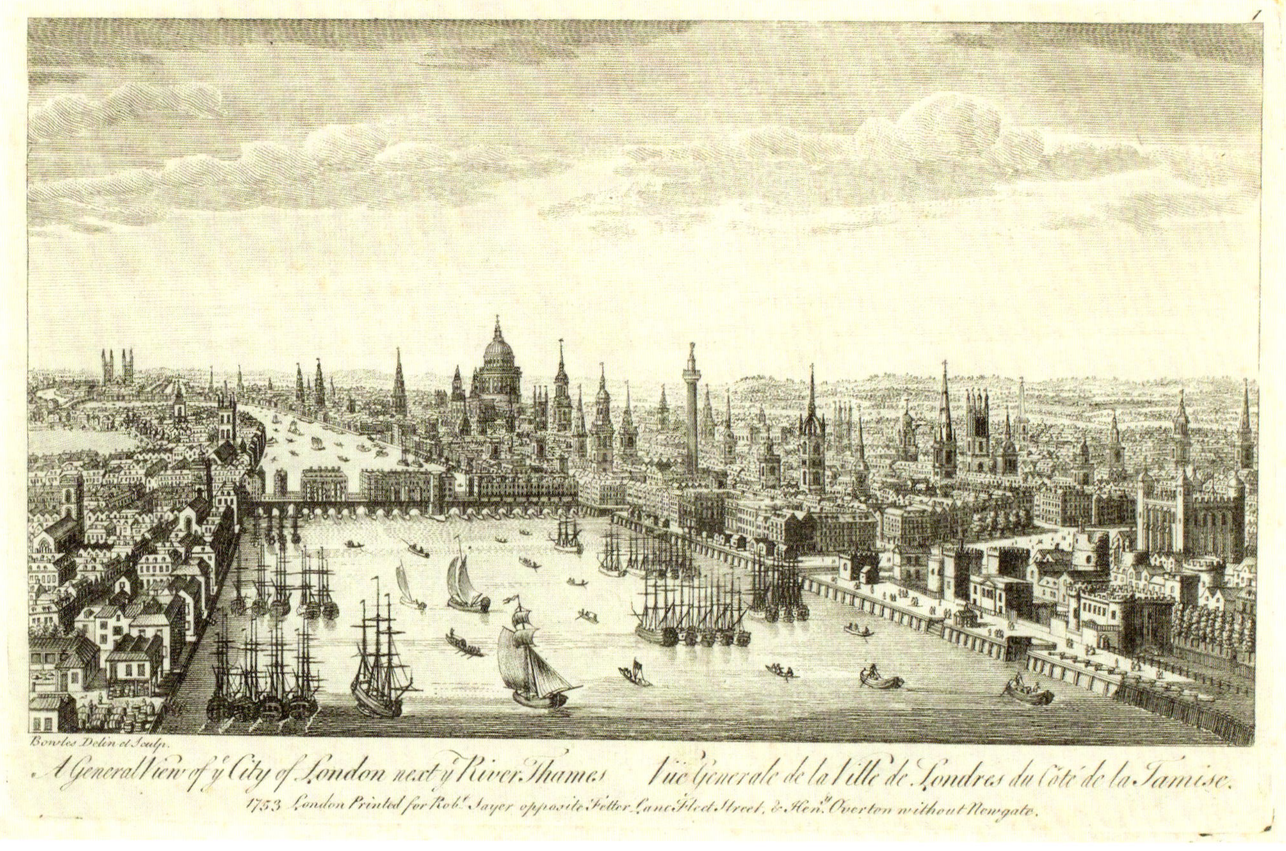

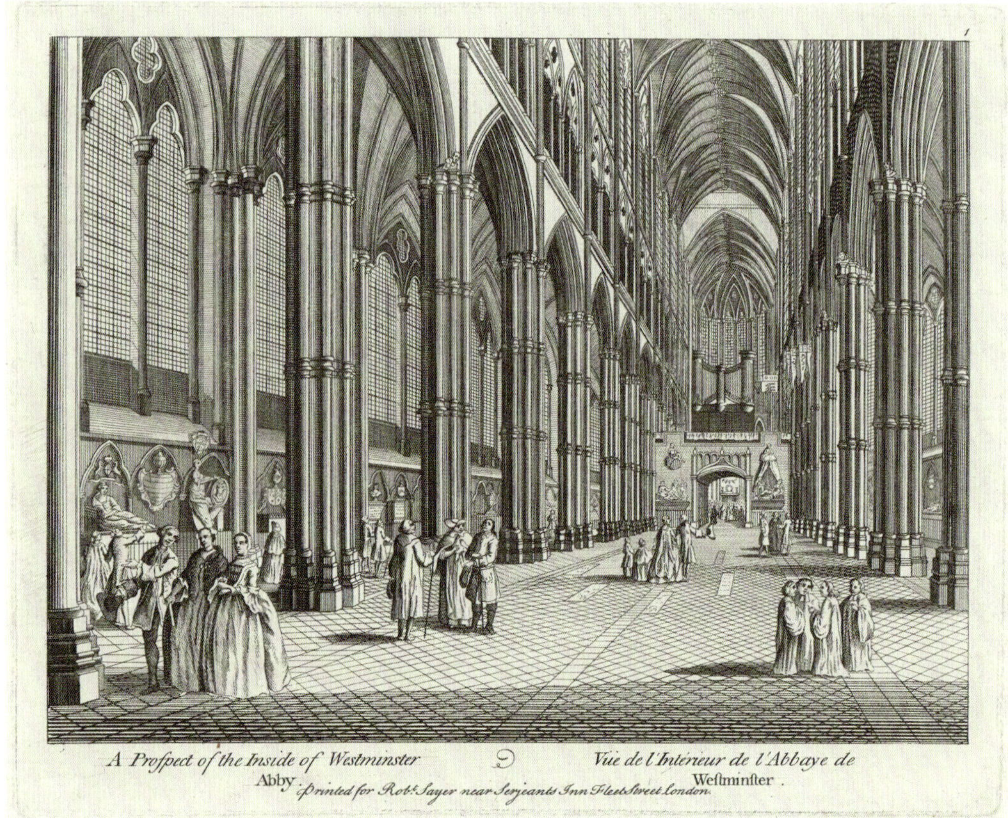

Figure 1 Thomas Bowles II (British, 1695–1767), *A General View of the City of London next the Thames River* in Robert Sayer and Henry Overton III's *Views in London*, 1753. Etching and engraving, 14.9 × 26.4 cm (5 $\frac{13}{16}$ × 10 $\frac{3}{8}$ in.) London, Royal Academy of Arts, 08/4287

Figure 2 Unknown Artist, *A Prospect of the Inside of Westminster Abbey*, 1750–70. Etching and engraving, 20 × 25.4 cm (7 $\frac{7}{8}$ × 10 in.). London, British Museum, 1875,0710.4916

the loss of thirteen North American colonies. Despite the astronomical costs of these wars, Britain as a whole experienced great prosperity thanks to its economic activities in the colonies and increasing industrialization. But the wealth was distributed unequally, and the disparity between the classes grew, resulting in social unrest. Religion continued to remain a source of division. Catholics, Jews, and Dissenters (Protestants who did not conform to the practices of the Anglican Church) had limited rights. Anxiety about the turn of the century crystalized among Nonconformist groups, who interpreted concurrent historical events such as the American and French Revolutions as signs of an impending apocalypse.

Blake bore witness to these changes. He watched the city of London transform in front of his eyes, growing grander and more crowded with each day (fig. 1).[3] He saw the emergence of a professional middle class that, with its accumulated wealth, became a driving force of consumerism and art patronage. Raised in a Dissenter family, he was critical of the political and religious establishment. He was receptive to esoteric religious ideas, even becoming involved with the Swedenborgians, a group dedicated to the doctrines of Emanuel Swedenborg (1688–1772), who believed he communicated directly with spirits. Blake associated with progressive thinkers, echoing their thoughts in his work. He understood history in millenarian terms and, with the creative power of his imagination, transformed violent upheavals and revolutions into universal struggles between great forces in his art.

Even at an early age Blake showed a strong inclination for the arts. When he was only ten years old, he enrolled in the Pars Drawing School run by the brothers Henry and William Pars.[4] Wishing to boost the production of luxury goods in Britain, the school sought to equip young boys with the necessary drawing skills to undertake jobs in trade and manufacturing. Basic instruction was provided to the students, who increased their dexterity and developed a graphic vocabulary by copying two- and three-dimensional models. Blake was an eager pupil with supportive parents. According to Benjamin Heath Malkin (1769–1842), author of the earliest partial biography of the artist, Blake's father purchased plaster casts for him and gave him an allowance to build his own collection of old master prints so that the boy could practice in his free time.[5]

At age fourteen, Blake began an apprenticeship with the engraver James Basire (1730–1804).[6] Specializing in antiquarian and scientific prints, Basire worked for both the Society of Antiquaries and Royal Society. In the course of a customary seven-year-long apprenticeship, Blake lived and worked with the master engraver. He learned to prepare printing materials and tools, mastered the two intaglio techniques—engraving and etching—and became a skilled printer. Through Basire, Blake became involved in Richard Gough's ambitious project *Sepulchral Monuments in Great Britain*.[7] He was tasked with making detailed drawings of the Gothic royal tombs in Westminster Abbey (fig. 2), which had a lasting impact on his artistic output.[8] According to his friend the artist Frederick Tatham (1805–1878),

> *Blake pursued his Task & his absorption gathered to itself impressions that were never forgotten. His Imagination ever after wandered as in a cloister, or clothing itself in the dark Stole of mural sanctity, it dwelt amidst the Druid terrors. His mind being simplified by Gothic Forms, & his Fancy imbued with the livid twilight of past days, it chose for its quaint Company, such sublime but antiquated associates as the Fearful Merlin, Arthur & the Knights of his Round Table, the just and wise Alfred, King John, and every other hero of English History & Romance. These Indigenous Abstractions for many of the following years occupied his hand, and ever after tinctured his thoughts &*

perceptions. The background of his pictures, nearly always exhibited Druidical Stones & other Symbols of English Antiquity. Albion was the Hero of his Pictures, Prints & Poems.[9]

While the apprenticeship with Basire prepared Blake to embark on a career in printmaking and printing, the young man aspired to become a history painter and leave the artisan world of London behind. For that reason, he enrolled in the Royal Academy of Arts in 1779.[10] Established in 1768 under the auspices of George III, the Academy did not provide a comprehensive artistic education but expected the students to arrive with practical skills acquired within the context of apprenticeships.[11] It did, however, offer drawing classes from plaster figures and live models in the evenings and held lectures intended to shape the students' taste and understanding of the history of art (fig. 3).

Although Blake would later direct disparaging remarks at the Royal Academy and its first president, Sir Joshua Reynolds (1723–1792), as a young artist he strived to become part of the establishment. He partook in academic exercises and studied the Academy's collection of works on paper. Between 1780 and 1785, he exhibited several watercolors at the institution's annual exhibitions. These works were of historical subjects, in accordance with the Academy's principles, which valued narrative art the highest among the genres for its ability to convey moral lessons to viewers.

Blake's affiliation with the Academy also opened doors to him that otherwise likely would have remained shut given his humble background. He made acquaintance with some of the leading figures of the English art world and a group of prosperous middle-class individuals, including Reverend Anthony Stephen Mathew and his wife, Harriet. The couple's literary gatherings provided Blake with a platform to present himself as a poet for the first time in his life. They also helped to finance the publication of Blake's first collection of poems, *Poetical Sketches*, in 1783. Written between the ages of twelve and twenty according to the accompanying advertisement, these compositions anticipate Blake's mature literary works with their indebtedness to the Bible and earlier English authors, including William Shakespeare, Edmund Spenser, John Milton, and Thomas Chatterton.[12]

Already during his student years at the Academy, Blake supported himself as a printmaker. By the 1790s, he became the favored reproductive engraver to artists like Henry Fuseli (1741–1825) and Thomas Stothard (1755–1834) and received regular employment from publishers as an engraver and a designer-engraver. Among the publishers with whom Blake worked closely was Joseph Johnson (1738–1809), who surrounded himself with radical thinkers: abolitionists, feminists, and religious and political dissenters.[13] Johnson published the groundbreaking text *A Vindication of the Rights of Woman* (1792), by Mary Wollstonecraft (the mother of Mary Shelley, author of the novel *Frankenstein*), which argued that women should be allowed the same education received by men, along with John Gabriel Stedman's autobiographical *Narrative of a Five Years' Expedition against the Revolted Negroes of Surinam* (1796), for which Blake created fourteen engravings based on the author's designs. Stedman's eyewitness account helped the abolitionist cause in Britain by confronting readers with the reality of slavery, despite being heavily edited to remove passages considered to be too scandalous and graphic.[14]

Striving for independence from publishers and possibly financial betterment, in 1784, Blake attempted to establish a print publishing company with James Parker (1750–1805), another one of Basire's former apprentices.[15] In London's highly competitive environment, the enterprise failed to achieve any real commercial success, and after publishing only two decorative plates after Stothard, the partnership came to an end. However, the partnership

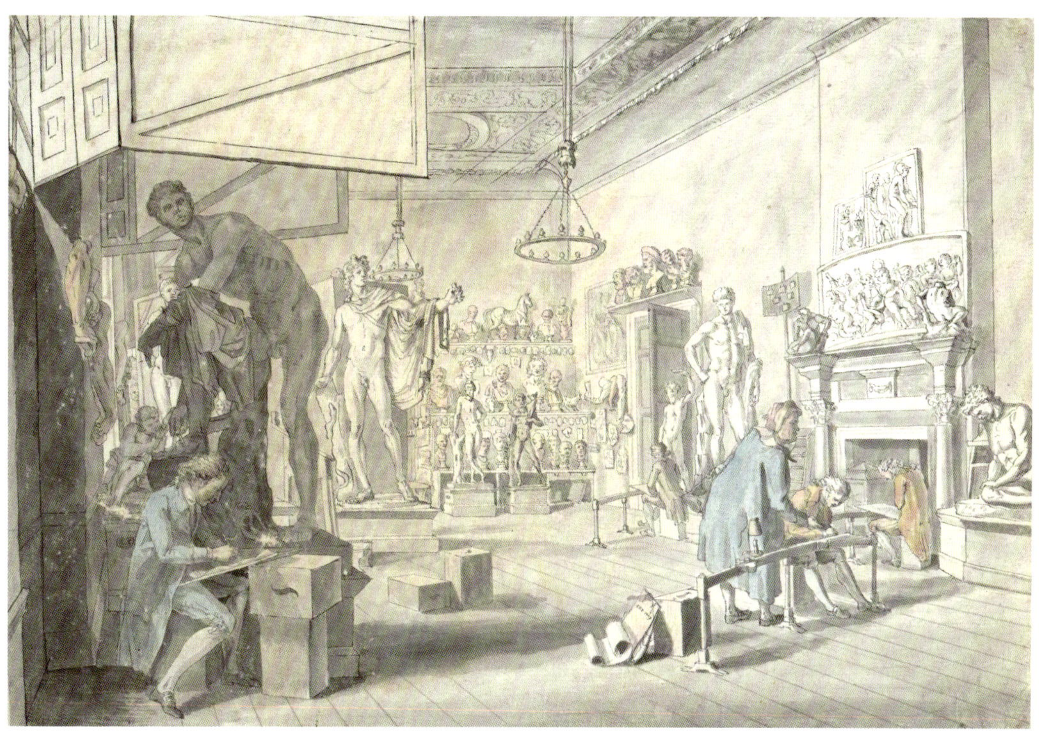

Figure 3 Edward Francis Burney (British, 1760–1848), *The Antique School at Old Somerset House*, 1779. Pen and ink with watercolor, 33.5 × 48.5 cm (13 3/16 × 19 1/8 in.). London, Royal Academy of Arts, 03/7485

yielded one important result for Blake: while in business with Parker, Blake purchased a rolling press. Having a press allowed Blake not only to print his plates and to self-publish them but also permitted endless experimentation in printmaking and printing.

Blake's wife, Catherine (plate 57), assumed the role of assistant and collaborator in his print-making activity, also coloring some of the prints, and in 1790 the couple moved to Lambeth, south of the Thames.[16] Here, Blake composed some of his most innovative works, including *America a Prophecy* (1793), *Europe a Prophecy* (1794), and *The Song of Los* (1795). Using highly allegorical language, these illuminated books, known as the "prophetic books," retold the American and French Revolutions as part of a universal mythology defined by Blake. He represented the historical events as struggles in which archetypal characters pursued liberation from political and spiritual imprisonment.

Throughout his life, Blake lived in relative obscurity. His art was appreciated by a small group of mostly wealthy and educated middle-class individuals. These were the primary consumers of his painted and printed original compositions. Among the most important of Blake's patrons was the army clerk Thomas Butts (1757–1845). Between about 1799 and 1809, Butts commissioned temperas and watercolors of biblical subjects, filling his Soho residence with pictures by Blake.[17] Butts also owned eight of the twelve large color prints and several illuminated books, including a copy of *Songs of Innocence and of Experience* (Copy E, now in the collection of the Huntington Library), and in order to provide the artist with a modest yet steady income, he employed Blake as his son's engraving instructor in 1806.[18] But Butts did not only give financial support to Blake. According to their correspondence, the two became friends, the patron often lending a sympathetic ear to the artist.

The popular poet William Hayley (1745–1820) was another influential patron in Blake's life. Hayley invited Blake and his wife to stay with him in the seaside village of Felpham in Sussex, and the couple moved there in 1800 (fig. 4). At first, the artist welcomed the prospect of steady employment and expressed enthusiasm about the change of scenery, writing to Butts, "the sweet air & the voices of winds trees & birds & the odours of the happy ground makes it a dwelling for immortals.

Work will go on here with God speed."[19] But within a few years the relationship between the two soured. Blake found Hayley's behavior overbearing and controlling and thought that the assigned projects, which comprised decorative paintings for the patron's library and engravings for his publications, were menial—mere distractions from his artistic endeavors. By the summer of 1803, Blake was determined to sever ties with Hayley, "to be no longer Pesterd with his Genteel Ignorance & Polite Disapprobation."[20] But the situation was aggravated one day in August when Blake quarreled with and forcibly evicted a soldier he found in his garden. The soldier accused him of assault and sedition: he claimed Blake had damned the King, which carried severe penalties. Fearing imprisonment, the artist had to rely on his patron one more time to secure legal counsel and was finally acquitted the following January. Blake worked through the trauma caused by the suffocating relationship with Hayley and his trial by creating *Milton a Poem*, dated 1804 but released (in only three copies) seven years later. In this illustrated epic, he expands the universe of his prophetic books into a deeply personal dimension. He recounts the journey of artistic and spiritual liberation from Satan, who with his "incomparable mildness," "primitive tyrannical attempts," and "soft endearing love" is a poetic portrait of Hayley.[21]

Late in his life, around 1818, Blake secured the patronage of the successful young painter-printmaker John Linnell (1792–1882), which greatly alleviated his consistently dire financial situation and brought him a sympathetic friend. In 1823, Linnell commissioned Blake to create a set of twenty-two engravings, *Illustrations of the Book of Job* (published in 1826), and in 1824, to design and engrave illustrations for Dante Alighieri's *Divine Comedy*.[22] The choice of technique in the case of both projects was prompted by Linnell's and Blake's admiration for old master printmakers like Albrecht Dürer (1471–1528), Marcantonio Raimondi (ca. 1470/1482–1527/1534), and the lesser-known Giulio Bonasone (ca. 1510–after 1576).[23] Thanks to Linnell, Blake also came in contact with a group of young artists, including Samuel Palmer and Frederick Tatham, who referred to themselves as "the Ancients" and came to consider the aging artist their spiritual leader. Blake was still working on the series of illustrations for *The Divine Comedy*—of which

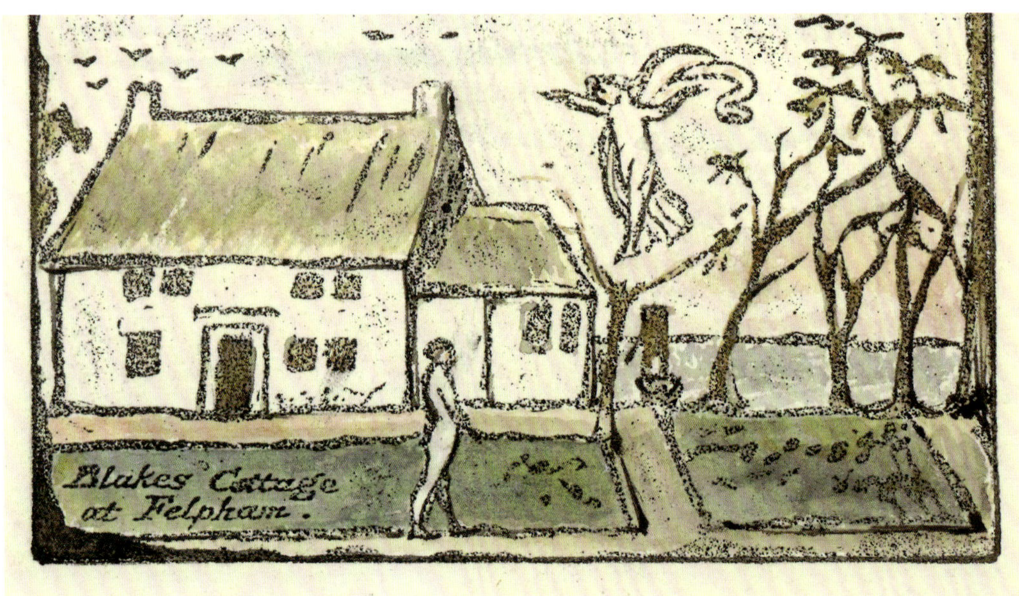

Figure 4 William Blake (British, 1757–1827), *Milton a Poem*, plate 36, detail showing Blake's cottage in Felpham, 1804–11. Relief etching, hand colored, 14.1 × 10.2 cm (5⁹⁄₁₆ × 4 in.). London, British Museum, 1859,0625.36

he produced 102 watercolors—when he died on August 12, 1827. His final years had seen recurring bouts of "that sickness to which there is no name," the symptoms of which, as described in Blake's letters, seem to accord with biliary cirrhosis, likely resulting from persistent exposure to the acid fumes produced by the etching process.[24]

Aside from the Ancients' veneration, Blake was largely unappreciated in his lifetime. The temperas and watercolors that he showed at six of the Academy's exhibitions attracted little attention. His 1809 solo exhibition held in an apartment above his brother's shop prompted only one review, which dismissed the display as a "farrago of nonsense, unintelligibleness, and egregious vanity, the wild effusions of a distempered brain."[25] Though Blake supported himself and his wife throughout their lives by his commercial illustrations and commissions from a few patrons, he rarely attempted to respond to the demands of the marketplace. For him there could be no compromise.

To enter William Blake's world is to journey into a deftly crafted, frequently morphing universe, replete with rich symbols, obscure mythologies, shape-shifting theatrical characters with exaggerated and wild gestures, and a combination of reality and fantasy unusual for its time. For the modern reader and viewer, extraordinary revelations abound—not always those intended by the artist. It becomes easy to see why Blake's contemporaries and even kindred spirits were baffled. But travelers in Blake's world are nourished by his superlative imagination. They are offered fantastical visions in the form of large jewel-like watercolors with the luminosity of stained glass and colored prints—often with added watercolor—with complex and beautiful effects that astound and puzzle with their technique, while defying imitation.

1 All titles and quotations by William Blake follow his spelling and punctuation.
2 Alexander Gilchrist, *Life of William Blake, "Pictor Ignotus"* (London and Cambridge: Macmillan and Co., 1863), 301–2.
3 Blake made the following observation in a letter to George Cumberland on July 2, 1800: "It is very Extraordinary that London in so few years from a City of meer Necessaries or at l[e]ast a commerce of the lowest order of luxuries should have become a City of Elegance in some degree & that its once stupid inhabitants should enter into an Emulation of Grecian manners." David F. Erdman, ed., *The Complete Poetry and Prose of William Blake*, rev. ed. (Berkeley and Los Angeles: University of California Press, 1982), 706.
4 Benjamin Heath Malkin, *A Father's Memoirs of His Child* (London: Longman, Hurst, Rees and Orme, 1806), xx–xxi.
5 Malkin 1806, xix.
6 Malkin 1806, xix.
7 Malkin 1806, xix–xxi.
8 See Edina Adam's essay in this volume.
9 Frederick Tatham, "MS 'Life of Blake' c. 1832" in Gerald Eades Bentley Jr., *Blake Records: Documents (1714–1841) Concerning the Life of William Blake (1757–1827) and His Family*, 2nd ed. (New Haven and London: Published for the Paul Mellon Centre for Studies in British Art by Yale University Press, 2004), 667.
10 Bentley 2004, 18–19.
11 James Fenton, *School of Genius: A History of the Royal Academy* (London: Royal Academy of Arts, 2006), 89–101.
12 Geoffrey Keynes, "Poetical Sketches," in *Blake Studies: Notes on His Life and Works in Seventeen Chapters* (London: Rupert Hart-Davis, 1949), 23–39; and Margaret Ruth Lowery, *Windows of the Morning: A Critical Study of William Blake's "Poetical Sketches," 1783* (New Haven: Yale University Press, 1940).
13 Robert N. Essick, *William Blake's Commercial Book Illustrations: A Catalogue and Study of the Plates Engraved by Blake after Designs by Other Artists* (Oxford: Oxford University Press, 1991), 7; Gerald P. Tyson, *Joseph Johnson: A Liberal Publisher* (Iowa City: University of Iowa Press, 1979).
14 Helen Thomas, *Romanticism and Slave Narratives: Transatlantic Testimonies* (Cambridge: Cambridge University Press, 2000), 125–33.
15 Bentley 2004, 33–34.
16 Bentley 2004, 744.
17 Martin Butlin, *The Paintings and Drawings of William Blake* (New Haven and London: Published for the Paul Mellon Centre for Studies in British Art by Yale University Press, 1981), vol. 1, 316–71.
18 Bentley 2004, 222–23.
19 Erdman 1982, 711.
20 Erdman 1982, 730.
21 Erdman 1982, 100.
22 Dante's poem became fully accessible in the English-speaking world following Henry Francis Cary's and Henry Boyd's translations in 1797–1812 and 1802, respectively. David Lummus, "Dante's Inferno: Critical Reception and Influence," in *The Inferno*, ed. Patrick Hunt (Pasadena: Salem Press, 2012), 68.
23 Gilchrist 1863, 289.
24 Erdman 1982, 781.
25 Bentley 2004, 286.

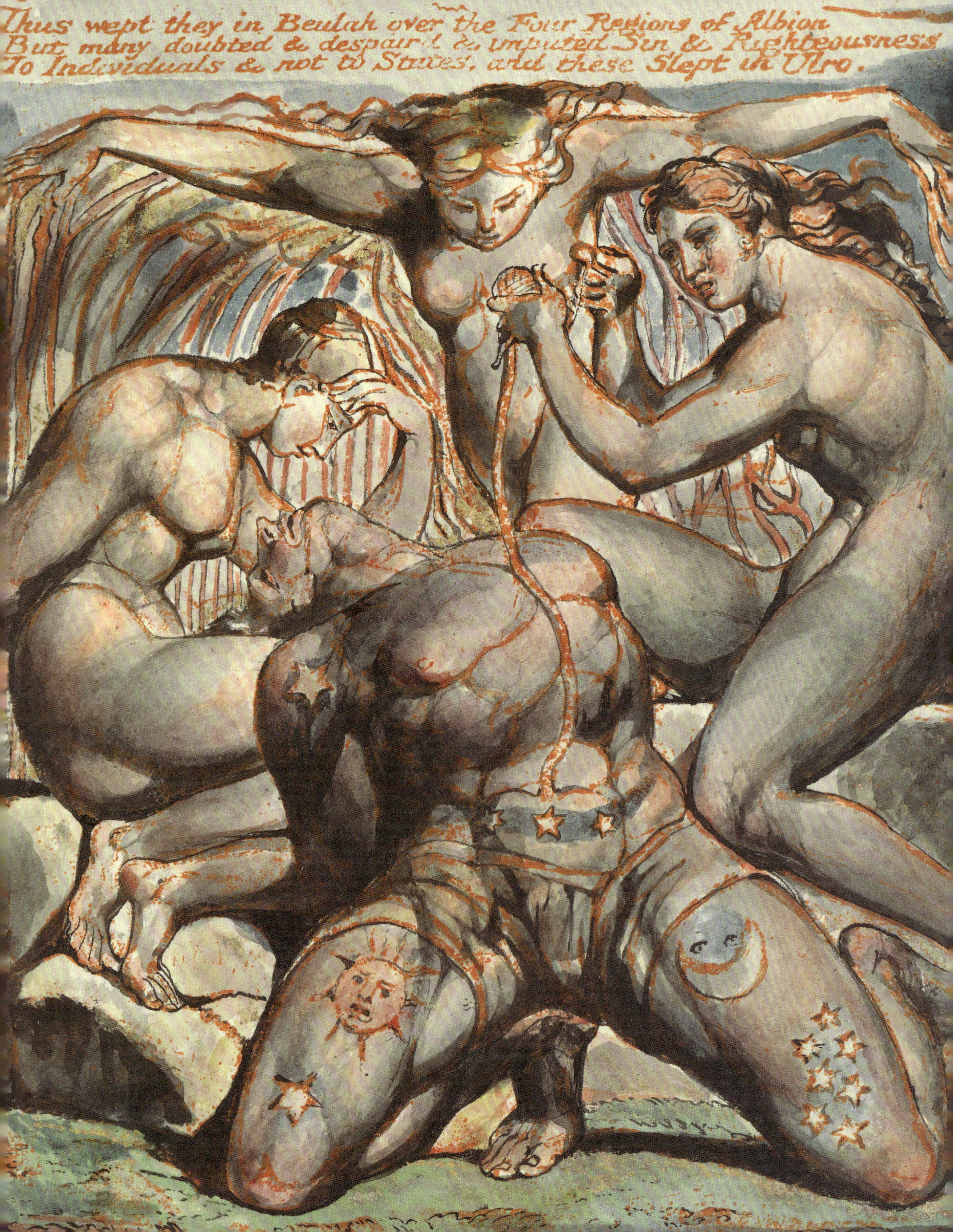
Thus wept they in Beulah over the Four Regions of Albion
But many doubted & despaird & imputed Sin & Righteousness
To Individuals & not to States, and these Slept in Ulro.

William Blake's "Bounding Outline": On the Sources of Artistic Originality

EDINA ADAM

The images of the British artist William Blake often perplex viewers with their enigmatic subjects and idiosyncratic forms. Flipping through this catalogue, readers encounter a bearded man in a state of terror, who crawls on all fours in a dark, tight space, perhaps a cave. His carefully delineated, sinewy body is partially covered in long hair; his nails are overgrown and sharp like those of an animal (plate 46). On a different page, one sees a kneeling muscular young man, surrounded by three weeping nude women. The figures' bodies are circumscribed in orange and black, colored in unnatural hues. One woman pulls the man's intestine from his body and winds it into a ball, causing him extreme agony (plate 105). Blake's writing is equally difficult: his language is highly allegorical, rooted in sixteenth- and seventeenth-century English literature and the traditions of political and religious dissent. Instead of explicating the accompanying imagery, the texts often further confuse the viewer. Above the group of women torturing the youth, dense script printed in orange reads in part: "Thus wept they in Beulah over the Four Regions of Albion / But many doubted & despaird & imputed Sin & Righteousness / To Individuals & not to States, and these Slept in Ulro."

Our response to Blake's art is further complicated by the two centuries that separate us from his world: the artisan and bourgeois classes of London; the brief optimism following the Seven Years' War (1756–63); Protestant fundamentalism; religious tension that escalated in the Gordon Riots (1780); and the shock and anxieties brought forth by the American (1765–83) and French (1789–99) Revolutions. Blake's images and poems were already challenging to his contemporaries. They described him as a madman and a drunkard, for they considered his art incomprehensible.[1] He was, in fact, a man of boundless imagination, coupled with a strong belief that as an artist he had to remain true to his aesthetic principles despite contemporary taste and conventions.[2]

Characterizing Blake's art, his first biographer, Alexander Gilchrist, claimed that the artist's originality was partially due to his emulation of past models, "a return to those of earlier and simpler times."[3] This was not merely Gilchrist's opinion, but was repeatedly voiced by Blake. Already in 1799, in a letter to a potential patron, the Reverend John Trusler, Blake emphatically stated his intention to draw on older models: "I find more & more that my Style of Designing is a Species by itself. & in this which I send you have been compelld by my Genius or Angel to follow where he led if I were to act otherwise it would not fulfill the purpose for which alone I live. which is in conjunction with such men as my friend Cumberland to renew the lost Art of the Greeks."[4]

While in a pamphlet advertising his "fresco paintings" displayed at his 1809 solo exhibition, Blake boldly claimed that "The Art has been lost: I have recovered it."[5] But why did the arts have to be revived? What prompted Blake to undertake this mission? And how did this manifest in his artistic production?

Blake believed that, following a thriving period, art began to decline in the sixteenth century.[10] He thought that the representatives of the Venetian School, notably Titian (1488–1576), and its followers, including Peter Paul Rubens (1577–1640), Anthony van Dyck (1599–1641), and Rembrandt van Rijn (1606–1669), corrupted the arts. He claimed that these masters failed to properly circumscribe forms and consequently erred in coloring. To mask their weaknesses, they employed chiaroscuro, further obfuscating their compositions. The lack of clarity in their paintings was unforgivable for Blake, who considered the visual arts a form of language. For Blake, "broken lines, broken masses, and broken colours"[11] meant the loss of indexicality and consequently chaos:

> *How do we distinguish the oak from the beech, the horse from the ox, but by the bounding outline? How do we distinguish one face or countenance from another, but by the bounding line and its infinite inflexions and movements? What is it that distinguishes honesty from knavery, but the hard and wirey line of rectitude and certainty in the actions and intentions. Leave out this line and you leave out life itself. All is chaos again, and the l[i]ne of the almighty must be drawn out upon before man or beast can exist.*[12]

Blake's idea of the deterioration of the arts was firmly rooted in a cyclical view of the history of art, according to which, art is a living organism that, following a period of growth, reaches its apex, then declines and ultimately regenerates. This paradigm originates from the Tuscan painter-biographer Giorgio Vasari (1511–1574), who characterizes Italian art from the thirteenth to the sixteenth century as a rebirth of classical antiquity following the "dark" Middle Ages in his seminal *Lives of the Most Excellent Painters, Sculptors, and Architects* (1550/68).[6] Given that the *Lives* was not available in English until 1850–52 and that Blake acquired a rudimentary knowledge of Italian only in the 1820s, it is likely that he indirectly learned about Vasari's framework.[7] His source might have been the erudite Swiss artist Henry Fuseli (1741–1825), whom he befriended around 1787.[8] As a professor of painting, Fuseli articulated similar ideas in a series of lectures delivered at the Royal Academy of Arts in 1801. The second lecture, titled "Art of the Moderns," is peppered with frequent references to Vasari's *Lives*.[9] Fuseli employs the Tuscan artist's theory to describe an era of restoration followed by a period of decline constituted mostly by derivative imitators.

Despite the shared framework, there are two major differences between Fuseli's and Blake's views on the history of art: firstly, their assessments of the Venetian School, and secondly, their opinions of their fellow British artists. Echoing popular opinion, Fuseli saw great merit in the art of Titian and his followers, in particular their use of sensuous coloring, and considered the painter a leading figure of the era of restoration.[13] Blake vehemently rejected the Venetian School and its offshoots. Furthermore, Fuseli believed that he and his contemporaries were witnessing a revival of British arts that was set in motion by the establishment of the Royal Academy in 1768 and by its president, the leading portraitist Sir Joshua Reynolds. Blake's general outlook grew increasingly pessimistic.[14] Fueled by frustration caused by his lack of critical and commercial success, Blake described the contemporary milieu in disapproving terms: "The Enquiry in England is not whether a Man has Talents & Genius But whether he is Passive & Polite & a Virtuous Ass: & obedient to Noblemans

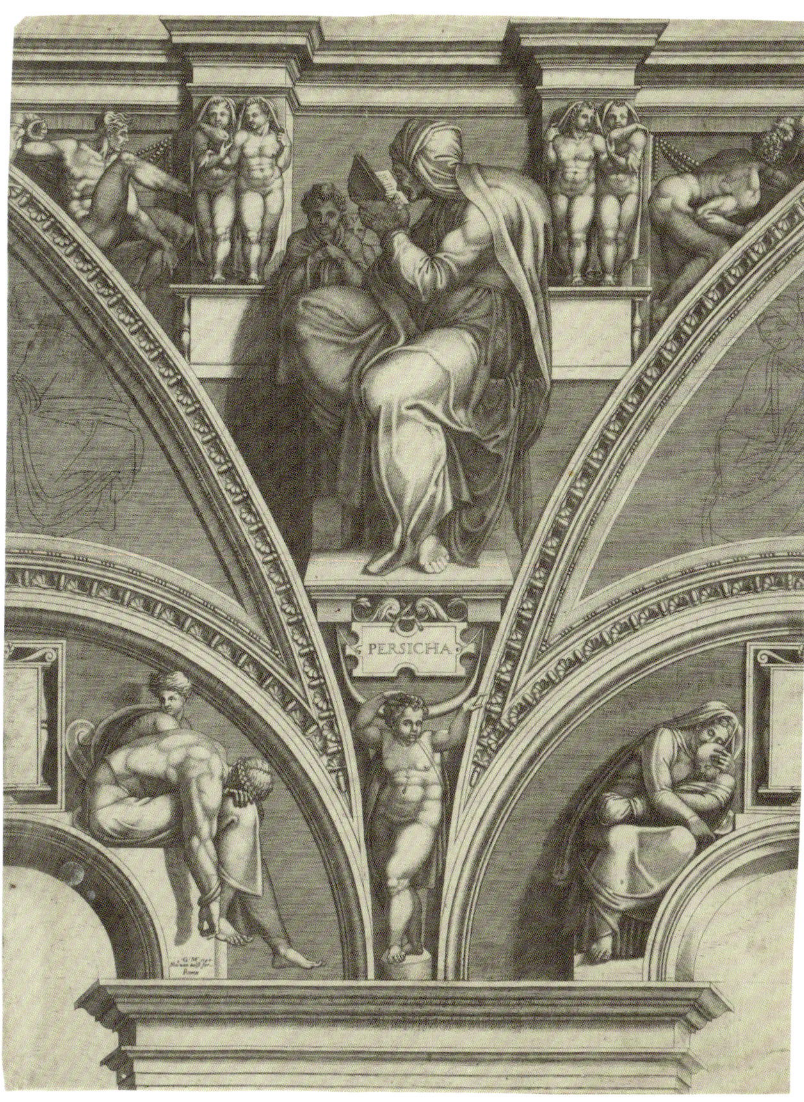

Figure 5 Giorgio Ghisi (Italian, 1520–1582) after Michelangelo (Italian, 1475–1564), Section of the Sistine Ceiling, early 1570s. Engraving, 55.5 × 43 cm (21⅞ × 16¹⁵⁄₁₆ in.). Amsterdam, Rijksmuseum, RP-P-OB-36.280

opinions in Art and Science. If he is; he is a Good Man: If not he must be starved."[15] Blake believed that in this stagnant and backward environment, it was his duty to restore the arts to a state of perfection, which he admired primarily in the clearly delineated works of certain Renaissance masters, notably Albrecht Dürer, Raphael (1483–1520), and Michelangelo Buonarroti (1475–1564), as well as in the art of the late Middle Ages.[16]

If Vasari and Fuseli provided Blake with a framework, it was the artwork he encountered that cemented his views. Unlike many of his contemporaries, Blake never embarked on a journey across the Continent; he never visited Italy's renowned sites or saw its countless Renaissance treasures. In England, prior to the establishment of the National Gallery in London (1824), he could only consult the works of old masters in private collections and public institutions. Guidebooks, like the one published by Thomas Martyn in 1766, would have provided him with information on which palace, governmental building, or hospital to visit in London in search of masterpieces.[17] Despite these riches scattered across the city,

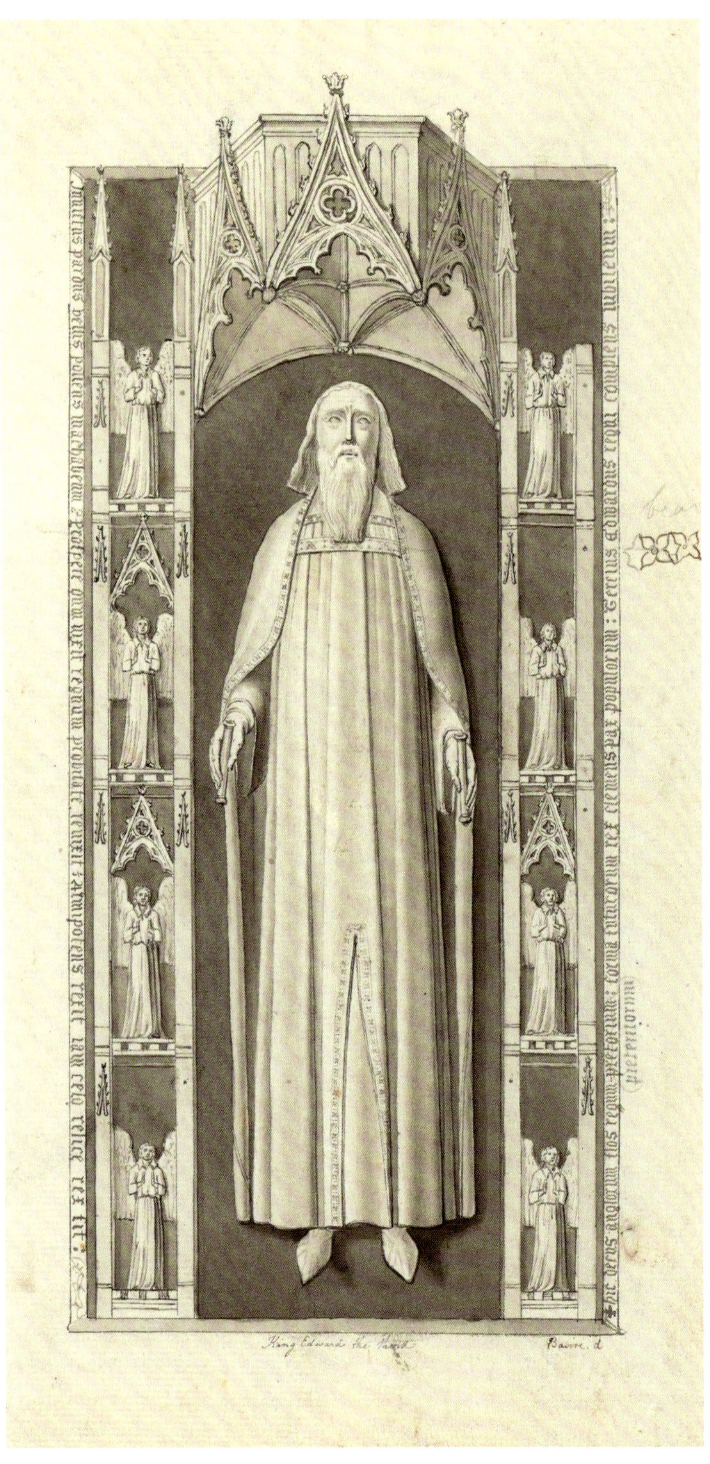

Figure 6 William Blake (British, 1757–1827), *Edward III, His Effigy Seen from Above*, ca. 1774. Pen and sepia wash, 26.6 × 12 cm (10½ × 4¾ in.). Oxford, Bodleian Library, Gough Maps 225

Blake's familiarity with the old masters was primarily based on prints. As a student at the Royal Academy, he studied the institution's considerable didactic collection, delighting in early engravings.[18] Prints were also abundant on the London art market in the late eighteenth and early nineteenth centuries.[19] Indeed, Blake immersed himself in the world of auction houses and print shops already as a child, even earning himself the nickname "little connoisseur" from auctioneer Abraham Langford.[20]

Comparison of these prints with the original works suggests some may have provided Blake with a skewed understanding of Renaissance masters, especially Michelangelo. While Dürer was an accomplished printmaker himself, and Raphael closely collaborated with the engraver Marcantonio Raimondi, Michelangelo had no control over the reproductive prints made after his works, which often resulted in inexact reproductions.[21] Some contained misinterpreted motifs, but more frequently they depicted the musculature in a schematic manner. Unlike in Michelangelo's anatomically accurate representations, the transition between muscles became more pronounced, resulting in a pattern-like effect (fig. 5). Furthermore, the prints were unable to convey certain characteristics of Michelangelo's art, such as his antinaturalistic coloring (*cangiantismo*) that switched hues for highlights and shades.

While Blake's understanding of Renaissance masters was mediated mainly through prints, his experience with Gothic art was firsthand. As an apprentice to the engraver James Basire, the young Blake spent a period of five years from 1774 to 1779 in Westminster Abbey creating drawings of Gothic tombs that were to be engraved for Richard Gough's publication *Sepulchral Monuments in Great Britain* (plate 2) and Joseph Ayloffe's *Some Ancient Monuments in Westminster Abbey*.[22] In addition to these funerary monuments, he likely saw paintings, especially following the French Revolution and the dissolution of religious orders when

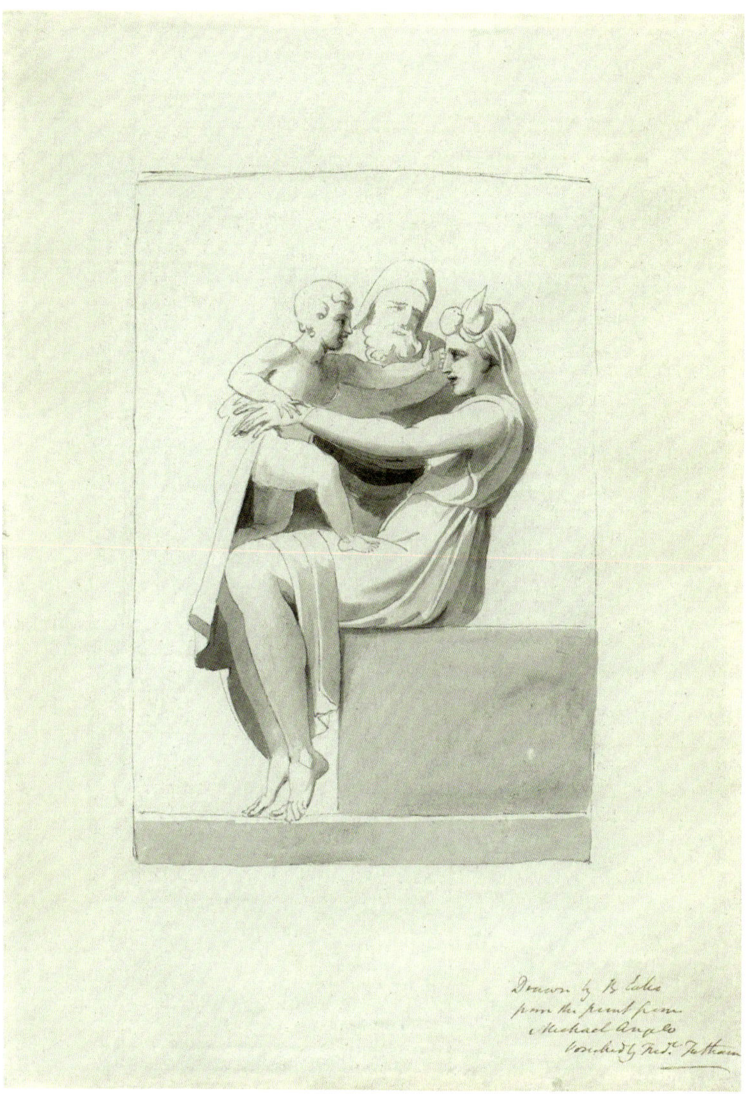

Figure 7 William Blake (British, 1757–1827), *Matthan*, ca. 1785. Pen and gray ink and gray wash, 24.2 × 17.4 cm (9 9/16 × 6 7/8 in.). London, British Museum, 1867,102.206 recto

illuminated manuscripts flooded the British art market.[23] In Gothic art, Blake found "a treasure, which he knew how to value. He saw the simple and plain road to the style of art . . . , unentangled in the intricate windings of modern practice."[24]

Blake engaged with these objects primarily through the act of copying, which he considered seminal to an artist's training and development.[25] In his studies of medieval funerary monuments, he meticulously and accurately recorded inscriptions, heraldry, architecture, and effigies of the deceased (fig. 6). But unlike in these antiquarian drawings, elsewhere Blake took liberties.[26] Around 1785, he made a set of copies possibly after Giorgio Ghisi and Cherubino Alberti's engravings of Michelangelo's Sistine Ceiling (see fig. 5).[27] Instead of the monumental figures of prophets, sibyls, and *ignudi*, Blake was drawn to the composition's peripheral characters, focusing mainly on Christ's ancestors seated on blocks in a variety of postures. He rendered them in a stylized manner and transformed the black-and-white matrix of the prints into pen-and-ink drawings, modeling the forms in gray wash of various

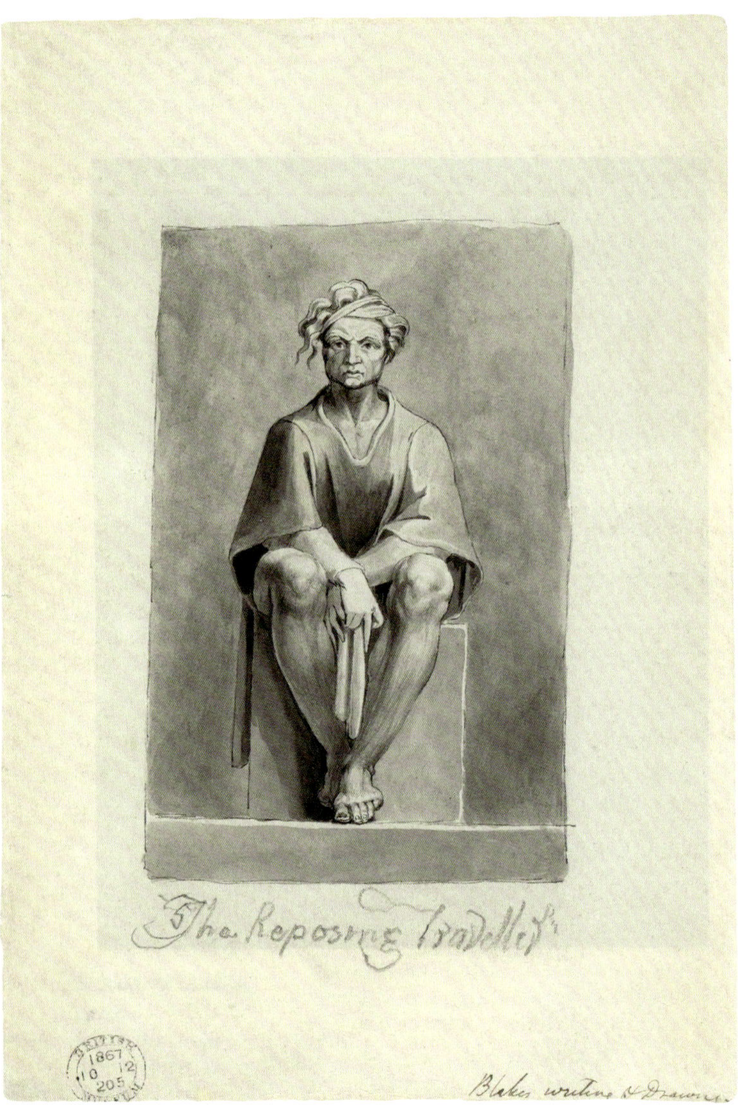

Figure 8 William Blake (British, 1757–1827), *Aminadab*, ca. 1785. Brush drawing in gray wash, with pen and gray ink, 24.4 × 17.3 cm (9⅝ × 6 13/16 in.). London, British Museum, 1867,102.205 verso

densities.[28] In the drawing of Matthan, the artist created an image of an idyllic family by changing the father's facial expression from shock to an adoring gaze (fig. 7); in handling Aminadab, he imbued the figure with a new meaning by inserting the title "The Reposing Traveller" (fig. 8).

These Renaissance and medieval models permeated every aspect of Blake's art. In the process of copying, he not only increased his dexterity but also memorized many of the forms, incorporating them into his core artistic vocabulary. As Frederick Tatham stated about Blake's internalization of historical models: "his absorption gathered to itself impressions that were never forgotten."[29] Accordingly, Blake populated his compositions with a mix of monumental, Michelangelesque figures in expressive poses—Satan hovering over Eve in a large color print (plate 48); men in contorted postures helplessly falling toward the ground in America (plate 78); the striding Albion shown from behind in Jerusalem (plate 111)—and elongated, lithe bodies with long limbs and relatively short torsos that recall Gothic imagery.[30] In emulation of medieval examples, Blake also developed a penchant for flat and symmetrical compositions. He placed his figures in abstract, shallow spaces and, disregarding the principles of perspective, rendered them at a scale determined by their role and importance. On occasions when Blake depicted his figures in an architectural setting, he used elaborate Gothic forms. For instance, in his *Chaucers Canterbury Pilgrims* composition, Tabard Inn is embellished with pointed arches and tracery and the background is scattered with structures topped with spired towers (plate 50).

Blake's prophetic mission of restoring the arts informed not only his iconography but his selection of media and his methods. From early on in his career, he refused to work in oil paint, which he primarily associated with the obfuscation of contours, the destruction of arts, and the masters he loathed. His decision was likely justified by the example of Michelangelo, who, according to Fuseli, considered oil painting "the art of women and disturbed and fraudulent men," even though he had an appreciation for "its glow, its juice, its richness, its pulp."[31] Instead, Blake worked in watercolor, tempera, and print media, but he used his own distinctive processes in order to achieve clear outlines and forms.

When working in watercolor, Blake first rendered the forms in pencil, black chalk, or charcoal, then carefully and evenly applied the paint within the contours.[32] Instead of mixing pigments on the palette to create new hues, a general practice among his contemporaries, Blake preferred to overlay pure colors.[33] He employed little shading and modeling. As a final step, he reinforced the outlines in pen and ink. A rare exception to this type of use of watercolor is his *Landscape near Felpham* (plate 102), which he completed during his stay in Sussex from 1800 to 1803, where he was a guest of his patron, William Hayley.[34] Here he sketched the elements of the landscape—the mill, the parish church, and several small buildings—then loosely and unevenly applied the watercolor onto the paper, disregarding the pencil outlines, blending colors, and creating accidental pools of pigment. From a technical point of view, this drawing is closer to how Blake's contemporaries would have used watercolor.

Blake strived to emulate Gothic and Renaissance models in his tempera painting, too. To prevent colors from blending and bleeding, which would have resulted in a muddling of forms, he applied a thin coat of animal glue over every layer of paint.[35] Starting from the 1800s, he began to use shell-gold and silver-gold alloy leaf on his temperas, presumably to imitate the gilding in medieval manuscripts and paintings like the Westminster Retable, which he might have seen while working in Westminster Abbey.[36] In *The Ghost of a Flea* (plate 97), he used it not only to render the stars and the comet in the background but also as an underlayer for the curtains and the body of the monstrous apparition, giving the painting an overall shimmering effect. Blake referred to his temperas as "portable frescoes" and considered them the revival of the correct method that Michelangelo and Raphael employed. But while traditional fresco painting entailed the application of pigments onto wet plaster, for Blake it meant using pigments mixed with binders other than oil, such as animal glue and gum, on a white priming layer. Whether this was a misunderstanding on the artist's part is difficult to tell.[37] Around 1821, Blake received a copy of the fourteenth-century Florentine artist Cennino Cennini's *The Book of Art* (1390s), which provides a detailed account of the technique. Upon reading the handbook, he boasted to his friend, the painter John Linnell, that he used the same materials and methods as described by Cennini, failing to acknowledge the discrepancies between his "frescoes" and those created in Renaissance Italy.[38]

In his printmaking practice, too, Blake attempted to return to the art of the past. Using his sui generis relief-etching technique developed around 1788, Blake created some of his most renowned works, including the *Songs of Innocence and of Experience*, *America a Prophecy*, *Europe a Prophecy*, *The Song of Los*, and *Jerusalem the Emanation of the Giant Albion*, which he called "illuminated books" to underscore their kinship to illuminated manuscripts.[39] Many of the prints bear formal resemblance to medieval examples. The letters are alive with sinuous forms like decorative initials, and small creatures and figures inhabit the margins and the space between the lines of the script. Furthermore, the surviving impressions are often printed in colored ink, painted in luminous watercolor, and embellished in gold. In emulation of late fifteenth- and early sixteenth-century printmakers whose works he adored, Blake refrained from the use of swelling lines and dot-and-lozenge systems in a number of his later engravings, including *Chaucers Canterbury Pilgrims*, *Illustrations of the Book of Job*, and *Divine Comedy*. In these works (plates 50, 11–16, 25), he clearly delineated each form and achieved tonal effects only through hatched and crosshatched marks in order to mimic "correct and finished Line manner, of Engraving, similar to those original Copper Plates of Albert Durer [*sic*], Hisben [Hans Holbein the Younger], Aldegreve [Heinrich Aldegrever] and the old original Engravers, who were great Masters in Painting and Designing, whose method, alone, can delineate Character as it is in this Picture, where all the Lineaments are distinct."[40]

Blake's engagement with the art of the past fueled his originality. It informed the formal characteristics, iconography, and technique of his works. Alluding to and learning from masters of bygone eras was of course not specific to him, but rather was common among his contemporaries. Reynolds, for instance, built a collection of paintings which he studied and restored in order to gain an understanding of techniques and materials, while Fuseli made numerous copies after ancient and Renaissance works during his extensive stay in Italy.[41] What set Blake apart were the models he chose and the ways he encountered them. Unlike Reynolds, Fuseli, and others, Blake derived knowledge of the works of these canonical masters largely from reproductive prints rather than original works, which led to misapprehensions of their aesthetic qualities. Consequently, the masters Blake knew were markedly different from the ones his contemporaries were familiar with. His selective understanding of Cennini's handbook suggests that his insistence on having recovered forgotten materials and techniques represented a practice of deliberately misconstruing the past. In a letter to Reverend Trusler, Blake writes that everyone perceives the world differently:

> *To the Eyes of a Miser a Guinea is more beautiful than the Sun & a bag worn with the use of Money has more beautiful proportions than a Vine filled with Grapes. The tree which moves some to tears of joy is in the Eyes of others only a Green thing that stands in the way . . . As a man is So he Sees.*[42]

It appears that for Blake artistic subjectivity was not limited to the present. Whether through misapprehension or deliberate reinvention, he created his own version of the past, which he then used to shape his remarkable art.

1 For instance, John Hoppner compared Blake's submission for the 1796 exhibition to "conceits of a drunken fellow or a Madman." Kenneth Garlick and Angus Macintyre, eds., *The Diary of Joseph Farington* (New Haven and London: Published by Yale University Press, for the Paul Mellon Centre for Studies in British Art, 1978–84), vol. 2, 507; vol. 3, 745–46. Robert Hunt, in his review of Blake's 1809 exhibition, described Blake's art and his *Descriptive Catalogue* as products of a "distempered brain." Gerald Eades Bentley Jr., *Blake Records: Documents (1714–1841) Concerning the Life of William Blake (1757–1827) and His Family*, 2nd ed. (New Haven and London: Published for the Paul Mellon Centre for Studies in British Art by Yale University Press, 2004), 282.

2 Martin Myrone, *The Blake Book* (London: Tate Publishing, 2007), 12–13.

3 Alexander Gilchrist, *Life of William Blake, "Pictor Ignotus"* (London and Cambridge: Macmillan and Co., 1863), 3.

4 David F. Erdman, ed. *The Complete Poetry and Prose of William Blake*, rev. ed., (Berkeley and Los Angeles: University of California Press, 1982), 701.

5 Erdman 1982, 527.
6 Henry Fuseli, *Lectures on Painting: Delivered at the Royal Academy, March 1801* (London: Joseph Johnson, 1801), 51–100.
7 The first English translation of the *Lives* is by Mrs. Jonathan Foster. Patricia Rubin, "'Not . . . what I would fain offer, but . . . what I am able to present': Mrs. Jonathan Foster's translation of Vasari's *Lives*," in *Le vite del Vasari: Genesi, topoi, ricezione* (Venice: Marsilio, 2010), 317–31.
8 On Blake's and Fuseli's relationship, see Carol Louise Hall, *Blake and Fuseli: A Study in the Transmission of Ideas* (New York and London: Garland Publishing Inc., 1985), in particular 56ff.
9 Fuseli 1801, 51–100.
10 E.g. Erdman 1982, 528–30.
11 Erdman 1982, 538.
12 Erdman 1982, 550.
13 Fuseli 1801, 65–66.
14 Fuseli 1801, 98–100.
15 Erdman 1982, 642.
16 As attested by the letter written to Trusler, Blake also admired Greek and Roman art at an early stage of his career, but his attitude toward classical art changed dramatically around 1803. He came to consider it derivative of Hebraic archetypes. In contrast, his appreciation for Gothic and Renaissance art was lifelong.
17 Thomas Martyn, *The English Connoisseur: Containing an Account of Whatever is Curious Painting Sculpture, Etc.* (London: L. Davis and C. Reymers, 1766).
18 Erdman 1982, 639. Painted copies after Renaissance masterpieces started to enter the Academy's collection only from 1800 onward. Jonathan Yarker, "Copies," in Robin Simon, ed., *The Royal Academy of Arts: History and Collections* (New Haven and London: Yale University Press, 2018), 491–503.
19 According to the Getty Provenance Index, over 2,500 sales included prints in London between 1757 and 1827. Among these was the auction of the Venetian Sagredo family's print collection in 1768.
20 Benjamin Heath Malkin, *A Father's Memoirs of His Child* (London: Longman, Hurst, Rees & Orme, 1806), xix.
21 Bernardine Barnes, *Michelangelo in Print: Reproductions as Response in the Sixteenth Century* (Farnham: Ashgate, 2009), 15.
22 Martin Butlin, *The Paintings and Drawings of William Blake* (New Haven and London: Published for the Paul Mellon Centre for Studies in British Art by Yale University Press, 1981), vol. 1, 1–14, nos. 1–47. Malkin 1806, xx–xxi.
23 Roger Wieck, "Folia Fugitiva: The Pursuit of the Illuminated Manuscript Leaf," *The Journal of the Walters Art Gallery* 54 (1996): 237–40.
24 Malkin 1806, xx.
25 In his annotations of *The Works of Sir Joshua Reynolds*, Blake wrote: "for no one can ever Design till he has learnd the Language of Art by making many Finishd Copies both of Nature & Art & of whatever comes in his way from Earliest Childhood. The difference between a bad Artist & a Good One Is the Bad Artist Seems to Copy a Great Deal: The Good one Really Does Copy a Great Deal." Erdman 1982, 645.
26 Jenijoy La Belle, "Blake's Visions and Revisions of Michelangelo," in Robert Essick and Donald Pearce, eds., *Blake in His Time: Studies in Aesthetic Theory and Practice*, (Bloomington: Indiana University Press, 1978), 13–22.
27 Alessia Alberti, Alessandro Rovetta, and Claudio Salsi, *D'après Michelangelo* (Venice: Marsilio, 2015), 72, 75–79; Butlin 1981, nos. 167–70.
28 During this early period in particular, Blake's graphic style closely resembled that of Fuseli. Fuseli also made copies after the Sistine Chapel frescoes during his Roman sojourn and subsequently incorporated figures derived from Michelangelo's paintings into his compositions. Gert Schiff, *Johann Heinrich Füssli, 1741–1825* (Zurich: Verlag Berichthaus, 1973), vol. 1, nos. 667–79.
29 Frederick Tatham, "MS 'Life of Blake' c. 1832," in Bentley 2004, 667.
30 For Blake's use of motifs taken from Michelangelo, see Anthony Blunt, *The Art of William Blake* (New York: Columbia University Press, 1959), 35; and Irene H. Chayes, "Blake's Ways with Art Sources: Michelangelo's *The Last Judgment*," *Colby Literary Quarterly* 20 (June 1984): 60–89.
31 Fuseli 1801, 62–63, n.K.
32 Noa Cahaner McManus and Joyce H. Townsend, "Watercolour Methods, and Materials Use in Context," in Joyce H. Townsend, ed., *William Blake: The Painter at Work*, (London: Princeton University Press, 2003), 62–63.
33 McManus and Townsend in Townsend 2003, 64.
34 Butlin 1981, no. 368.
35 This solution has proven detrimental to many of his paintings by causing severe discoloration and darkening of the paint. Bronwyn Ormsby with Brian Singer and John Dean, "The Painting of Temperas," in Townsend 2003, 114–15, 151, 153.
36 Ormsby with Singer and Dean in Townsend 2003, 137–38. The Retable, which was removed from the high altar of Westminster Abbey following Henry VIII's dissolution of monasteries, was rediscovered in the Abbey's Islip's Chapel by George Vertue, a member and official engraver of the Society of Antiquaries. At the time, the Retable made up part of an effigy press that housed wax funerary figures. Vertue's findings were published posthumously in 1770. Warwick Rodwell and Jenny Rose, "Post-Reformation Documentation and Use," and Jenny Rose, "Eighteenth- to Twentieth-Century Documentation," in Paul Binski and Ann Massing, eds.,*The Westminster Retable: History, Technique, Conservation*, (London: Harvey Miller Publishers, 2009), 156–71, 172–81.
37 Traditional fresco painting was not practiced in England, but Blake might have seen a small fragment attributed to Giotto at the time in the collection of Charles Townley. Robin Hamlyn, "William Blake at Work: 'Every thing which is in Harmony,'" in Townsend 2003, 15, 175nn35–36.
38 Gilchrist 1863, 369. According to Joan K. Stemmler, Blake might have been familiar with the treatise as early as the 1790s through his friend George Cumberland, who was granted access to Cennini's text during his Italian sojourn between 1785 and 1790. Joan K. Stemmler, "Cennino, Cumberland, Blake, and Early Painting Techniques," *Blake/An Illustrated Quarterly* 17 (1984): 145–49.
39 Erdman 1982, 693. See page 93 for the description of the technique.
40 Erdman 1982, 567.
41 Lucy Davis, "Interacting with the Masters: Reynolds at the Wallace Collection," in Lucy Davis and Mark Hallett, eds., *Joshua Reynolds: Experiments in Paint* (London: Trustees of the Wallace Collection, 2015), 28–41; Bernhard von Waldkirch, "Fuseli's Early Drawings: Transformations in Expression," in Franziska Lentzsch et al., *Fuseli: The Wild Swiss* (Zurich: Scheidegger & Spiess, 2005), 62–74.
42 Erdman 1982, 702.

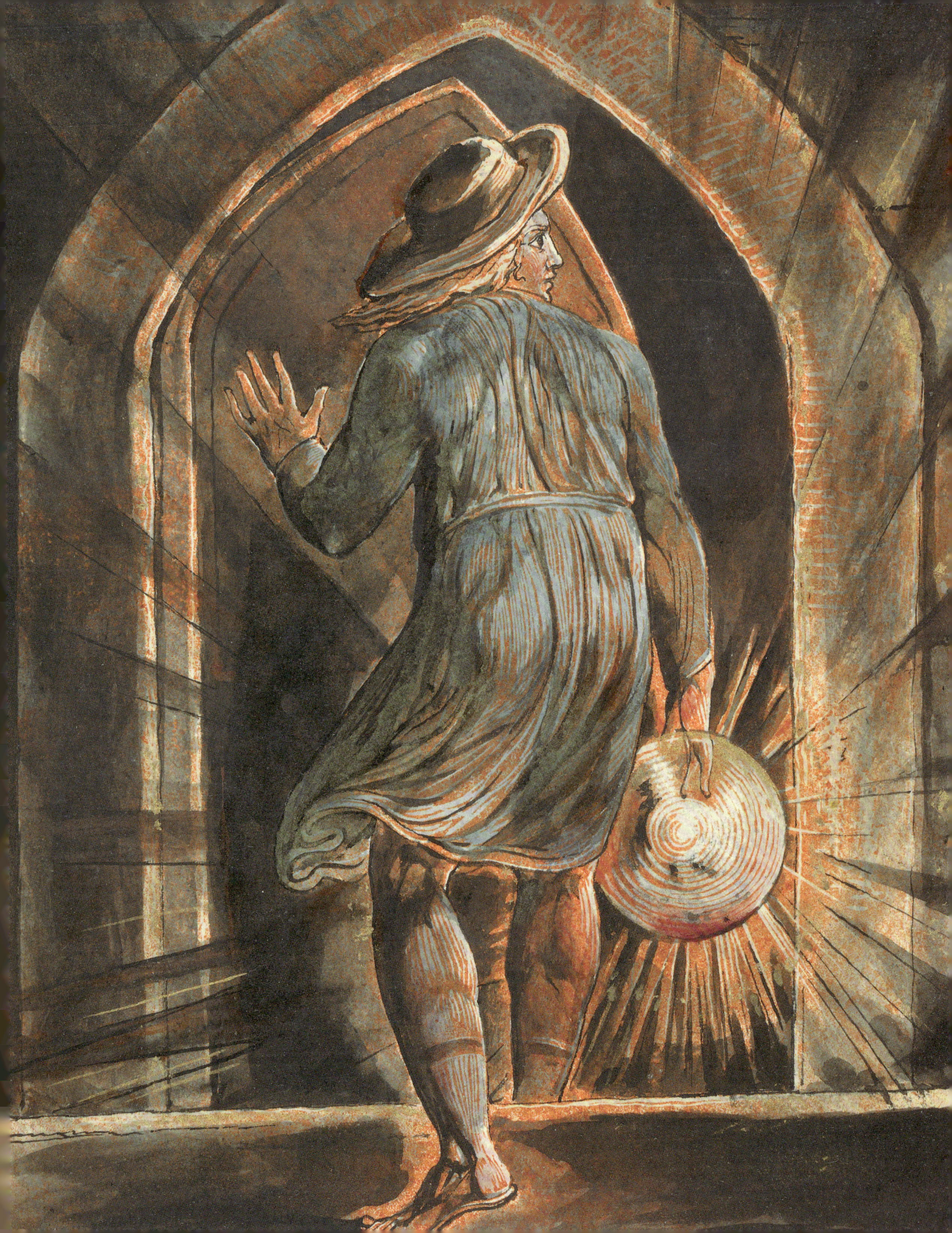

America's Blake

MATTHEW HARGRAVES

Americans have dominated William Blake collecting for one hundred and fifty years.[1] From the East Coast Transcendentalists of the nineteenth century who introduced the passion for Blake, to the West Coast collectors of today, no nation has rivaled the United States in its enthusiasm for this poet-artist.[2] Though the cultural value of Blake may have shifted over time, the demand for his work among collectors has never dimmed.

The American interest in accumulating Blake first appeared in elite Harvard circles in the 1870s. This was largely because Transcendentalists in Massachusetts had kept his spirit alive in the 1840s at a time when he was virtually forgotten in Britain.[3] Their taste for Blake's poetical works was essentially textual, having little or nothing to do with the graphic or pictorial qualities inherent in his art, but his appeal to the spiritual life and individual freedom chimed with Transcendentalist concerns. Consequently, Alexander Gilchrist's *Life of Blake*, published in 1863, found an eager and receptive audience in progressive New England circles. Indeed, Anne Gilchrist, who actually completed the *Life of Blake* after her husband's death, corresponded with Transcendentalists and formed a deep attachment to Walt Whitman in the 1870s before moving briefly to Concord and Boston in 1878, bringing work by Blake with her. In his review of *Life of Blake* for the *North American Review* in 1864, eminent Bostonian Horace Scudder (1838–1902) wrote a pioneering critical essay on the artist.[4] "The Job . . . it is that enshrines Blake's genius, and as a whole it is doubtless the most perfect work of art which came from his pencil," he asserted, and sometime before 1880 Scudder bought a copy of the *Illustrations of the Book of Job*.[5]

Another member of Boston's elite, Henry Adams (1838–1913), bought an impression of *Nebuchadnezzar* (fig. 9) while in Britain in around 1873, one of the large, color-printed drawings, which he later donated to the Museum of Fine Arts (MFA), Boston. The young Adams, thoroughly European in outlook and notably hostile to Transcendentalist ideas, had spent the 1860s in London as secretary to his father, President Lincoln's ambassador to the Court of St. James, and enjoyed close friendships with two prominent British admirers of Blake, Richard Monckton Milnes and Francis Turner Palgrave. It was their example that prompted his own modest forays into acquiring work by Blake. But the first great American Blake collector was Edward William Hooper (1839–1901), treasurer of Harvard from 1876 to 1889, whose mother was the committed Transcendentalist poet Ellen Sturgis (1812–1848), a close associate of Ralph Waldo Emerson.[6] Through Bernard Quaritch, the London book dealer crucial for

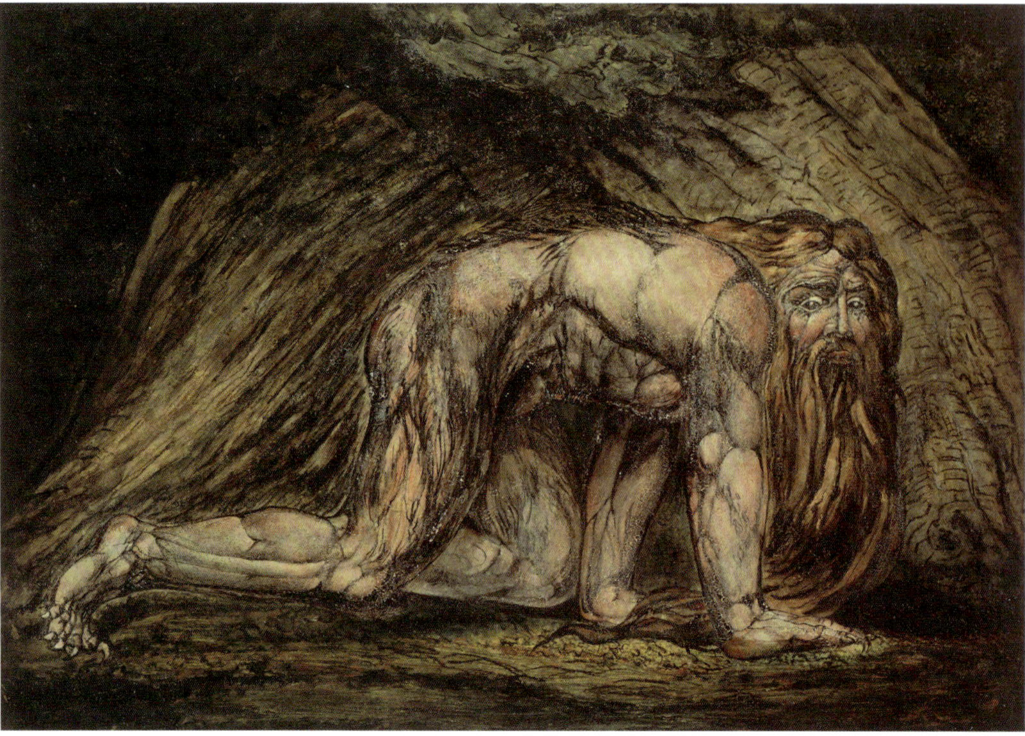

Figure 9 William Blake (British, 1757–1827), *Nebuchadnezzar*, about 1795. Monotype finished in black chalk, pen and watercolor, coated with gum or size, 41.8 × 60.3 cm (16 7/16 × 23¾ in.). Boston, Museum of Fine Arts, 27.354

American collectors, Hooper secured prize illuminated books such as *Jerusalem* (Copy D, Houghton Library).[7] He was also the first to acquire a pictorial masterpiece by Blake: *The Virgin Hushing the Young John the Baptist* (fig. 10), one of around fifty temperas commissioned by Thomas Butts, of which thirty survive today.[8] Hooper bought it from Palgrave before 1880 when it was shown, along with the Scudder *Job* and the Adams *Nebuchadnezzar*, in a small Blake exhibition at the MFA Boston, the first of its kind in the United States.[9] Then, in 1890, the first group of Blakes entered an American institutional collection when the MFA Boston bought thirty-three drawings, a purchase marked by a second exhibition at the museum.[10] It included eight designs for Milton's *Comus*, commissioned by Butts in around 1815, nine illustrations from the Bible, also for Butts, and nine for Milton's *Paradise Lost*.[11]

What explains this enthusiasm for Blake in nineteenth-century Boston? In the aftermath of the Civil War, Blake offered New England humanists a view of society that appealed for its urgent, emancipated quality. They found in him a European champion of independent thought, imaginative faculty, and democratic principles, but also someone who offered the ingredients for forging a distinctively American culture that was, attractively, of a dissenting Christian ethos with deeply biblical roots. In his review of Gilchrist's *Life*, Scudder declared that he chose "to class Blake in the small number of distinctively Christian men of genius."[12] For these cultured Bostonians, Blake was also pleasingly difficult, esoteric, and elitist. Gilchrist had opined of Blake's work that "one must almost be born with a sympathy for it," as if it was a matter of social refinement or sensibility.[13]

Among these pioneering Blake enthusiasts emerging from Boston circles, "perhaps the greatest Blake collector of all was W. A. White . . . who assembled a range of work far greater than was then to be found in The British Museum."[14] William Augustus White (1843–1927) was a Unitarian banker from Brooklyn who had graduated from Harvard in 1863 and began buying rare books in the mid-1880s. Though White is best known for his Elizabethan books, his Blake holdings were princely. Neither did White neglect Blake's pictorial art. In 1908 he acquired *The Great Red Dragon* (fig. 11), the twelve lyrical drawings for Milton's pastoral poems *L'Allegro* and *Il Penseroso*

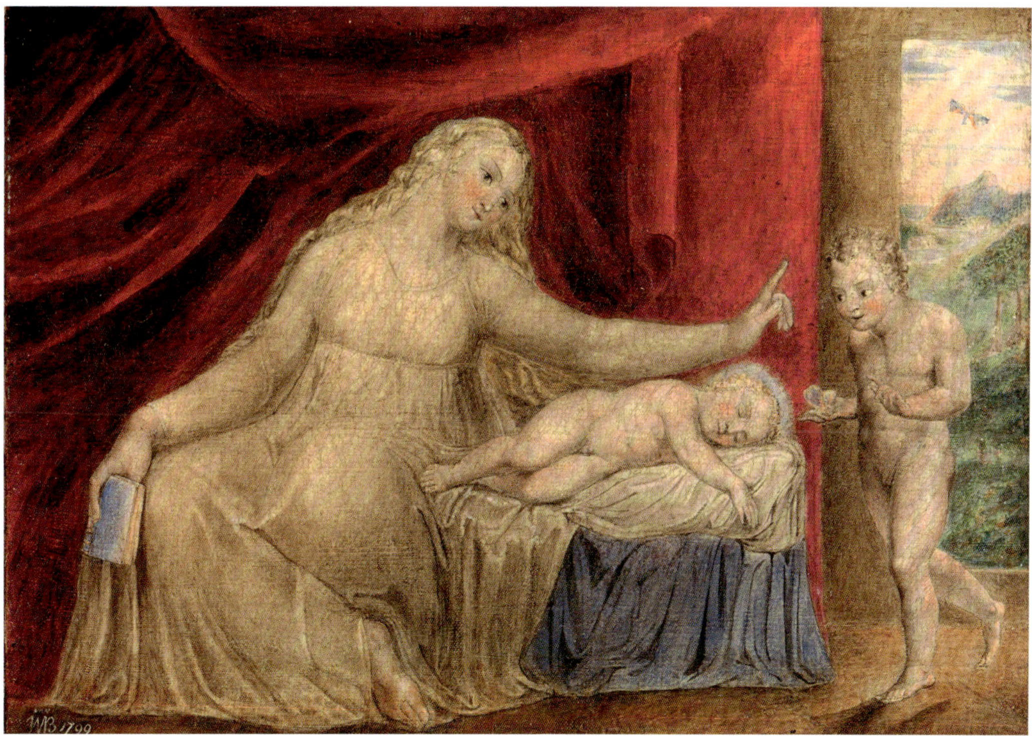

Figure 10 William Blake (British, 1757–1827), *The Virgin Hushing the Young John the Baptist*, 1799. Pen and ink and oil on paper on linen, laid down on canvas, 27 × 38 cm (10⅝ × 5 in.). Private collection

(ca. 1816–20, Morgan Library & Museum), and also—his greatest achievement as a collector: the 537 watercolors for Edward Young's *Night Thoughts* (ca. 1795–97, British Museum). They passed to his daughter in 1926 but subsequently re-crossed the Atlantic when she donated them to the British Museum in 1929.

But White marks something of a transition in Blake collecting in America. Between 1880 and 1900 Blake's reputation was rehabilitated rapidly as he went from being of interest to a narrow caste of Bostonians to attract the attention of America's mighty new millionaire bibliophiles. The gradual rehabilitation of Blake's reputation in Britain, especially after the 1880 second edition of Gilchrist's *Life*, made what few copies of his illuminated books that survived valuable commodities, to say nothing of his equally scarce drawings and manuscripts. The two chief American bibliophiles who began pursuing Blake were J. P. Morgan (1837–1913) and Henry Huntington (1850–1927). In terms of book collecting, Blake presented them with an opportunity for true connoisseurship since each of his illuminated books is unique, and those books quickly became the province of any respectable collector of note.

Morgan began purchasing the requisite illuminated books in 1899 through both Quaritch and Abraham Rosenbach, the leading American rare-book dealer. These were balanced by exceptional drawings. He acquired the twenty-one watercolors making up the *Illustrations of the Book of Job* (1805–6, the Butts Set) in 1903.[15] Huntington likewise bought copies of most of the major books, sometimes singly but often through the acquisition of entire libraries.[16] *Milton a Poem* (Copy B, Huntington Library, plates 98–101), for instance, was bought singly in 1911, one of only four copies known. Meanwhile his copy of the *Song of Los* (Copy E, Huntington Library, plate 92) was acquired when he bought the American bibliophile Frederic Robert Halsey's library en bloc in 1915. Huntington also acquired three outstanding sets of watercolors: the Reverend Joseph Thomas set of twelve drawings for Milton's *Paradise Lost* (1807) in 1914, and in 1916, eight drawings illustrating Milton's *Comus* (ca. 1801) and six drawings illustrating Milton's *On the Morning of Christ's Nativity* (ca. 1815), also made for Thomas Butts.[17]

Aside from Blake's new prestige, the gradual decline of British economic power

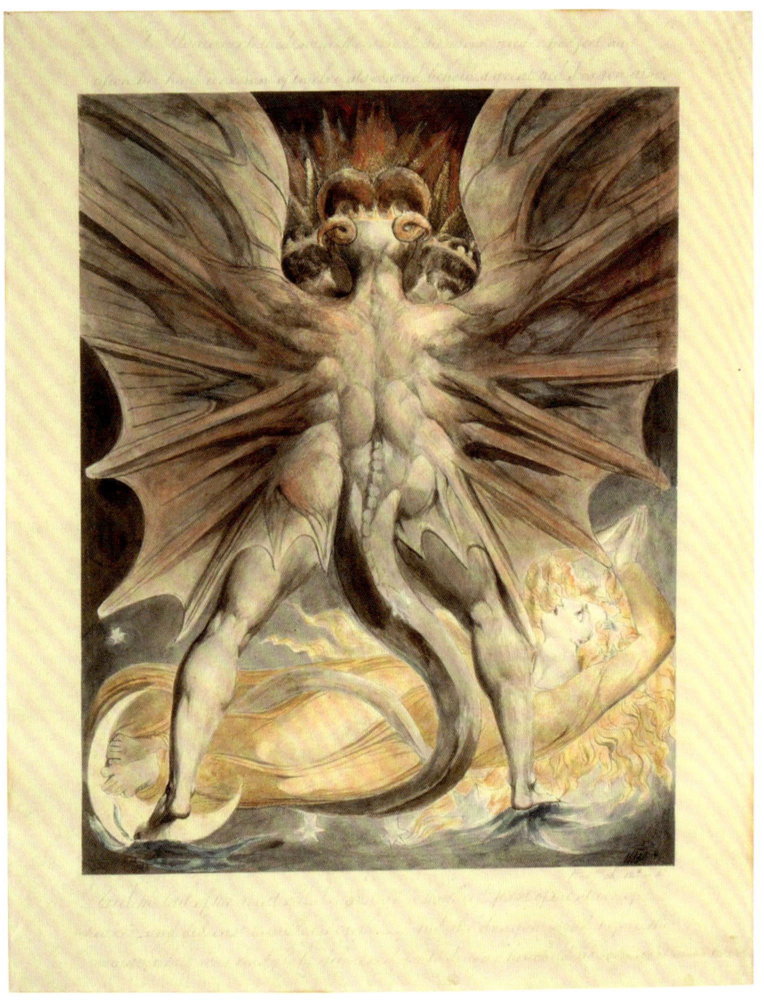

Figure 11 William Blake (British, 1757–1827), *The Great Red Dragon and the Woman Clothed with the Sun*, ca. 1803–5. Black ink and watercolor over traces of graphite and incised lines on wove paper, 43.7 × 34.8 cm ($17\frac{3}{16} \times 13\frac{11}{16}$ in.). New York, Brooklyn Museum, 15.368

after 1880, the concomitant dispersal of British collections, and the shift of the world's financial capital to New York City all played key factors in shaping the market for his work among American millionaires.[18] But of central importance was their attachment to English culture.[19] As David Cannadine has explained, the impetus for the acquisition of British cultural heritage had much to do with an ideology about "the common Atlantic bonds of the Anglo-Saxon race."[20] Huntington, for instance, the first great Blake collector residing on the West Coast, specifically intended to bring English culture to a former outpost of colonial Spain. But these common bonds began to fray as the sale of Blake's work to America provoked growing resentment in Britain. Attempts were made to halt its export abroad. In 1909, after stepping down from his fashionable Carfax Gallery in London, Robbie Ross wrote an appreciation of the poet-artist for the *Burlington Magazine*. Speaking on Blake's behalf, Ross declared: "no one would have resented more than he the attempts of any national Art-Collections Fund to stay the tide of his Prophetic Books ebbing to America."[21] For Ross, Blake was a transnational figure who belonged to all times and places. But Edwardian Britain was busy defining Blake in ever more nationalistic terms. Hubert Parry's 1915 setting of Blake's "And did those Feet" from his preface to *Milton a Poem* (ca. 1804–11) turned Blake into a patriotic champion. Paradoxically, or perhaps characteristically, Ross was soon contradicting his earlier assertion of Blake's transnational character. In 1918 he was central to a nationalistic effort to thwart the exodus of Blake material to America. The impending sale of the John Linnell collection at Christie's on March 15, 1918, "a sale that laid the foundation for several twentieth-century Blake collections" in the United States, raised the possibility of the prized Dante watercolors going to an American bibliophile.[22] As Cathy Leahy has explained, Ross, working as the London-based adviser to the Felton Bequest Committee at Australia's National Gallery of Victoria, coordinated an effort to stop the Americans and keep these Blakes "within the Empire" by mounting a successful consortial bid through the National Art Collections Fund to buy and split the entire set between Melbourne and a group of British public collections.[23] But efforts like this were exercises in shutting the door after the horse had bolted. American bibliophiles had both the means and determination to bring Blake's finest work to the United States in what became a golden age of Blake collecting.

The most significant American Blake collector of the period was Lessing Rosenwald (1891–1979), the Chicago-born heir of the Sears fortune,[24] who was able to buy a Blake collection

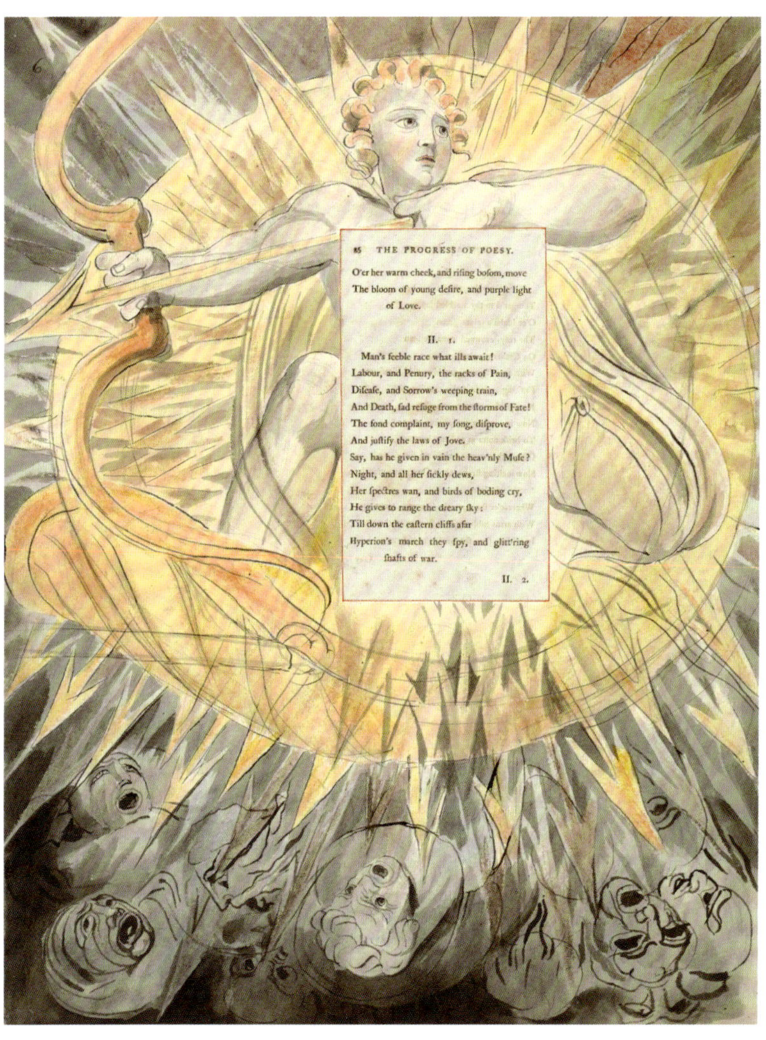

85 THE PROGRESS OF POESY.

O'er her warm cheek, and riſing boſom, move
The bloom of young deſire, and purple light
of Love.

II. 1.

Man's feeble race what ills await!
Labour, and Penury, the racks of Pain,
Diſeaſe, and Sorrow's weeping train,
And Death, ſad refuge from the ſtorms of Fate!
The fond complaint, my ſong, diſprove,
And juſtify the laws of Jove.
Say, has he given in vain the heav'nly Muſe?
Night, and all her ſickly dews,
Her ſpectres wan, and birds of boding cry,
He gives to range the dreary ſky:
Till down the eaſtern cliffs afar
Hyperion's march they ſpy, and glitt'ring
ſhafts of war.

II. 2.

Figure 12 William Blake (British, 1757–1827), *The Poems of Thomas Gray*, design 46, verso: "The Progress of Poesy," 1797–98. Watercolor with pen and black ink and graphite on wove paper with inlaid letterpress page, 41.9 × 32.4 cm (16½ × 12¾ in.). New Haven, Yale Center for British Art, B1992.8.11(23)

unrivaled on either side of the Atlantic. Among Rosenwald's greatest book treasures were three of only nineteen known copies of *The Book of Thel*, though his Blake drawings and prints were equally extraordinary. Rosenwald's entire holdings were given to the National Gallery of Art and the Library of Congress between 1941 and 1943 but remained at his Alverthorpe Gallery in a suburb of Philadelphia until his death.[25]

Rosenwald's gift to the nation came quickly on the heels of the landmark show in Philadelphia in 1939. The battle for Blake was eagerly joined as the organizers declared with patriotic pride: "it will be observed that no loans were invited from Europe, one object of the exhibition being to show what a great wealth of material is now in America."[26] Looking back on this event in 1969, Charles Ryskamp, legendary director of the Morgan Library and himself a Blake collector, described it as "in all likelihood the most comprehensive showing of his works ever arranged" but noted two remarkable new private collections formed in the United States since the 1940s: those of Mrs. Landon Thorne (1890–1974) and Paul Mellon (1907–1999).[27]

Julia Atterbury Loomis Thorne was the first woman to become a major Blake collector in America. A New Yorker, she married the financier Landon Ketchum Thorne in 1911.[28] Thorne's holdings were exceptional if conventional in their focus on the illuminated books, her choicest item being the only copy of the *Song of Los* in a private collection, one that had come from W. A. White's collection.[29] The Morgan Library exhibited Mrs. Thorne's collection in 1971 in advance of her gift of 1973, brokered through her friendship with Ryskamp. The other influential woman in Blake collecting was Mary Conover Mellon, who set her husband, Paul Mellon, whom she married in 1935, on the course to being a great collector. Paul would later recall that Blake's "haunting poetry with its arcane mythology and his beautiful illuminated books have always had a special appeal for me," one rooted in his early appreciation for English literature, which he studied at Yale in the late 1920s.[30] But it was Mary's intellectual passion for psychoanalysis, especially the ideas of Carl Jung, that induced the Mellons to move to Ascona to become patients of Jung himself. There Paul discovered a shared interest in Blake with Jung, and both Paul and Mary Mellon were so impressed by Jung's own collection of rare alchemical books that they began collecting themselves.[31]

Mellon had the means to compete with anyone in acquiring Blakes and made his first acquisition in 1941, *There is No Natural Religion* (Copy B, Yale Center for British Art), from W. A. White. Other books followed, but in 1953, as Mellon was exploring Freudian psychology with Anna Freud, he bought his greatest Blake book: *Jerusalem The Emanation of the Giant Albion* (Copy E, Yale Center for British Art, plates 103–112). Only five complete copies survive, and this unique, hand-colored copy was kept by Catherine Blake after her husband's death and bequeathed to Frederick Tatham when she died in 1831. Later, in 1966, Mellon made his most significant acquisition of Blake drawings, buying the entire set of 116 *Illustrations to Gray's Poems* (fig. 12). Almost all his Blakes were given to his beloved Yale Center for British Art during his lifetime, a few precious objects being retained until his death and bequeathed posthumously.

Mellon's affinity to Blake through his interest in psychology and psychoanalysis was a foretaste of how Blake was being redefined in the United States. From the esoteric and elitist Blake of the 1880s, to Blake as a bastion of English culture in the early to mid-twentieth century, Blake was becoming a countercultural figure of great prominence in America from the 1960s on. As W. J. T. Mitchell has put it, he became "the key to all mythologies, a prophetic voice for emancipation, and a visionary working-class hero."[32] It was also the moment when a new generation of Blake collectors emerged in the United States, some of whom remain active today. The two most significant have formed extraordinary collections by adopting entirely different strategies. A very private couple in the Midwest has built a group of Blake books to rival anything created by earlier Americans such as White or Rosenwald. Their collection includes a copy of almost every great illuminated book, including an exceptionally rare *First Book of Urizen* (Copy E) and, remarkably, *Jerusalem* (Copy C). By contrast, Blake scholar Robert N. Essick has formed the most comprehensive collection of Blake's work from across his entire career in all genres and media. Essick's collection is shaped by a desire that it should increase knowledge of Blake and supply gaps in our understanding of his thought and working method. Essick was not able to compete with the resources of a Rosenwald or a Mellon for the highest prizes but could turn his attention to objects that deepened our perception of the artist. The greatest strength of Essick's collection is Blake's commercial book illustrations, which had hitherto little interested scholars or collectors; now Essick holds the largest such collection in the world, larger even than that of the British Library. Among his greatest treasures is the only impression of Blake's *Deaths Door* (1805), previously in the collection of Samuel Palmer and printed for publisher Robert Cromek's edition of *The Grave* but rejected and never used (plate 7).[33]

Thanks to the breadth of Blake's work gathered in America over the last one hundred and fifty years, Blake and Blakean imagery have now entered the mainstream of American culture, not least because of the enthusiasm of the illustrator Maurice Sendak (1928–2012), who called Blake "my teacher in all things" and formed a significant collection of Blake's work, including *Songs of Innocence* (Copy J), which he bought in 1963, and *Songs of Experience* (Copy H).[34] Sendak, following Mellon's interest in the relationship between Blake's imagery and psychoanalytic thinking, saw Blake as an important advocate of the peculiar genius of childhood and the complexity of that transitional state of human life, drawing heavily on Blakean ideas and images in his own work from the late 1950s through the 1980s. Nevertheless, can America's enthusiasm for Blake remain unabated as it has over the last century and a half? It seems reasonable to ask what the future of Blake collecting might be. Will Blake, the lover of complexity and contradictions, still find admirers in an American culture that is seemingly becoming resistant to both? Or will he be redefined once again to answer the needs of the present moment, inspiring a new generation of collectors for the twenty-first century?

1 An essay of this length could not possibly hope to mention every Blake collector in the Unites States. The most comprehensive essay on the collecting of Blake globally remains Robert N. Essick's "Collecting Blake," in Karen Mullhallen, ed., *Blake in Our Time* (Toronto: University of Toronto Press, 2010), and I am grateful to him for so generously sharing his knowledge with me and also for reading and commenting on a draft of this essay.

2 "After about 1880 Blake's works began to cross the Atlantic regularly and since then most of the great Blake collectors have been from the United States." Charles Ryskamp, "The Great Collections of Blake's Books," in *The Blake Collection of Mrs. Landon K. Thorne* (New York: The Pierpont Morgan Library, 1971), 12.

3 Clare Frances Elliott, "William Blake's American Legacy: Transcendentalism and Visionary Poetics in Ralph Waldo Emerson and Walt Whitman" (PhD thesis, University of Glasgow, 2009).

4 Horace Scudder, "Reviewed Work: *Life of William Blake, 'Pictor Ignotus' with Selections from His Poems and Other Writings* by Alexander Gilchrist," *North American Review* 99, no. 205 (1864): 478.

5 Scudder 1864, 479.

6 As Charles Ryskamp (1971, 12) put it: "The first important American collector was Edward William Hooper."

7 Acquired sometime after it was used for John Pearson's 1877 facsimile edition printed in London. It is now in the Houghton Library. See G. E. Bentley Jr., *Blake Books* (Oxford: Clarendon Press, 1977), 259.

8 This object was indeed "one of the earliest works by Blake to enter an American collection." See Jonathan Yarker, "The Virgin Hushing the Young St. John the Baptist," in *Lowell Libson Ltd, 2015: New York Annual Exhibition, British Acquisitions* (January 2015), 69.

9 The other major lender was Anne Gilchrist herself: *Exhibition of Drawings, Water Colors, and Engravings by William Blake. Arranged in the First Print Room*, Museum of Fine Arts, Boston, June 1880.

10 *Books, Water Colors, Engravings, Etc. by William Blake*, Feb–March, 1891.

11 These drawings were purchased with funds donated by unnamed friends of the museum, although the Comus drawings were the joint gift-purchase of Isabella Stewart Gardner and George Nixon Black.

12 Scudder 1864, 480.

13 Alexander Gilchrist, *Life of William Blake,"Pictor Ignotus," with Selections from His Poems and Other Writings* (London: Macmillan and Co., 1863), vol. 1, 3.

14 Ryskamp 1971, 12.

15 Martin Butlin, *The Paintings and Drawings of William Blake* (New Haven and London: Published for the Paul Mellon Centre for Studies in British Art by Yale University Press, 1981), vol. 1, 411. Notably, the second Linnell set of Job drawings, made in 1821, soon also found its way to America when it was acquired in 1921 by the Harvard-educated Grenville Lindall Winthrop of New York, who gave the group to the Fogg in 1943. See A. Edward Newton, "Introduction," *William Blake 1757–1827*, xvi, and Colin Trodd, *Visions of Blake: William Blake in the Art World 1830–1930* (Liverpool: Liverpool University Press, 2010), 448. The third, "New Zealand set" of disputed attribution, now at Yale, was bought by Philip Hofer, curator of the Houghton Library, and later purchased by Paul Mellon.

16 The most complete catalogue of the Huntington collection is Robert N. Essick, *The Works of William Blake in the Huntington Collections: A Complete Catalogue* (San Marino: The Huntington Library, 1985).

17 Butlin 1981, 373, 378, 392.

18 For a succinct account see David Cannadine, "Pictures across the Pond: Perspectives and Retrospectives," in Inge Reist, ed., *British Models of Art Collecting and the American Response: Reflections across the Pond* (Farnham: Ashgate, 2014), 9–25.

19 Cannadine 2014, 17.

20 Cannadine 2014, 17. See also A. S. W. Rosenbach, "Why America Buys England's Books," *Atlantic Monthly*, 140, (July–December 1927), 452–59.

21 Robert Ross, "A Recent Criticism of Blake," *Burlington Magazine for Connoisseurs* 16, no. 80 (1909): 84.

22 Essick 2010, 21.

23 Catherine Leahy, "Melbourne's Blake Collection," in *William Blake* (Melbourne: National Gallery of Victoria, 2014), 6–7; and Louise Wilson, "To See a World in a Grain of Sand: A Closer Look at the 'Melbourne Blakes'," National Gallery of Victoria, online article. I am indebted to Richard Read for pointing out this episode to me and to Petra Kayser for supplying me with further information. Some were sold in 1921 and crossed the Atlantic when acquired by Grenville L. Winthrop, who gave them to the Harvard Art Museums in 1943. See Butlin 1981, 557.

24 Space does not permit more discussion of George C. Smith and A. E. Newton, both major Blake collectors in this period whose collections laid the foundation for future American collectors.

25 Essick 2010, 26.

26 *William Blake 1757–1827: A Descriptive Catalogue of an Exhibition of the Works of William Blake Selected from Collections in the United States* (Philadelphia: Philadelphia Museum of Art, 1939), xix.

27 *William Blake, Engraver* (Princeton: Princeton University Press, 1969), vii–viii.

28 For Mrs. Thorne see Jennet Conant, *Tuxedo Park: A Wall Street Tycoon and the Secret Palace of Science That Changed the Course of World War II* (New York: Simon & Schuster, 2003).

29 Ryskamp 1971, 6.

30 Paul Mellon with John Baskett, *Reflections in a Silver Spoon: A Memoir* (New York: William Morrow and Company, 1992), 284. I am grateful to John Baskett for sharing his knowledge of Paul Mellon's life and collecting with me on many occasions. This section owes much to my own "William Blake and Paul Mellon: The Life of the Mind," *The Public Domain Review*, online article.

31 For the chronology of Paul Mellon's William Blake collecting, I am indebted to Charles Ryskamp, "Paul Mellon and William Blake" in John Wilmerding, ed., *Essays in Honor of Paul Mellon: Collector and Benefactor* (Washington: National Gallery of Art, 1986), 329–37. For his book collecting, see William Reese, "Paul Mellon as a Book Collector," in *Paul Mellon's Legacy: A Passion for British Art* (New Haven and London: Yale Center for British Art, Royal Academy of Arts: Yale University Press, 2007), 57–71.

32 W. J. T. Mitchell, "Blake Now and Then," in Stephen F. Eisenman, ed., *William Blake and the Age of Aquarius* (Princeton: Princeton University Press, 2017), 202.

33 Essick 2010, 30; and Butlin 1981, 329.

34 For Blake's influence on Sendak see Mark Crosby, "Sendak, Blake, and the Image of Childhood" in Eisenman 2017, 184. For the provenances of these books see Bentley 1977, 407 and 416.

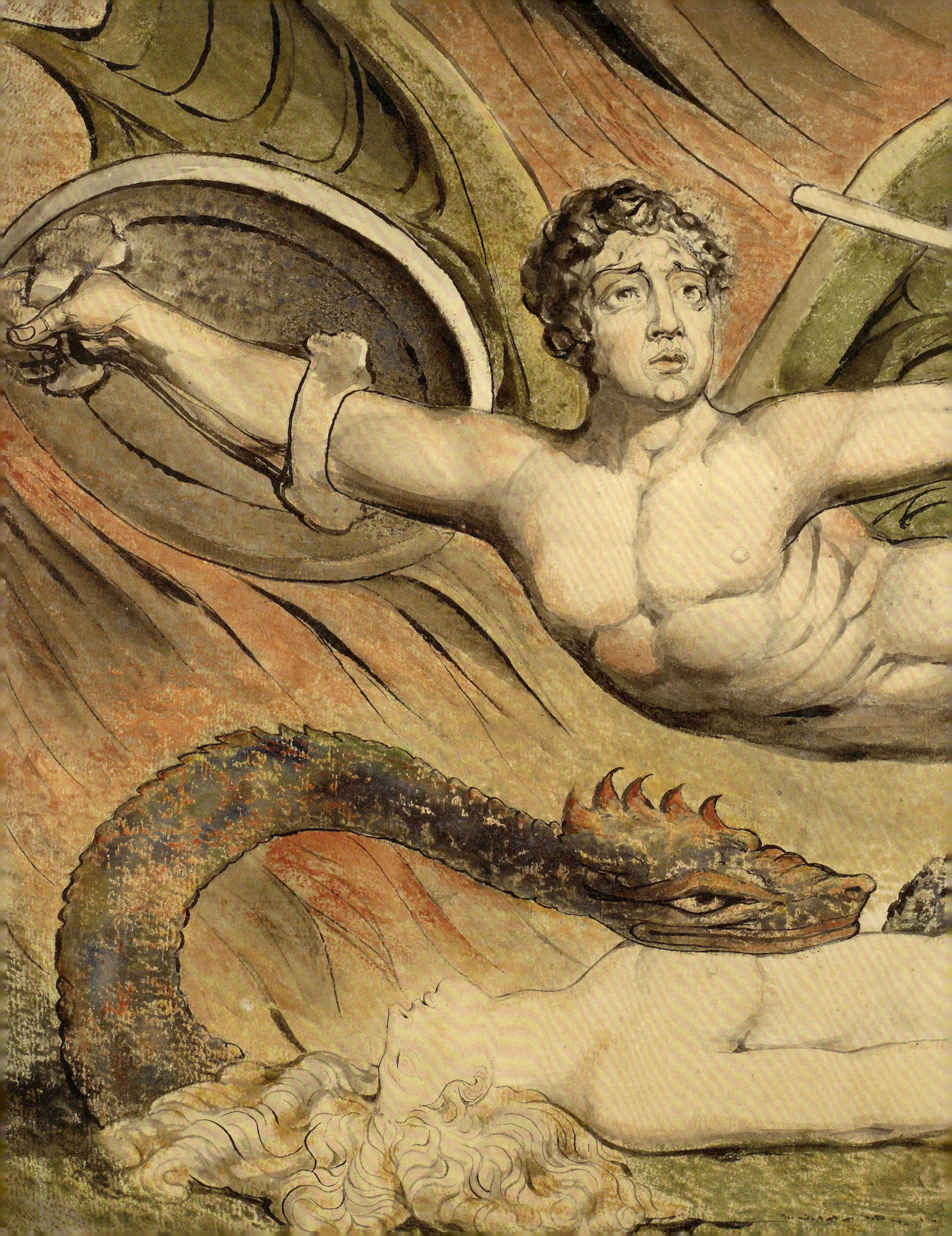

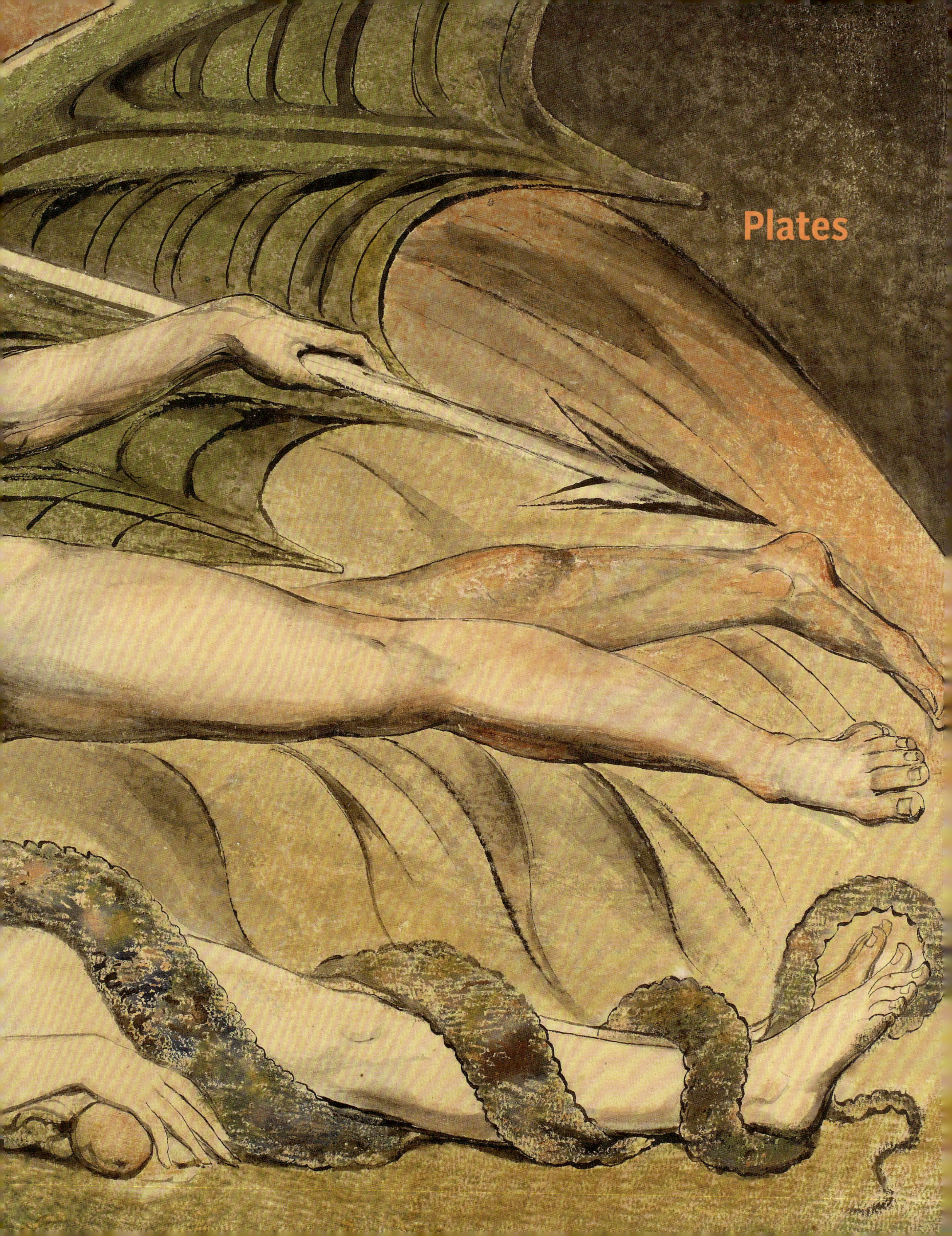

Plates

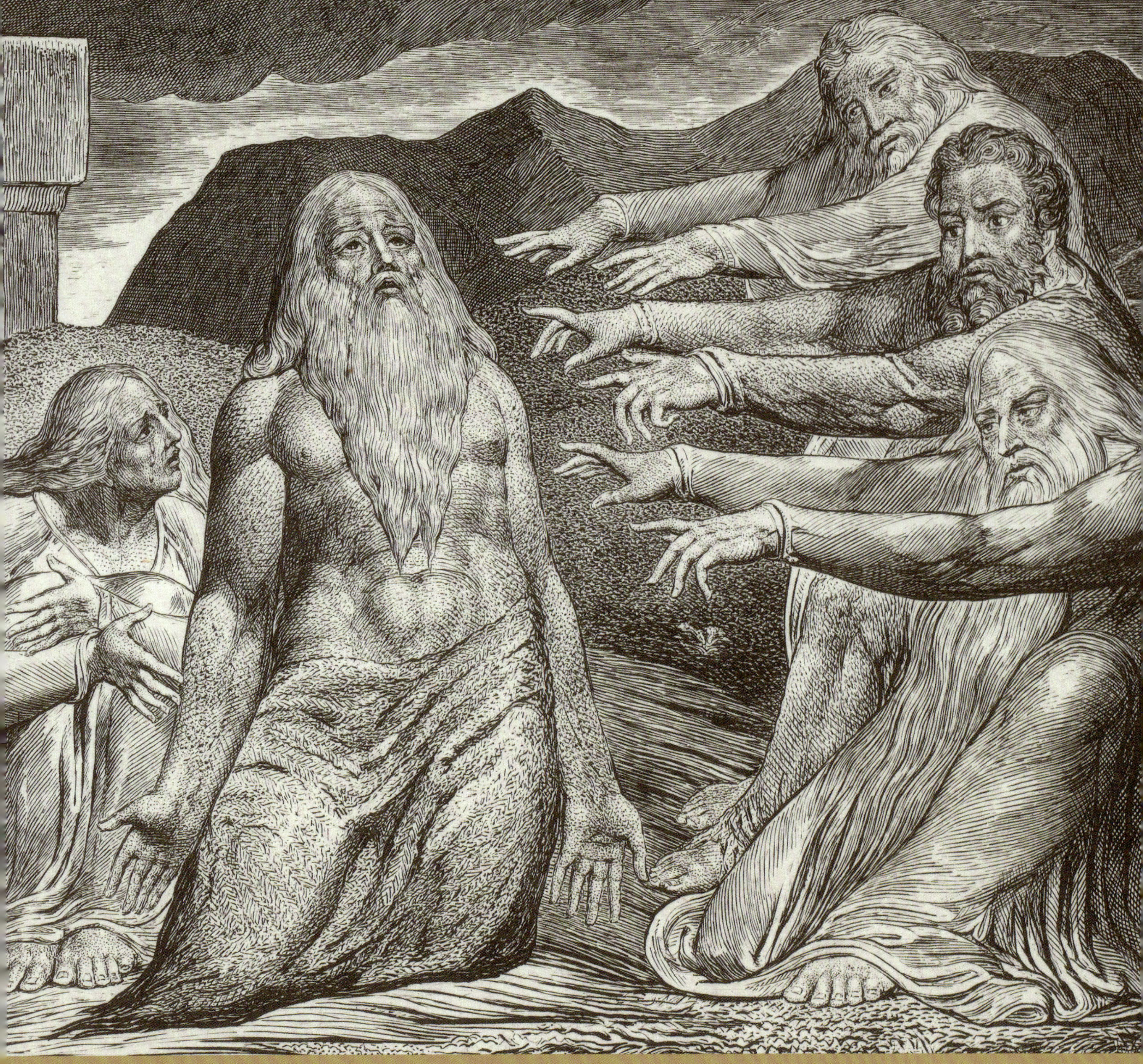

"Engraving is the profession I was apprenticed to, & should never have attempted to live by any thing else If orders had not come in for my Designs & Paintings . . ."

—William Blake to the Reverend Trusler, August 23, 1799

The Professional Printmaker

PLATES 1–25

Throughout his career, William Blake collaborated with artists and publishers, producing prints after the images of others, as well as designing and engraving his own pictorial inventions. Blake considered the former a commercial activity and the latter instead a part of his creative endeavor.

Blake received rigorous training in traditional printmaking techniques during his apprenticeship with James Basire (see Introduction), giving him a strong technical foundation on which to build. The *Portrait of Queen Philippa* (plate 2) amply demonstrates the young apprentice's considerable skill in the mixed method of etching and engraving, the conventional means of image reproduction at the time. It was this technique he used to translate William Hogarth's oil painting *Beggar's Opera* into a virtuosic and complex pattern of lines (plate 3).

Blake's *Michelangelo* was instead a collaboration between artist and printmaker (plate 5). Rather than a finished work, the Swiss-born artist Henry Fuseli provided Blake with only a quick pen-and-ink sketch (plate 4). The drawing contained very little visual information, and Blake himself transformed the design into a full-length representation of the Renaissance master with the Colosseum in the background.

Some projects required Blake to fulfill the role of the illustrator as well. Around 1795, the publisher Richard Edwards asked him to illustrate Edward Young's *Night Thoughts* for a deluxe edition of the fashionable poem that explored the themes of death and bereavement. Blake created an astonishing 537 watercolors, of which he engraved forty-three. Despite Blake's highly original images that surround the framed text panels, such as the ethereal figure of Narcissa with the coiled serpent (plate 8), the enterprise was a commercial failure and was abandoned after the first volume.

When working for publishers, Blake was required to comply with their demands, something he occasionally failed to do. He rendered his design *Deaths Door* for Robert Blair's *The Grave* in unusual white-line etching, but the publisher Robert Cromek rejected it and tasked the printmaker Luigi Schiavonetti to reproduce Blake's design using conventional etching and engraving (plates 6, 7). Blake's seventeen tiny wood engravings for Dr. Robert Thornton's student edition of *The Pastorals of Virgil* (1821), although masterfully evoking the elegiac mood of the text, were not received enthusiastically by his patron (plate 10).

Toward the end of Blake's life, the painter John Linnell commissioned him to design and engrave two major sets of illustrations, encouraging Blake to employ pure line engraving in the manner of old masters. For the first, the illustrations of the *Book of Job* (plates 11–16), Blake relied on his own earlier watercolor compositions, but added border designs with quotes and inscriptions. The illustrations are deeply imbued with Blake's private mythology, perhaps most visibly in the way the wrathful Old Testament God morphs into a redemptive Christlike presence by the end.

For the second, for Dante's *Divine Comedy*, he made 102 watercolors interpreting—and criticizing—the text (plates 17–24). These watercolors, which display various degrees of finish, are some of his most compelling works. Preoccupied with the idea of a vengeful god, Blake focused primarily on depicting Dante and Virgil's journey through Hell, the two wandering through an abstract landscape, witnessing the unimaginable suffering of sinners. The *Divine Comedy* engravings from the watercolors were left unfinished, with only seven plates completed by the time Blake died (plate 25).

EA

Plate 1
William Blake, *Self-Portrait*, 1802/1804

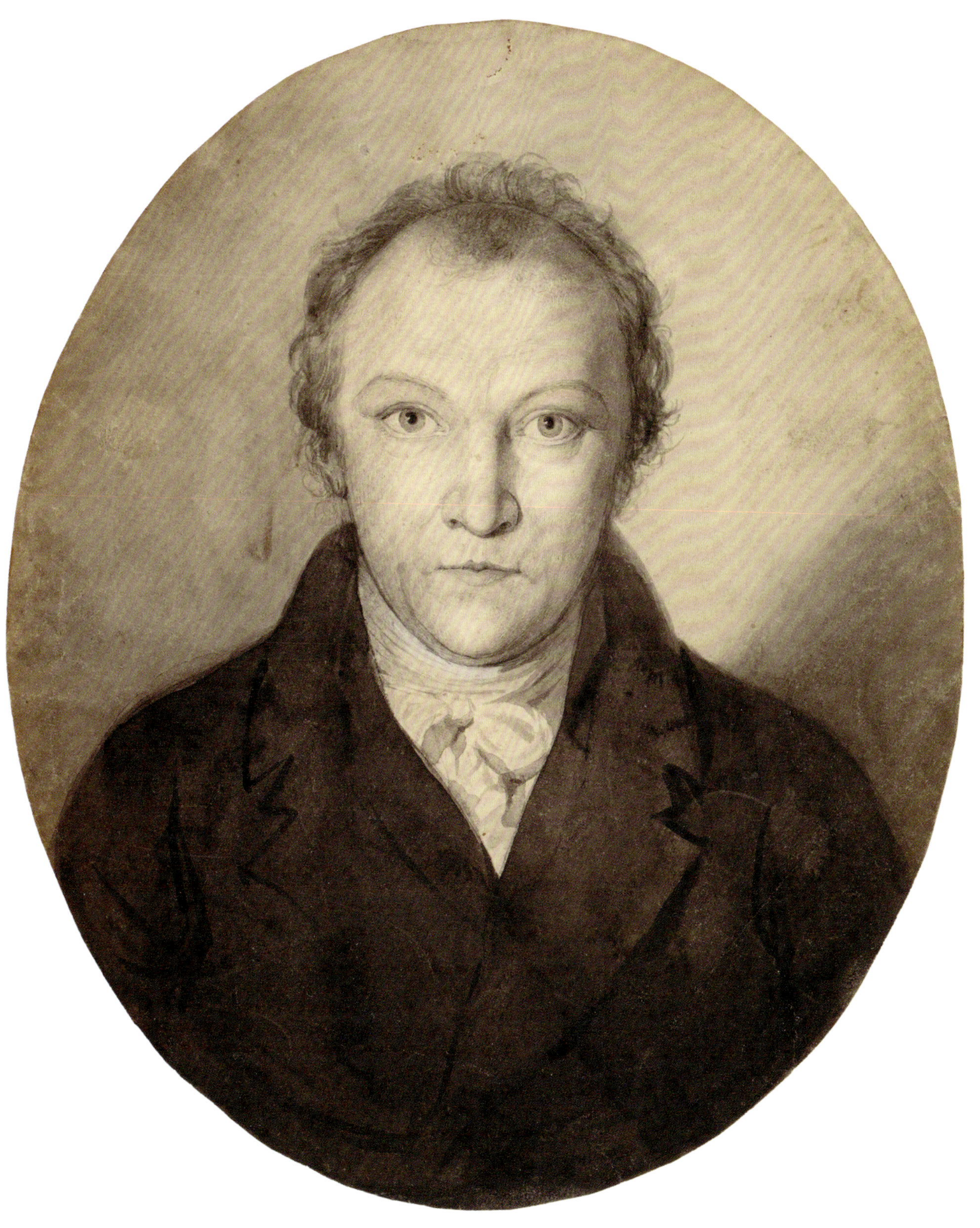

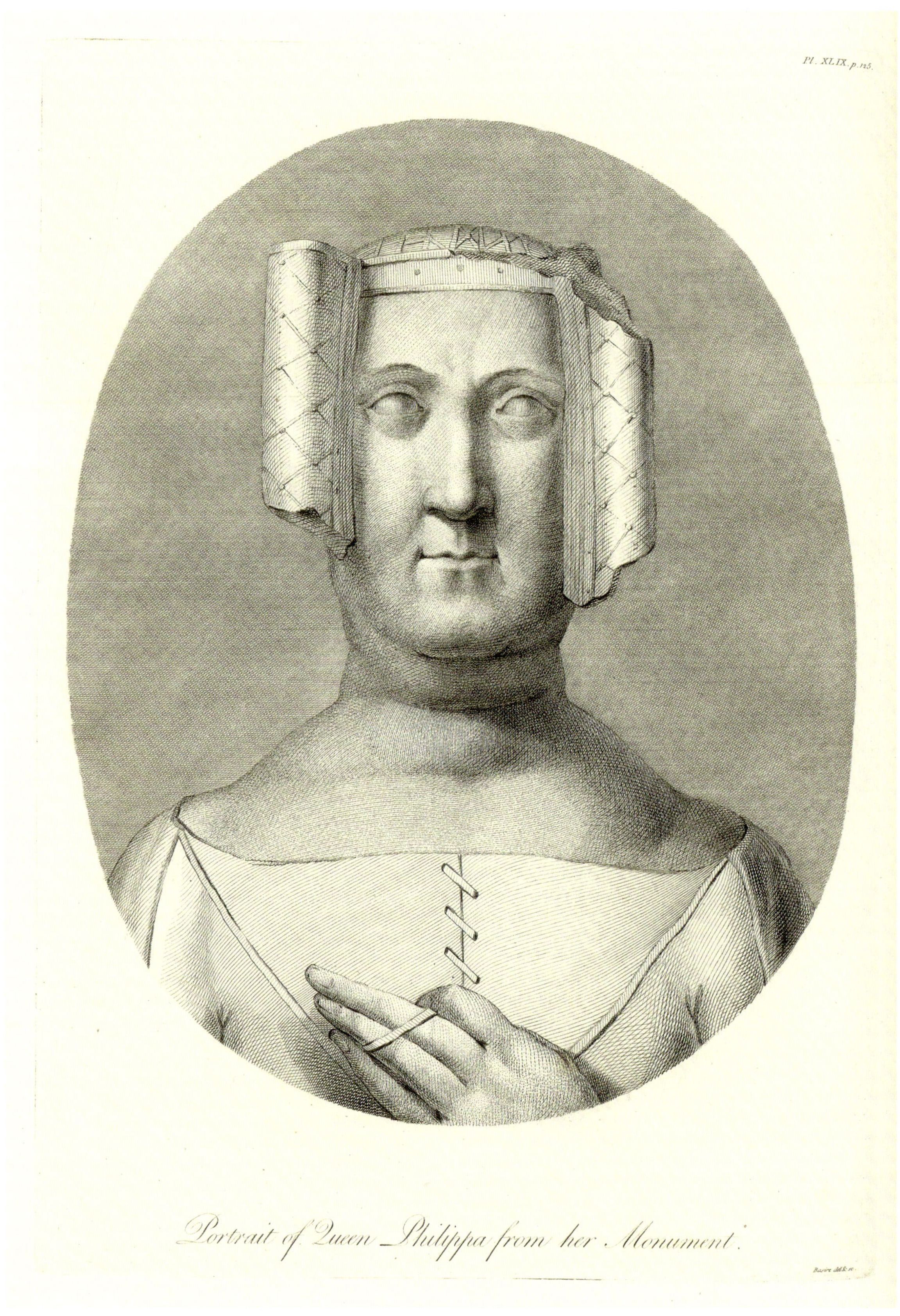
Pl. XLIX. p. 125.
Portrait of Queen Philippa from her Monument.
Basire del. & sc.

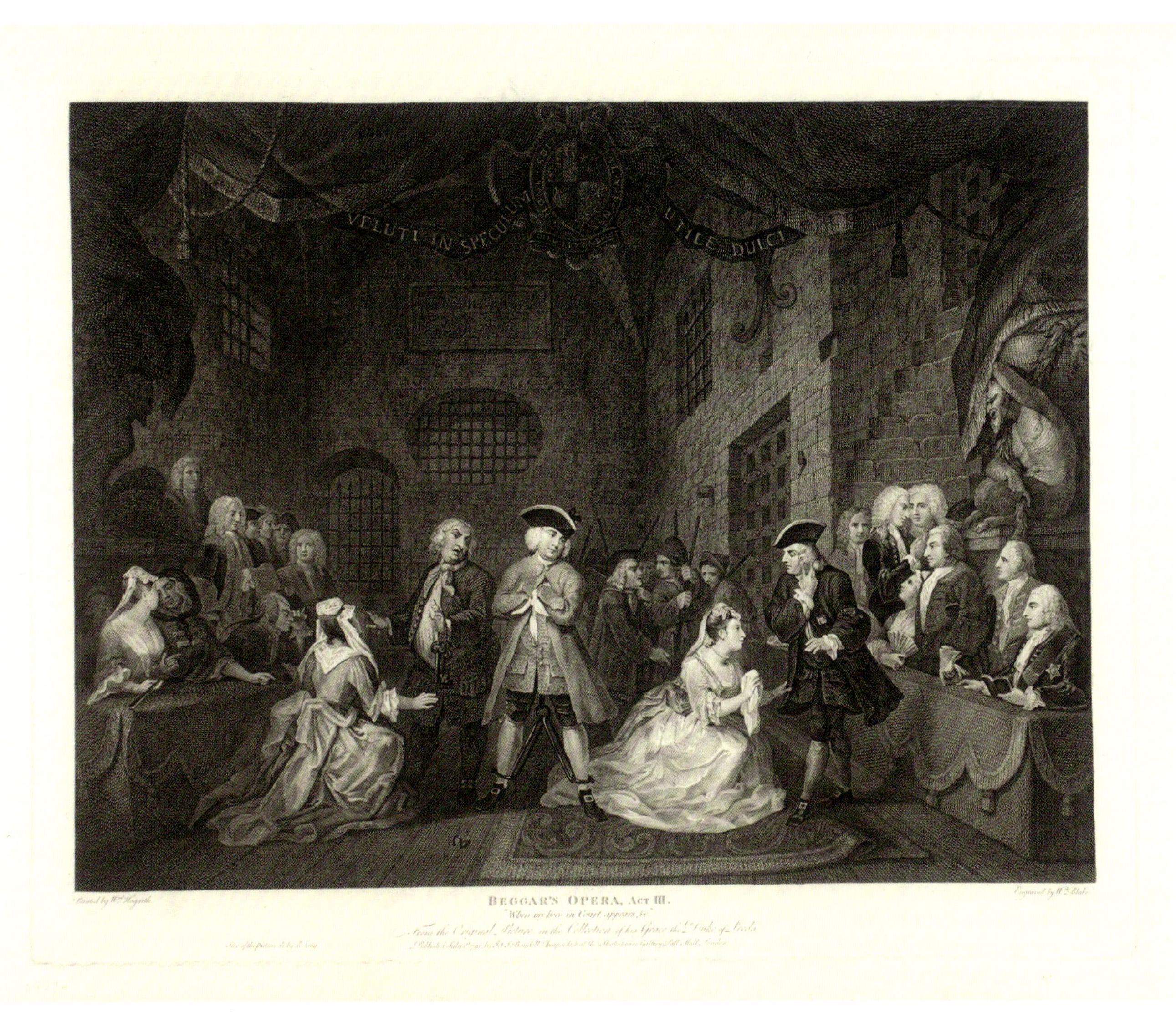

Plate 2
William Blake, *Portrait of Queen Philippa* in Richard Gough's *Sepulchral Monuments in Great Britain*, vol. 1, 1796

Plate 3
William Blake, after William Hogarth, *Beggar's Opera, Act III*, 1790

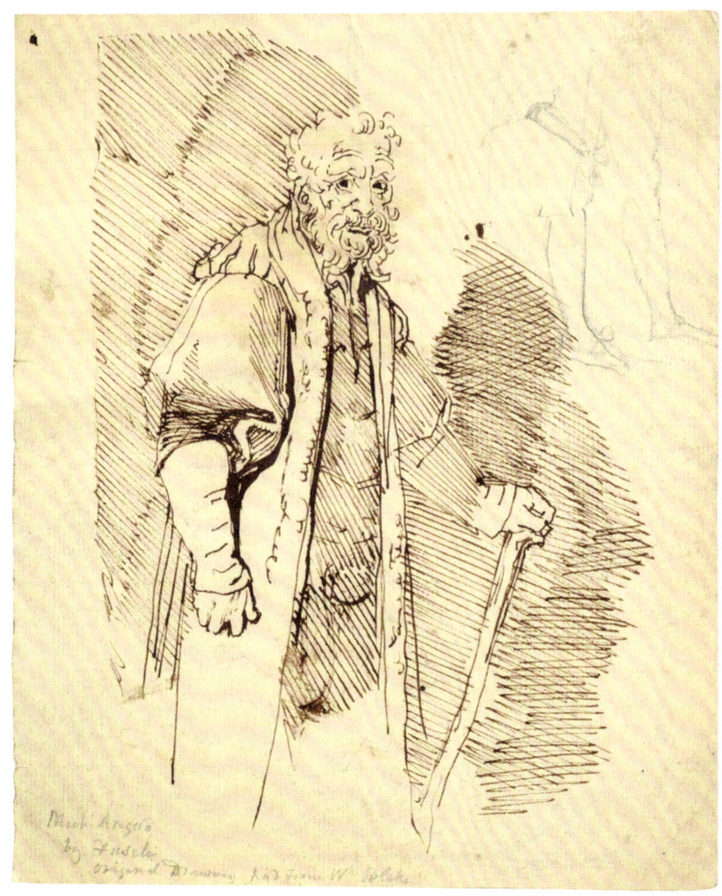

Plate 4
Henry Fuseli, *Portrait Sketch of Michelangelo* for *Lectures on Painting,* about 1788

Plate 5
William Blake, after Henry Fuseli, *Michelangelo* from Henry Fuseli's *Lectures on Painting*, 1801

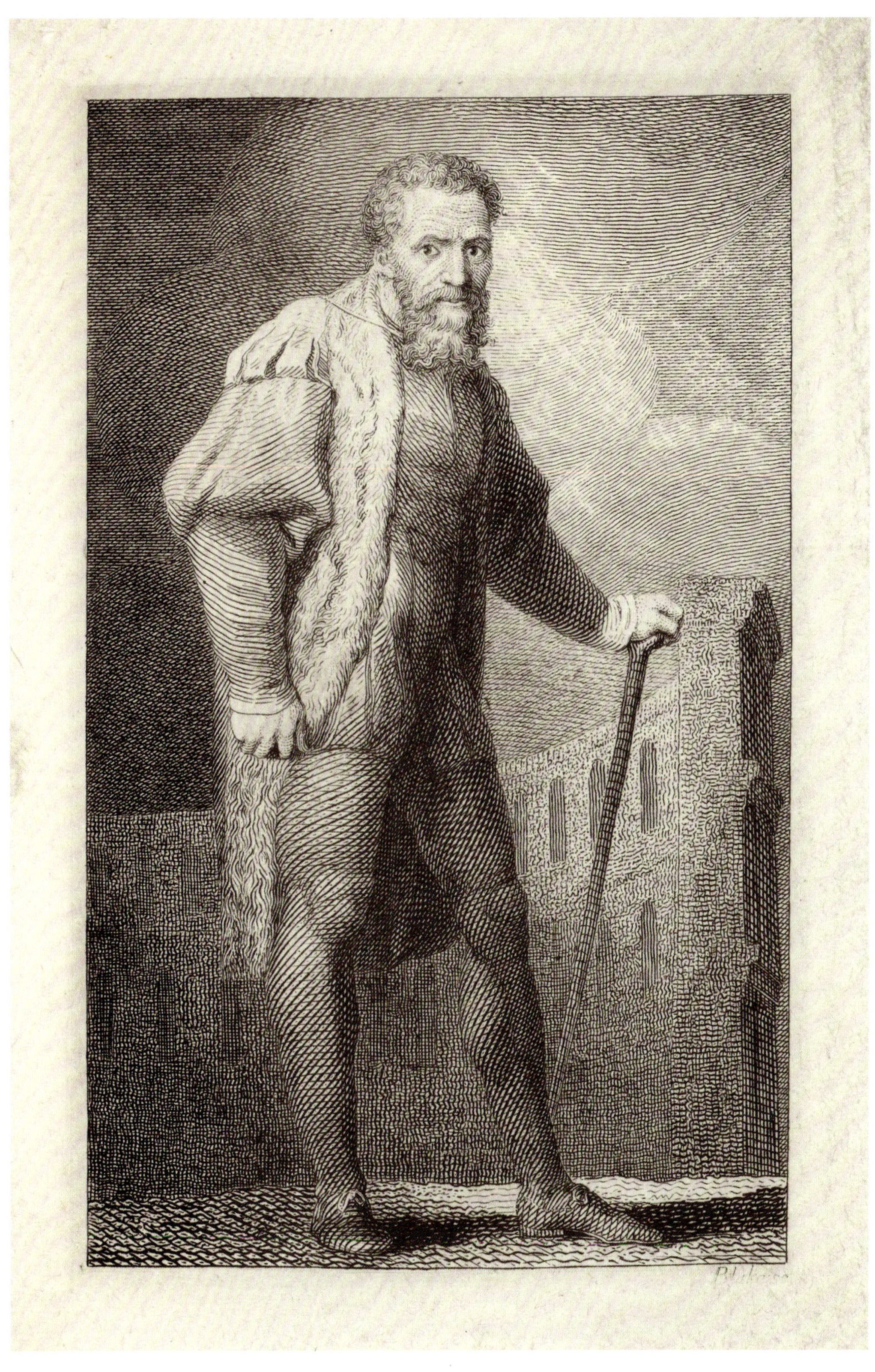

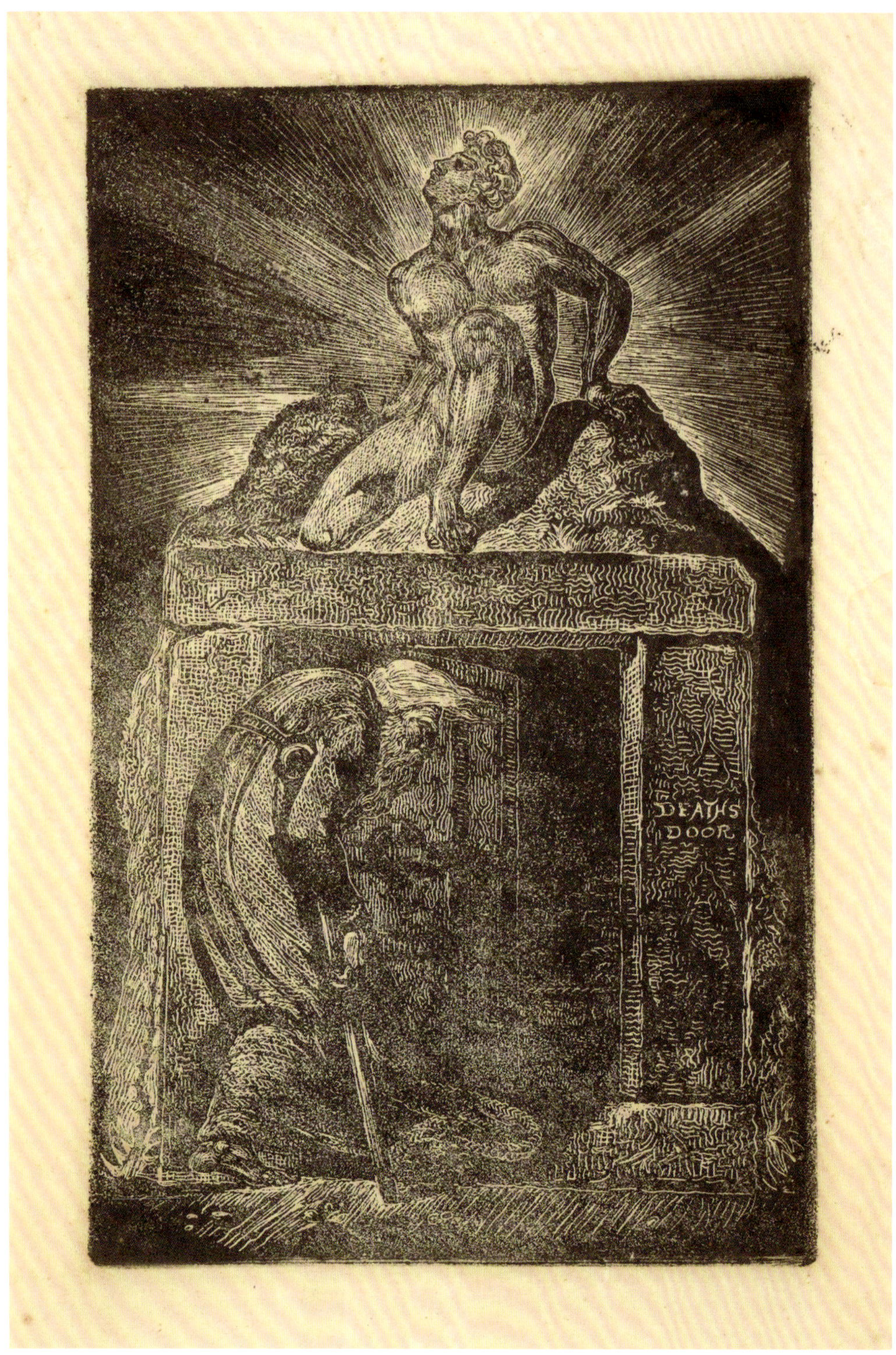

Plate 6
William Blake, *Deaths Door*, 1805

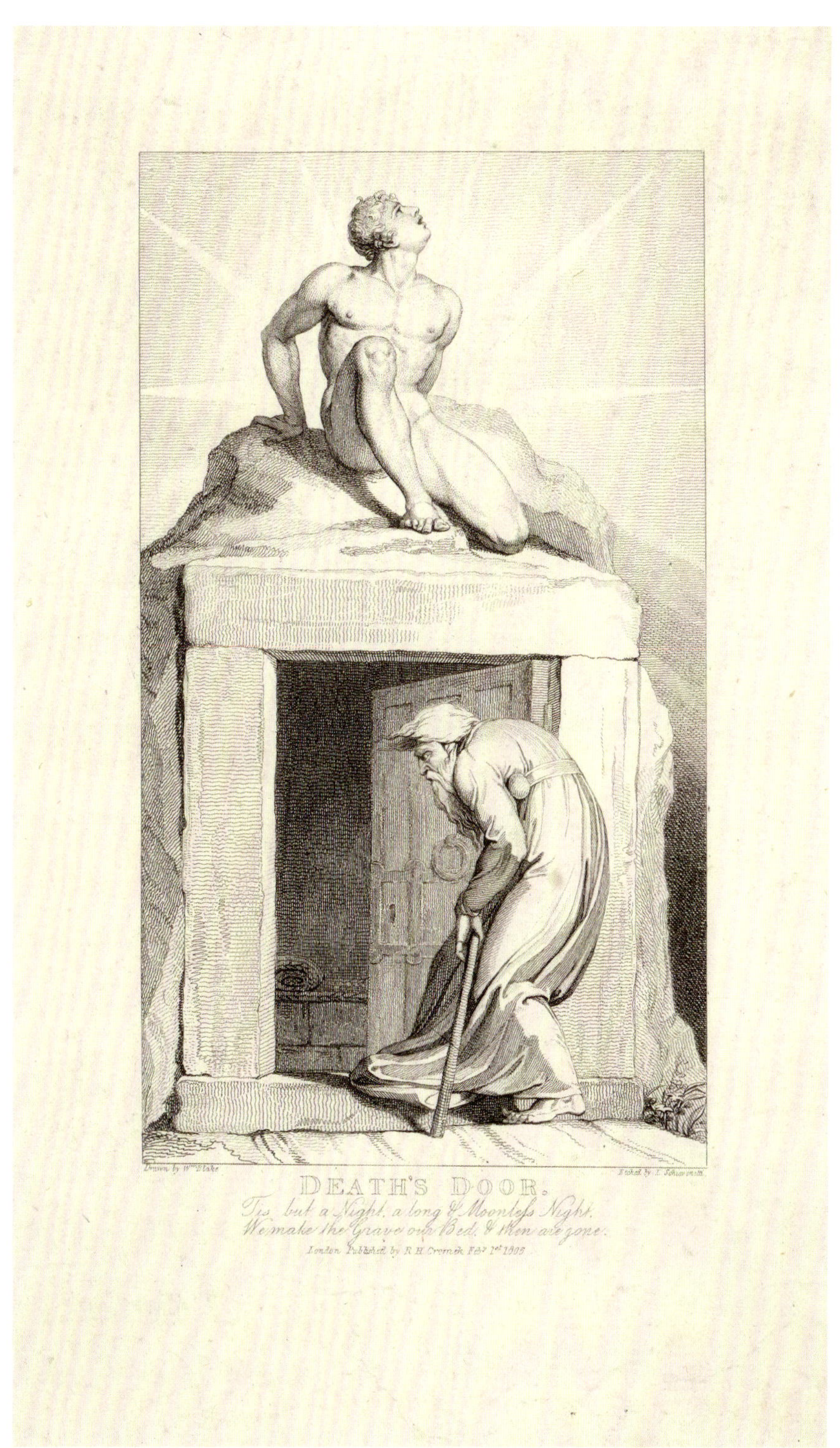

Plate 7
Luigi Schiavonetti, after William Blake, *Death's Door*, 1806

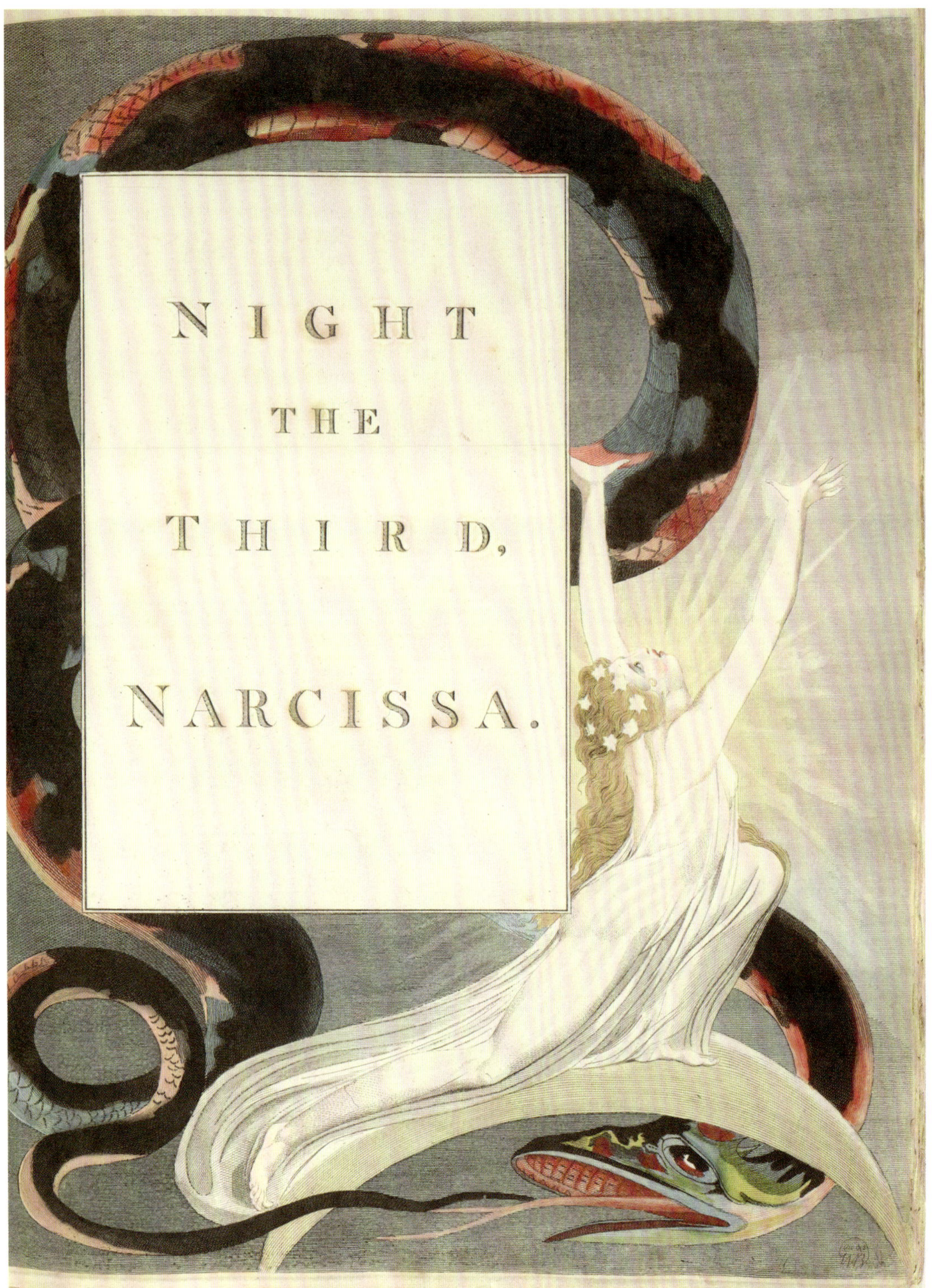

Plate 8
William Blake, *Edward Young's Night Thoughts*: "Night the Third, Narcissa," 1797

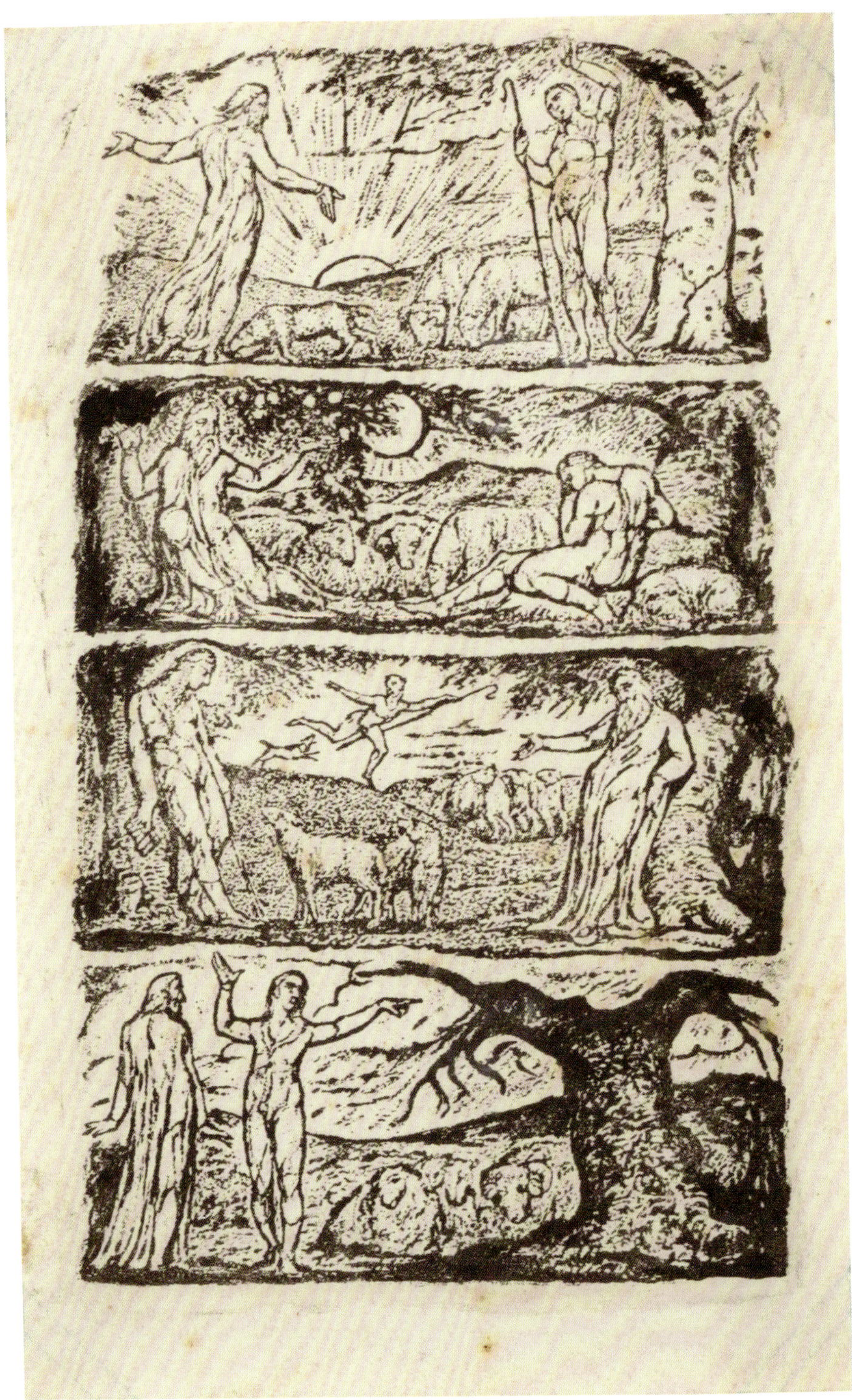

Plate 9
William Blake, *The Pastorals of Virgil*, 1821

To face page 13.

ILLUSTRATIONS

OF

IMITATION OF ECLOGUE I.

FRONTISPIECE.

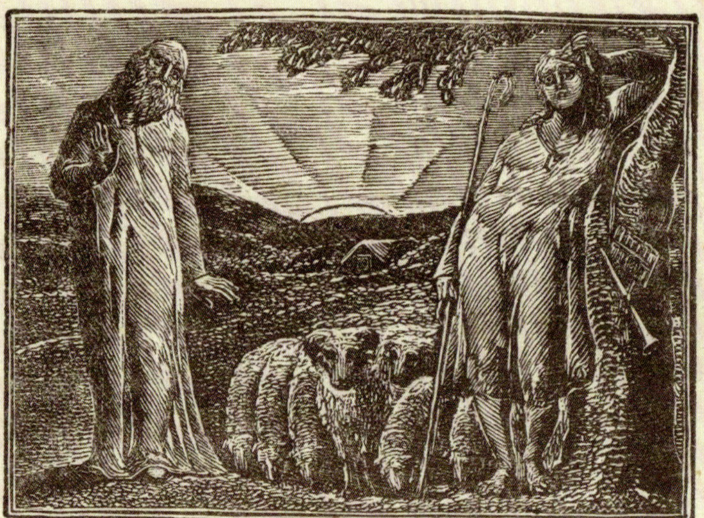

THENOT AND COLINET.

The Illustrations of this English Pastoral are by the famous BLAKE, the illustrator of *Young's* Night Thoughts, and *Blair's* Grave; who designed and engraved them himself. This is mentioned, as they display less of art than genius, and are much admired by some eminent painters.

Plate 10
William Blake, *The Pastorals of Virgil*, 1821

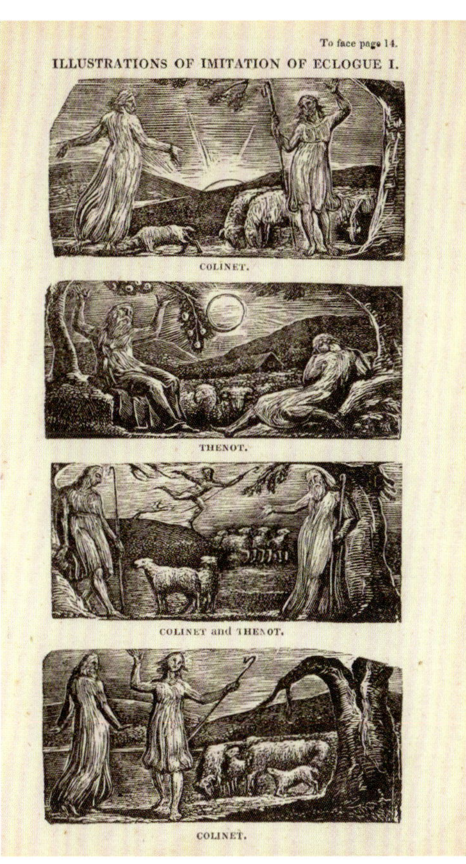
To face page 14.

ILLUSTRATIONS OF IMITATION OF ECLOGUE I.

COLINET.

THENOT.

COLINET and THENOT.

COLINET.

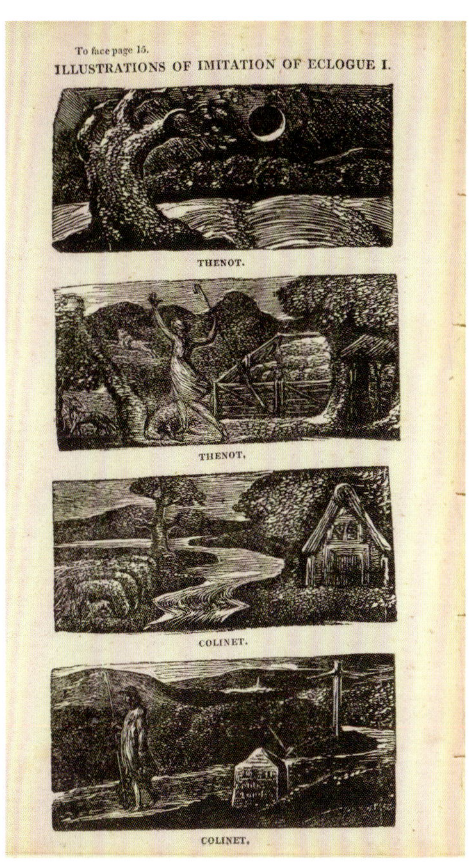
To face page 15.

ILLUSTRATIONS OF IMITATION OF ECLOGUE I.

THENOT.

THENOT.

COLINET.

COLINET.

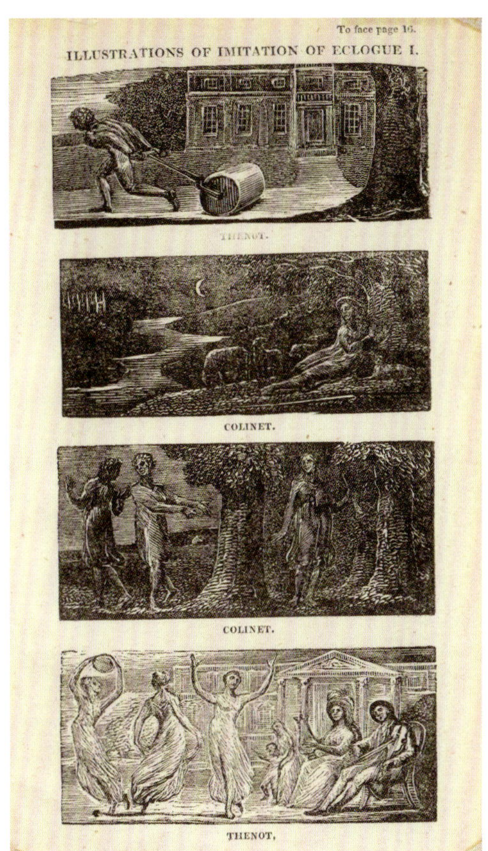
To face page 16.

ILLUSTRATIONS OF IMITATION OF ECLOGUE I.

THENOT.

COLINET.

COLINET.

THENOT.

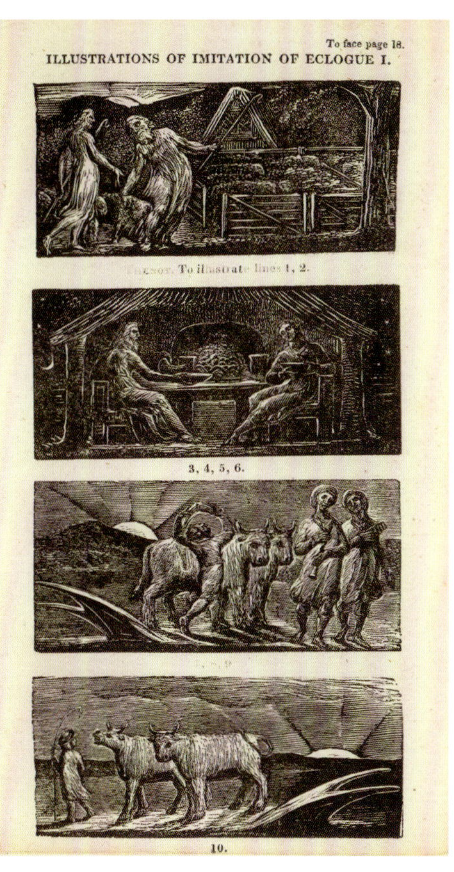
To face page 18.

ILLUSTRATIONS OF IMITATION OF ECLOGUE I.

THENOT. To illustrate lines 1, 2.

3, 4, 5, 6.

19.

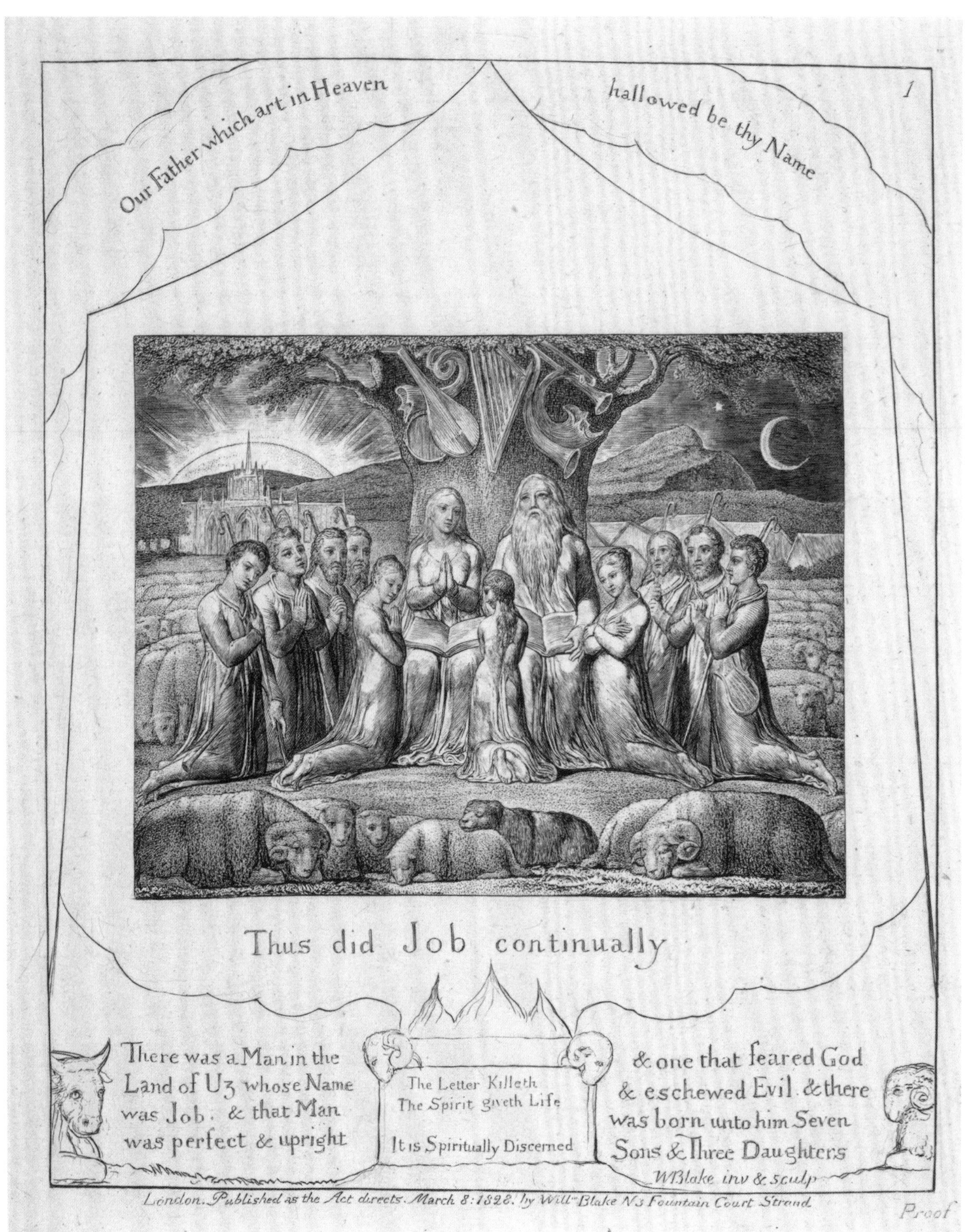

Plate 11
William Blake, *Illustrations of the Book of Job: Job and His Family*, 1825

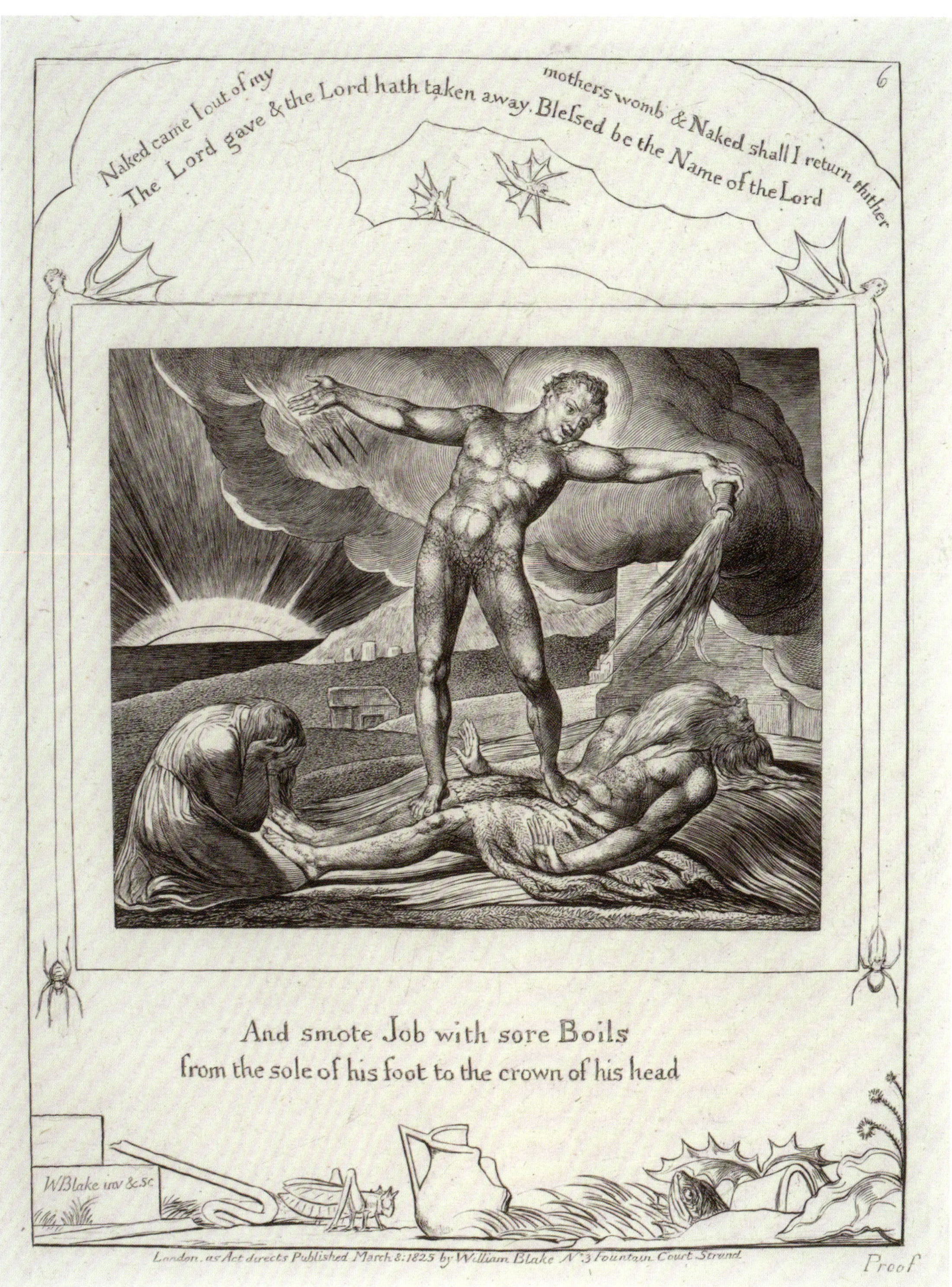

Plate 12
William Blake, *Illustrations of the Book of Job: Satan Smiting Job*, 1825

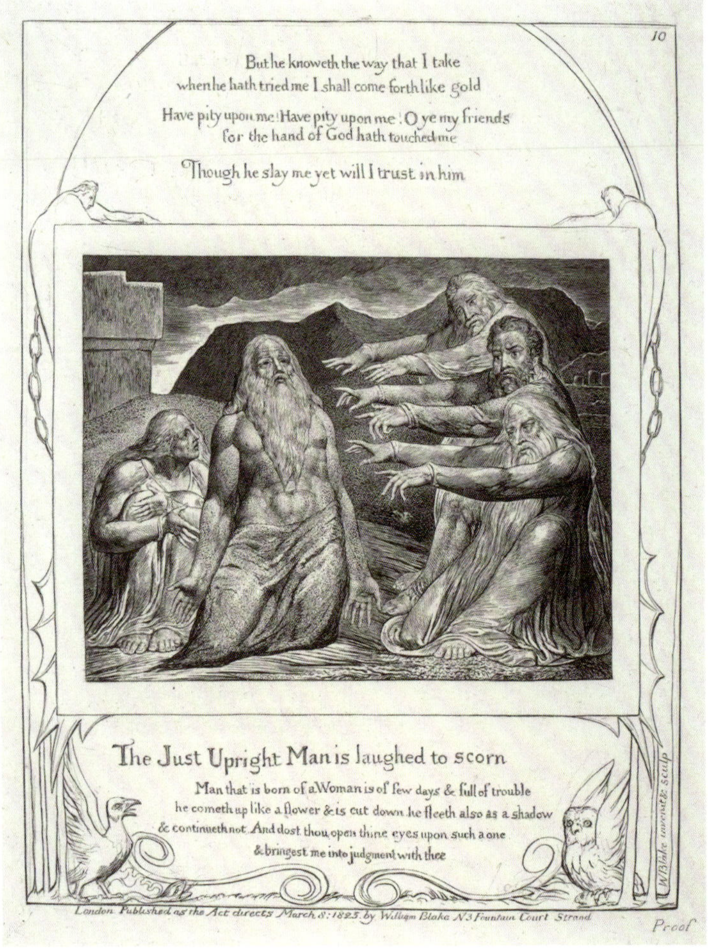

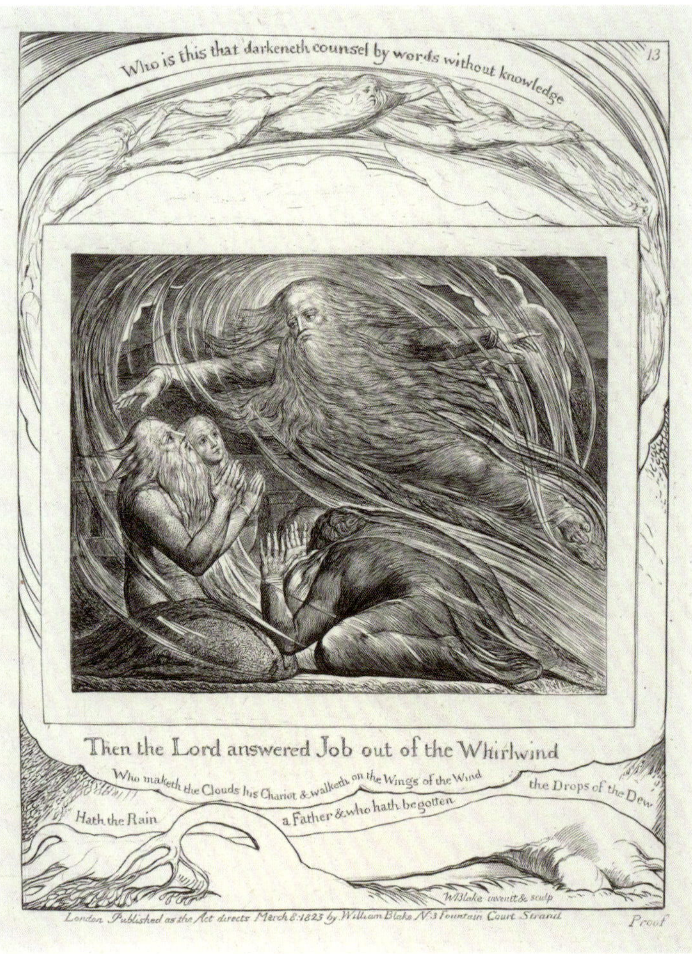

Plate 13
William Blake, *Illustrations of the Book of Job*: *Job Rebuked*, 1825

Plate 14
William Blake, *Illustrations of the Book of Job*: *The Lord Answering Job*, 1825

Plate 15
William Blake, *Illustrations of the Book of Job*: *Behemoth*, 1825

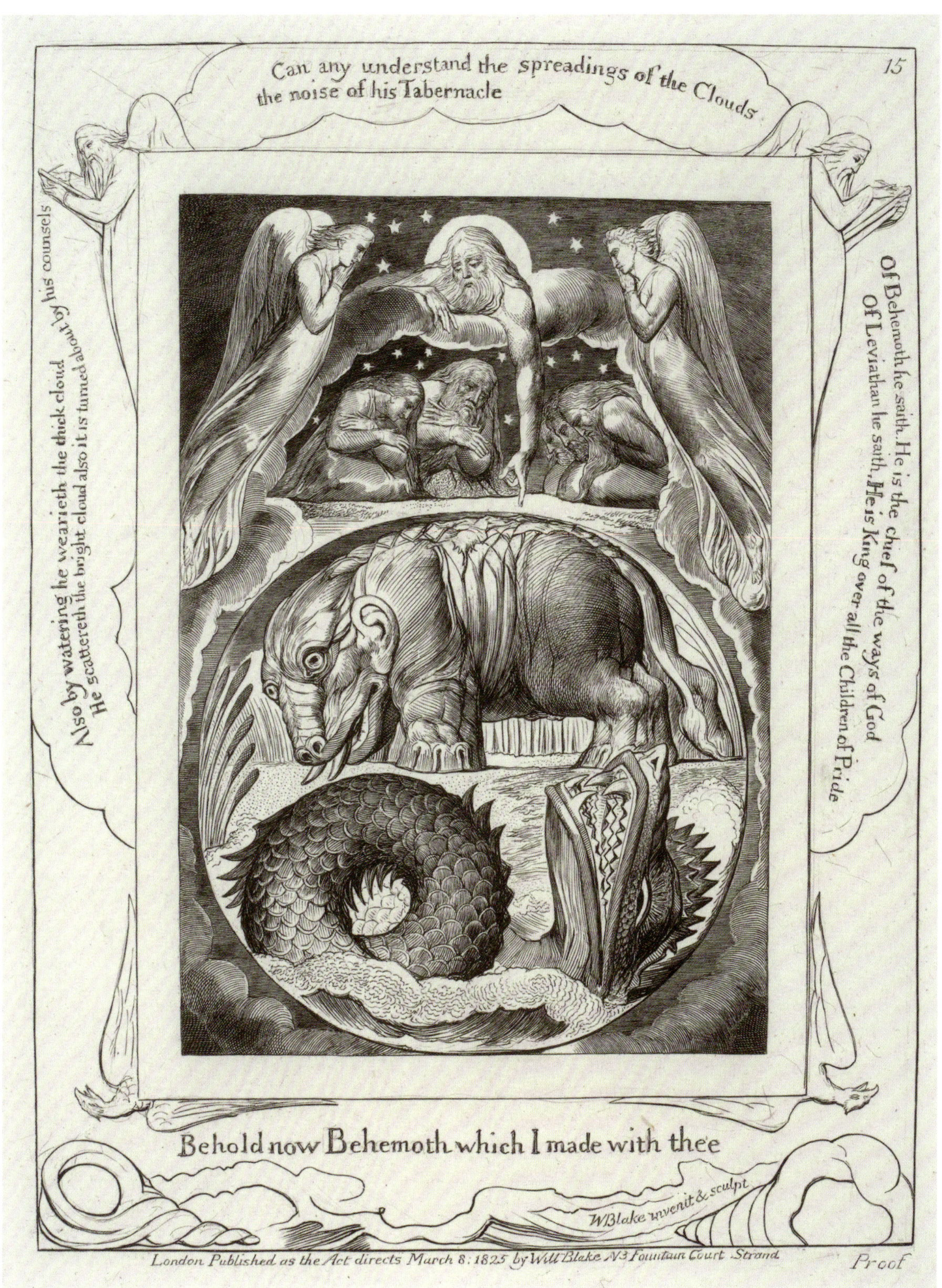
15
Can any understand the spreadings of the Clouds
the noise of his Tabernacle
Also by watering he wearieth the thick cloud
He scattereth the bright cloud also it is turned about by his counsels
Of Behemoth he saith, He is the chief of the ways of God
Of Leviathan he saith, He is King over all the Children of Pride
Behold now Behemoth which I made with thee
W Blake invenit & sculpt
London Published as the Act directs March 8: 1825 by Will Blake N3 Fountain Court Strand
Proof

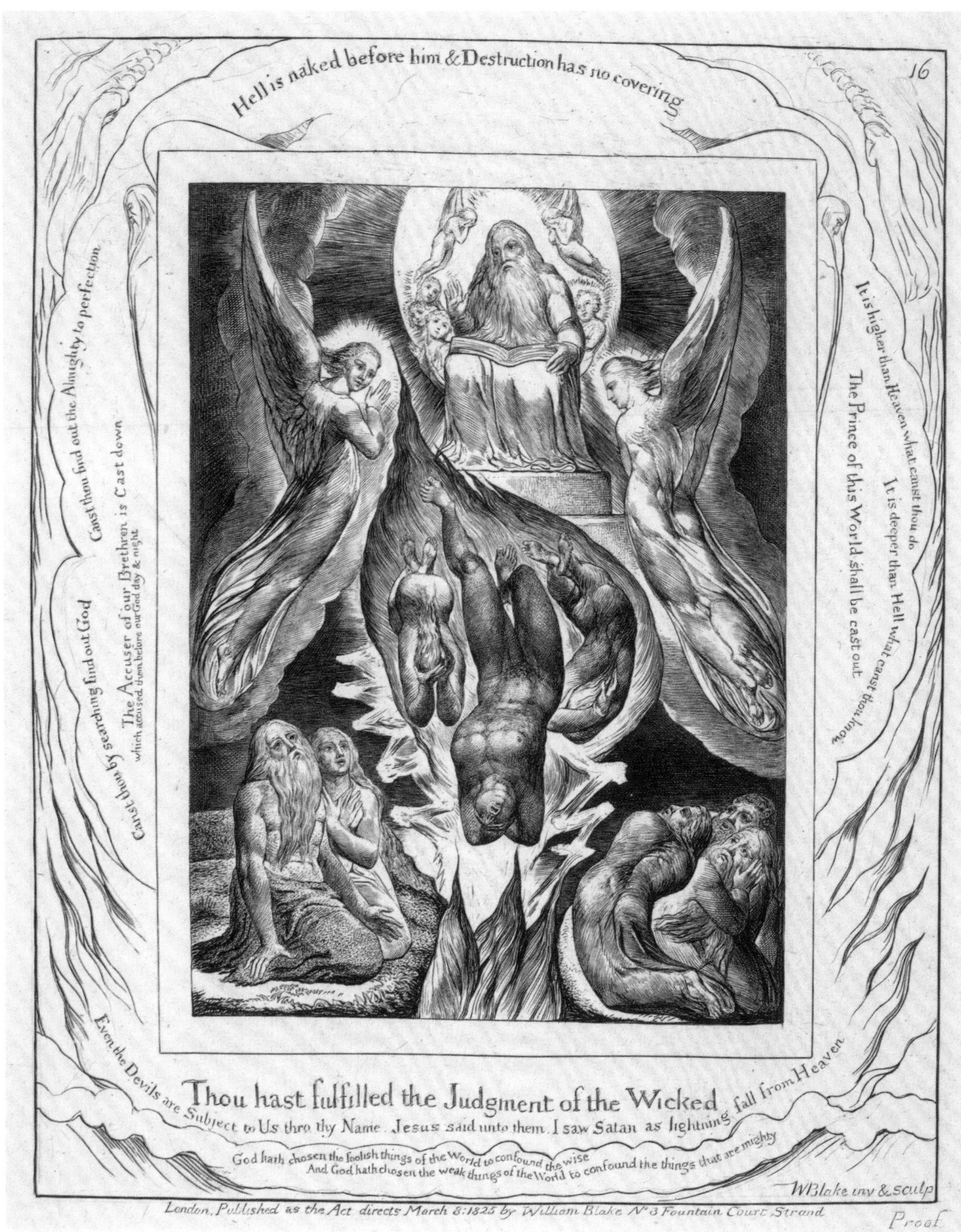

Plate 16
William Blake, *Illustrations of the Book of Job: Fall of Satan*, 1825

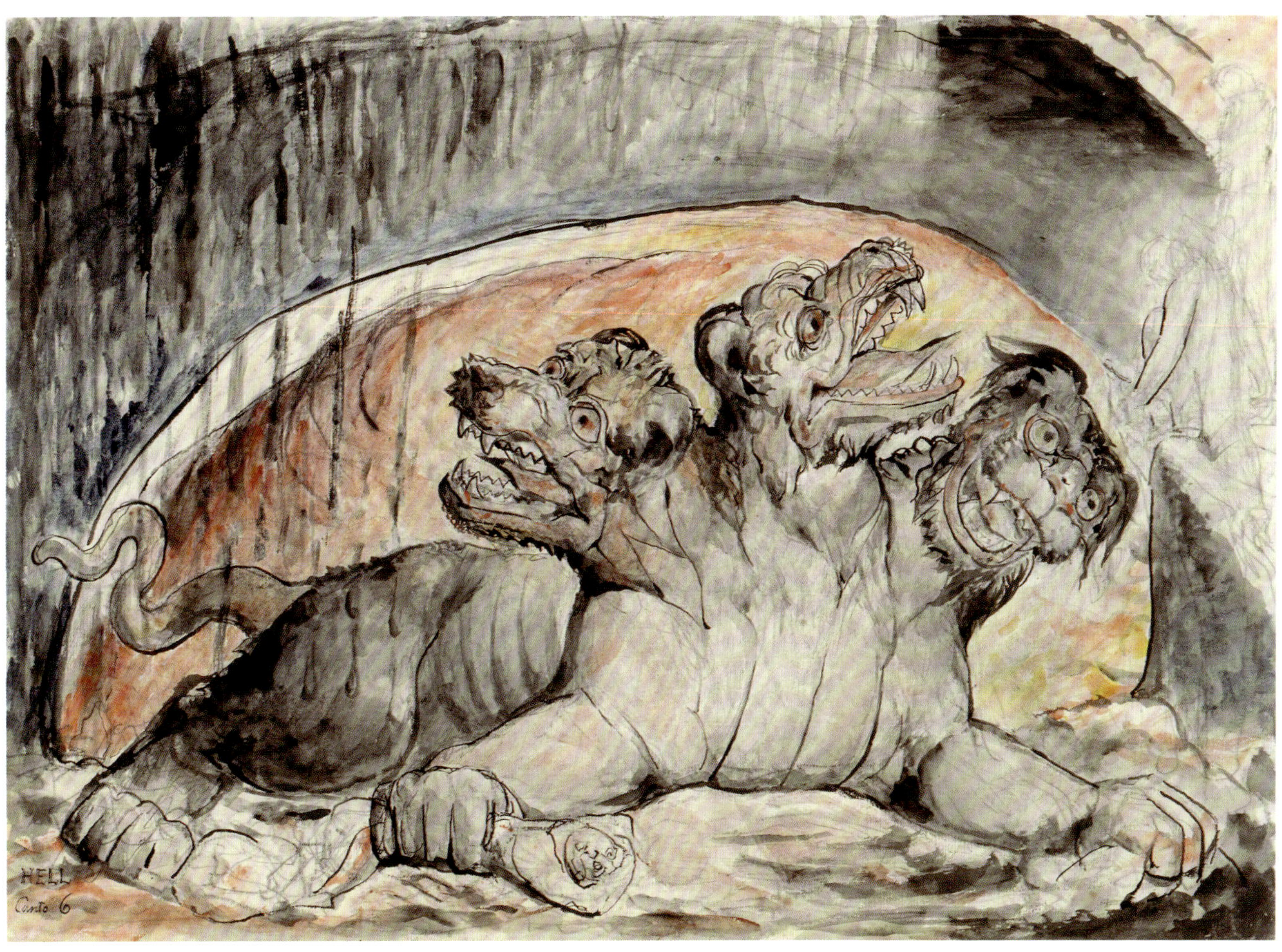

Plate 17
William Blake, *Cerberus*, 1824–27

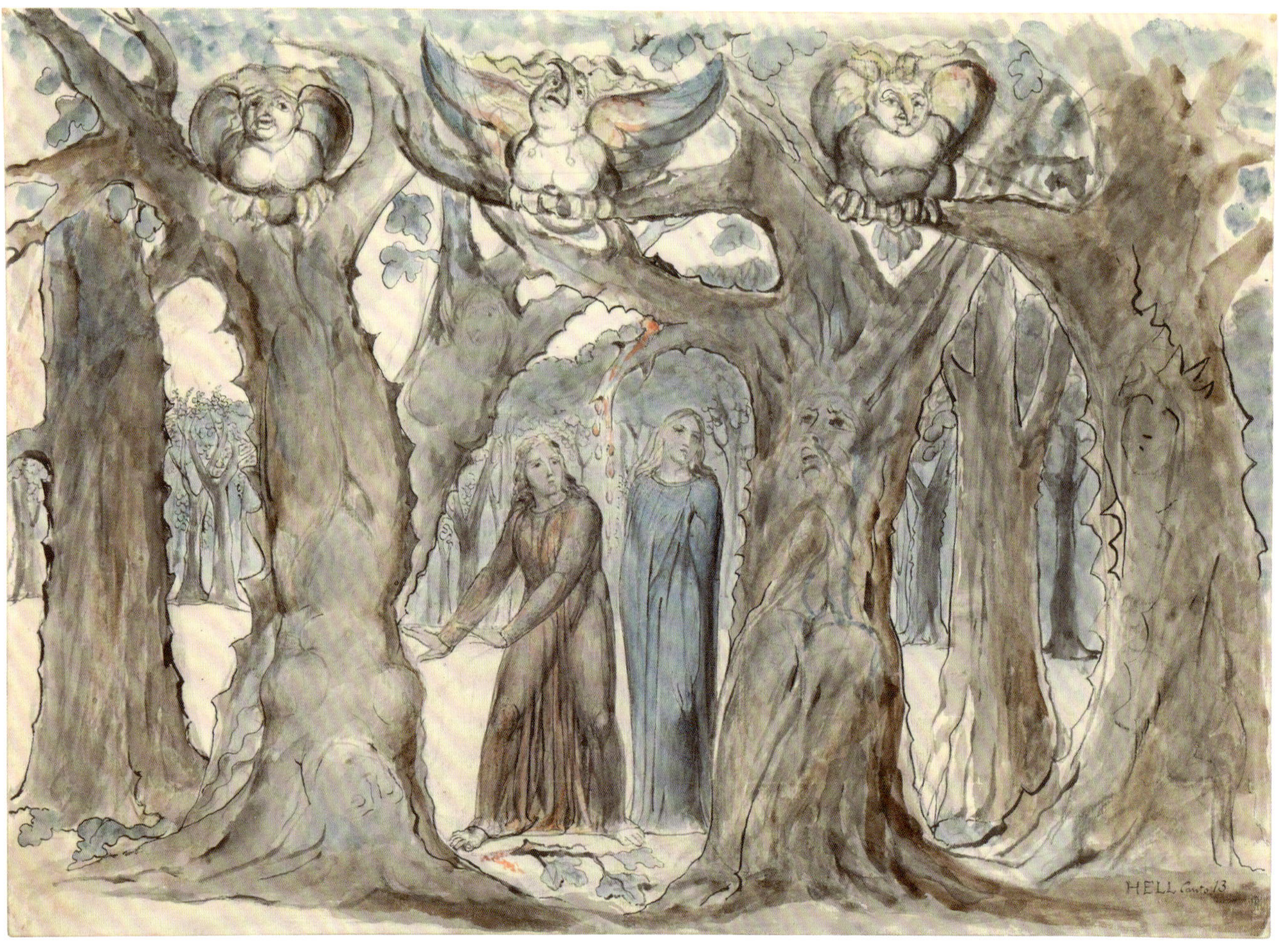

Plate 18
William Blake, *The Wood of Self-Murderers: The Harpies and the Suicides*, 1824–27

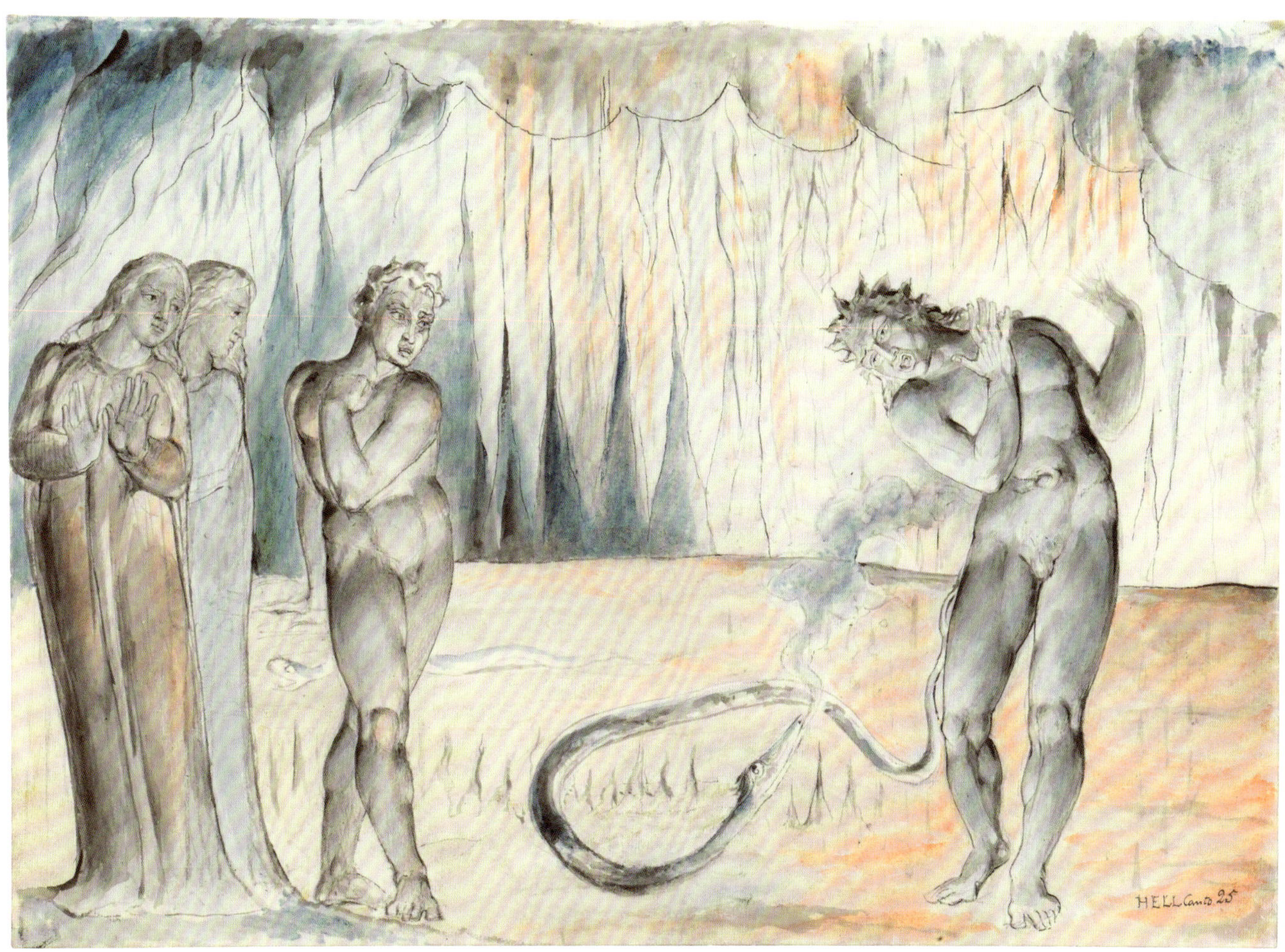

Plate 19
William Blake, *The Serpent Attacking Buoso Donati*, 1824–27

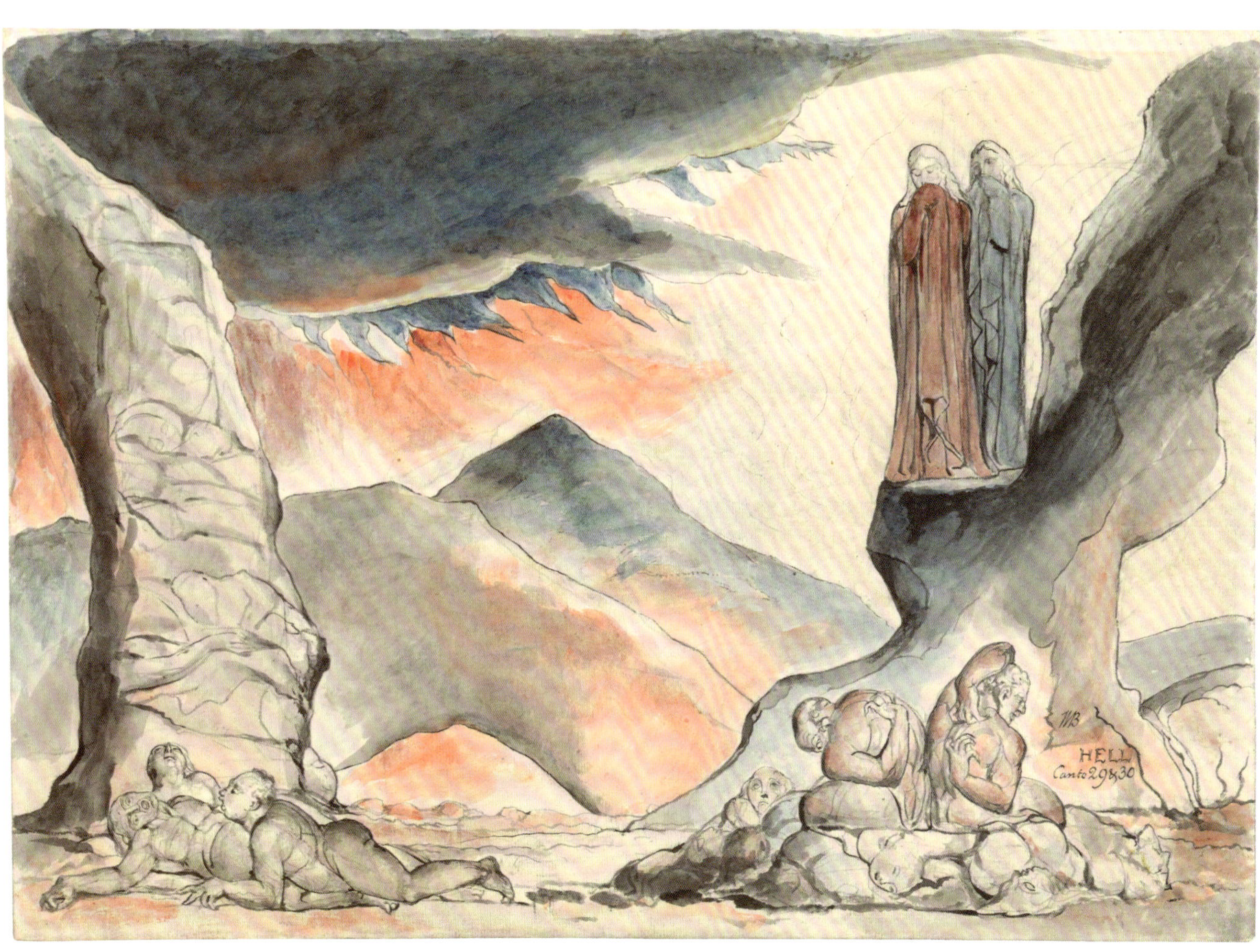

Plate 20
William Blake, *The Pit of Disease: The Falsifiers,* 1824–27

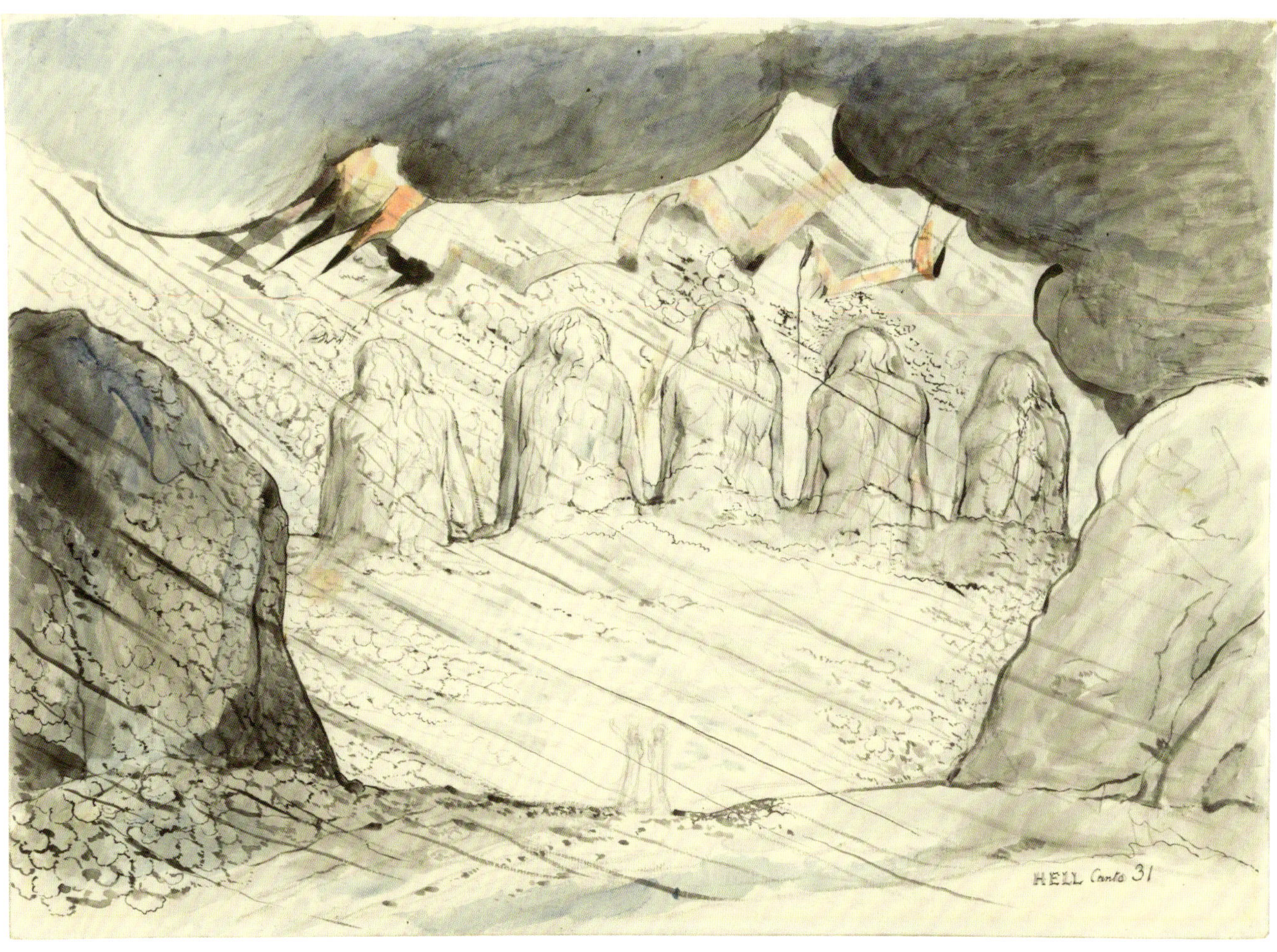

Plate 21
William Blake, *The Primaeval Giants Sunk in the Soil*, 1824–27

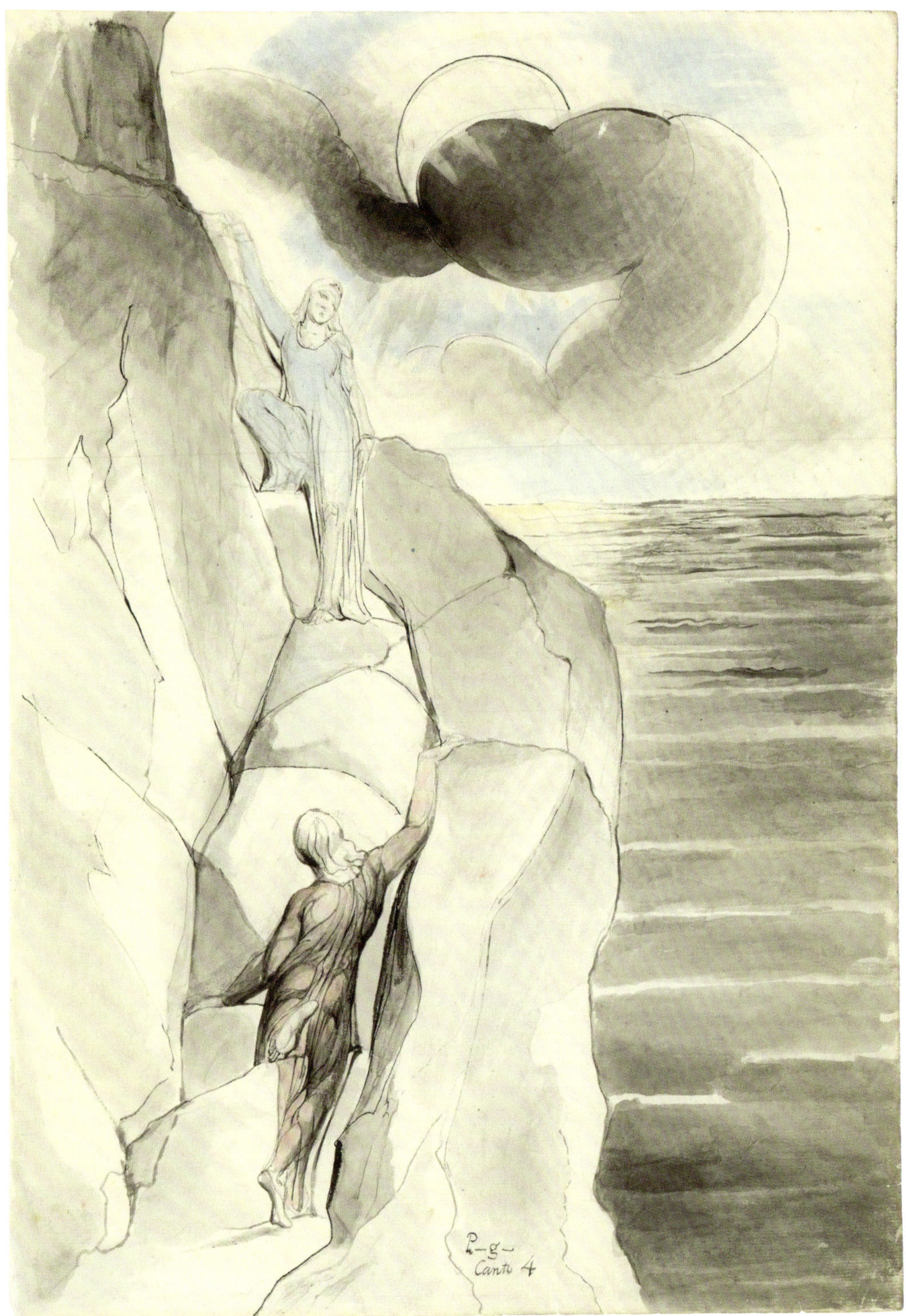

Plate 22
William Blake, *The Ascent of the Mountain of Purgatory*, 1824–27

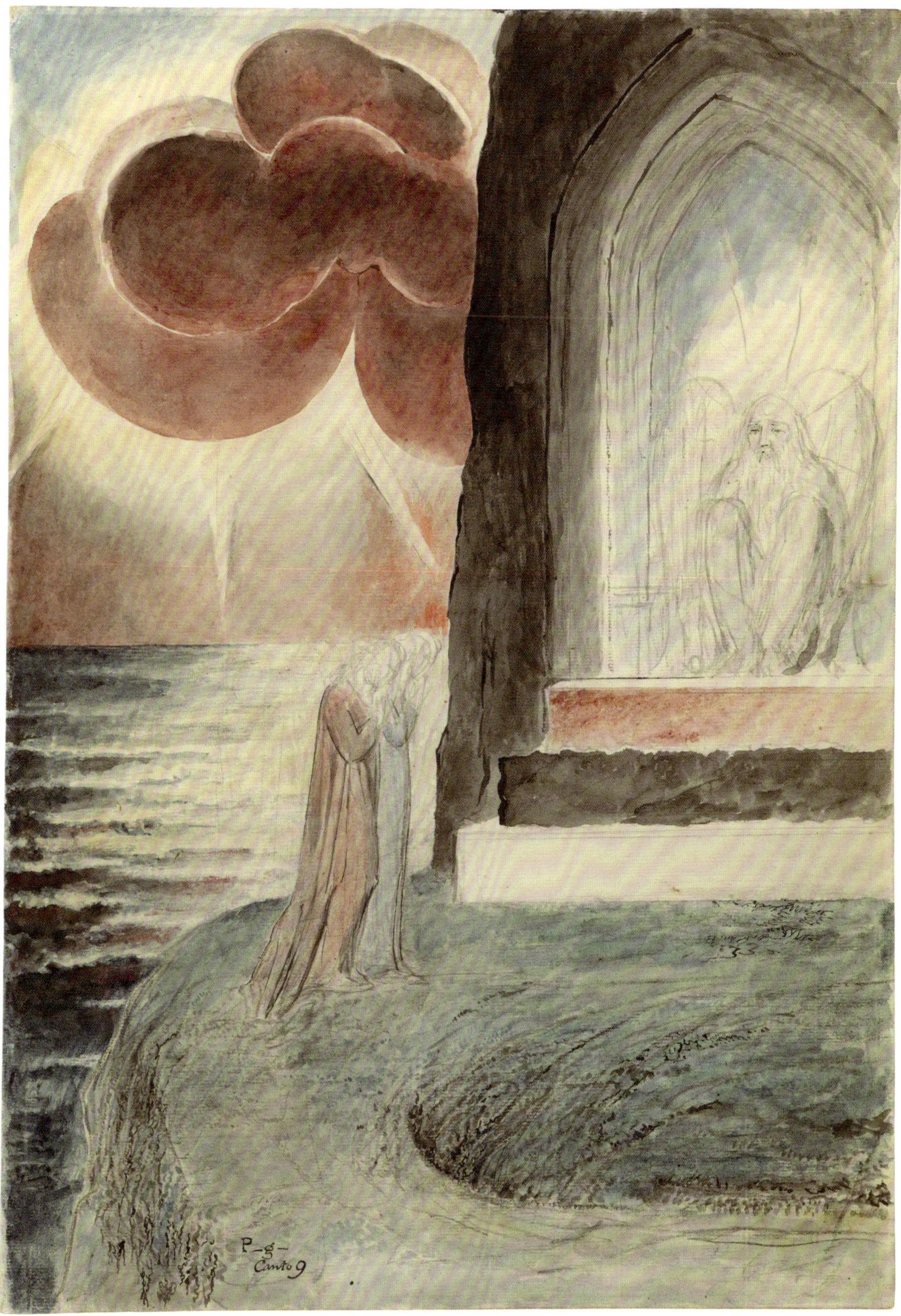

Plate 23
William Blake, *Dante and Virgil Approaching the Angel Who Guards the Entrance of Purgatory*, 1824–27

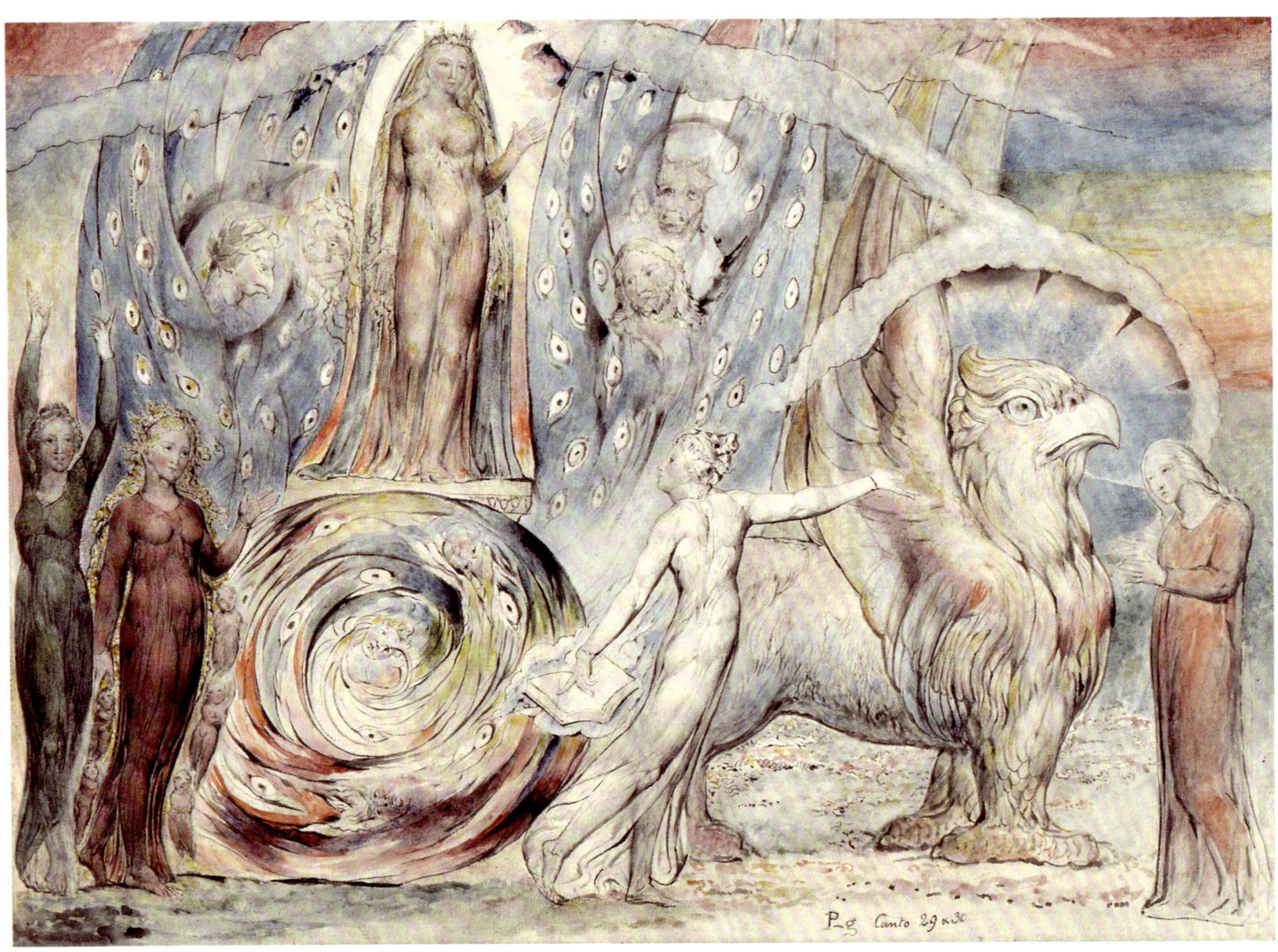

Plate 24
William Blake, *Beatrice Addressing Dante from the Car*, 1824–27

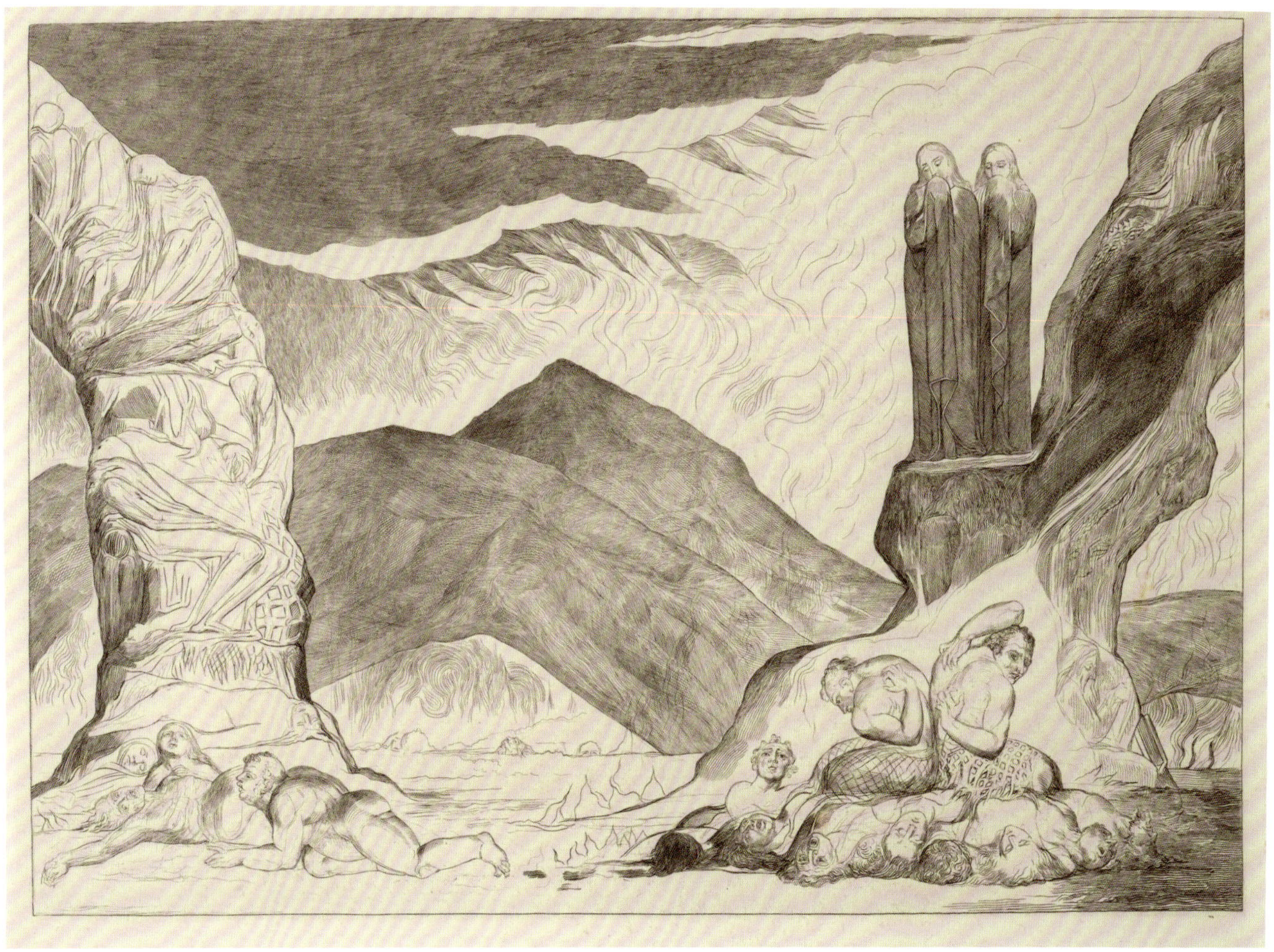

Plate 25
William Blake, *The Pit of Disease: The Falsifiers*, 1826–27

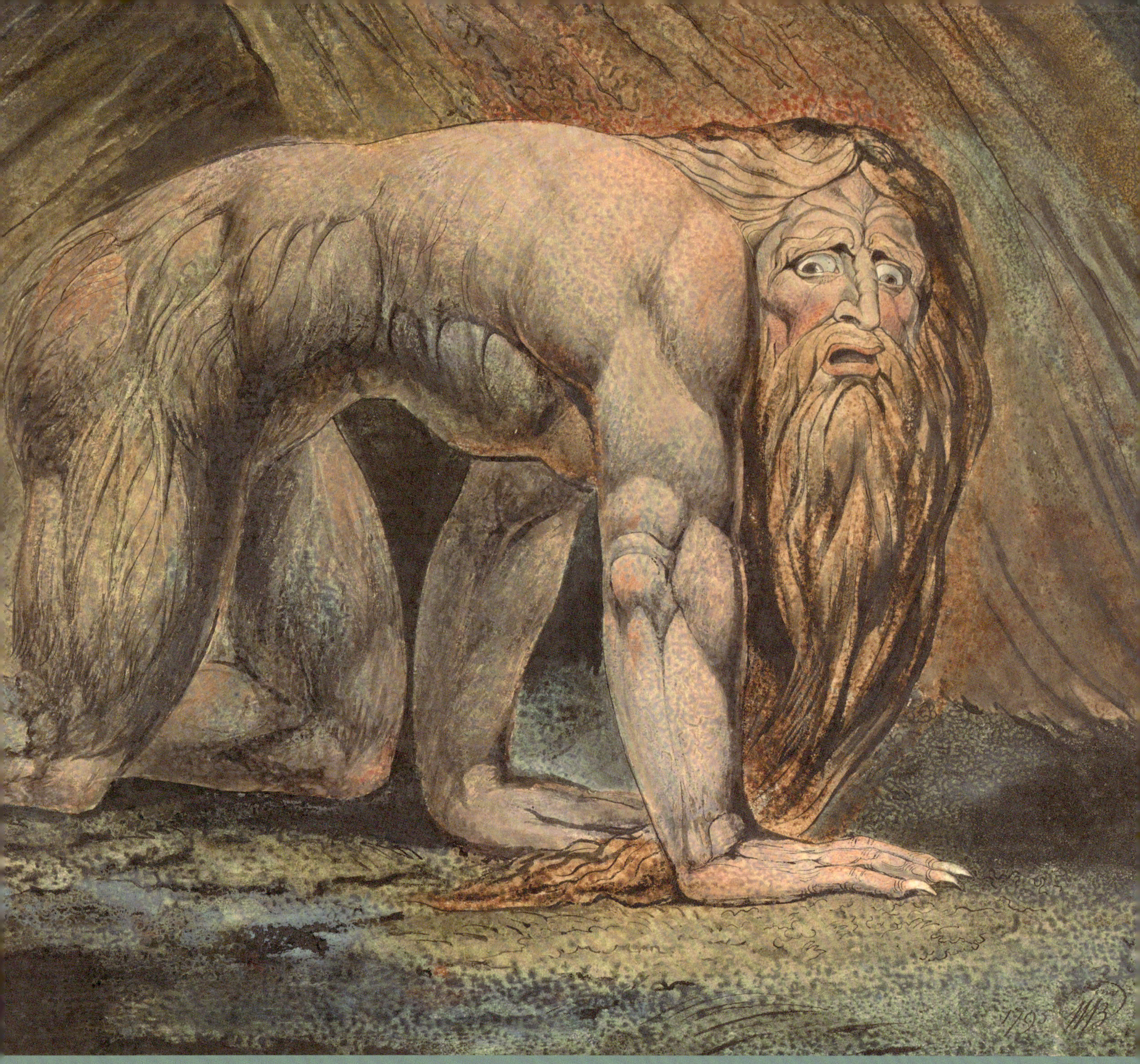

"I find more & more that my Style of Designing is a Species by Itself."

—William Blake to the Reverend Trusler, August 10, 1799

The Painter-Illustrator

PLATES 26–50

Beyond Blake's work as a professional printmaker (see p. 39), his output as an illustrator of other authors' texts is marked by a tendency to do more than directly illustrate. Sometimes his illustrations seem akin to adaptive theatrical performances of texts, or personal commentaries; often they are deeply spiritual meditations, intrigued explorations, or free associations.

A hugely significant patron for Blake, and one who appreciated his frequently innovative approach to subject matter, was the civil servant Thomas Butts. In 1799 Butts commissioned from Blake fifty paintings in tempera of biblical scenes. Thirty survive, though often in ruinous states as a result of Blake's tempera technique; among other aspects, his use of carpenter's glue as a binding medium caused intense darkening and discoloration over time (plates 31–35). Confusingly, Blake called the technique "fresco." Butts also commissioned biblical watercolors (plates 36–40), offering a guinea for each one produced over a period of about ten years; Blake produced about eighty for him. Like the temperas, the watercolors use deceptively simple, often symmetrical, compositions, but the vibrant, aqueous effects lend ethereality. Their wide-ranging biblical subject matter and nonsystematic production fit with the suggestion that they were intended as extra illustrations to be interleaved into a large Bible owned by Butts.

From 1795 Blake created a series of striking large color prints, also called large color printed drawings (plates 43–48), principally of biblical subjects, but including scenes from Milton, Shakespeare, and his own prophecies. These daunting works represent a landmark in Blake's experimentation with color printing. He made the powerful image of *God Judging Adam* from a partially relief-etched copper plate, evident in the slight embossing of God's figure (plate 47). For the others, Blake painted directly onto millboard, placed a damp sheet of paper on top, and ran it through his rolling press, thus transferring the design. He could pull two to three impressions from the same application of paint before it dried. Overall, he used twelve different designs to make thirty-three large color prints, of which thirty survive. Each is unique: even in the same design the density of the paint varies from one impression to the next, and Blake also completed the images differently in watercolor and ink.

JB

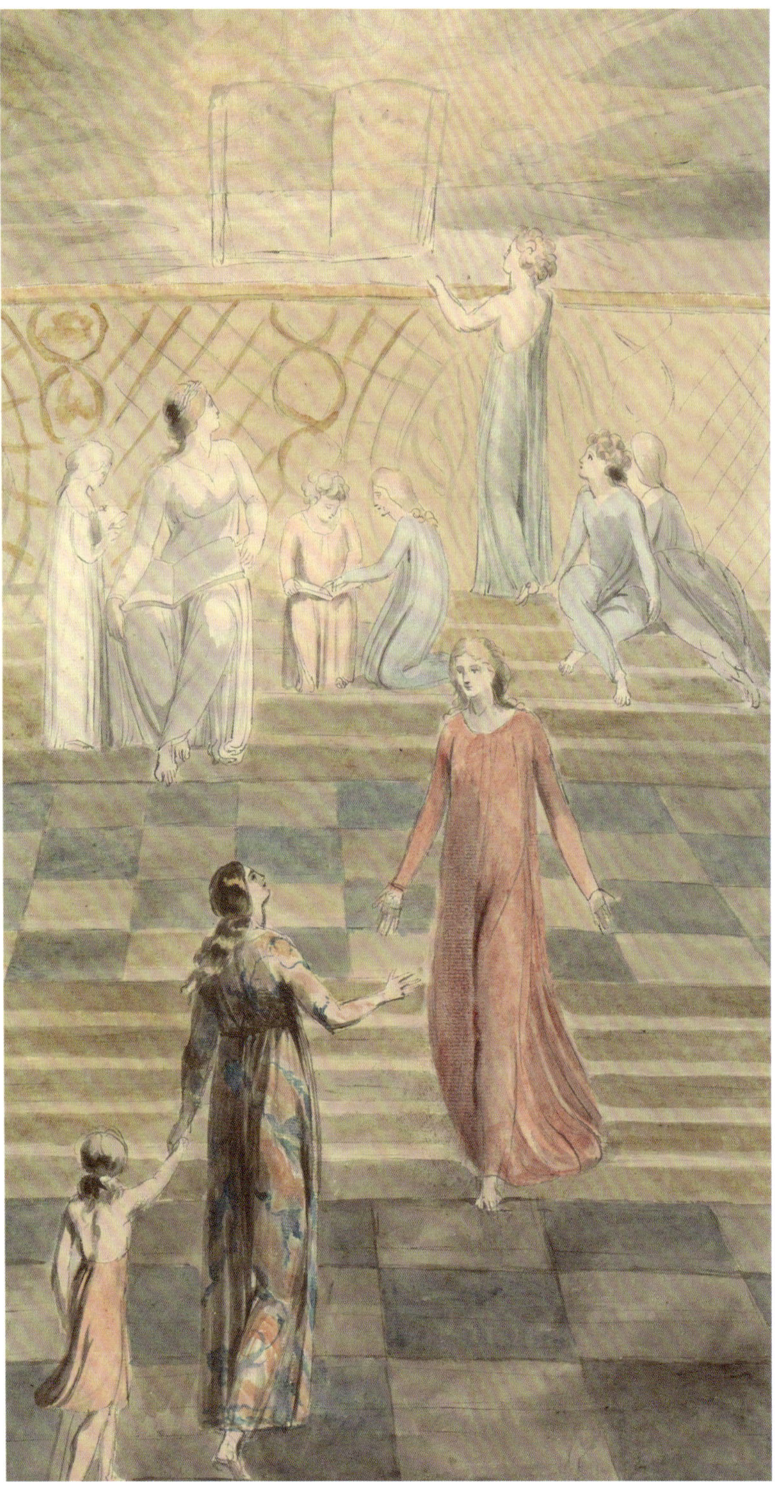

Plate 26
William Blake, *An Allegory of the Bible*, about 1780–85

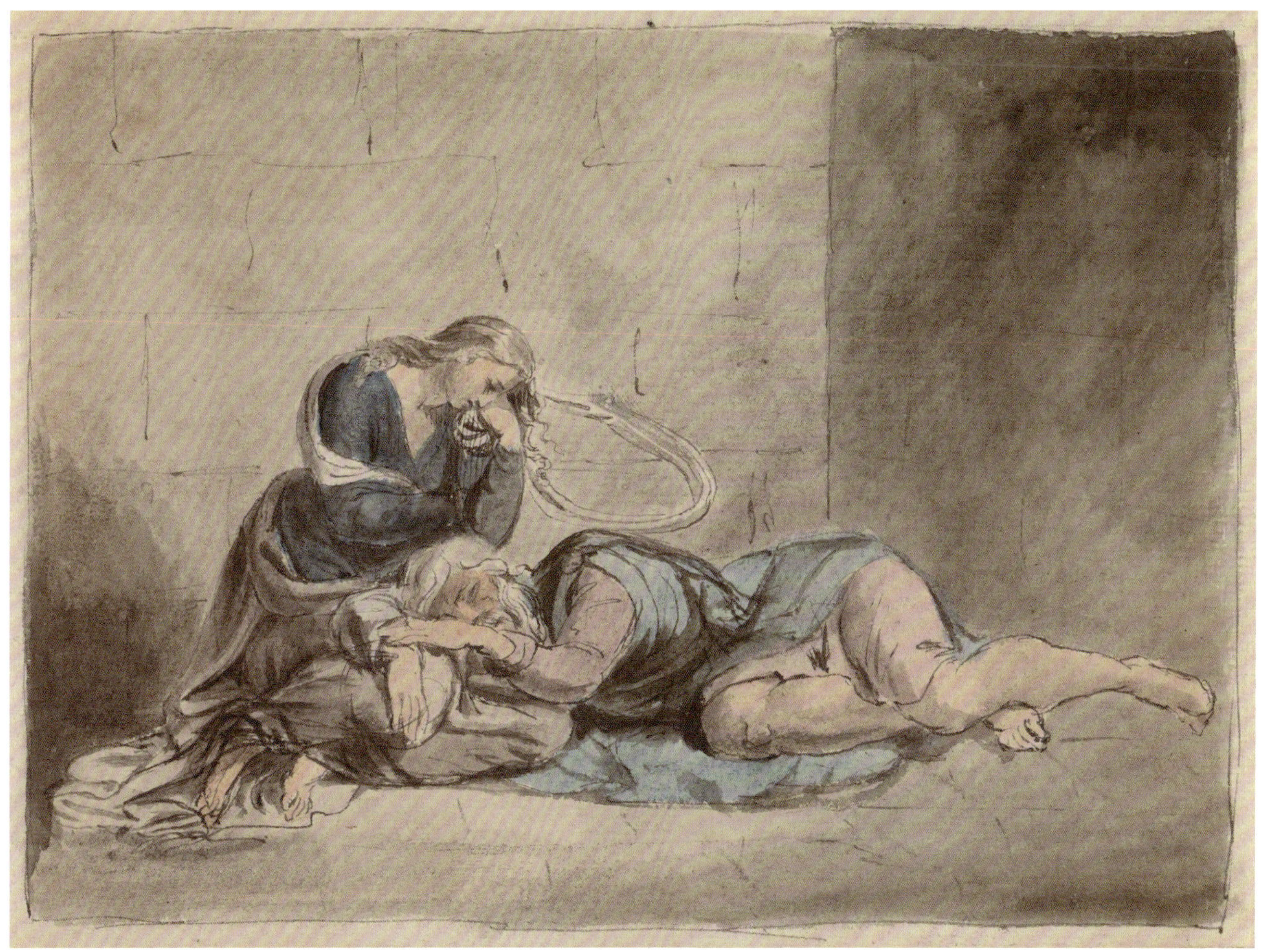

Plate 27
William Blake, *Lear and Cordelia in Prison*, about 1779

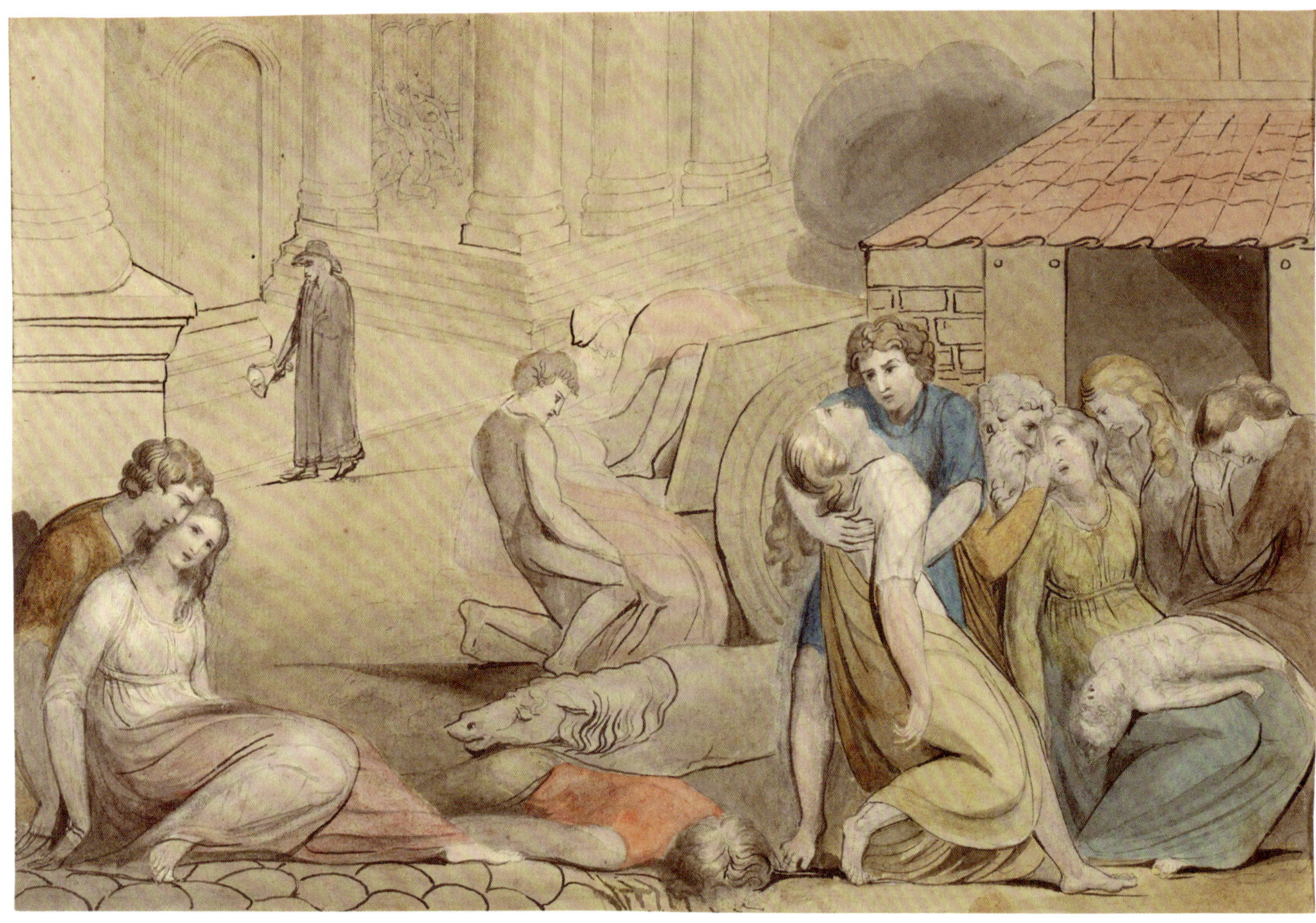

Plate 28
William Blake, *Pestilence*, about 1780–84

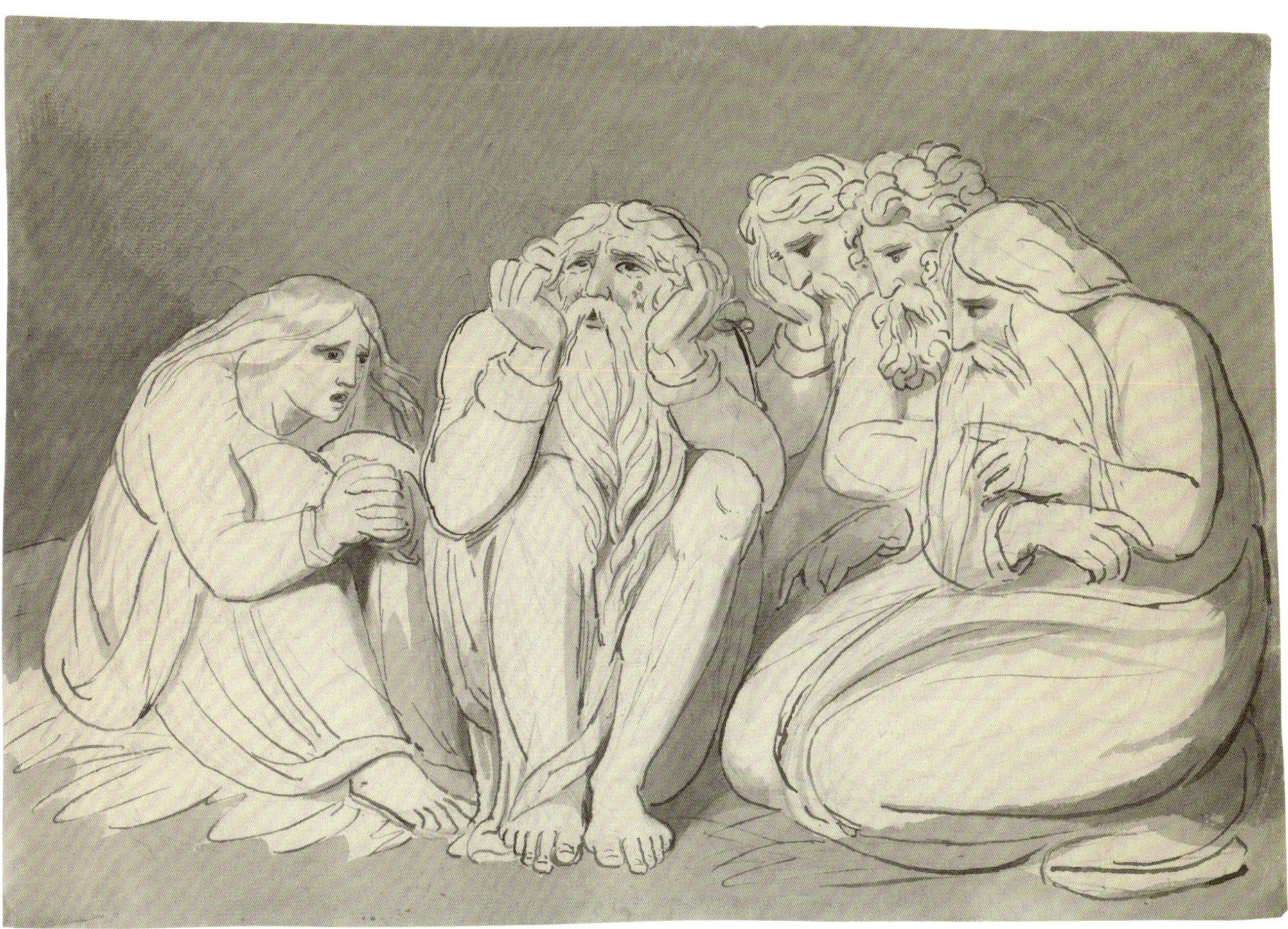

Plate 29
William Blake, *Job, His Wife and His Friends: The Complaint of Job*, about 1785

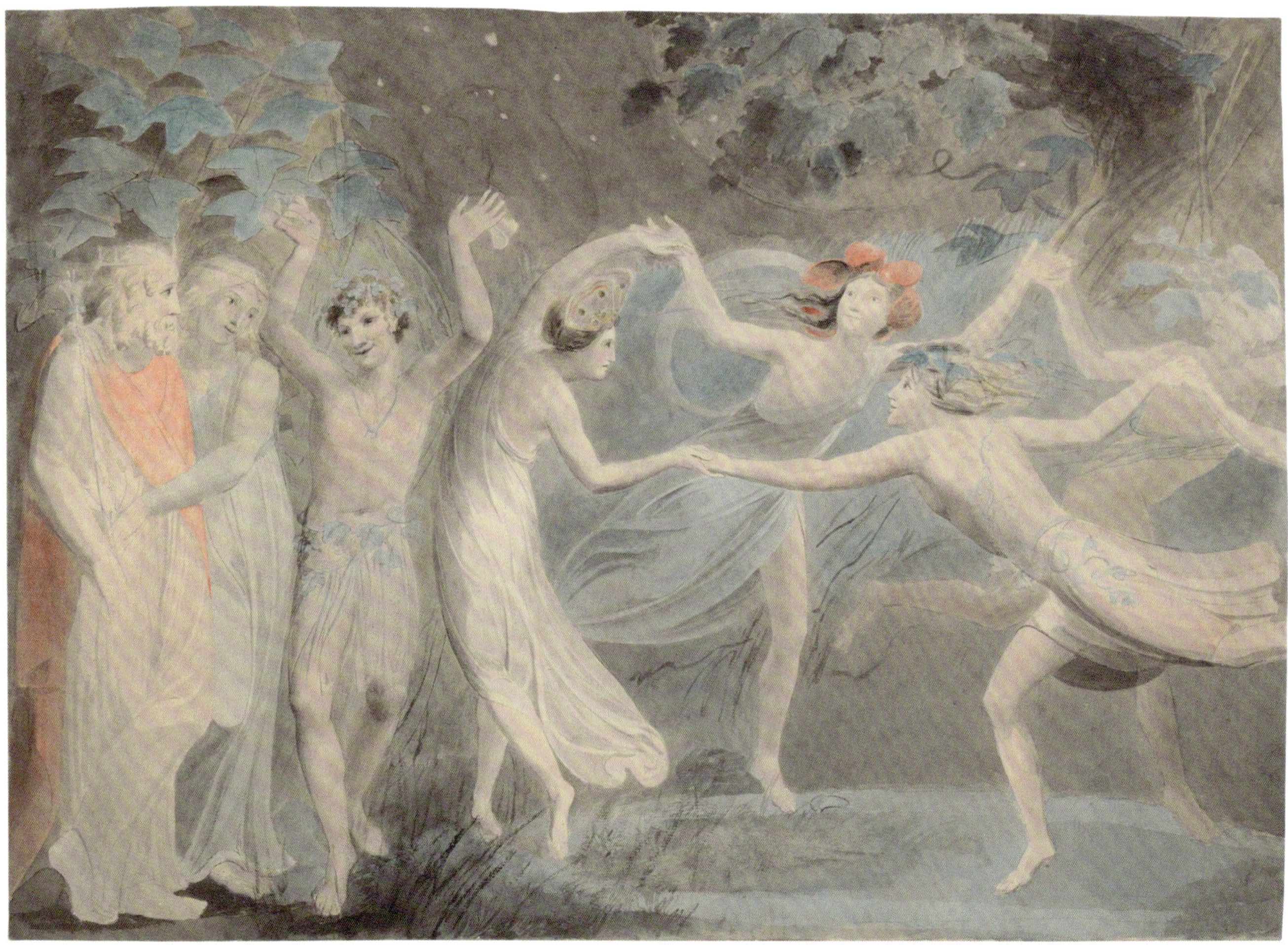

Plate 30
William Blake, *Oberon, Titania and Puck with Fairies Dancing*, about 1786

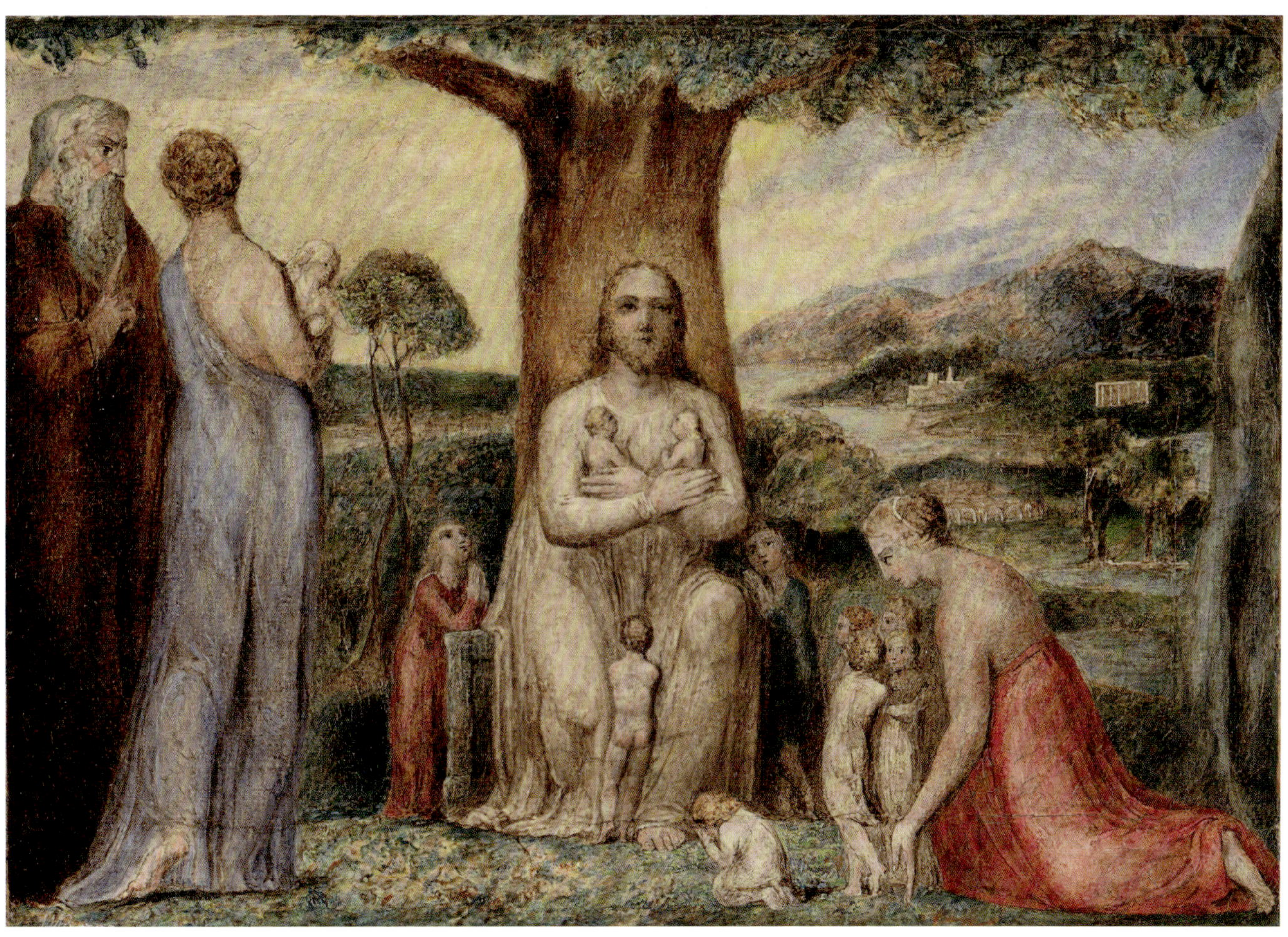

Plate 31
William Blake, *Christ Blessing the Little Children*, 1799

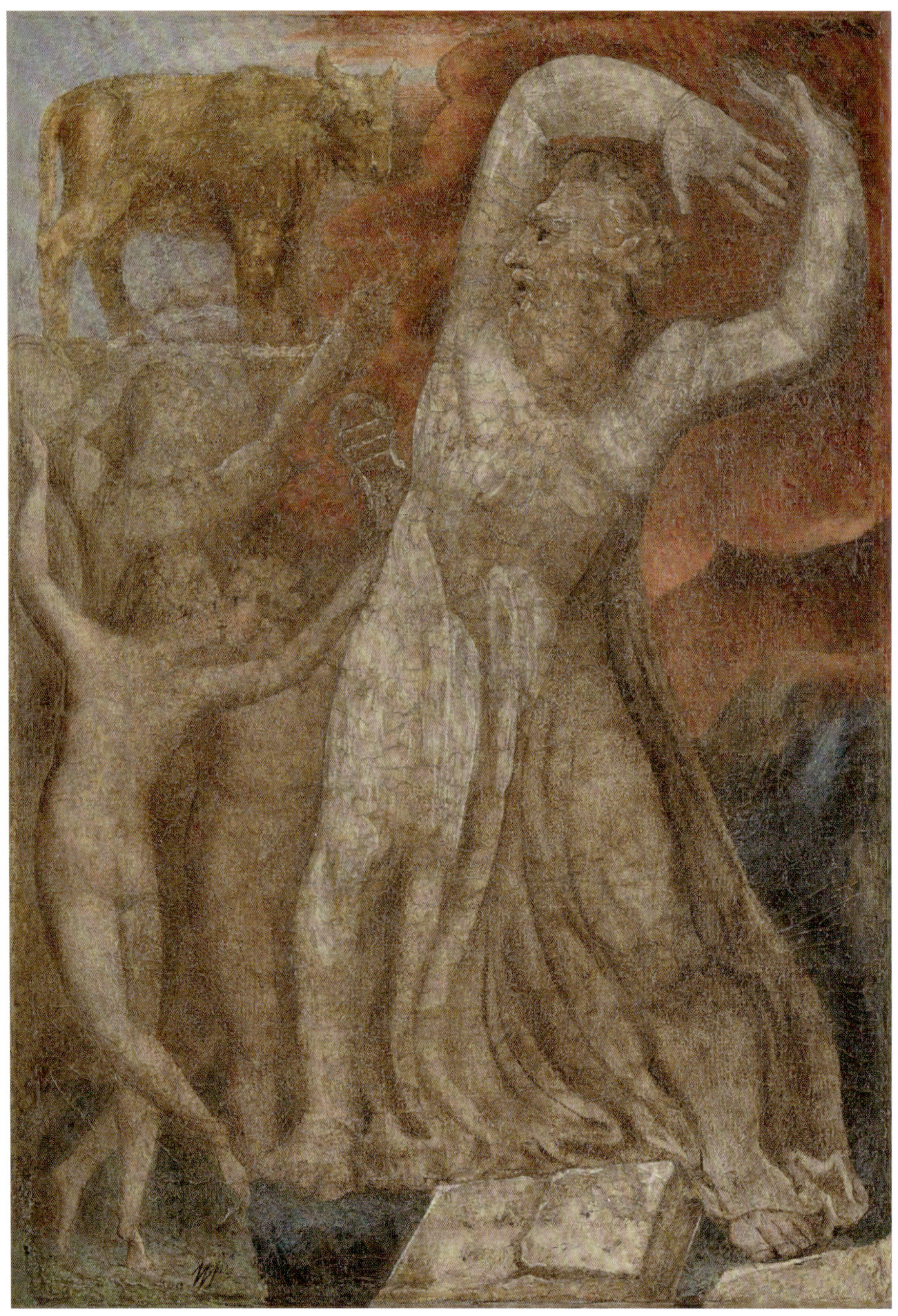

Plate 32
William Blake, *Moses Indignant at the Golden Calf*,
about 1799–1800

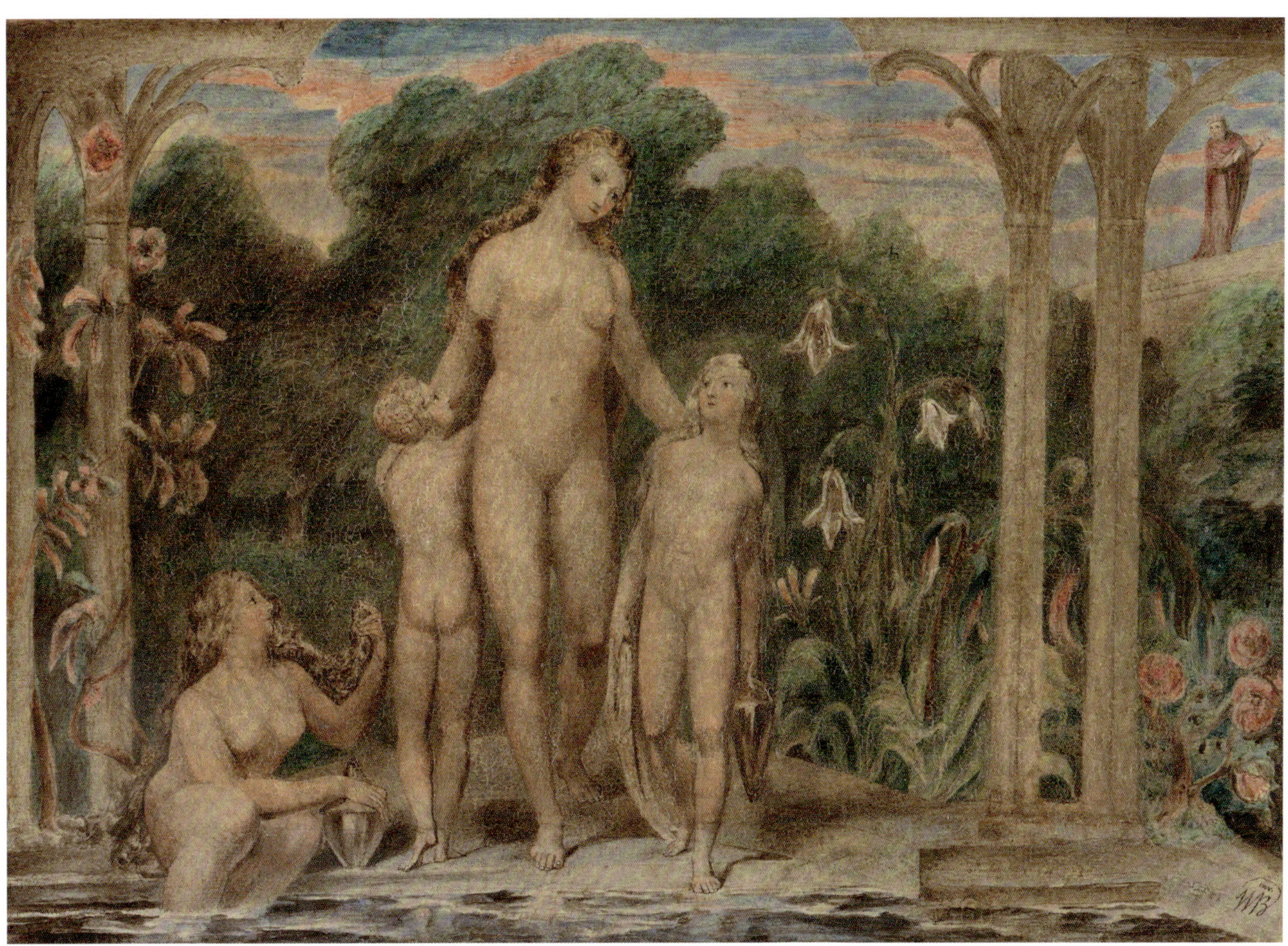

Plate 33
William Blake, *Bathsheba at the Bath*, about 1799–1800

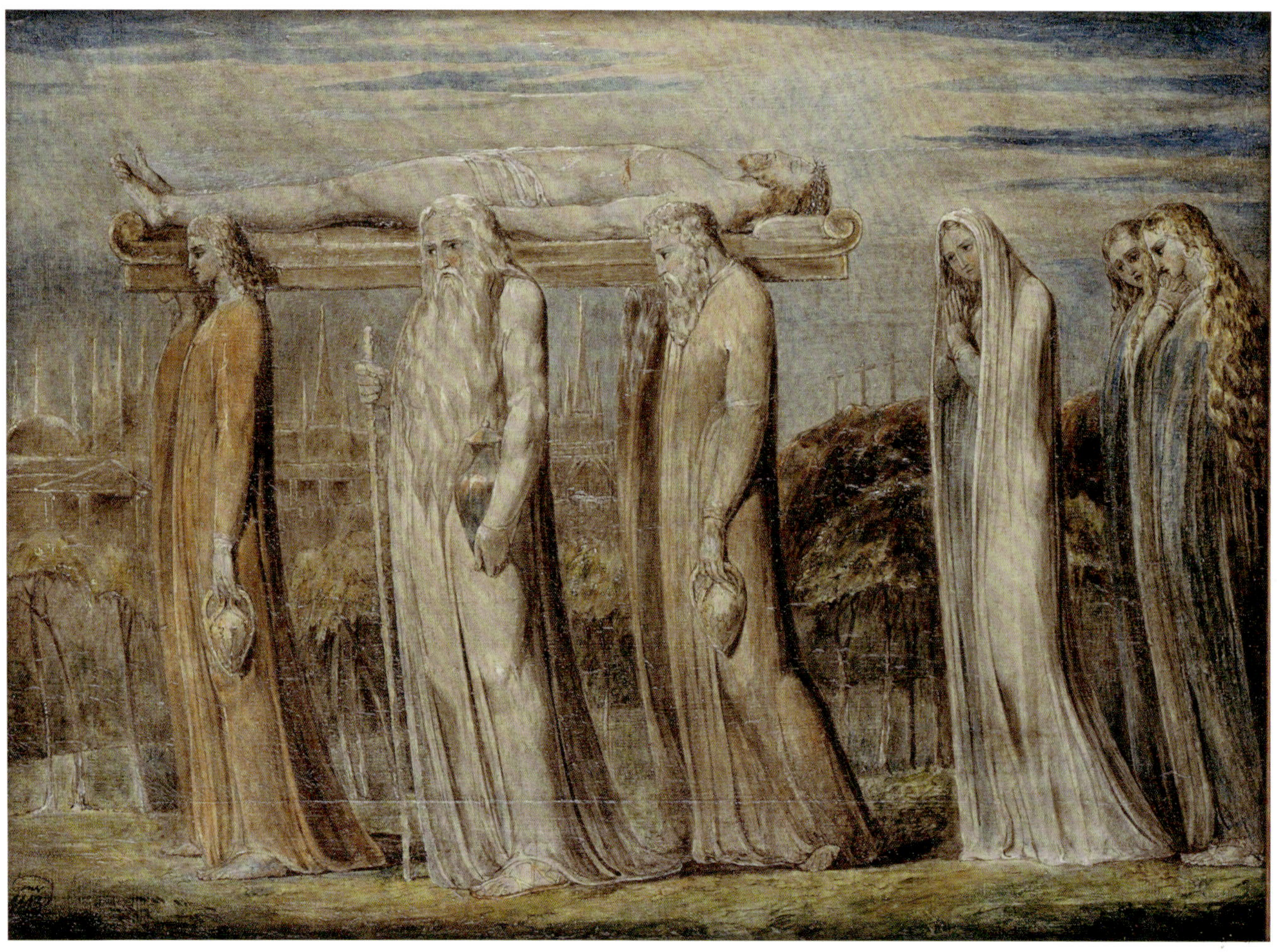

Plate 34
William Blake, *The Body of Christ Borne to the Tomb*, about 1799–1800

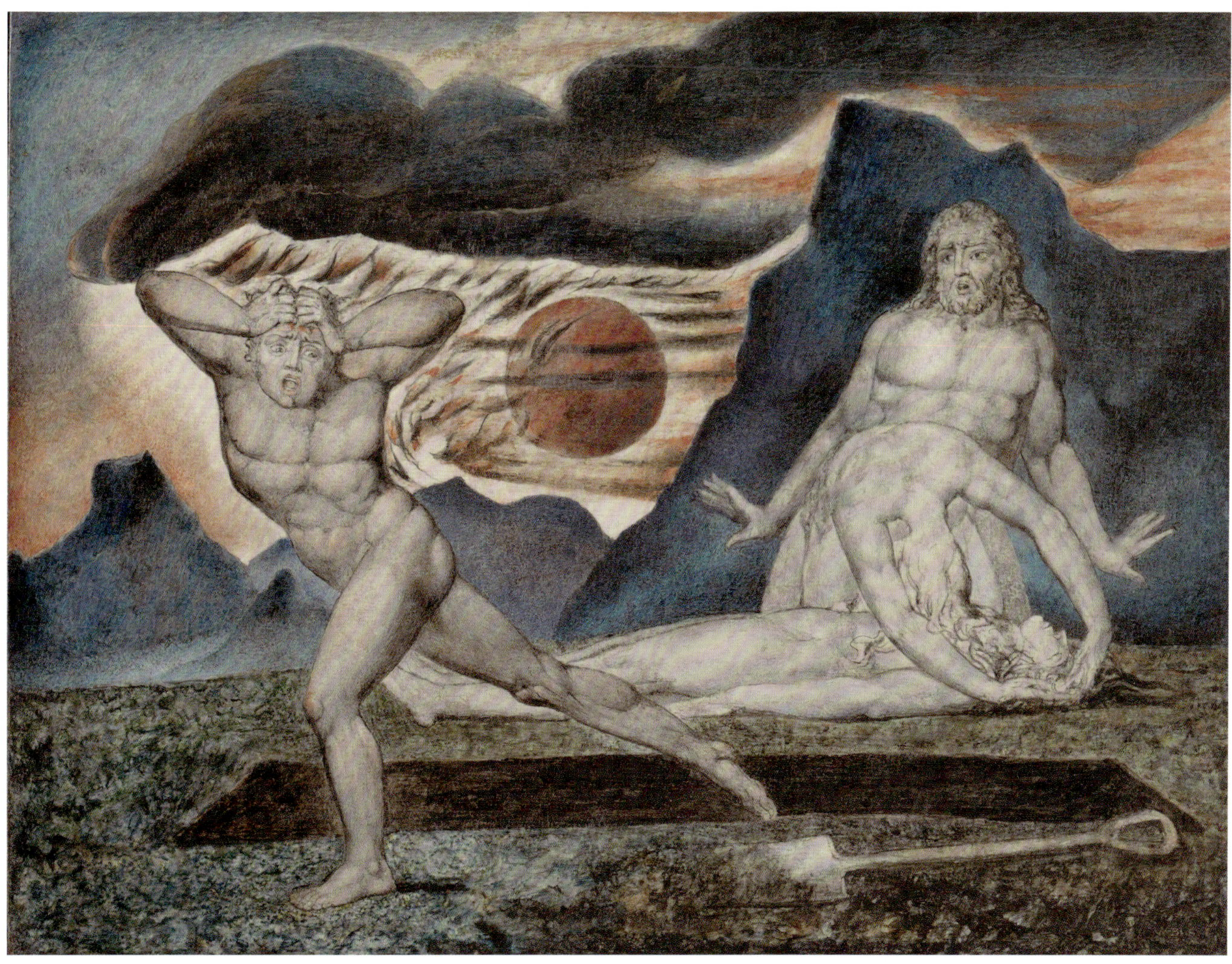

Plate 35
William Blake, *The Body of Abel Found by Adam and Eve*, about 1826

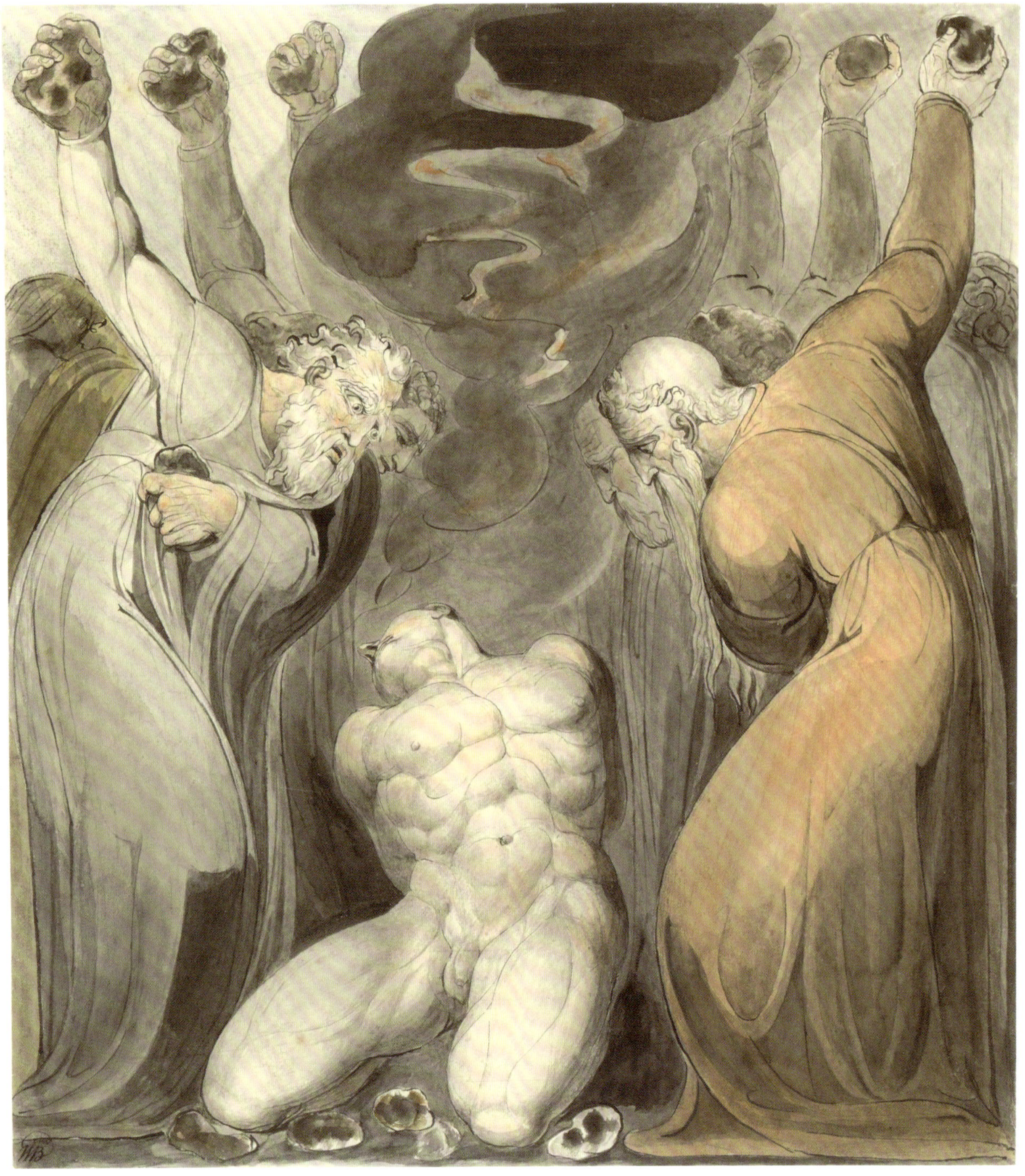

Plate 36
William Blake, *The Blasphemer*, about 1800

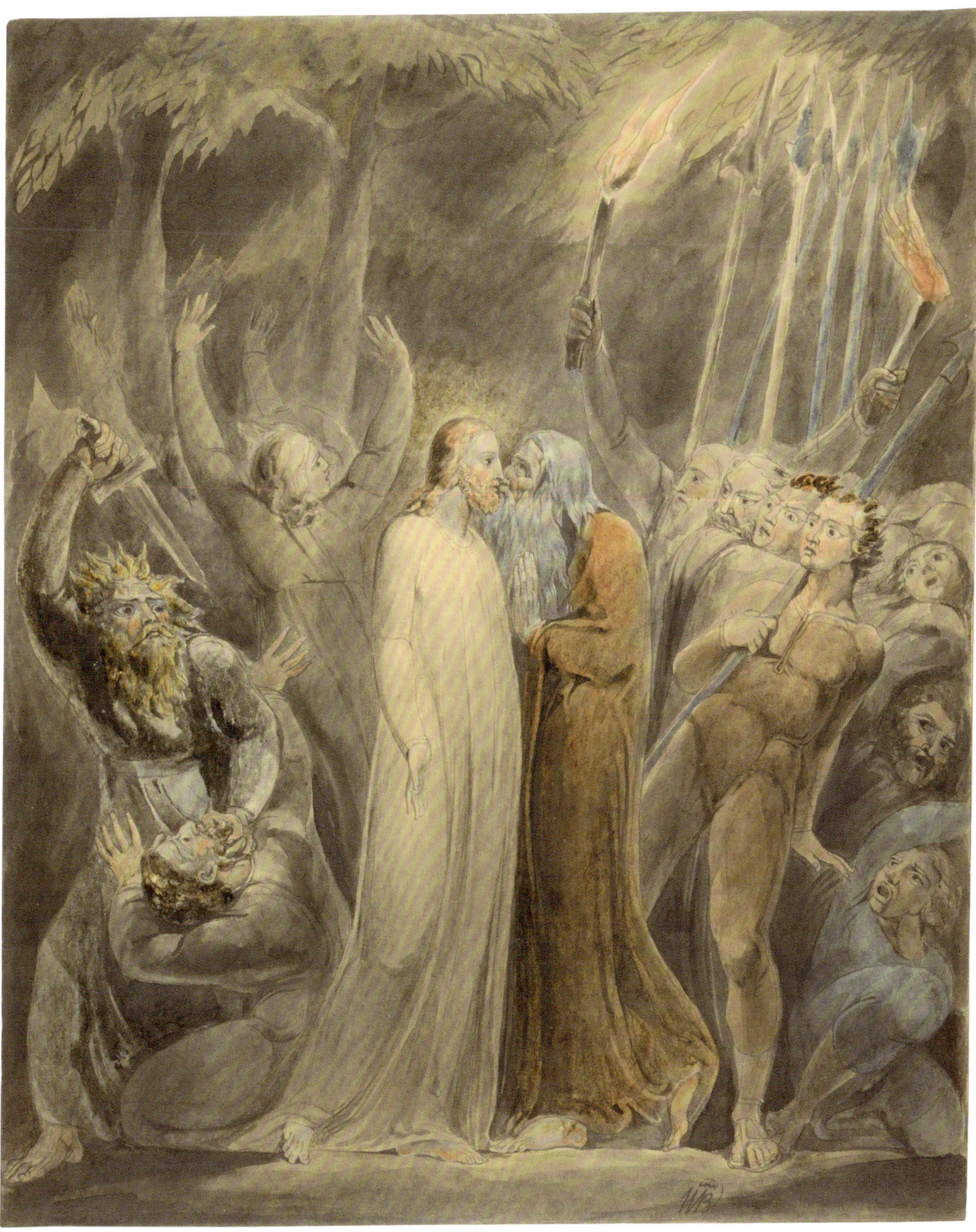

Plate 37
William Blake, *Judas Betrays Him*, about 1803–5

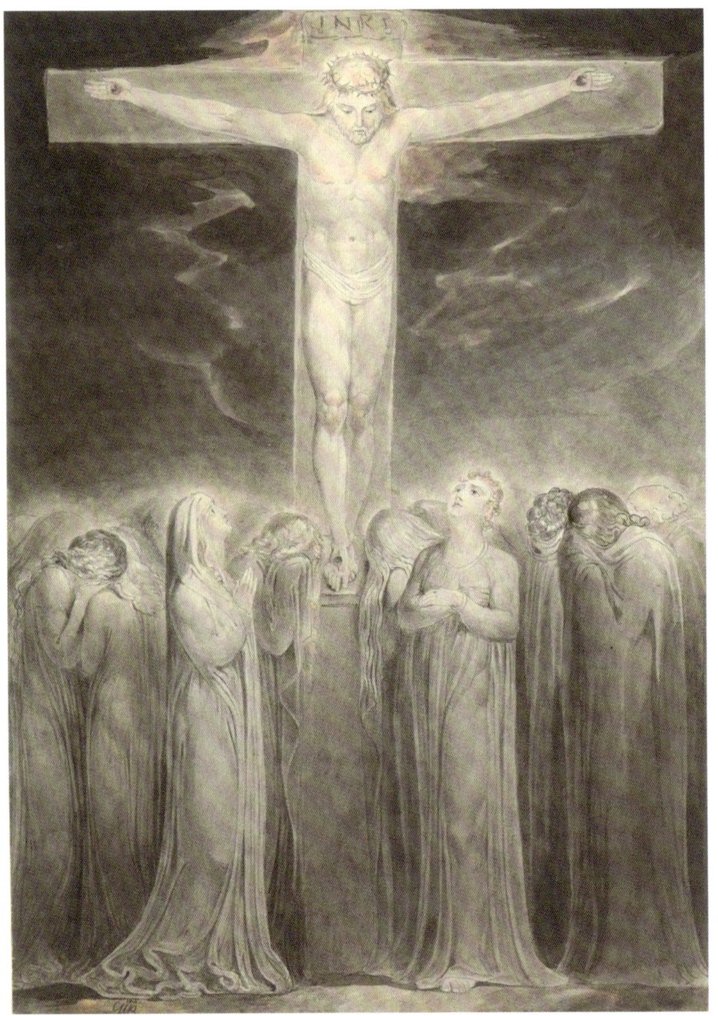

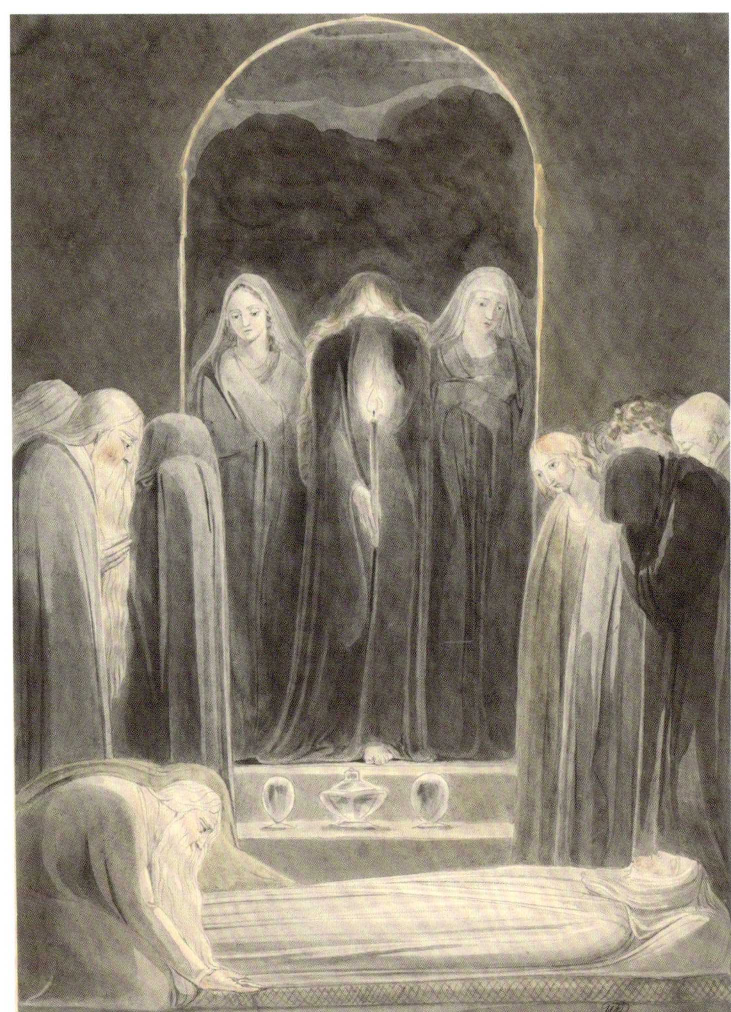

Plate 38
William Blake, *The Crucifixion: "Behold Thy Mother,"* about 1805

Plate 39
William Blake, *The Entombment*, about 1805

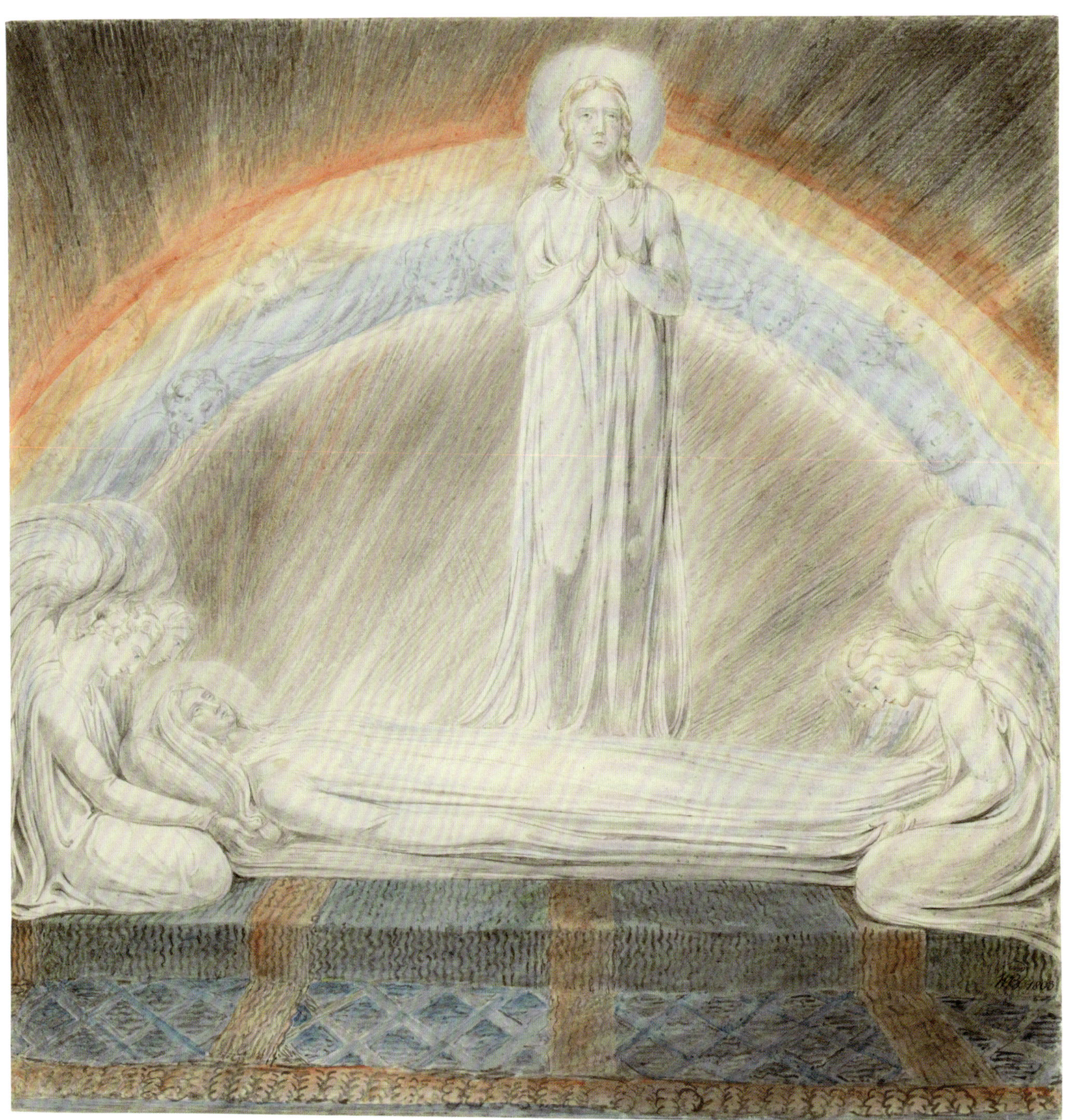

Plate 40
William Blake, *The Death of the Virgin*, 1803

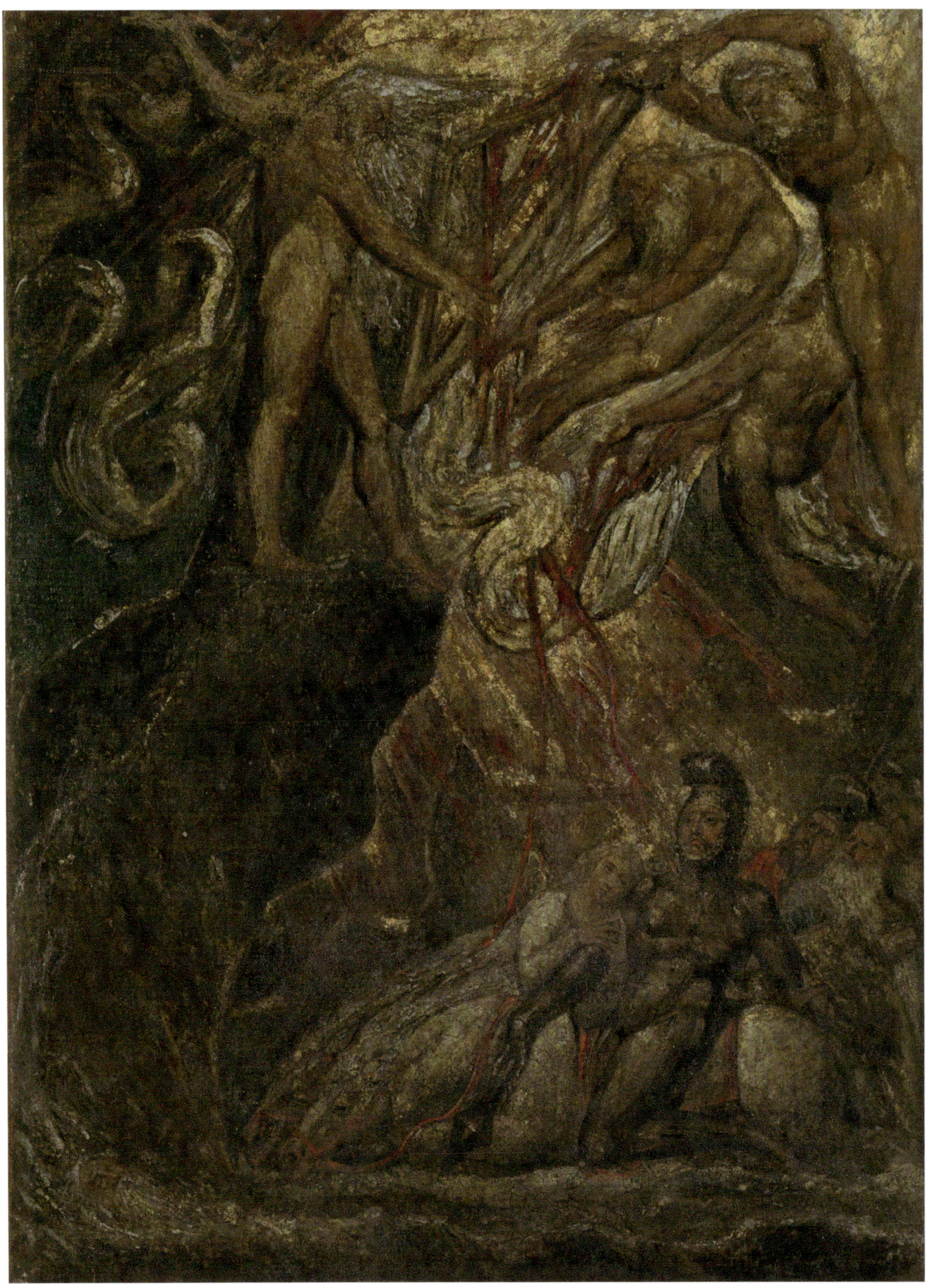

Plate 41
William Blake, *The Bard, from Gray*, 1809?

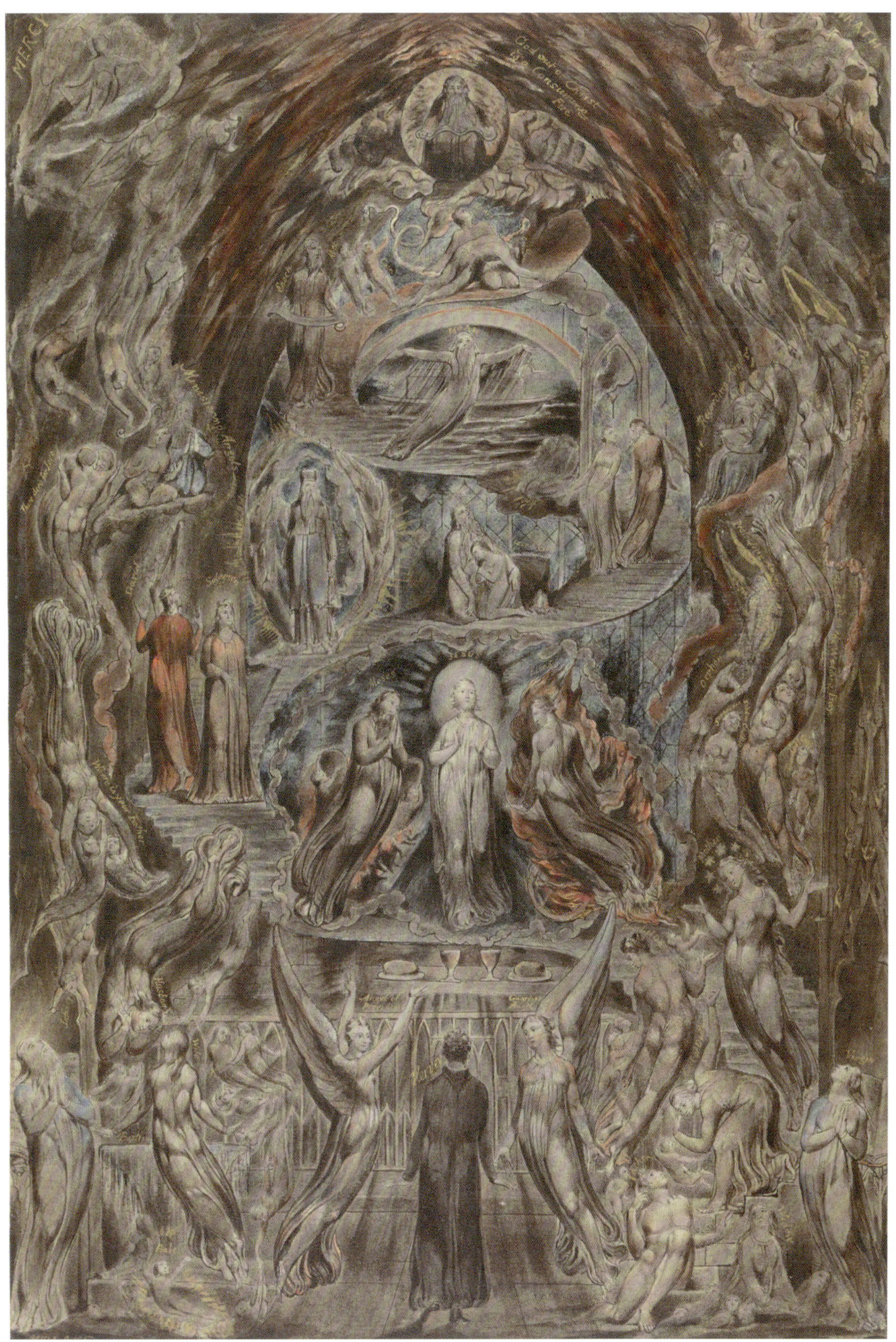

Plate 42
William Blake, *Epitome of James Hervey's "Meditations among the Tombs,"* about 1820–25

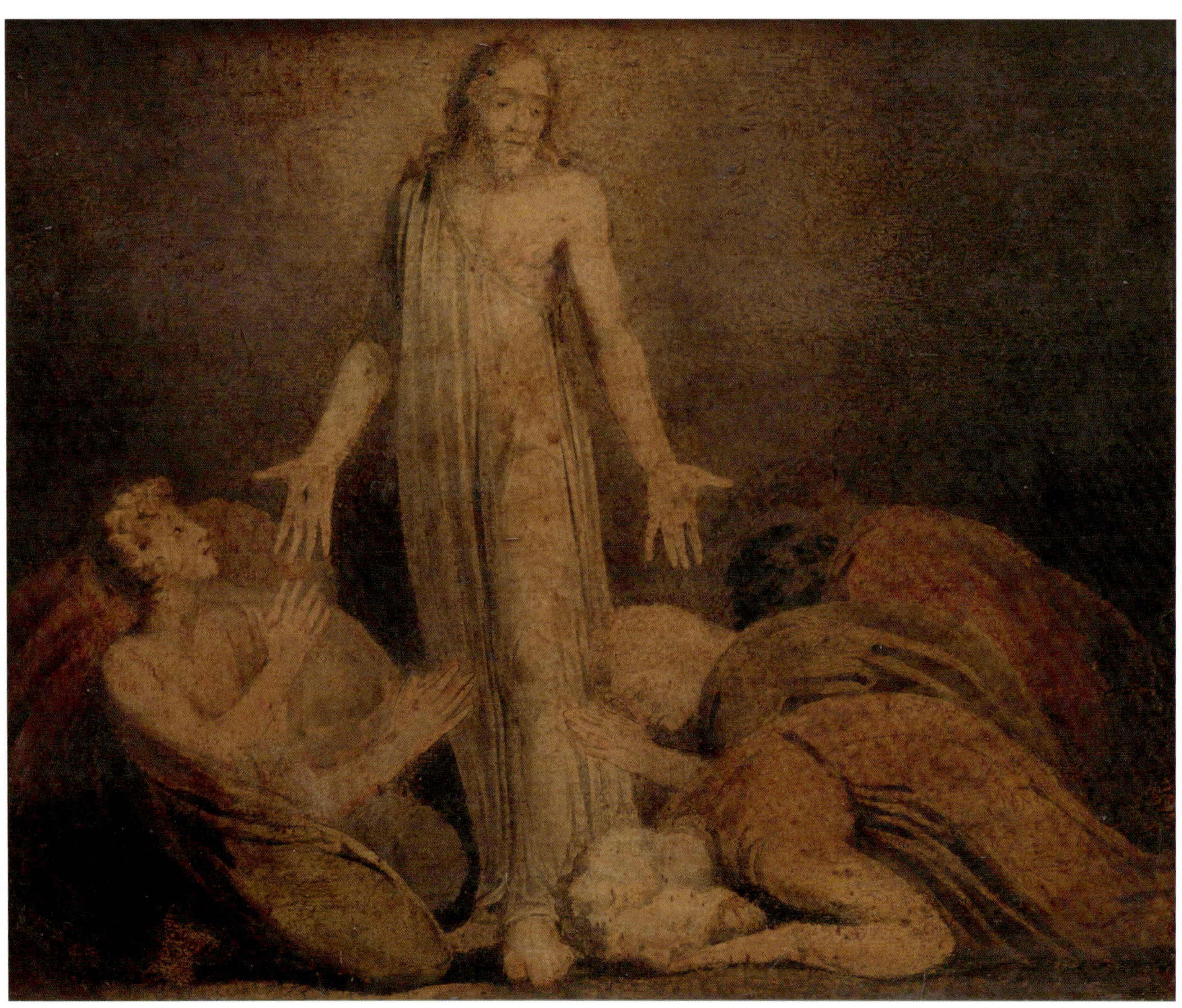

Plate 43
William Blake, *Christ Appearing to the Apostles after the Resurrection*, about 1795

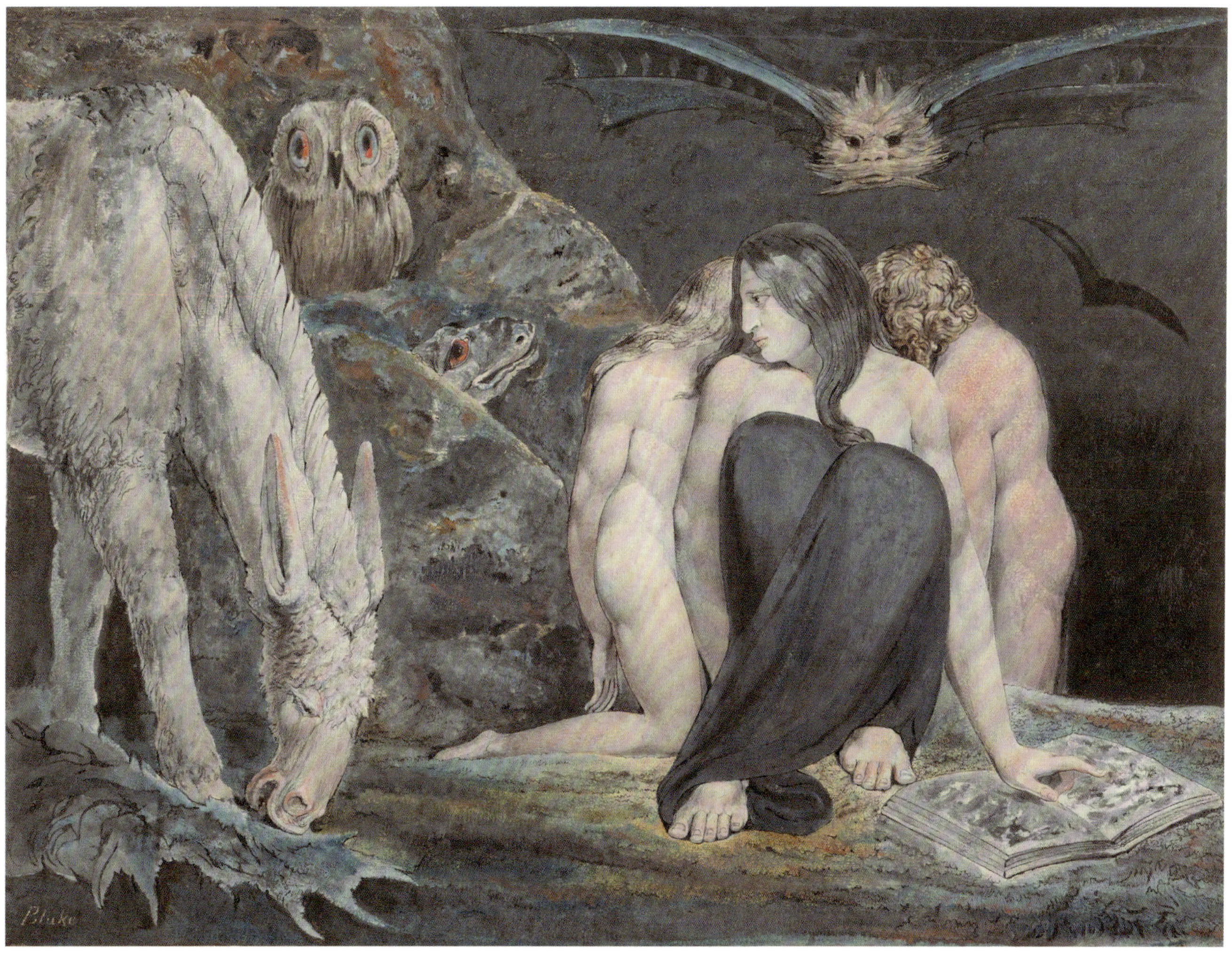

Plate 44
William Blake, *The Night of Enitharmon's Joy* or *Hecate*, about 1795

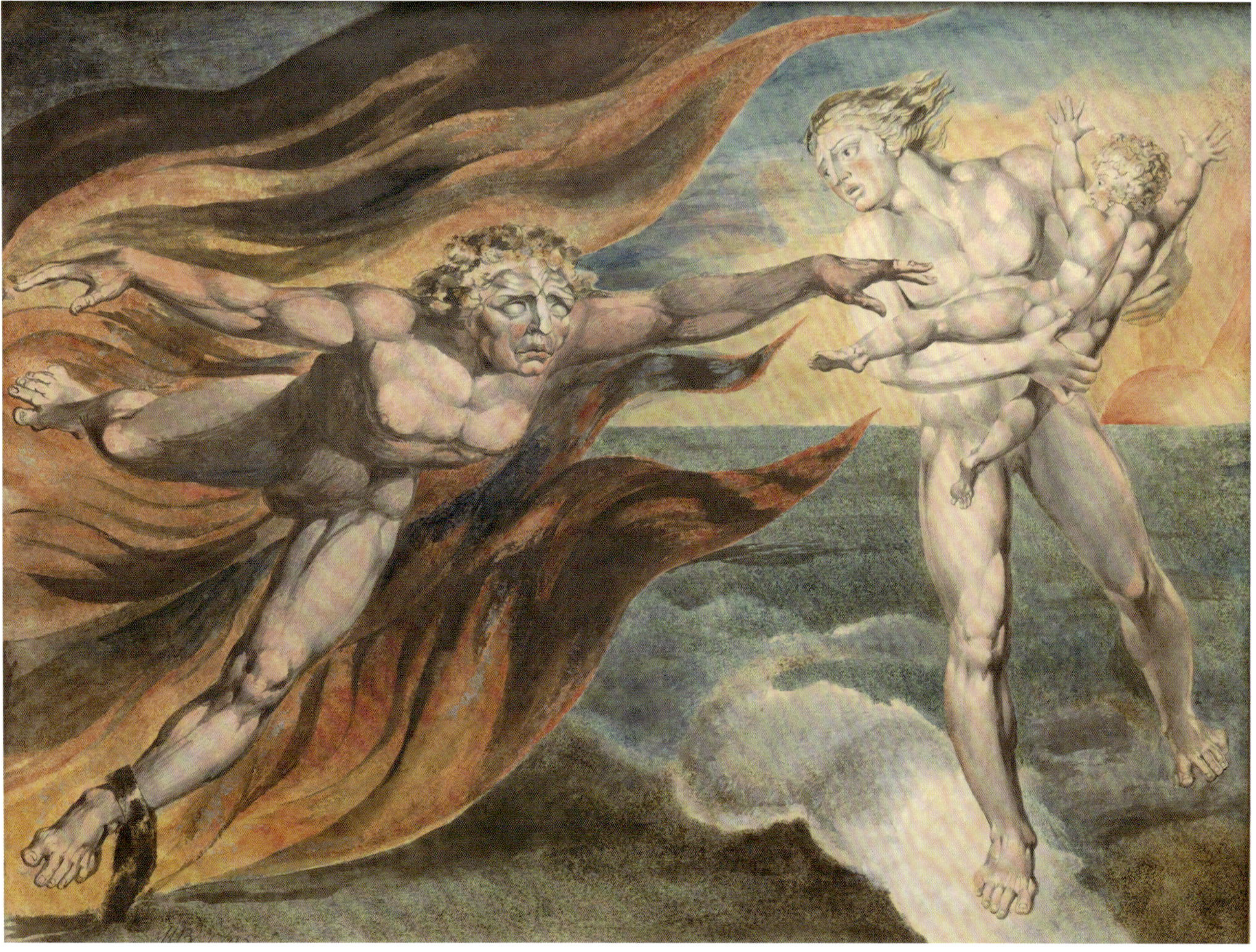

Plate 45
William Blake, *The Good and Evil Angels*, 1795–about 1805

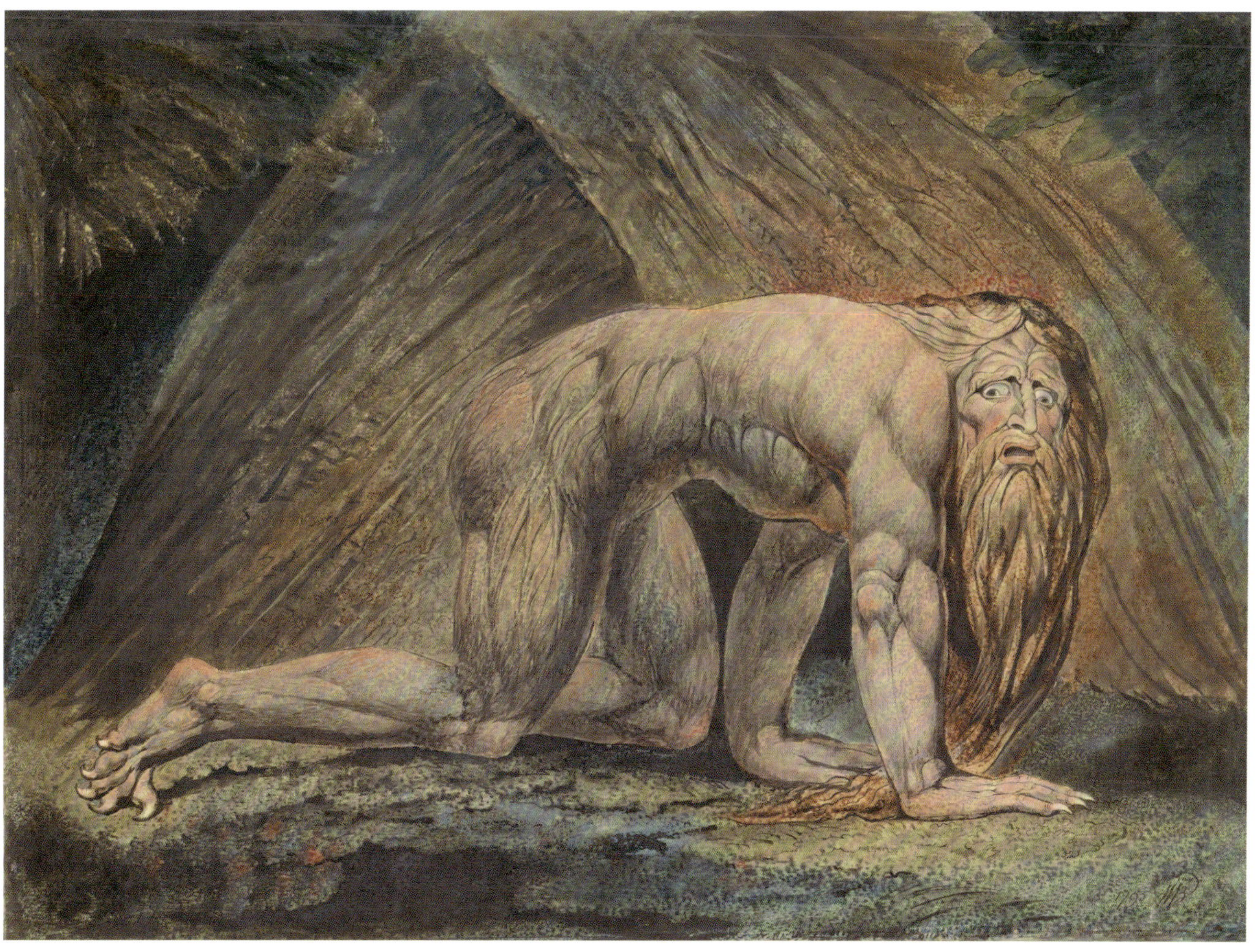

Plate 46
William Blake, *Nebuchadnezzar*, 1795–about 1805

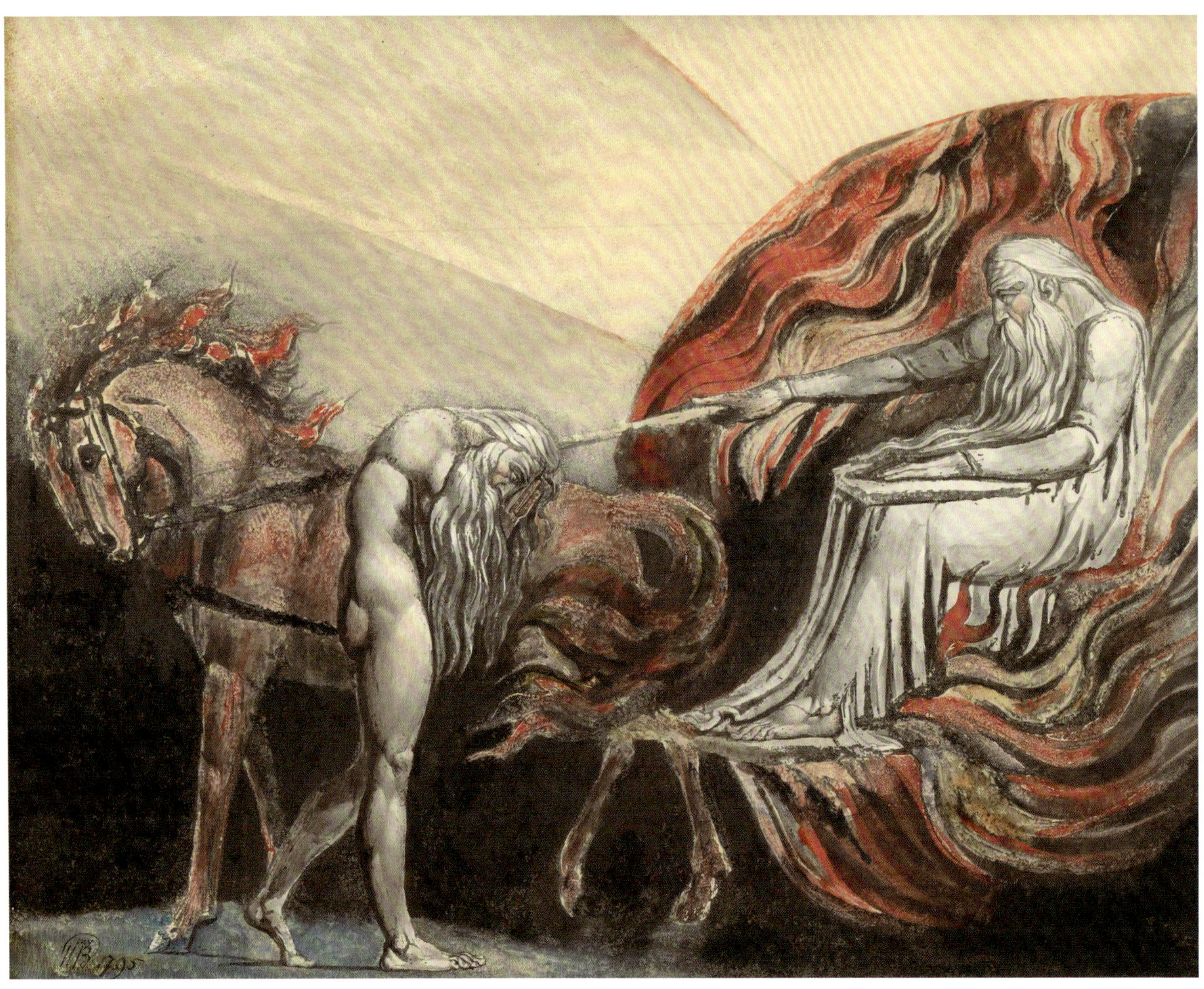

Plate 47
William Blake, *God Judging Adam*, 1795

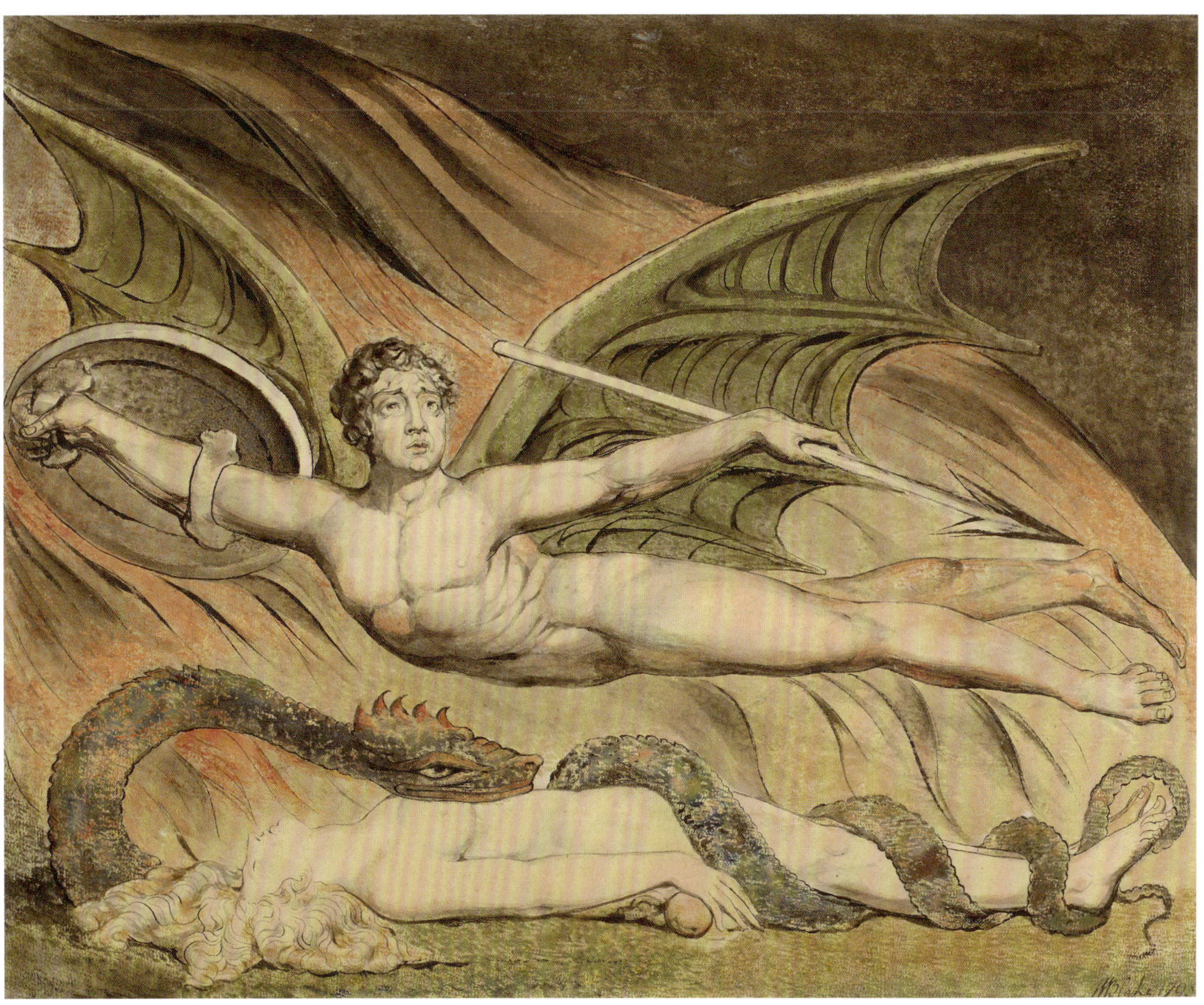

Plate 48
William Blake, *Satan Exulting over Eve*, 1795

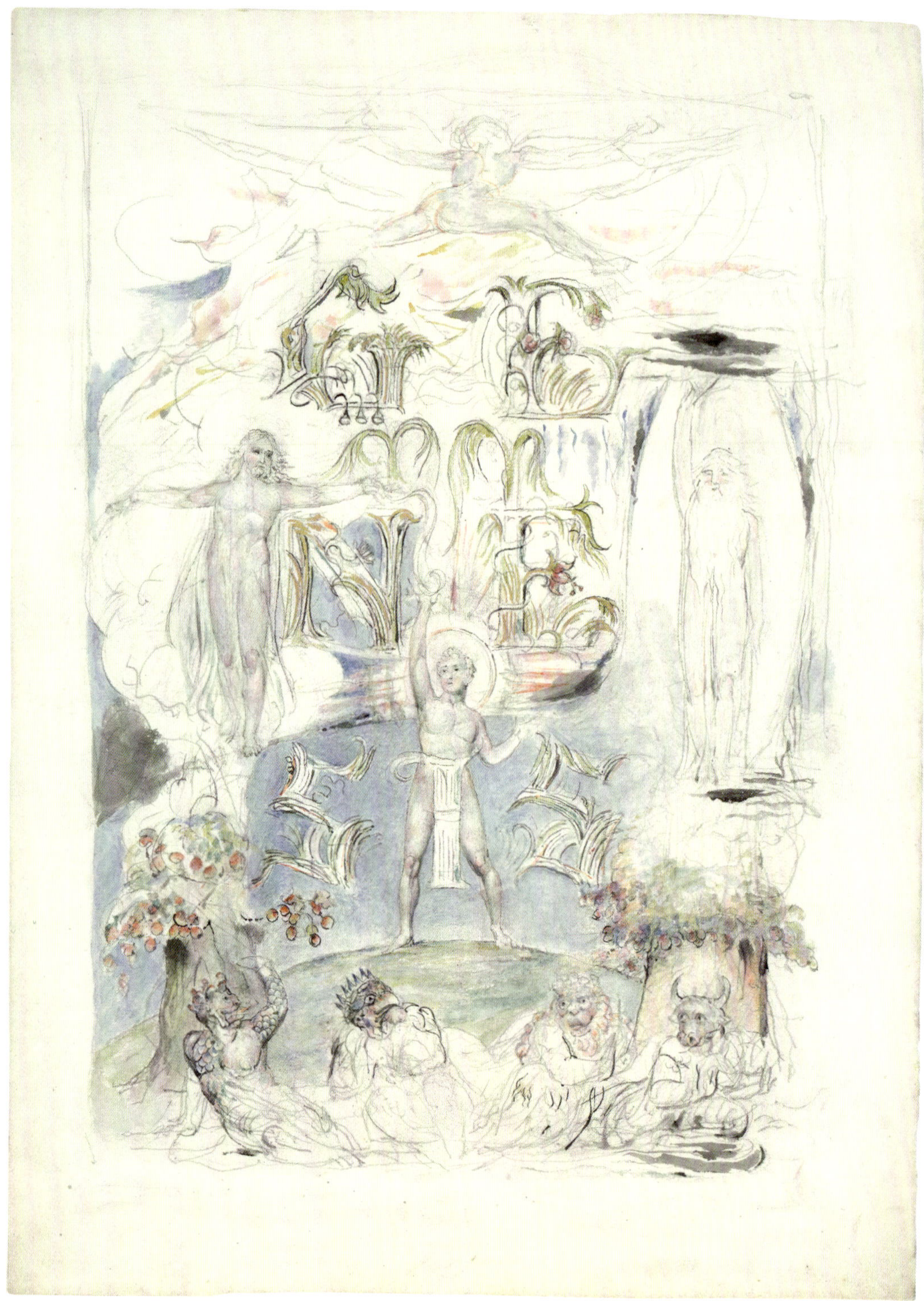

Plate 49
William Blake, *Genesis*, Second Title Page, about 1826–27

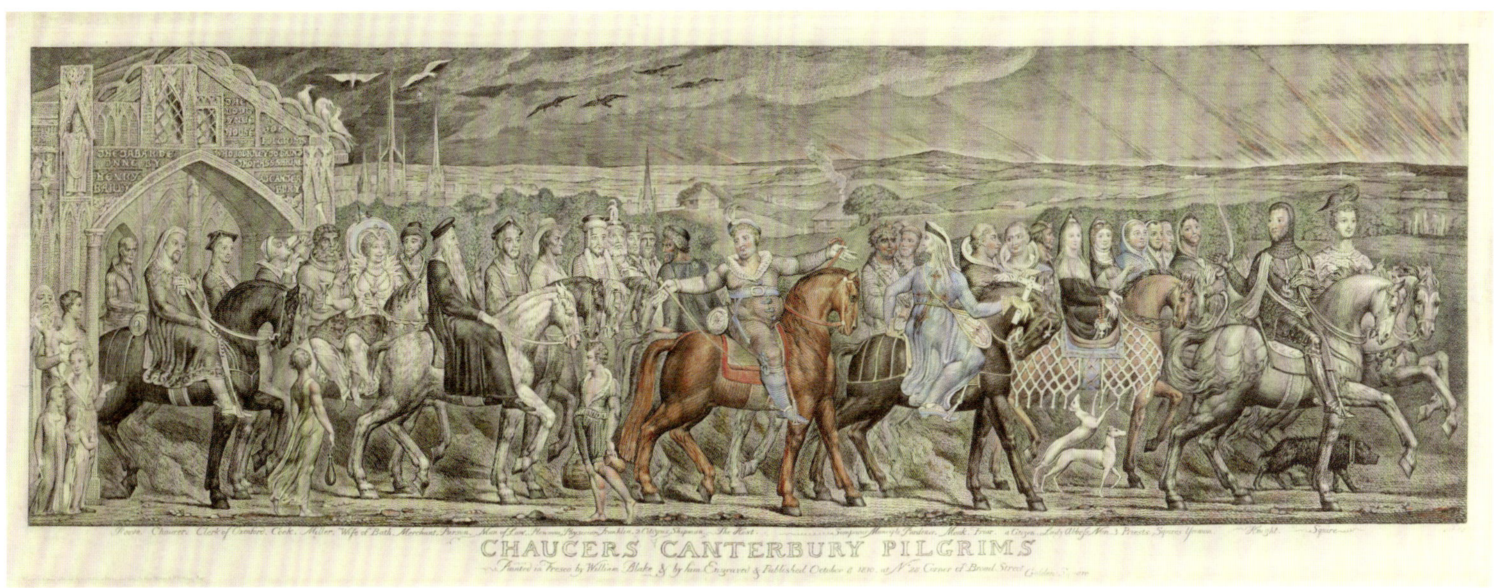

Plate 50
William Blake, *Chaucers Canterbury Pilgrims*, about 1810

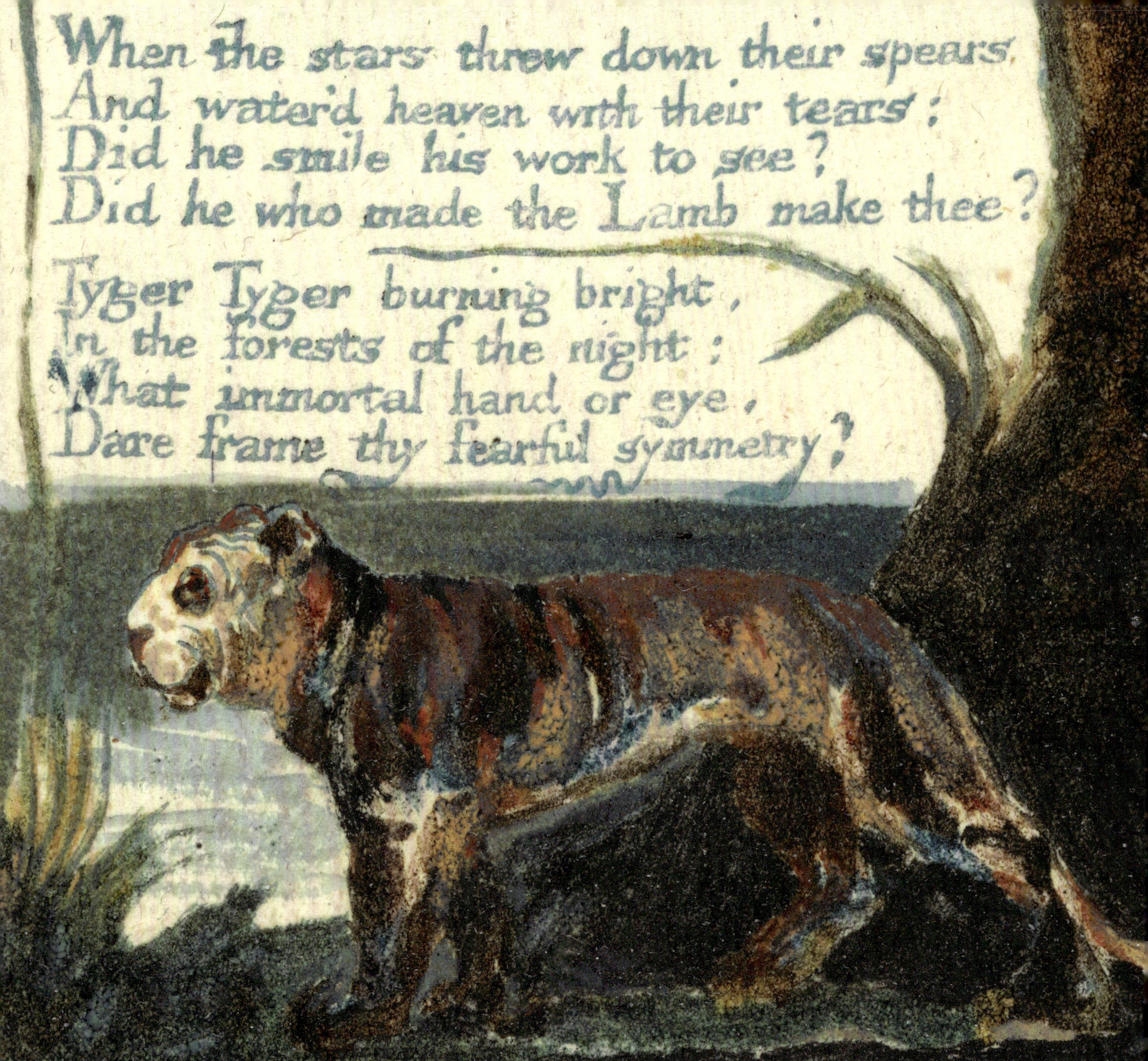

"If a method of Printing which combines the Painter and the Poet is a phenomenon worthy of public attention, provided that it exceeds in elegance all former methods, the Author is sure of his reward."

—William Blake, *To the Public*, 1799

The Painter-Poet

PLATES 51–63

Equipped with a solid grounding in traditional printmaking, around 1788 Blake developed a relief etching method. This allowed him to easily and effectively combine the activities of a painter and a poet without employing the specialized techniques of conventional etching and engraving. Prone to visions throughout his life, Blake claimed that his deceased brother Robert came to him in the form of an apparition and revealed the secret of the technique. Possibly as an homage, Blake first employed relief etching to make *The Approach of Doom* after Robert's design. Subsequently, he used it almost exclusively to publish his own poetry, calling these publications "illuminated books."

Blake's relief etching method was ingenious: it allowed him to write and draw on the copper plate as if he was working on paper and to print both text and image at the same time using the same matrix. The process involved four main steps. First, Blake rendered his poetical and pictorial inventions on the plate with brushes and pens in an acid-resistant substance, working in reverse to counteract the reversal that would occur in printing. Once he was satisfied with the composition, he immersed the plate in acid to eat away the nondesigned areas. Next, he inked the plate: in some instances, he limited himself to the raised surfaces, but in others, he applied colors to the etched areas to create highly painterly effects. Finally, he ran the plate through his rolling press with minimal pressure applied.

Using this technique, Blake composed the *Songs of Innocence* and the *Songs of Experience*, which he issued separately in 1789 and 1794, and together in the latter year (plates 51–56). These popular poems are the best known and most accessible of his poetic works. The accompanying illustrations—picturesque and dramatic tableaux surrounded by swirling vegetation—complement, clarify, and even contradict the texts.

Image and text were interdependent in Blake's illuminated books. Writing to Dawson Turner about *A Small Book of Designs* (plates 58–63), a compilation of plates from various illuminated books printed without the text portion, the artist stated that the elimination of his writing led to a major loss, a sundering of the whole. Around 1818, he added handwritten captions to one of the two known copies of *A Small Book of Designs*. By inscribing these impressions, he not only reinterpreted the meaning of the images but also restored the composite nature of his art.

EA

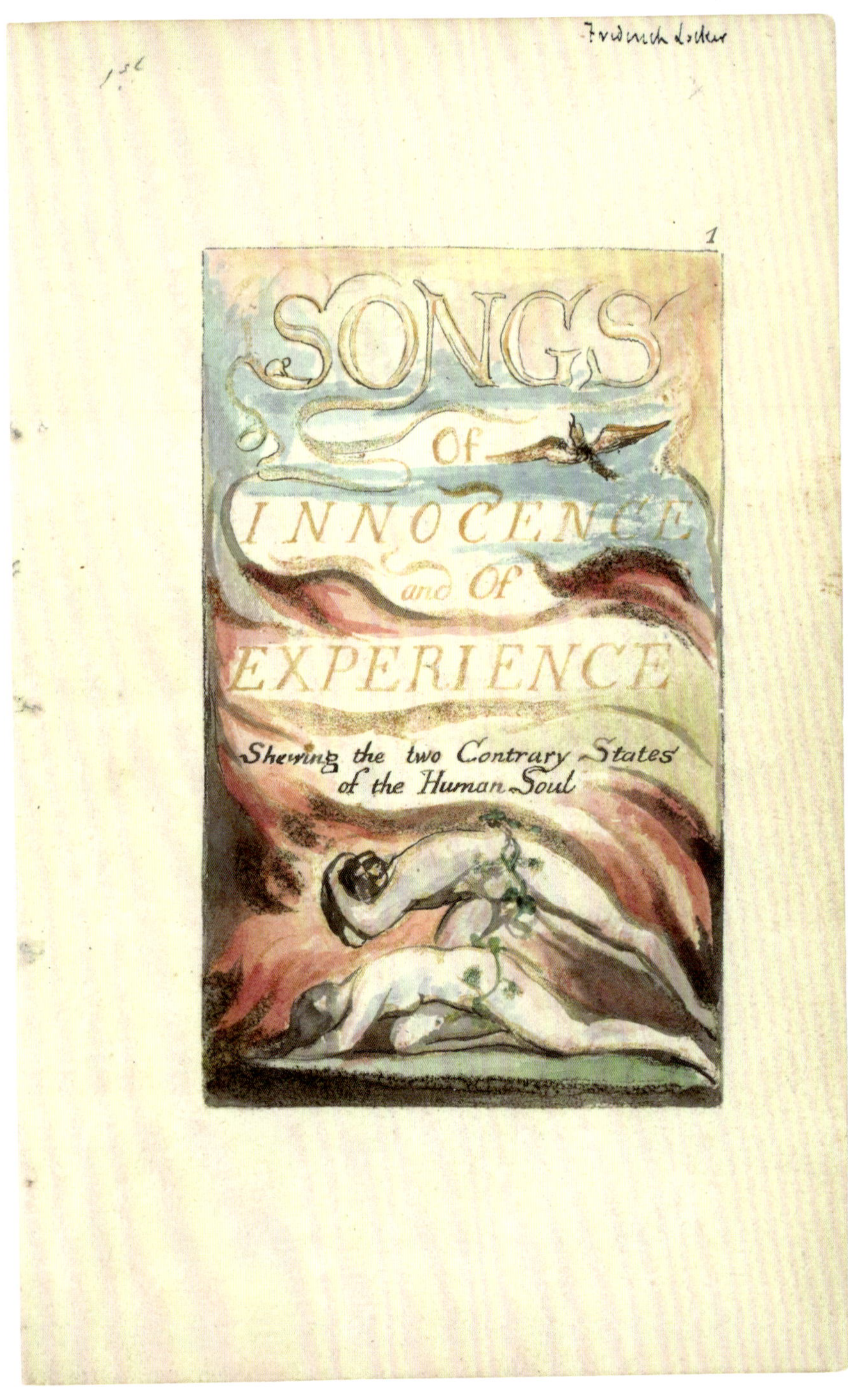

Plate 51
William Blake, *Songs of Innocence and of Experience*,
Title Page, 1794/95

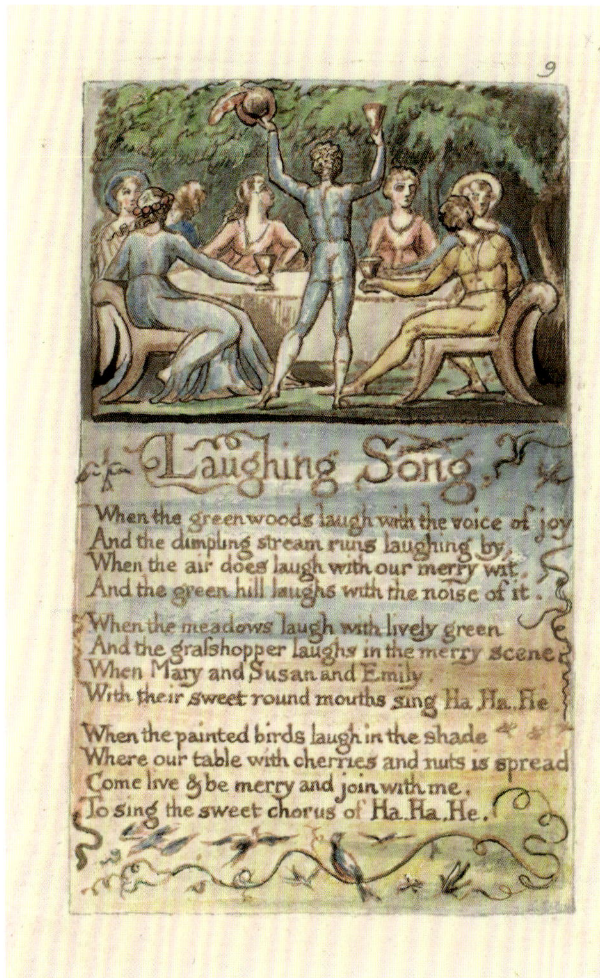

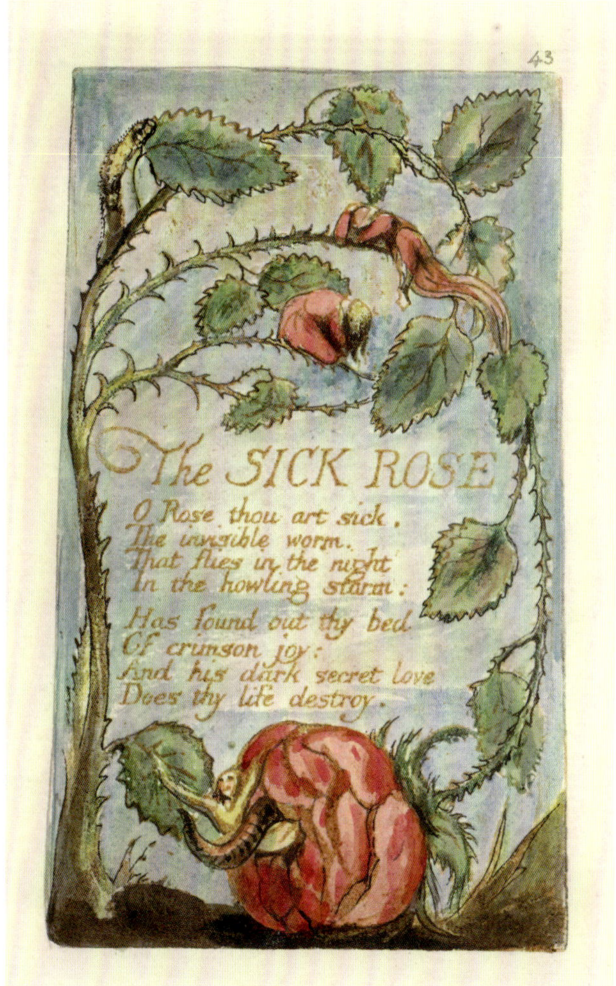

Plate 52
William Blake, *Songs of Innocence and of Experience*, "Laughing Song," 1789

Plate 53
William Blake, *Songs of Innocence and of Experience*, "The Sick Rose," 1794/95

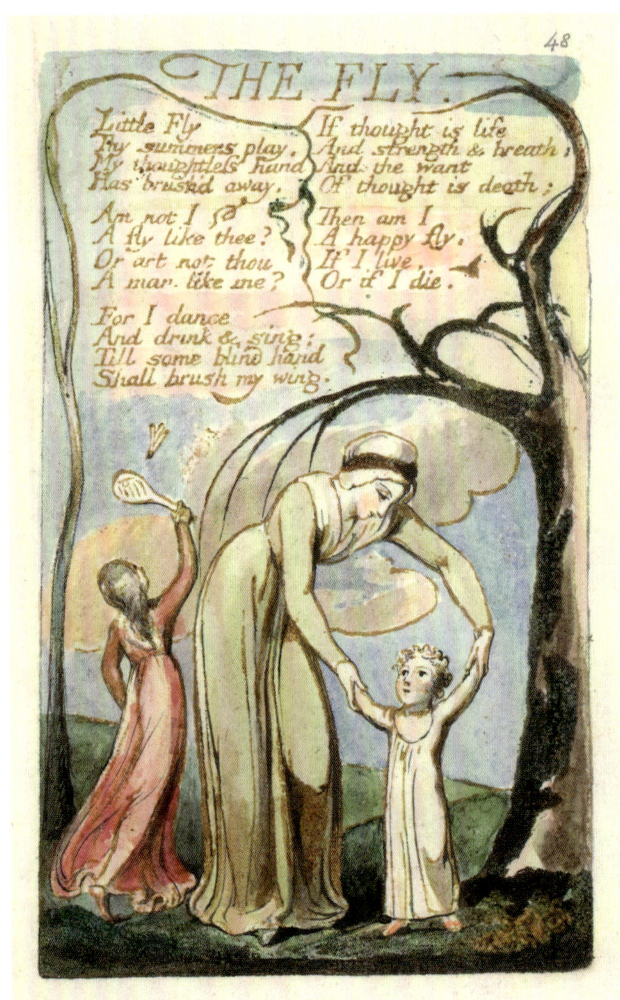

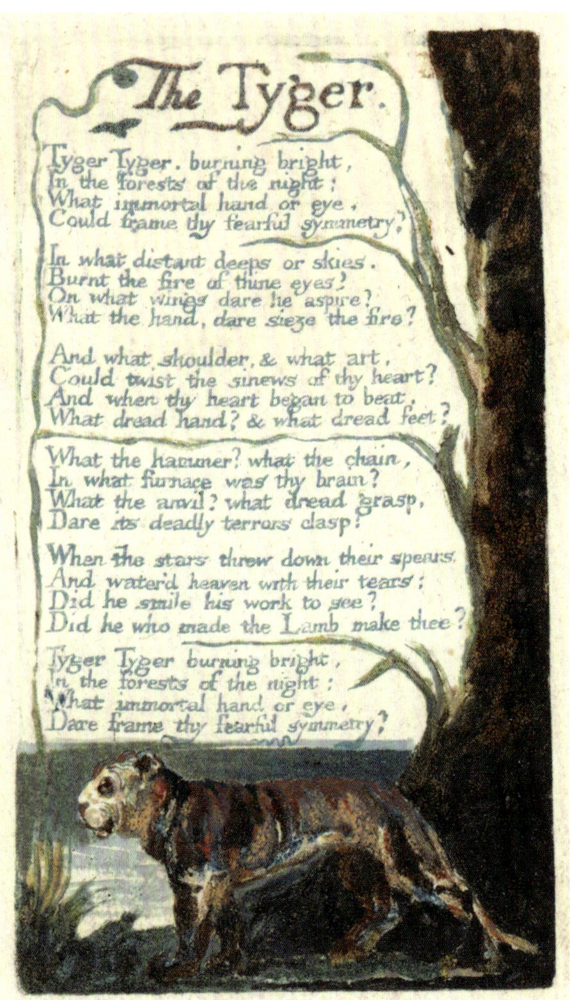

Plate 54
William Blake, *Songs of Innocence and of Experience*, "The Fly," 1794/95

Plate 55
William Blake, *Songs of Innocence and of Experience*, "The Tyger," 1794

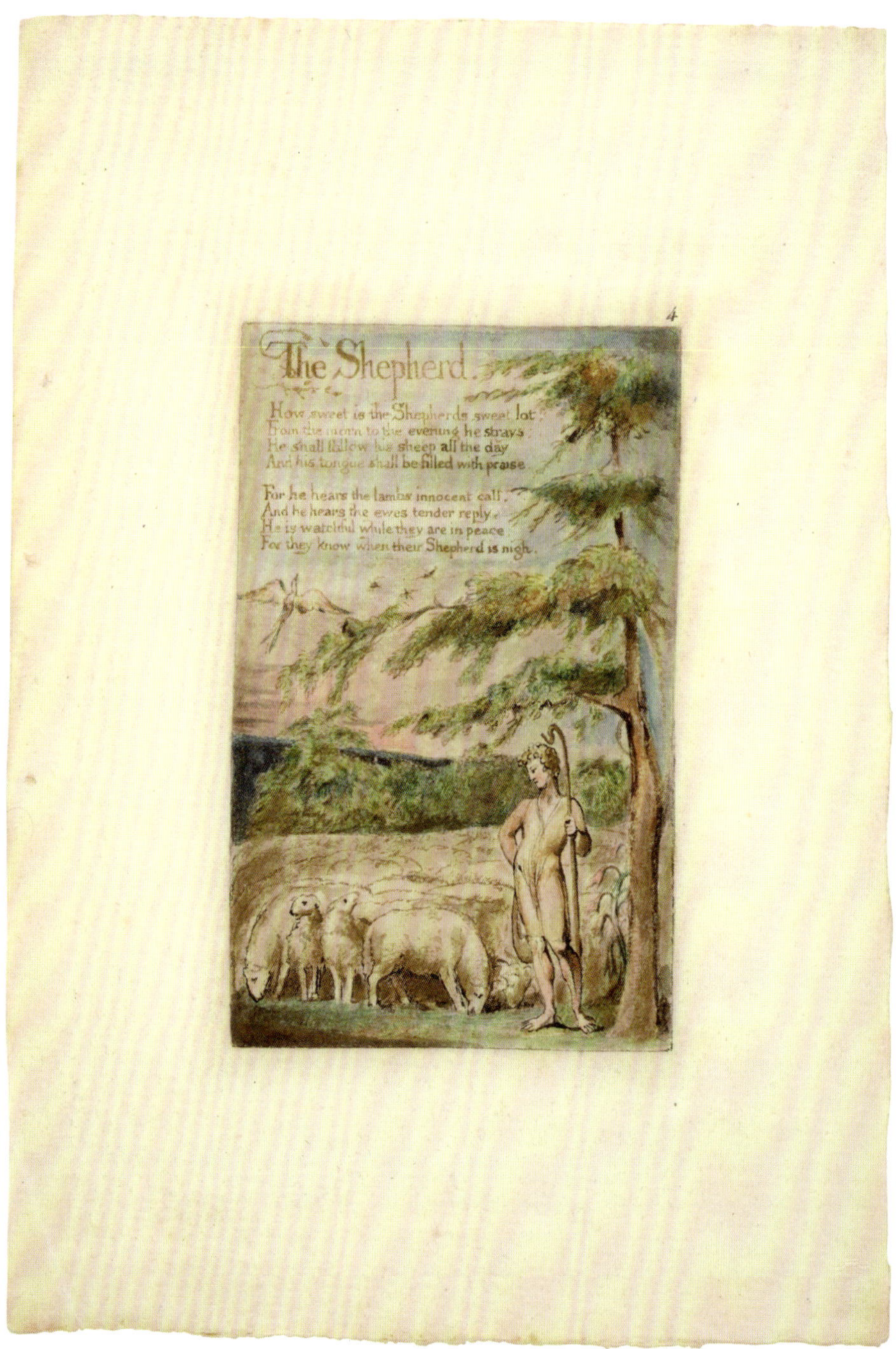

Plate 56
William Blake, *Songs of Innocence*, "The Shepherd,"
1789

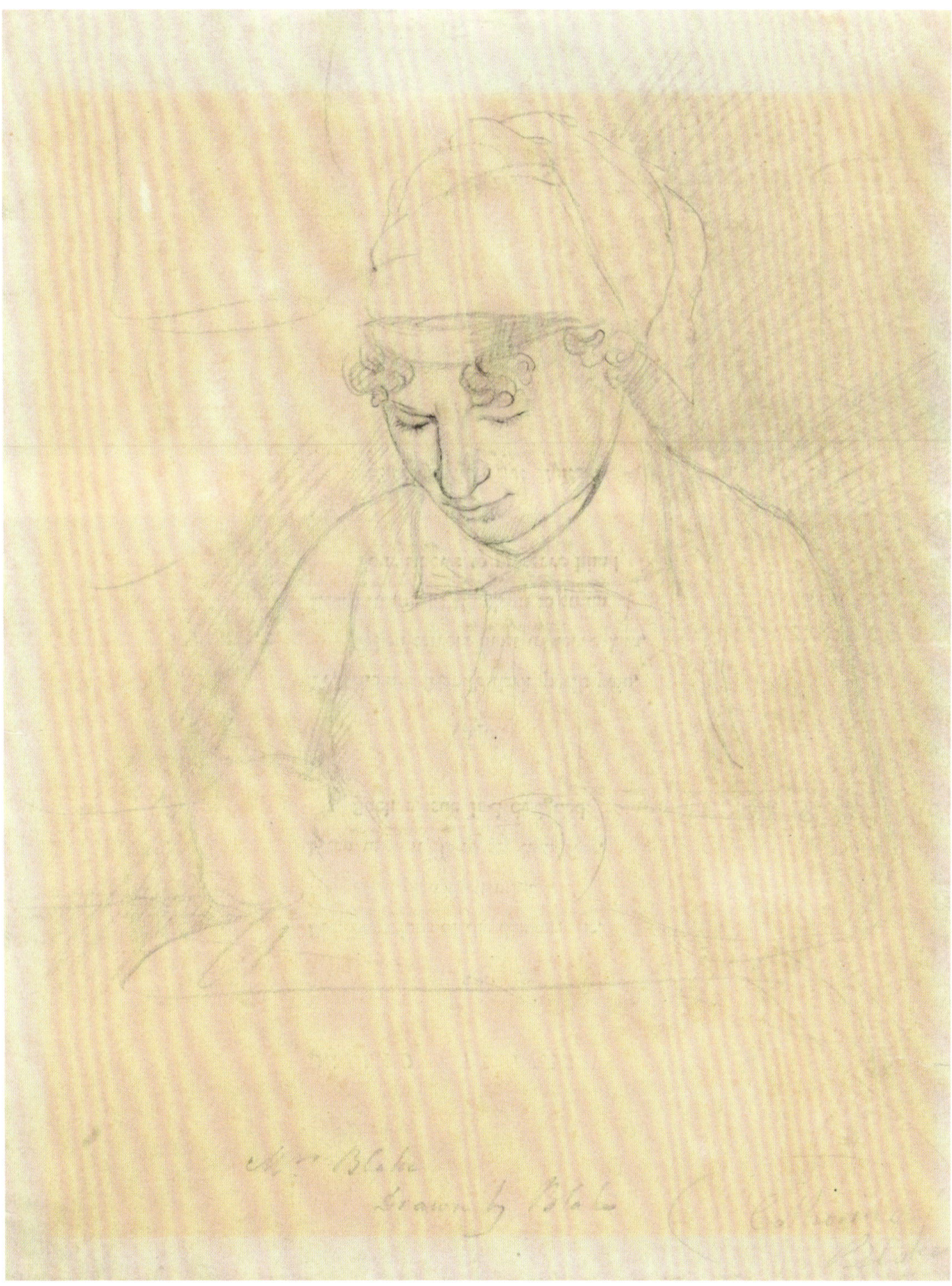

Plate 57
William Blake, *Catherine Blake*, about 1805

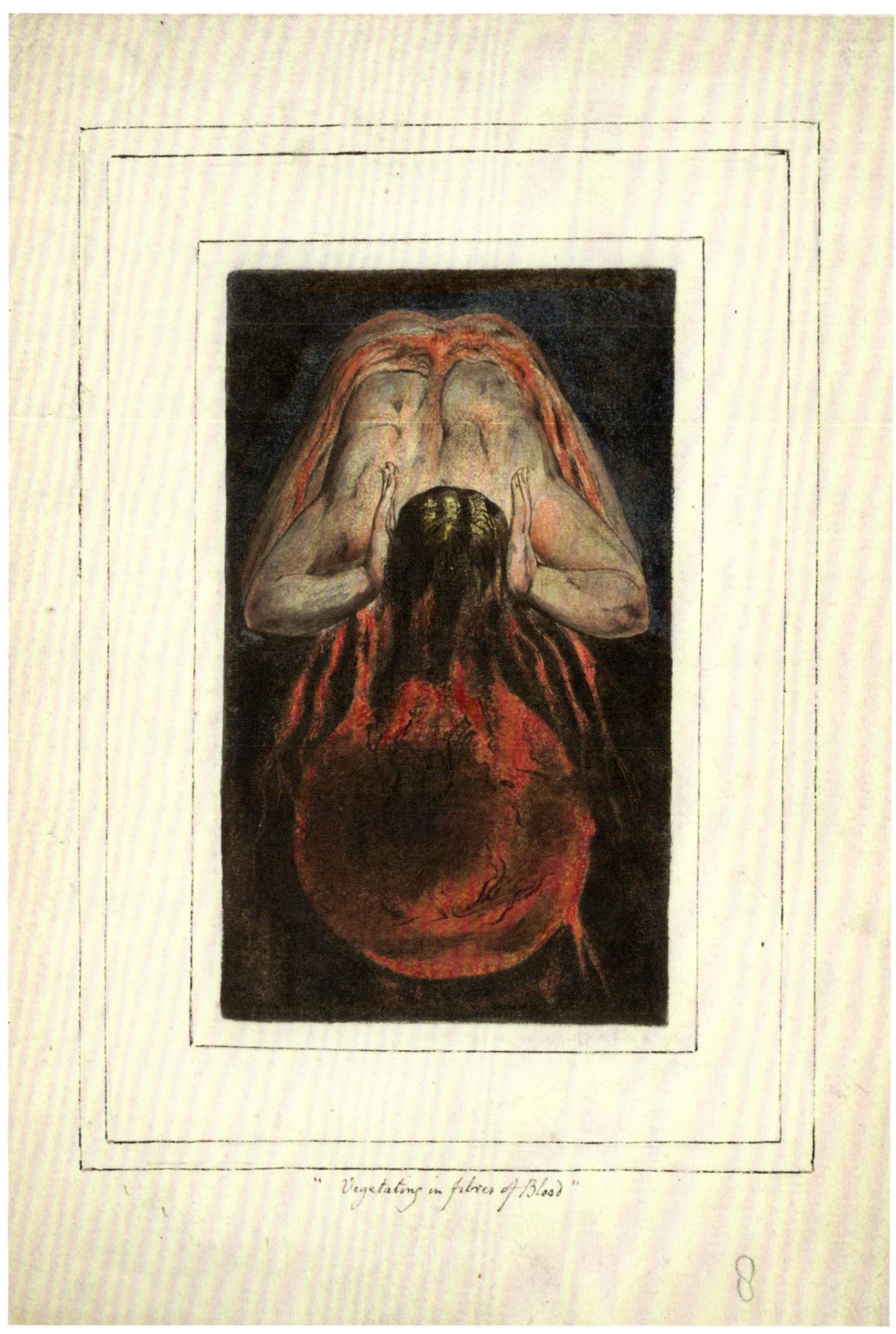

Plate 58
William Blake, *First Book of Urizen*, plate 15,
1796–about 1818

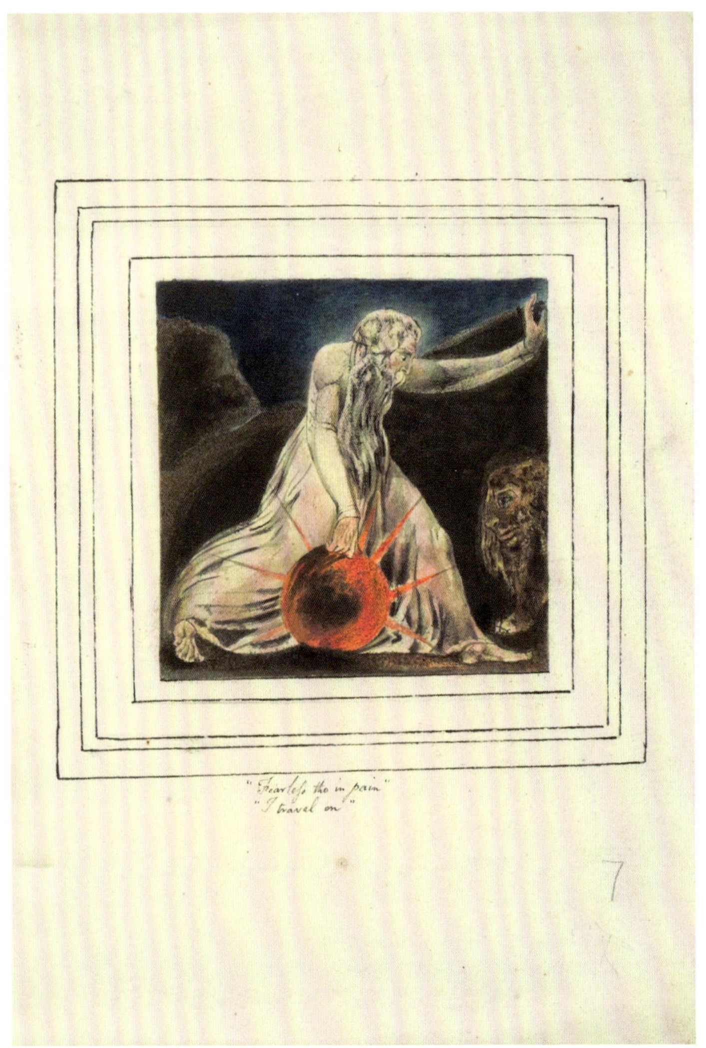

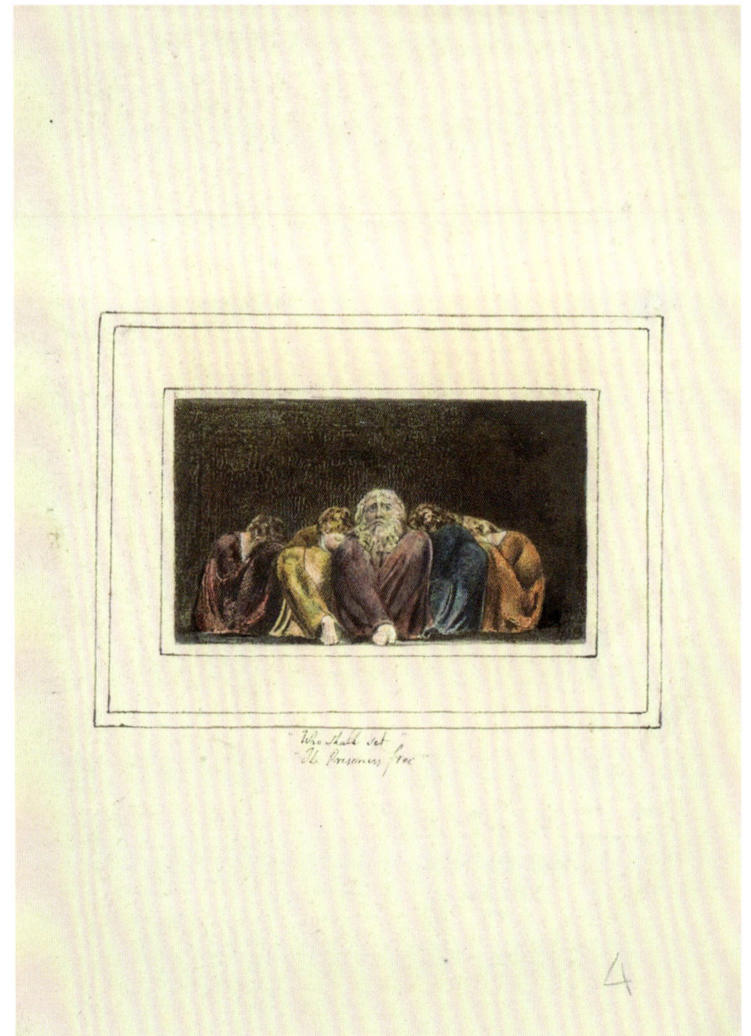

Plate 59
William Blake, *First Book of Urizen*, plate 21, 1796–about 1818

Plate 60
William Blake, *The Marriage of Heaven and Hell*, plate 16, 1796–about 1818

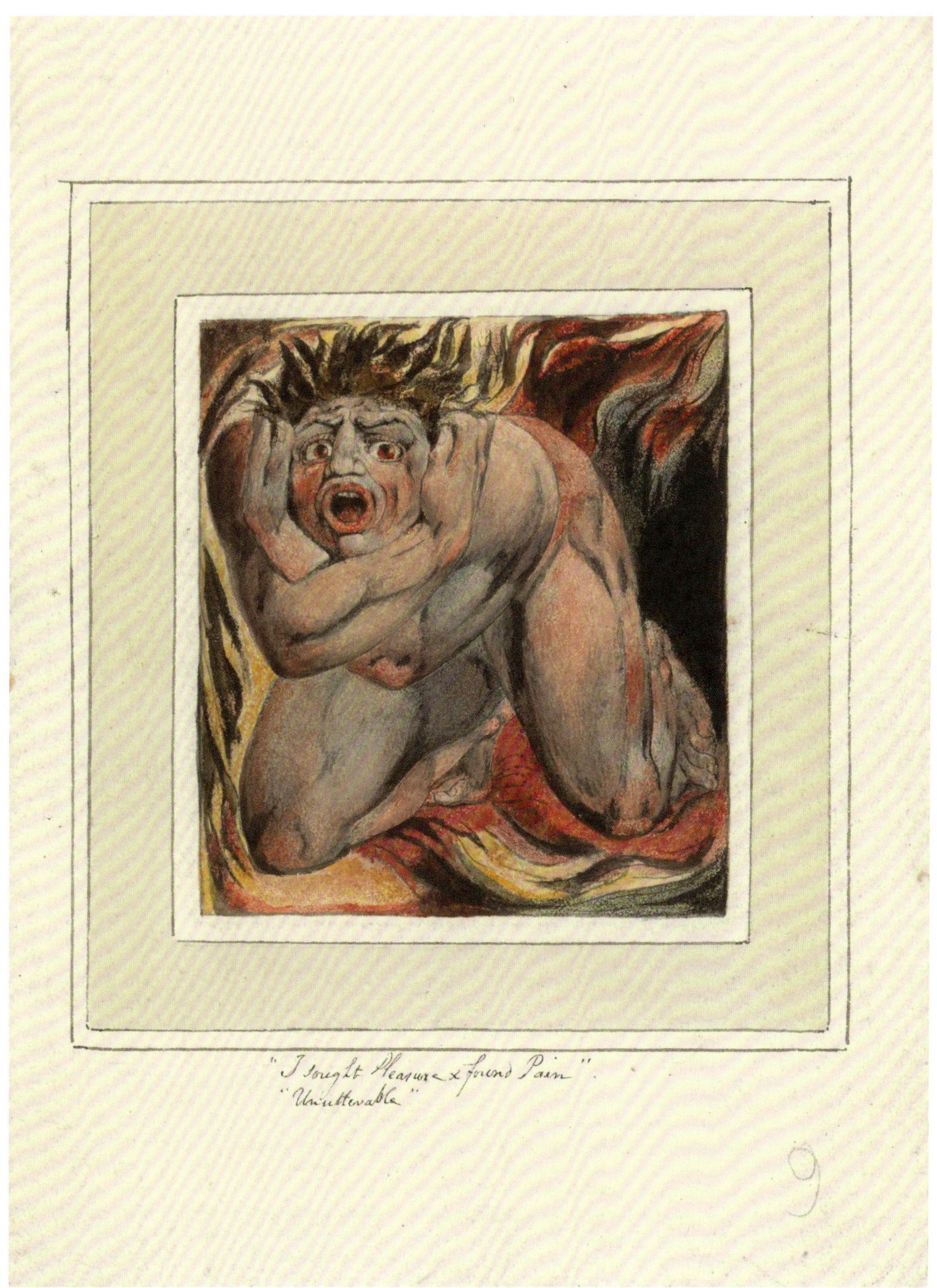

Plate 61
William Blake, *First Book of Urizen*, plate 6, 1796–about 1818

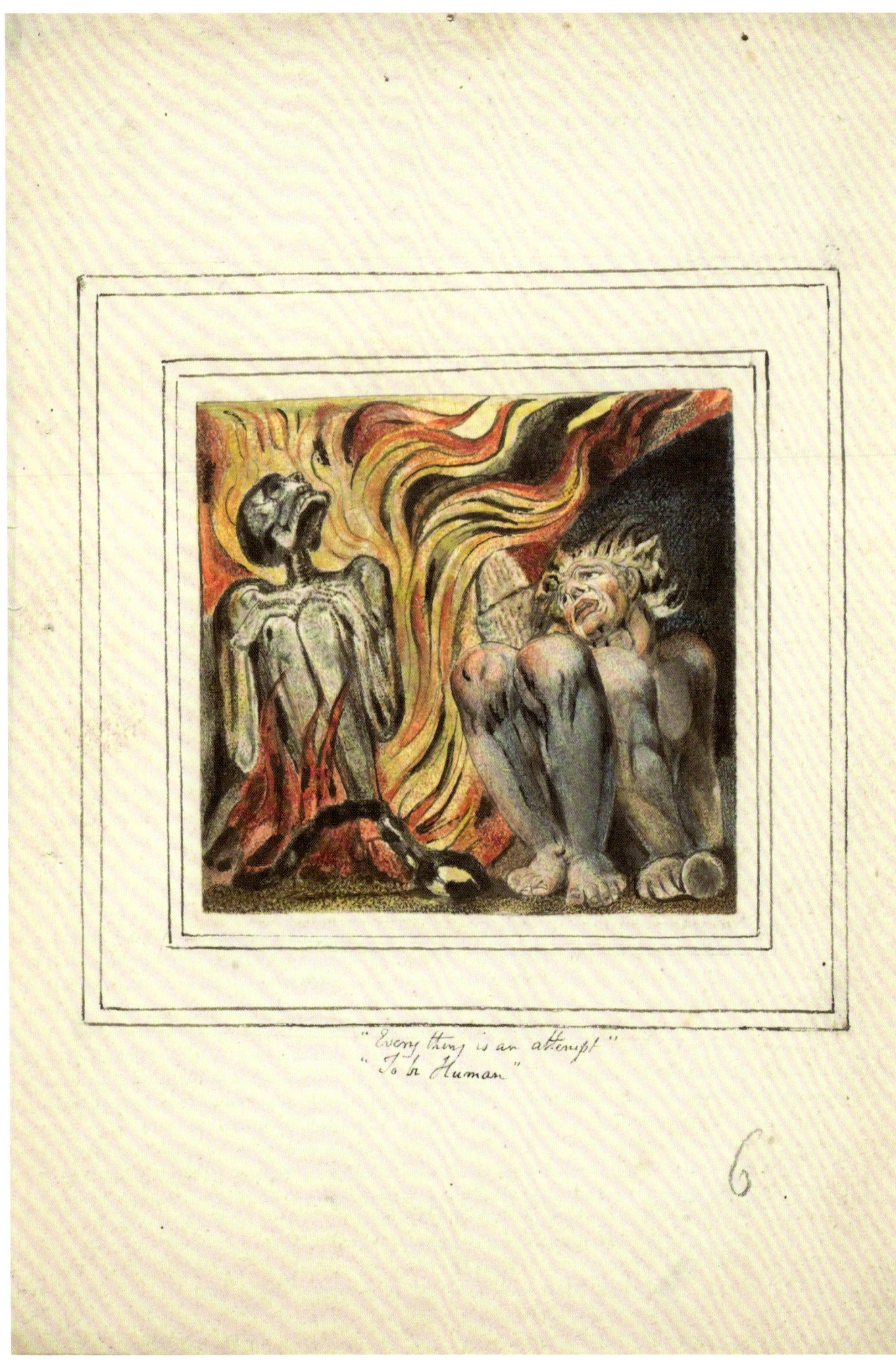

Plate 62
William Blake, *First Book of Urizen*, plate 10, 1796–about 1818

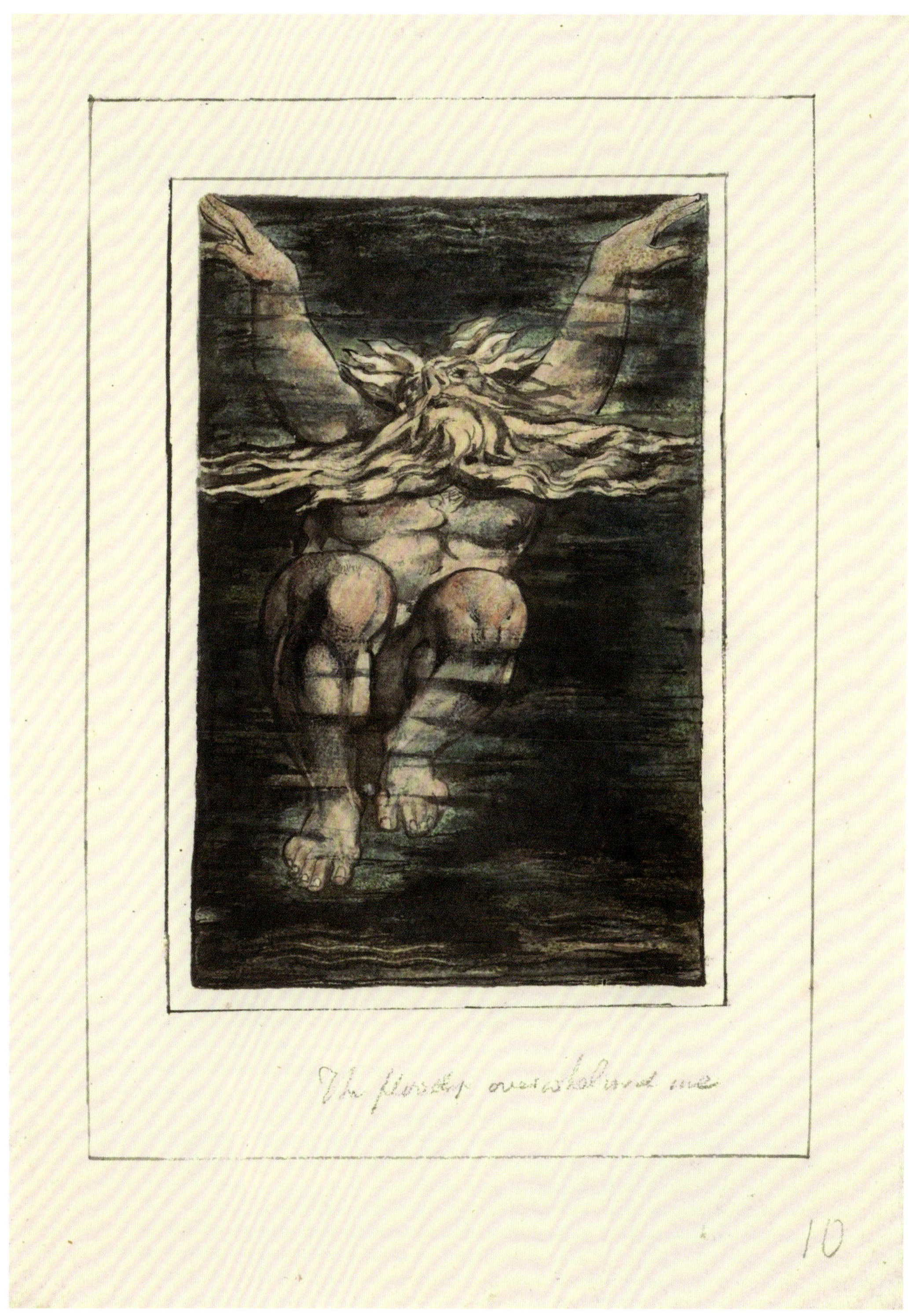

Plate 63
William Blake, *First Book of Urizen*, plate 11, 1796–about 1818

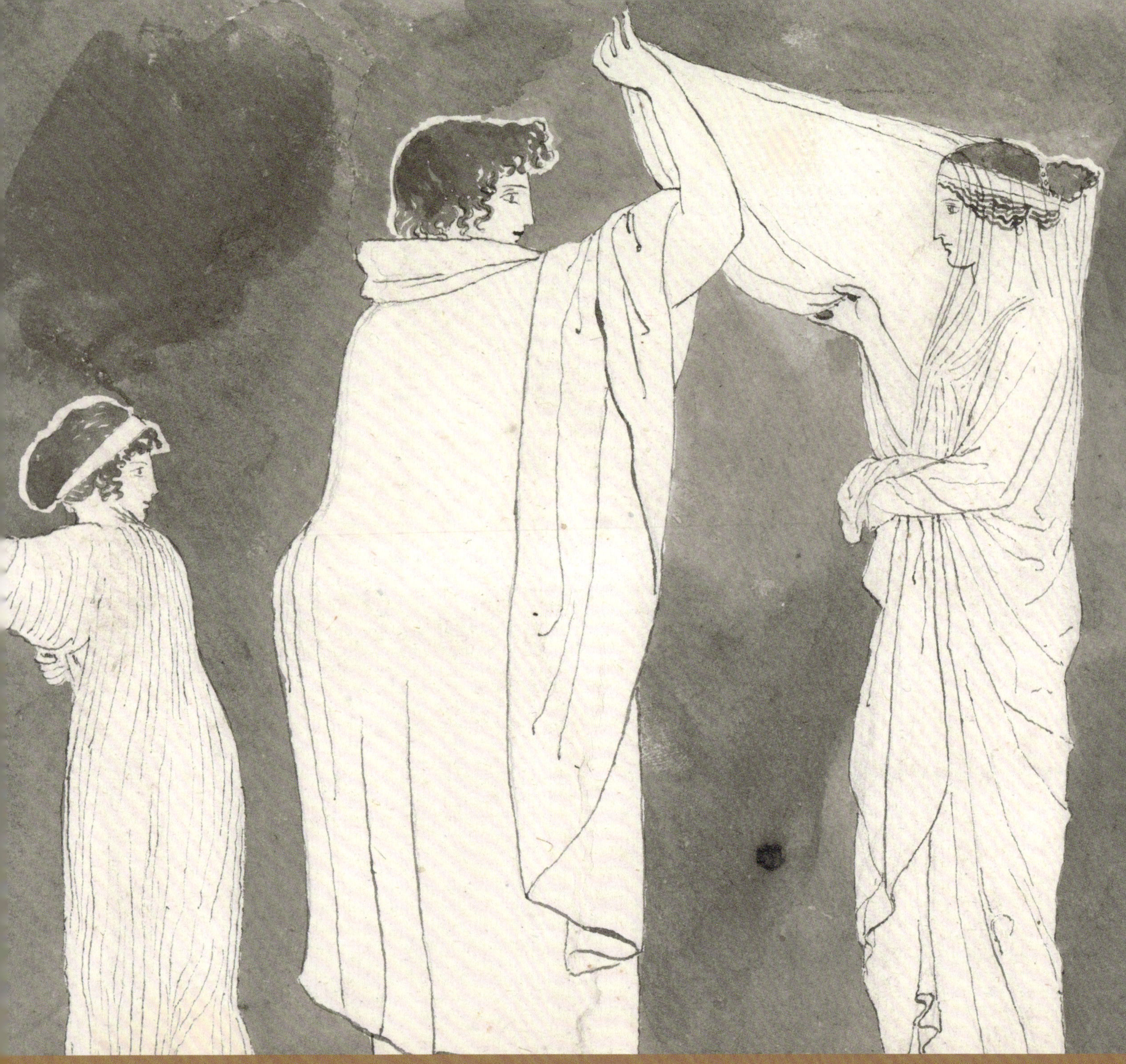

"It is to you I owe All my present Happiness It is to you I owe perhaps the Principal Happiness of my life."

—William Blake to John Flaxman, September 12, 1800

Blake's Contemporaries

PLATES 64–71

Blake's work was firmly rooted in the art of his age, which was actively shaped by the Royal Academy of Arts. Founded in 1768 with the backing of King George III, the institution aimed at elevating artistic production and taste in the country by providing training and organizing annual exhibitions.

As the Academy gave primacy to grand, historical paintings in the style of revered old masters, artists—aspiring for fame and fortune—turned to mythology, history, and literature for subjects. To acquire a classicizing visual vocabulary, it was common practice among Blake's contemporaries to travel to Italy, where they had the opportunity to study the remnants of Antiquity and the masterpieces of Renaissance artists. The Irishman James Barry (1741–1806), who was the Academy's professor of painting from 1782 to 1799, spent six years on the peninsula. While in Bologna, he made a study for an oil painting of the Greek warrior Philoctetes, who, due to his festering foot, was left behind by his fellow soldiers on their way to Troy (plate 65). Barry based the pose of the wounded hero on the Belvedere Torso, the celebrated fragmentary marble statue preserved in Rome.

Like Barry, other artists affiliated with the Academy emulated the art of the past. The sculptor and draftsman John Flaxman (1755-1826) developed a linear style in which the contrast between the dark-colored background and the light figures attests to his interest in Greek vases (plate 68), while the erudite painter Henry Fuseli based his striding, muscular males and the distressed woman on the Niobid sculptural group in the Uffizi in Florence (plate 66).

Although the Academy promoted narrative art as the noblest genre for its ability to convey moral instruction to its viewers, portraiture remained highly popular and commercially successful. One of the leading portraitists of the era was George Romney (1734–1802), who desperately tried to establish himself as a history painter and free himself from "cursed portrait-painting." He made the sketch depicting a scene from *The Tempest* in preparation for a large oil painting for the engraver and publisher John Boydell's ambitious project known as the Shakespeare Gallery (plate 69).

Outside the art establishment, visual satire experienced a golden age during Blake's lifetime. Employing primarily the medium of printmaking, satirical artists criticized social and political institutions through hyperbolic representations. James Gillray (1756–1815), a famed satirist, mercilessly lampooned political figures in his prints (plates 70, 71). His *Presages of the Millenium* shows the emaciated, nude Prime Minister William Pitt the Younger as a Horseman of the Apocalypse, with King George III depicted as a monkey, holding onto him and kissing his behind.

Throughout his life, but especially while enrolled in the Royal Academy, Blake formed meaningful and lasting friendships with a number of fellow British artists. These relationships provided professional help to Blake through much of his career by introducing him to potential patrons and by commissioning works from him. Blake's interactions with his colleagues informed his art and his views about art, the extent of both of which has yet to be fully explored.

EA

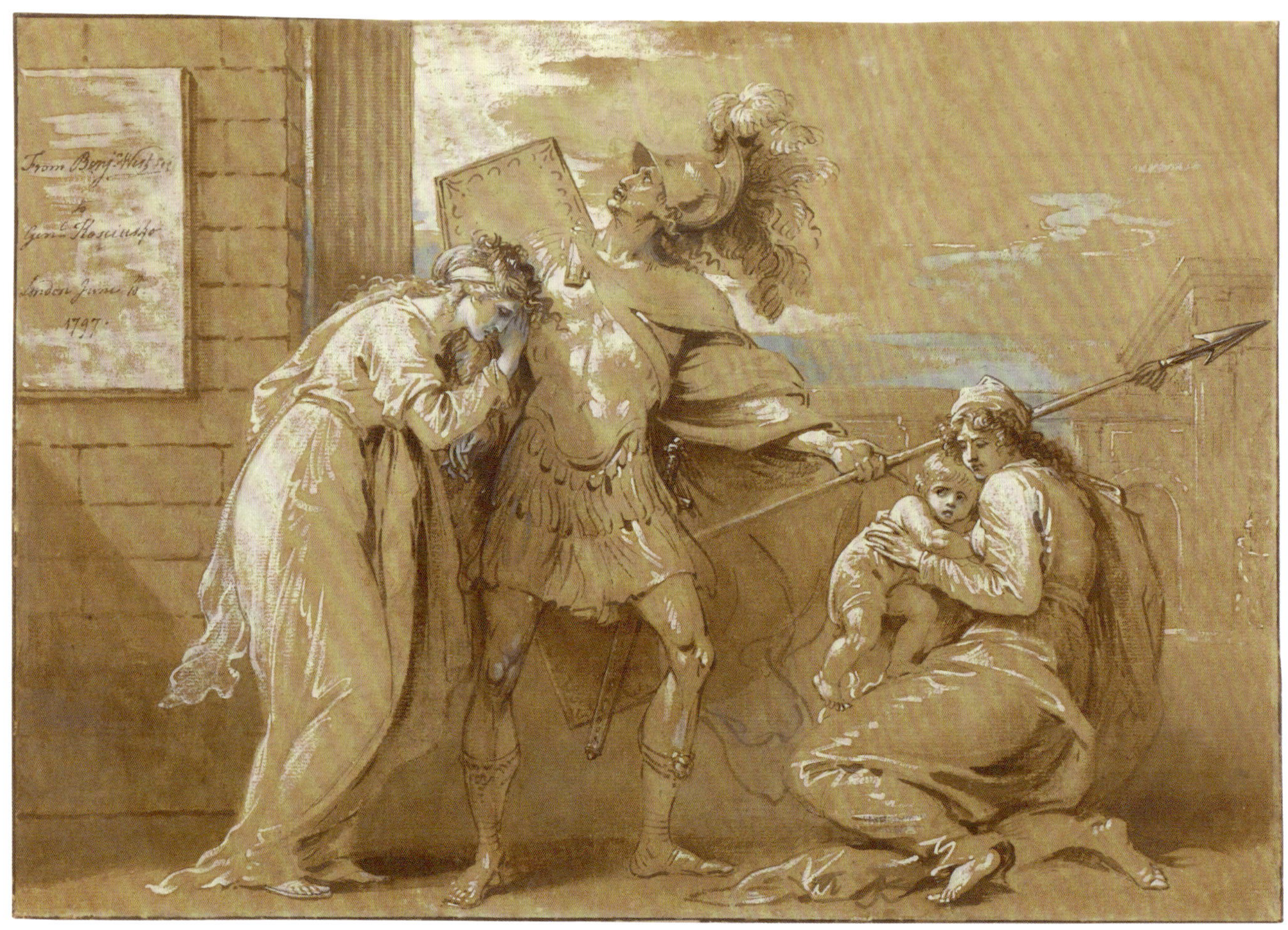

Plate 64
Benjamin West, *The Fright of Astyanax (Hector Bidding Farewell to Andromache)*, 1797

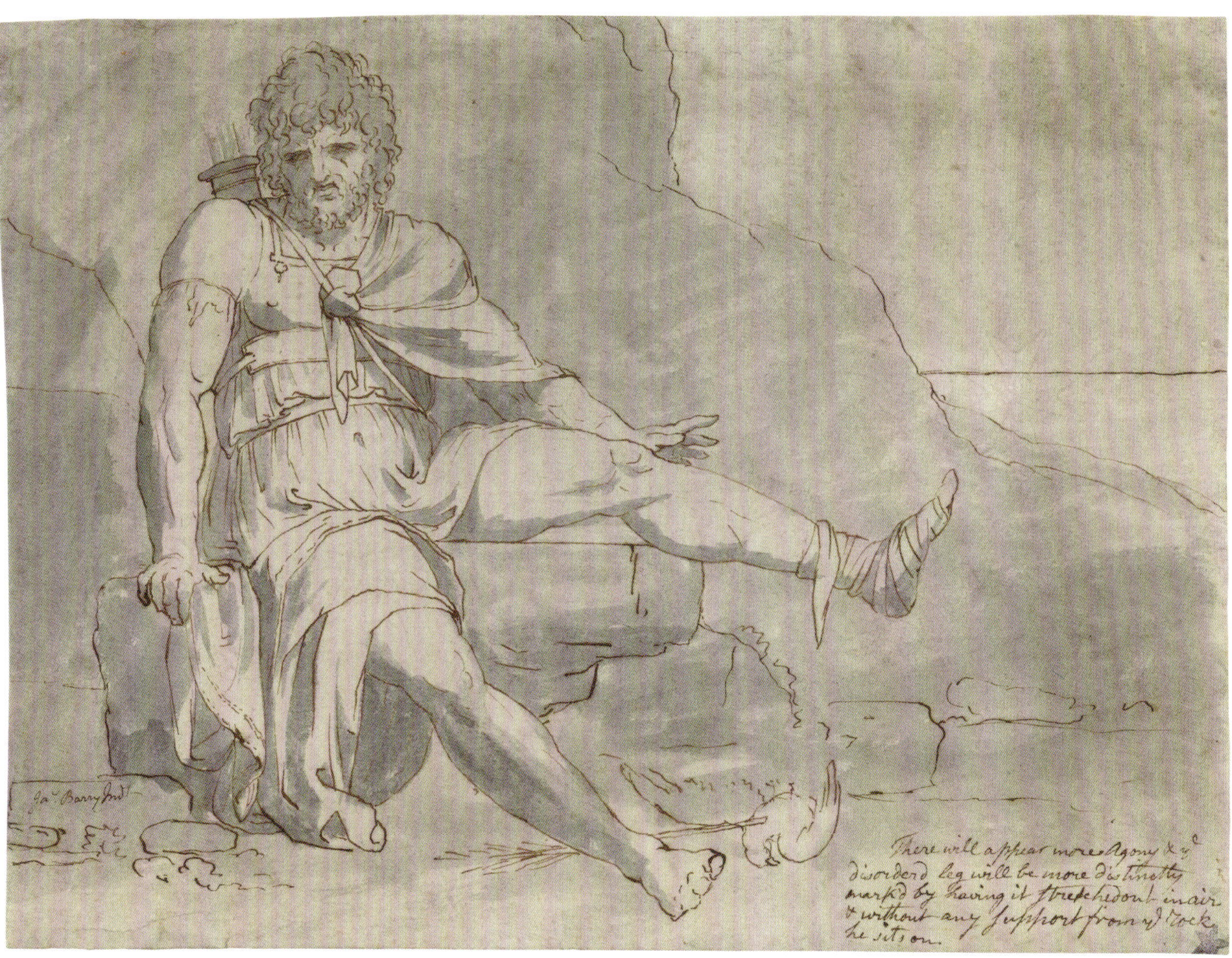

Plate 65
James Barry, *Study for "Philoctetes on the Island of Lemnos,"* 1770

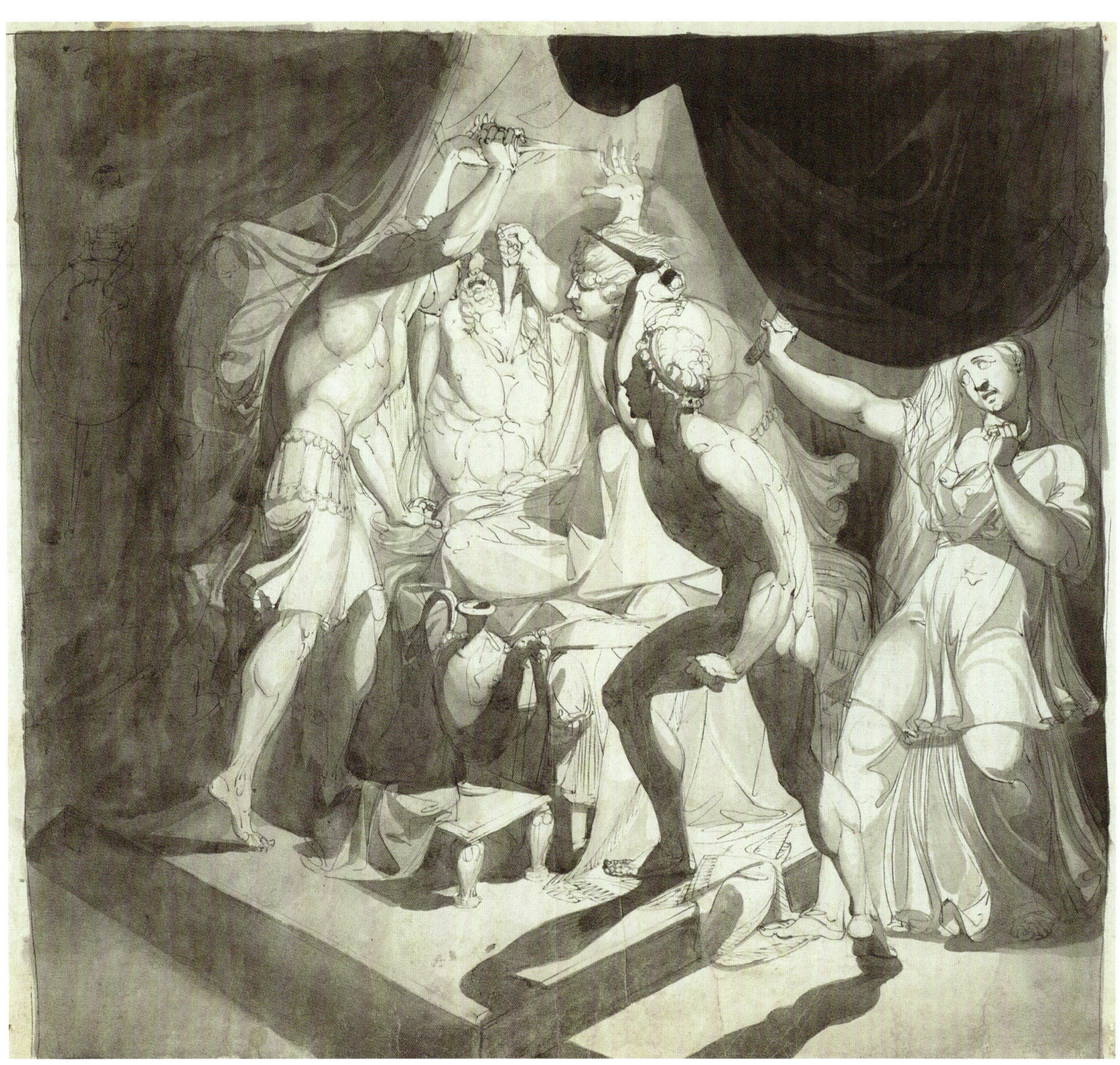

Plate 66
Henry Fuseli, *An Old Man Murdered by Three Younger Men*, early 1770s

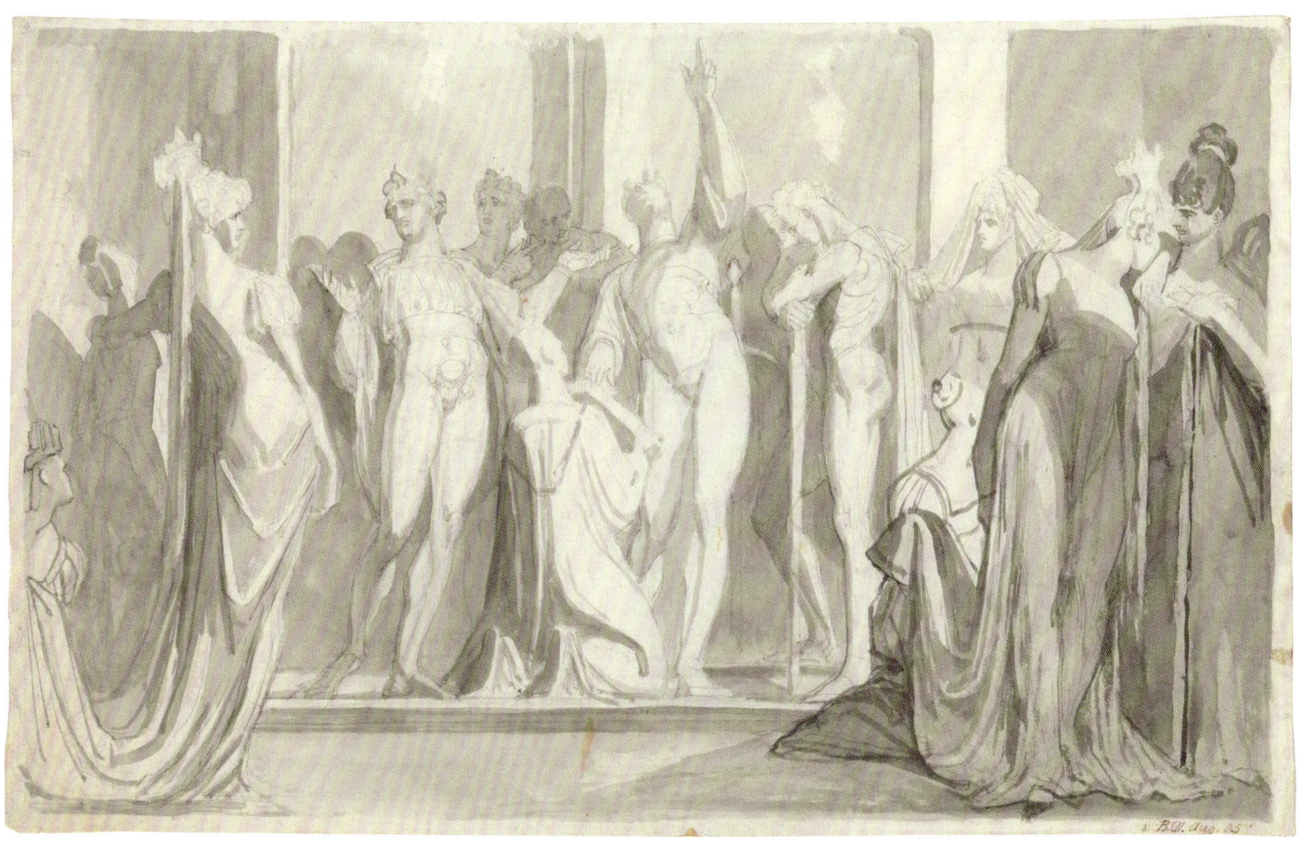

Plate 67
Henry Fuseli, *Siegfried About to Deny an Oath That Brunhild Had Been His Paramour*, 1805

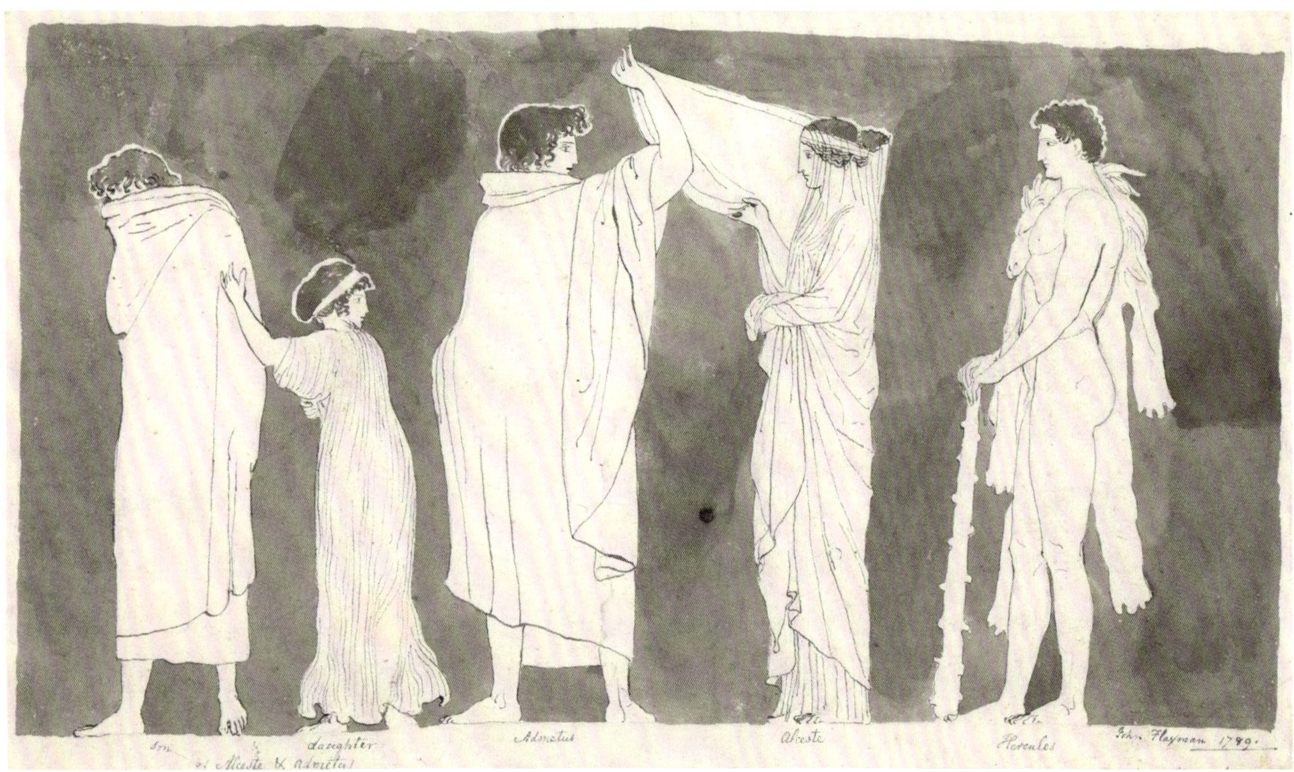

Plate 68
John Flaxman, *Alcestis and Admetus*, 1789

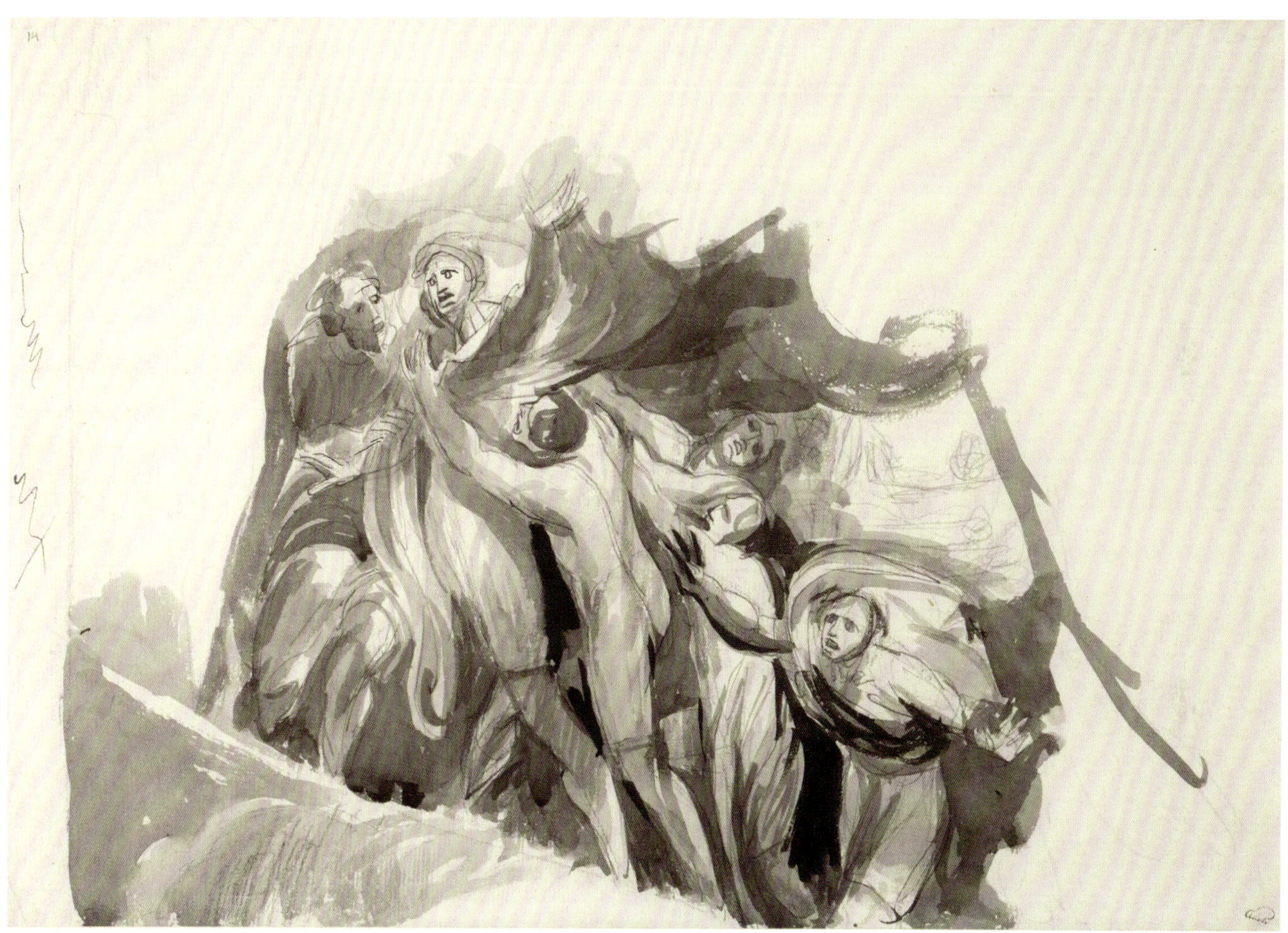

Plate 69
George Romney, *The Tempest, Act I*, about 1787

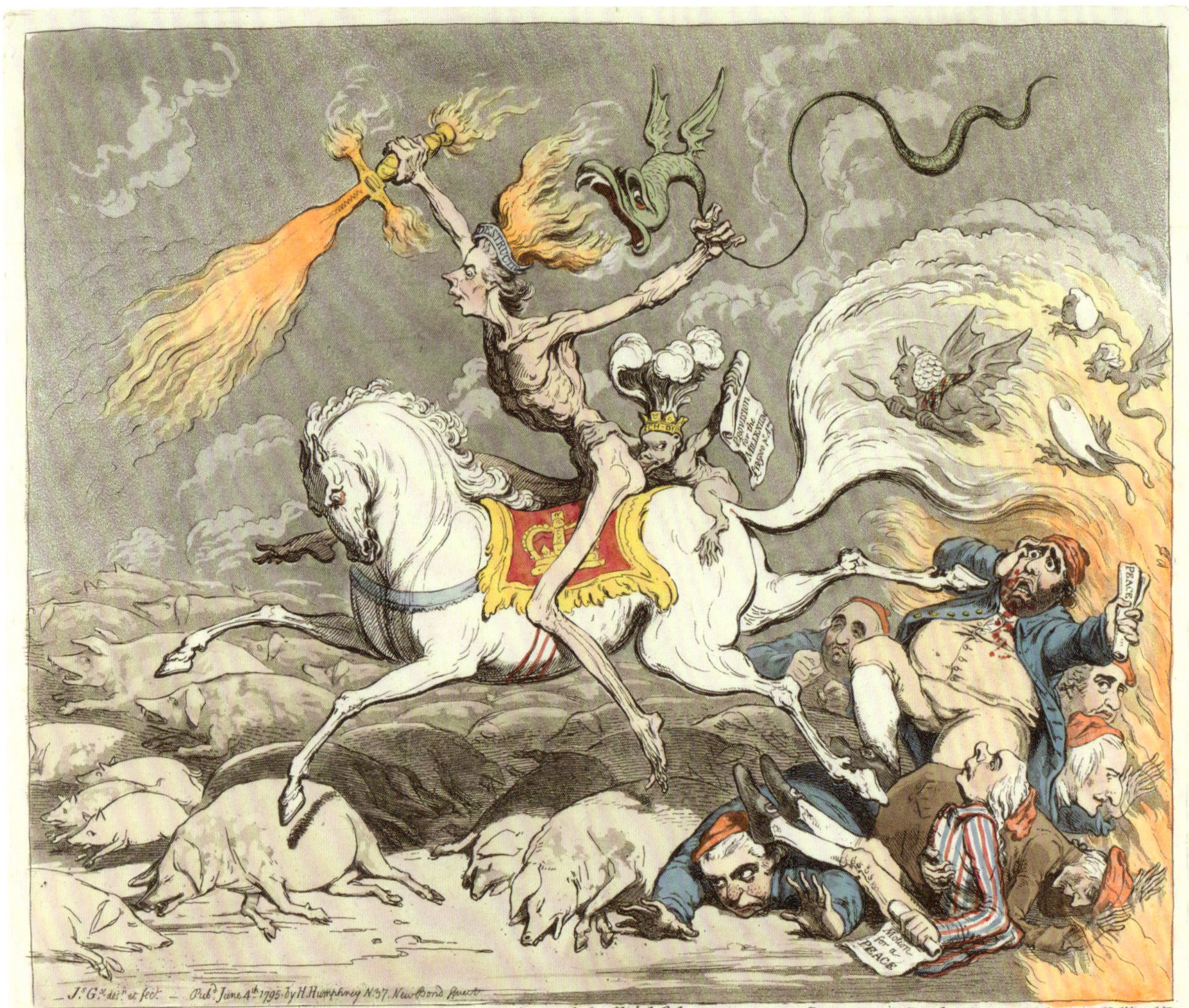

Plate 70
James Gillray, *Presages of the Millenium*, 1795

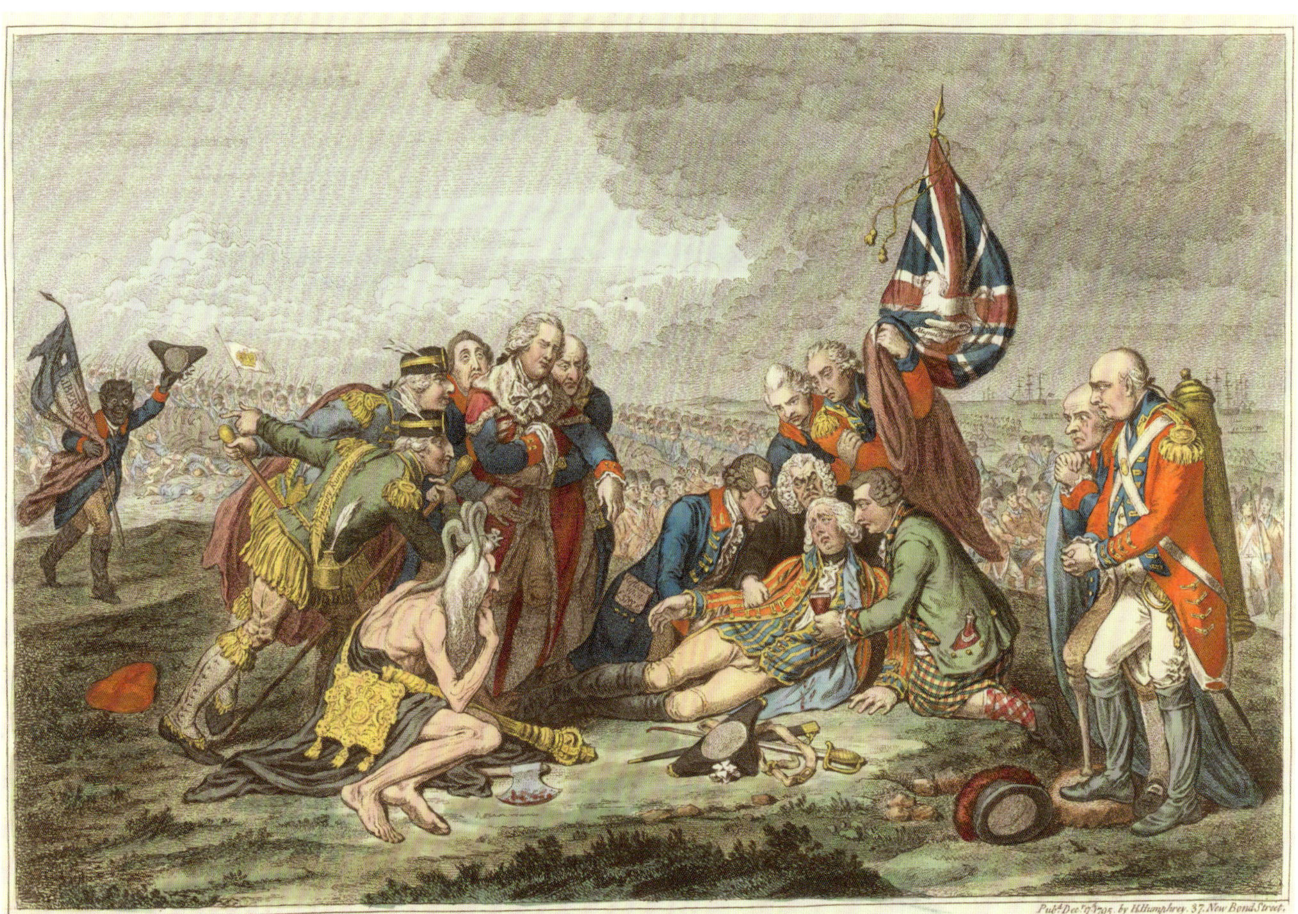

Plate 71
James Gillray, *The Death of the Great Wolf*, 1795

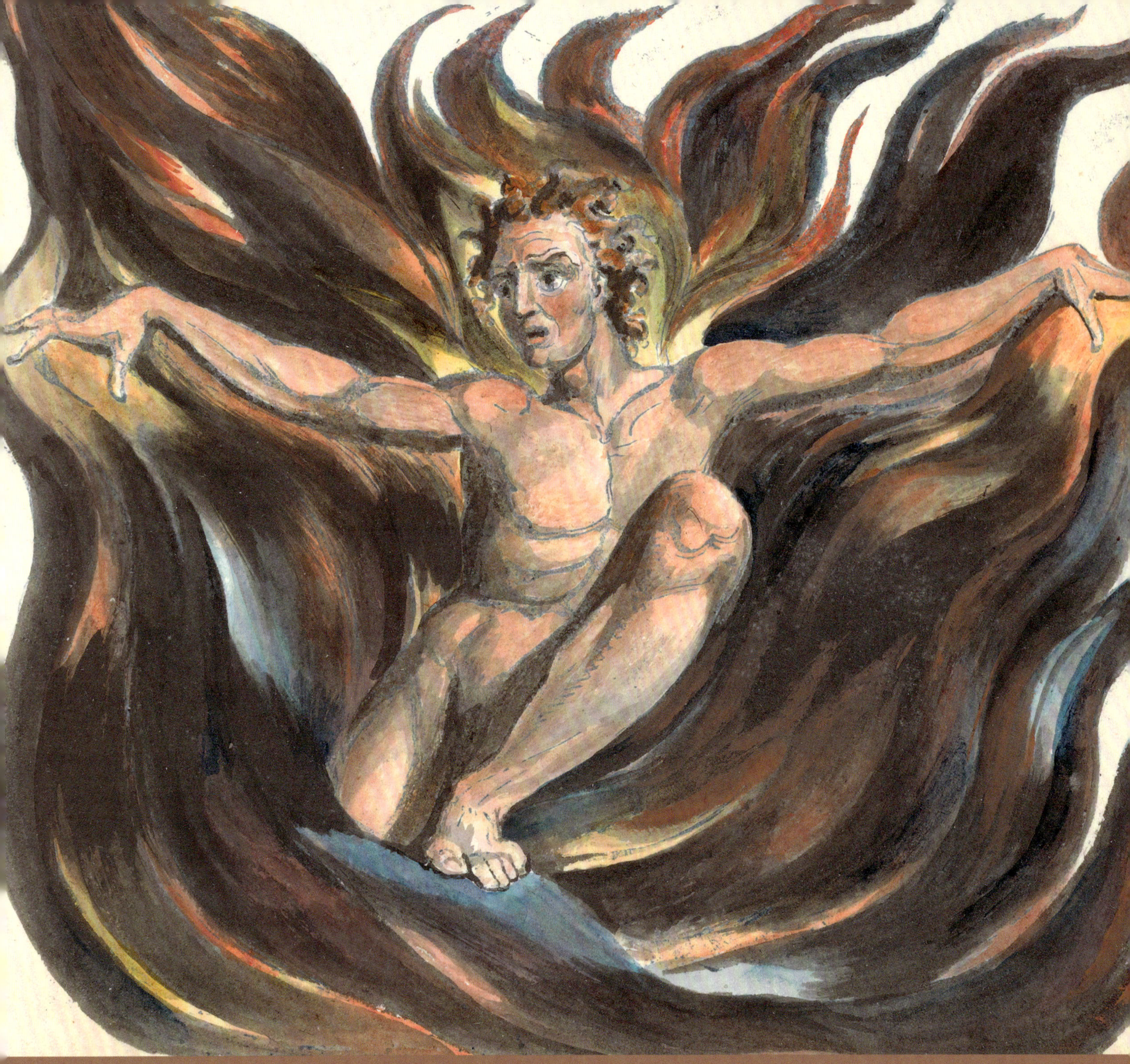

"See Visions, Dream Dreams, & prophecy & speak Parables unobserv'd & at liberty from the Doubts of other Mortals."

—William Blake to Thomas Butts, April 25, 1803

The Visionary

PLATES 72–97

Blake's seemingly limitless imagination saw full rein in his prophetic or "Lambeth" books, in which he used his relief etching technique to combine word and image freely on the page and to bypass traditional publishing hierarchies. These works are not prophetic in the modern sense of foretelling the future, but rather they set out a personal vision of the arc of human existence as Blake saw it, using his own cast of characters to represent universal forces of creation and destruction—physical, psychological, and historical. They reflect the tumultuous world in which Blake lived, dominated by news of the American Revolution and French Revolution. Through the books' opaque and demanding symbolism, they convey views that could not have been conventionally published in Britain at the time given their potentially seditious nature.

In *America a Prophecy* (1793, plates 72–89) the fallen structure of repressive British rule, in the form of Albion's Angel (underpinned by Urizen's organized religion, law, and reason), is challenged by Orc, the fiery energy that would sweep away the old order and impose a new one. Eighteen copies of *America a Prophecy* survive, most in monochrome. *Europe a Prophecy* (1794) followed swiftly. The images principally catalogue the woes of the old order, including plague, famine, and terror. The frontispiece (plate 90) depicting Urizen dividing the deep with a compass, separating light and dark, has become one of the iconic images of British art. *The Song of Los* (1795, plate 92), with eight rich and evocative plates, develops a complex overarching narrative, from humankind's initial submission to organized religion through to an apocalyptic resurrection. Los represents the creative spirit of the artist (including the literary arts), who strives for a vision of eternity.

The Visionary Heads (plates 94–96) are a peculiar series of over 100 drawings made by Blake around 1819–25. They record nighttime visions and interactions with characters, some historical or biblical, experienced by him and the watercolorist John Varley (plate 93, 1778–1848), who had a passion for astrology. One records the ghost of a flea, who told Blake all fleas were inhabited by the souls of men and were "bloodthirsty to excess" (plate 96). Blake subsequently worked his vision into a now-famous tempera painting, in which the ghost of a flea holds a cup for drinking blood (plate 97).

JB

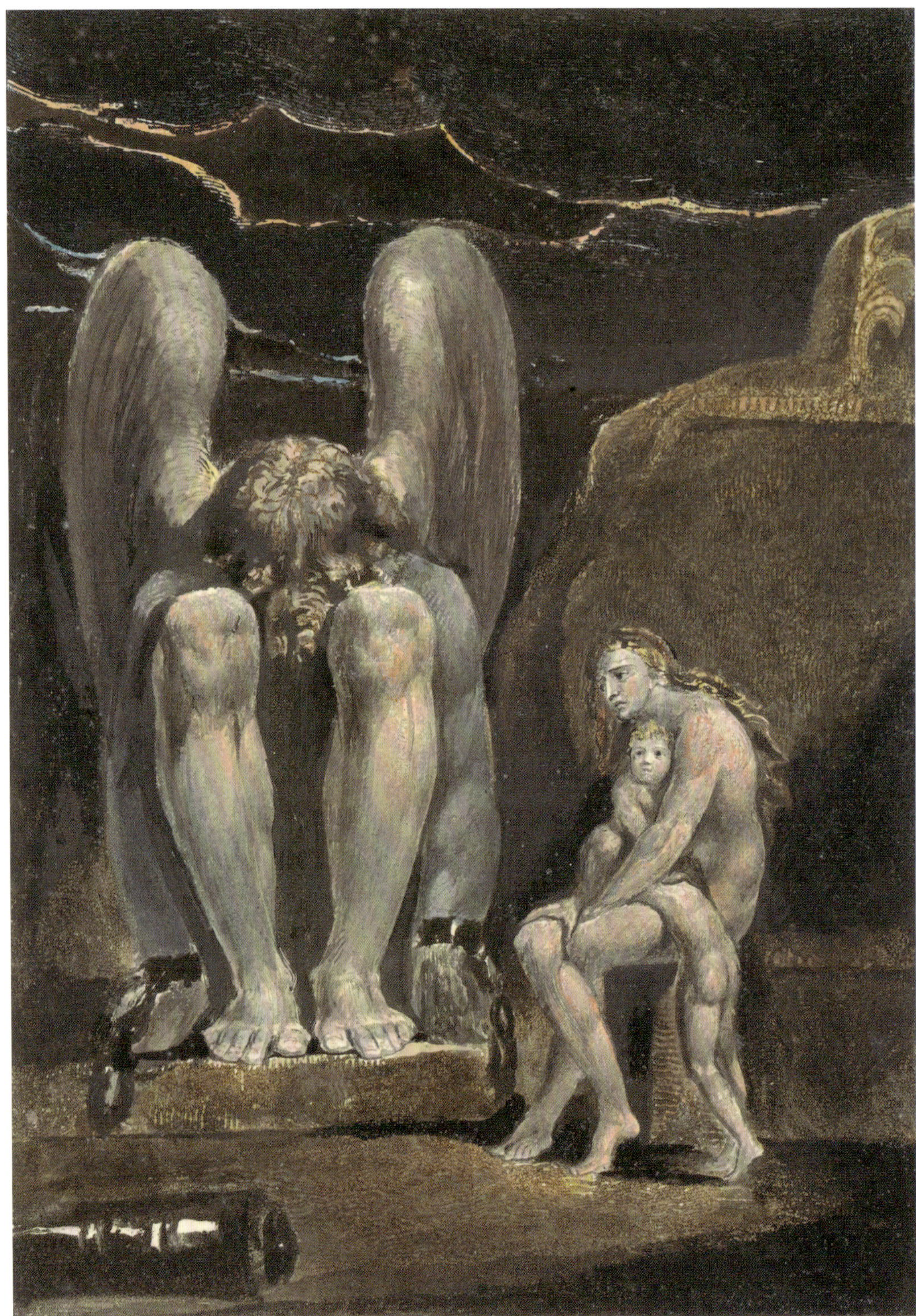

Plate 72
William Blake, *America a Prophecy*, plate 1, 1793

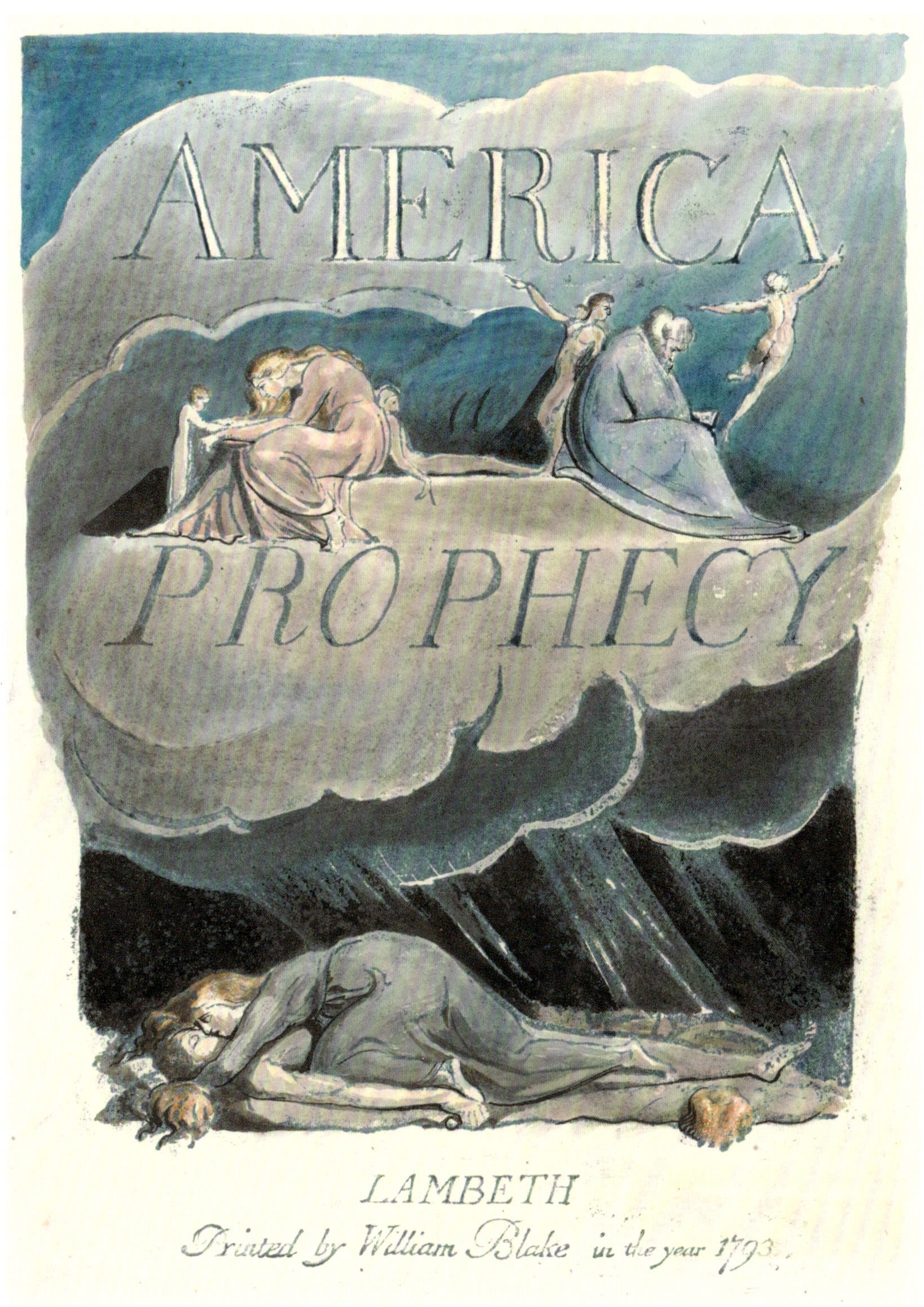

Plate 73
William Blake, *America a Prophecy*, plate 2, 1793

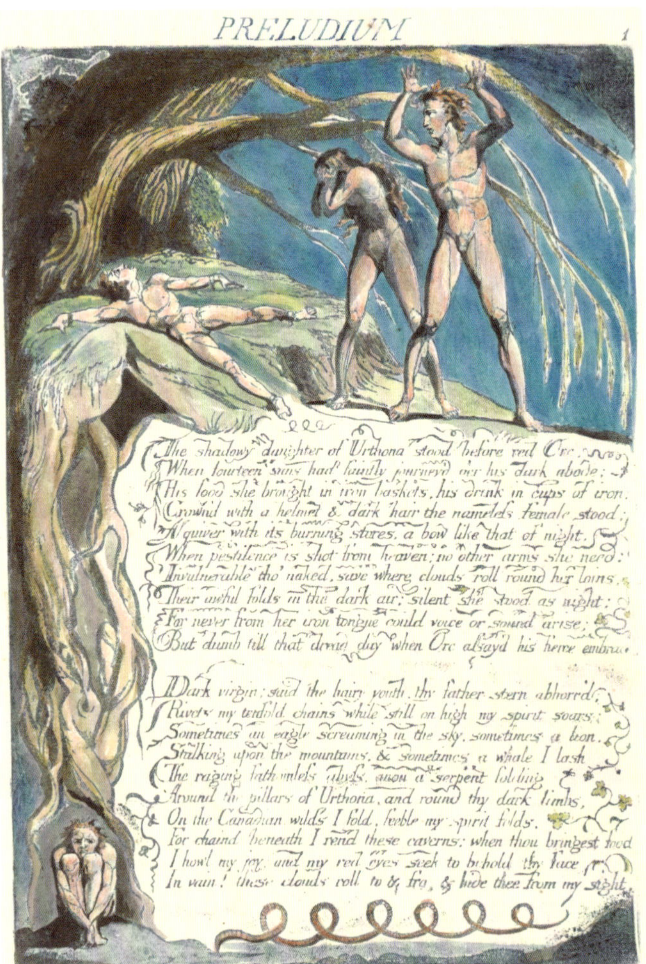

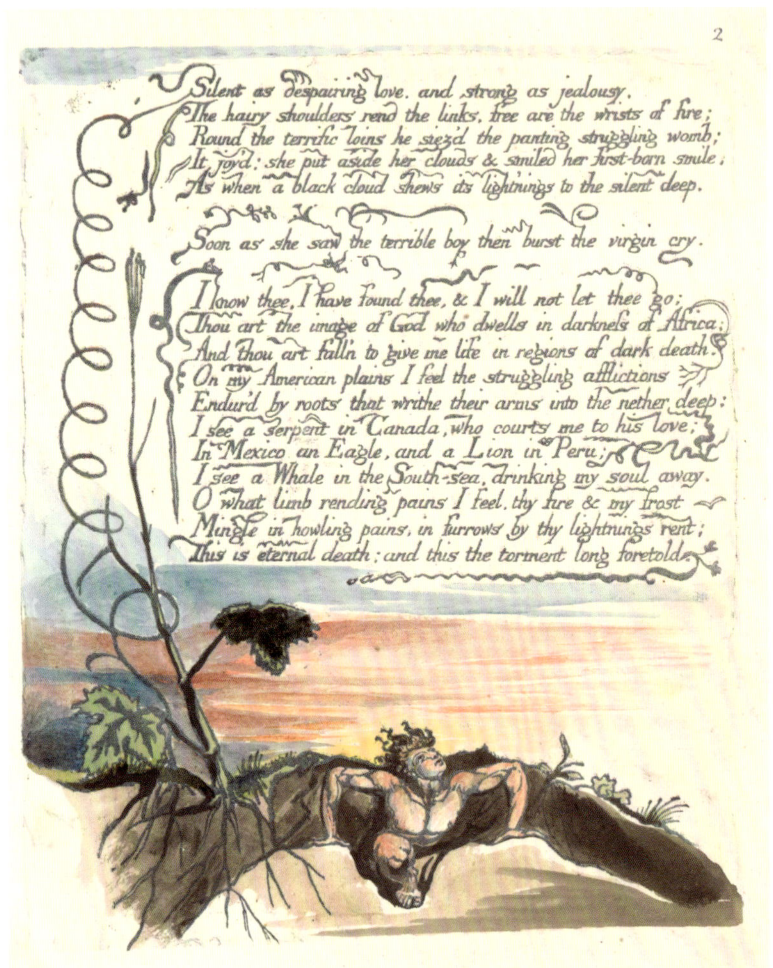

Plate 74
William Blake, *America a Prophecy*, plate 3, 1793

Plate 75
William Blake, *America a Prophecy*, plate 4, 1793

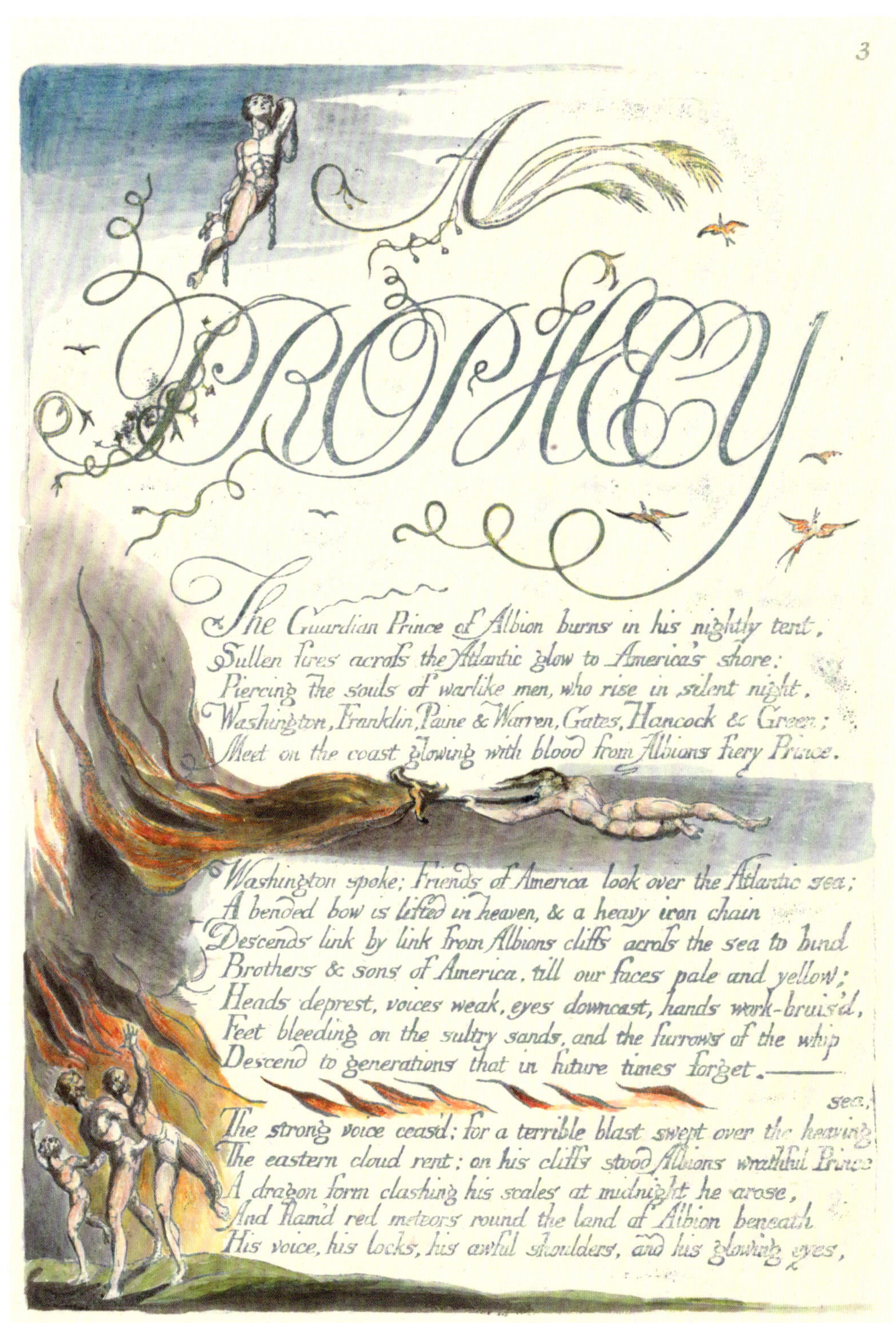

Plate 76
William Blake, *America a Prophecy,* plate 5, 1793

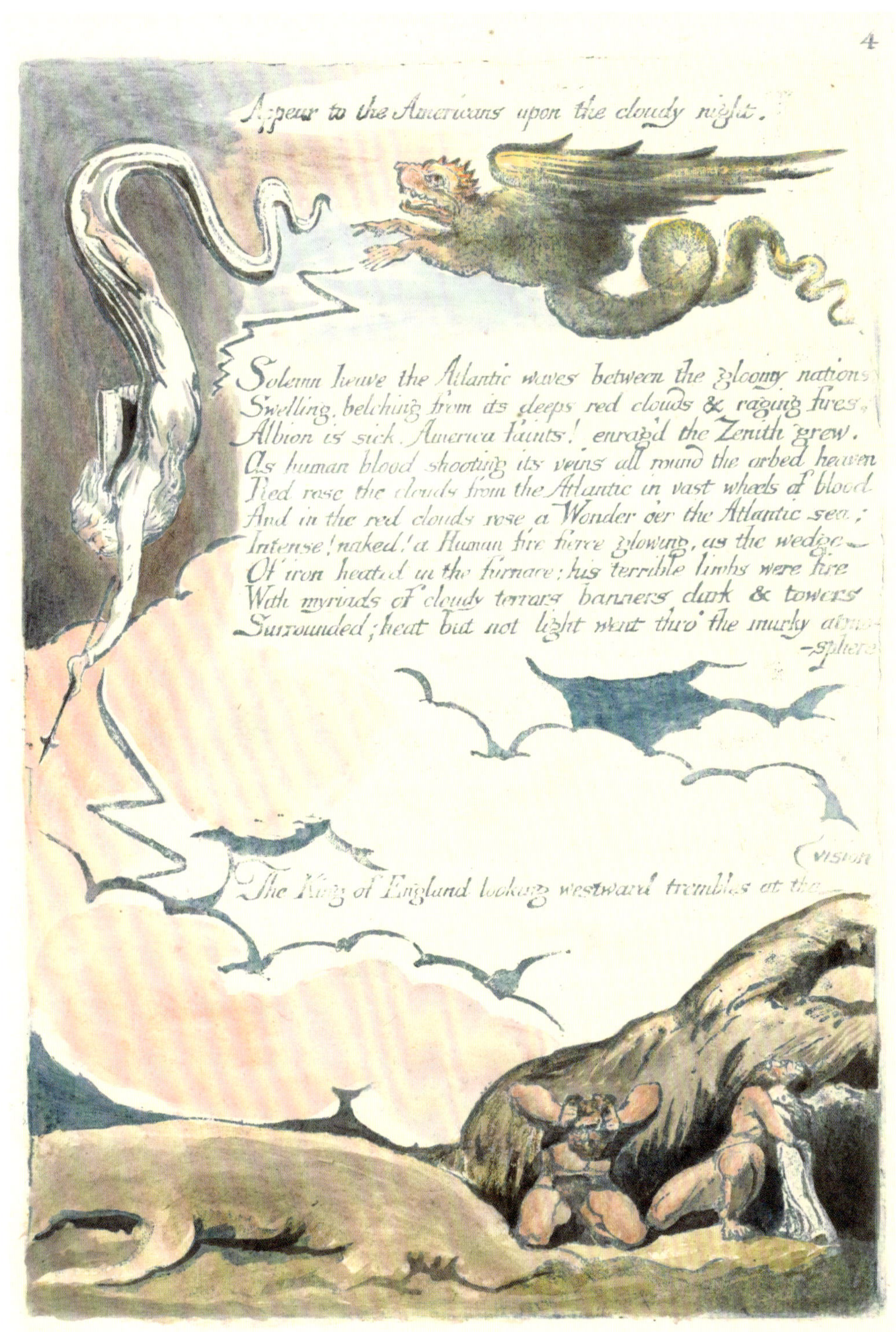

Plate 77
William Blake, *America a Prophecy*, plate 6, 1793

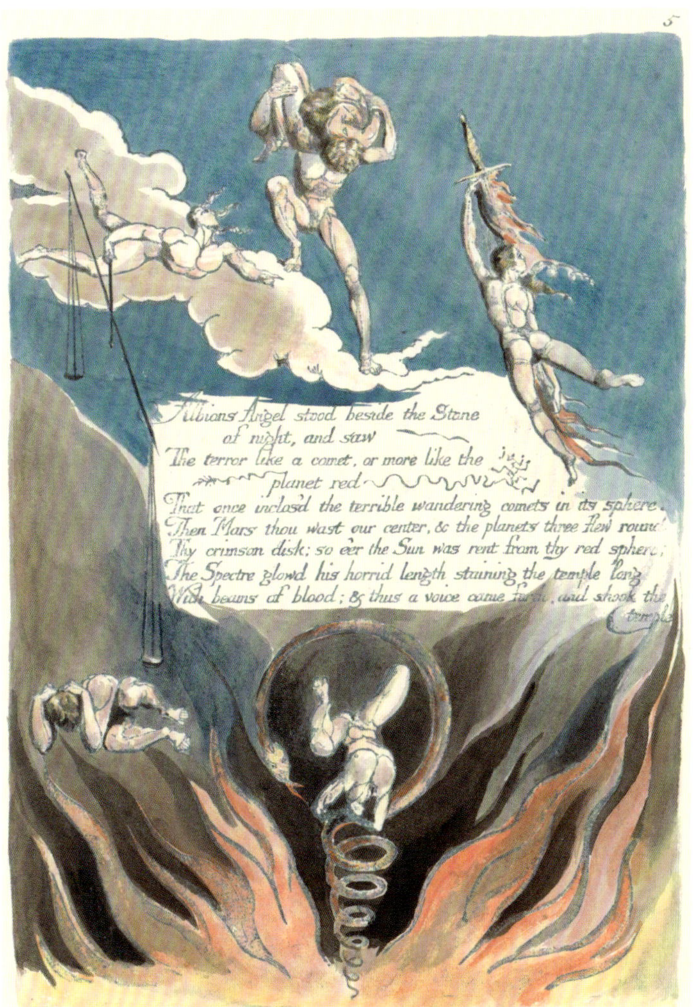

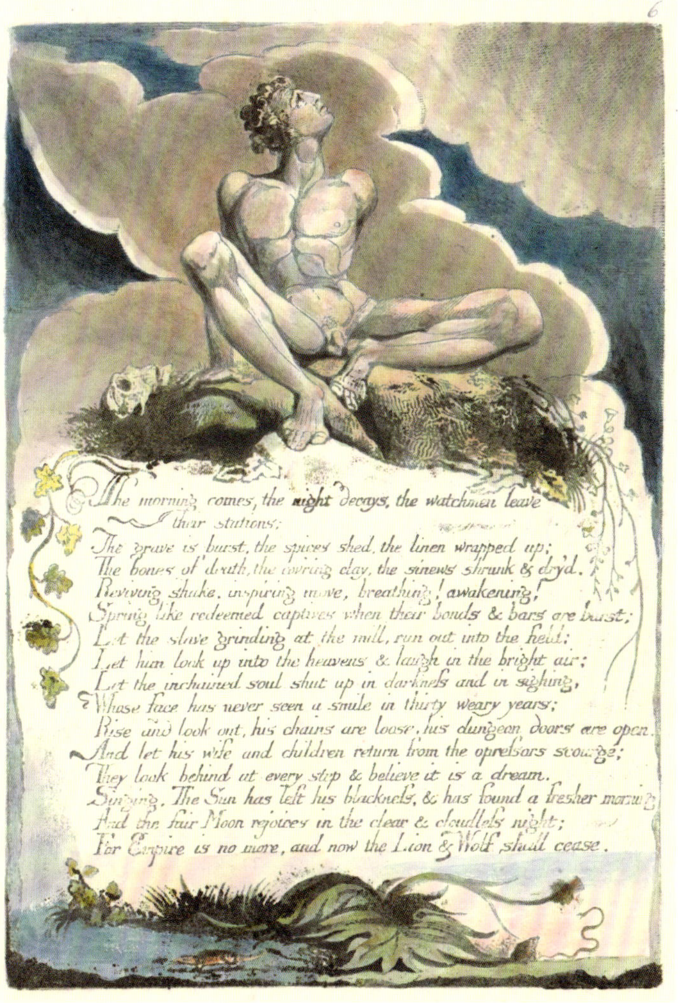

Plate 78
William Blake, *America a Prophecy*, plate 7, 1793

Plate 79
William Blake, *America a Prophecy*, plate 8, 1793

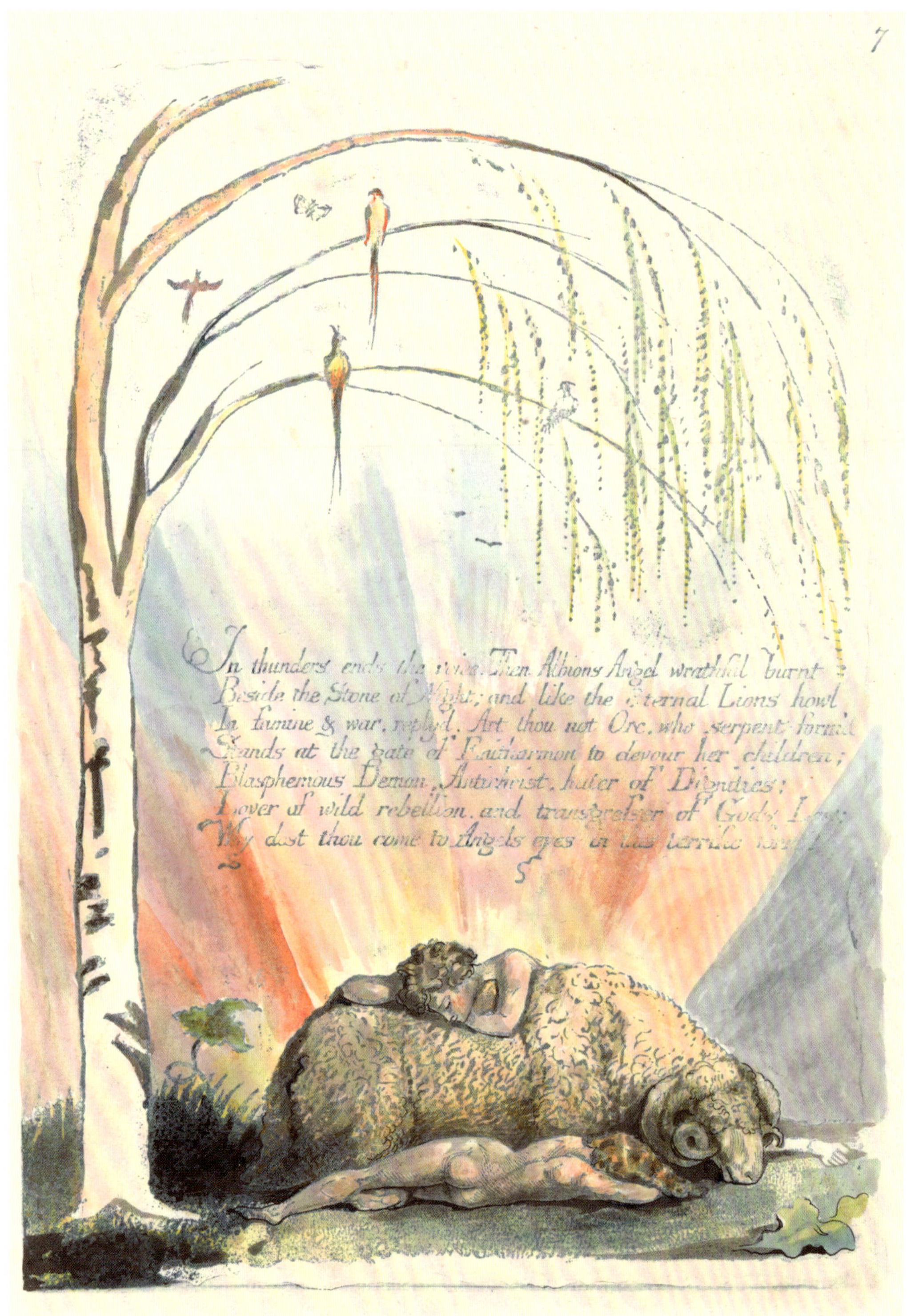

Plate 80
William Blake, *America a Prophecy*, plate 9, 1793

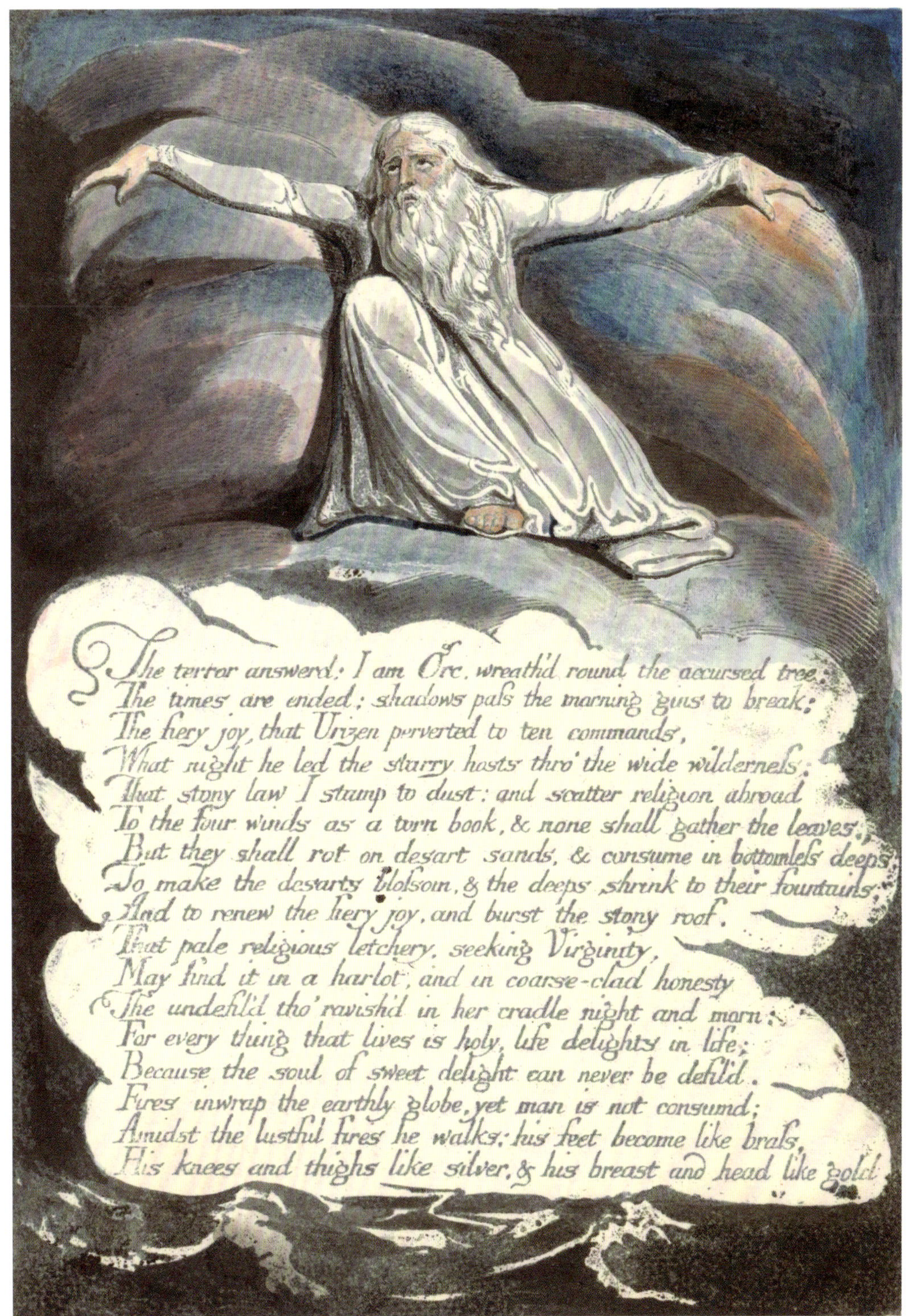

Plate 81
William Blake, *America a Prophecy*, plate 10, 1793

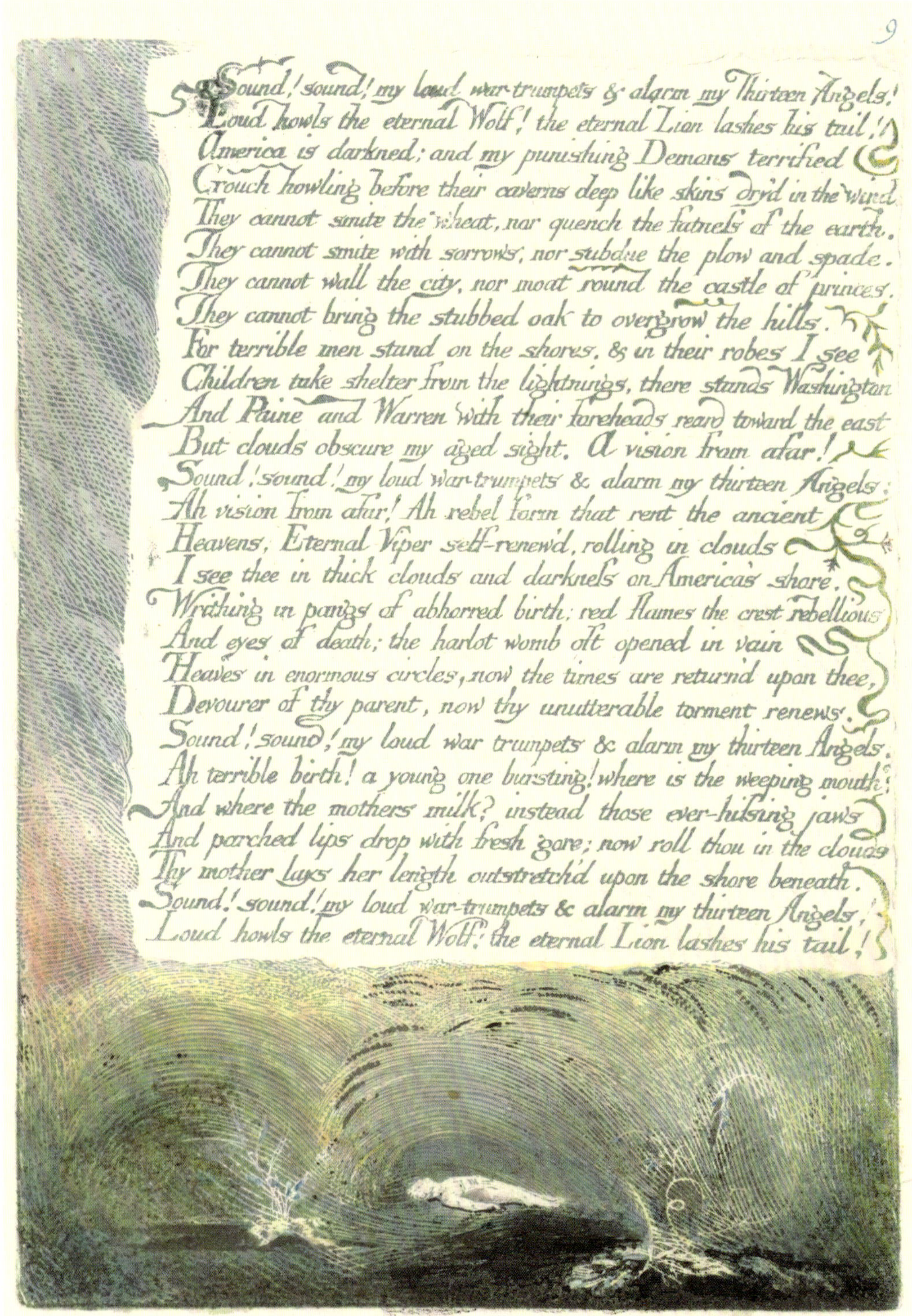

9

Sound! sound! my loud war-trumpets & alarm my Thirteen Angels!
Loud howls the eternal Wolf! the eternal Lion lashes his tail!
America is darkned; and my punishing Demons terrified
Crouch howling before their caverns deep like skins dry'd in the wind.
They cannot smite the wheat, nor quench the fatneſs of the earth.
They cannot smite with sorrows, nor subdue the plow and spade.
They cannot wall the city, nor moat round the castle of princes.
They cannot bring the stubbed oak to overgrow the hills.
For terrible men stand on the shores, & in their robes I see
Children take shelter from the lightnings, there stands Washington
And Paine and Warren with their foreheads reard toward the east
But clouds obscure my aged sight. A vision from afar!
Sound! sound! my loud war-trumpets & alarm my thirteen Angels:
Ah vision from afar! Ah rebel form that rent the ancient
Heavens; Eternal Viper self-renew'd, rolling in clouds
I see thee in thick clouds and darkneſs on America's shore.
Writhing in pangs of abhorred birth; red flames the crest rebellious
And eyes of death; the harlot womb oft opened in vain
Heaves in enormous circles, now the times are return'd upon thee,
Devourer of thy parent, now thy unutterable torment renews.
Sound! sound! my loud war trumpets & alarm my thirteen Angels!
Ah terrible birth! a young one bursting! where is the weeping mouth?
And where the mothers milk? instead those ever-hiſsing jaws
And parched lips drop with fresh gore; now roll thou in the clouds
Thy mother lays her length outstretch'd upon the shore beneath.
Sound! sound! my loud war-trumpets & alarm my thirteen Angels!
Loud howls the eternal Wolf! the eternal Lion lashes his tail!

Plate 82
William Blake, *America a Prophecy*, plate 11, 1793

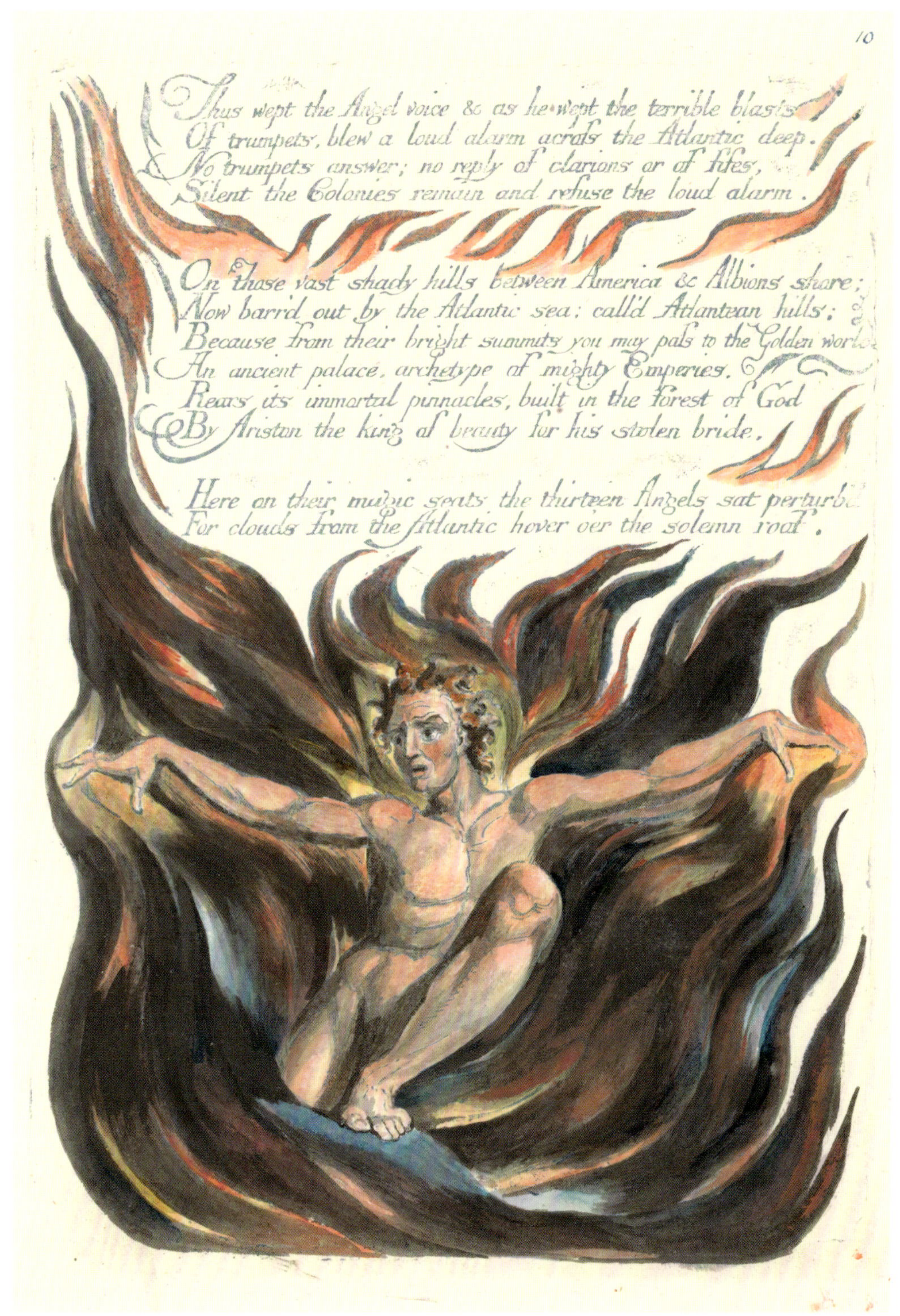

Plate 83
William Blake, *America a Prophecy*, plate 12, 1793

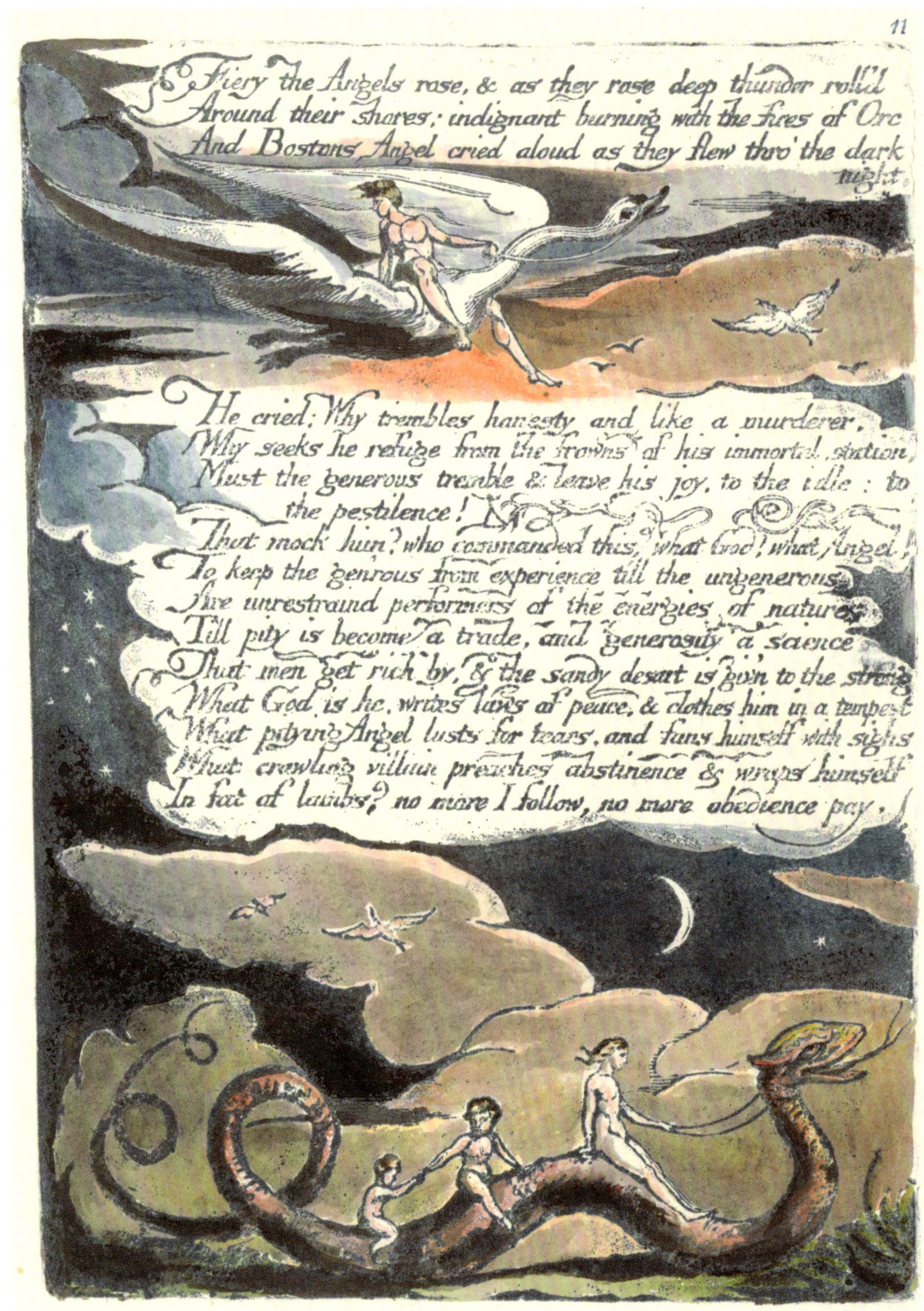
11

Fiery the Angels rose, & as they rose deep thunder roll'd
Around their shores: indignant burning with the fires of Orc
And Bostons Angel cried aloud as they flew thro' the dark
night.

He cried: Why trembles honesty and like a murderer,
Why seeks he refuge from the frowns of his immortal station!
Must the generous tremble & leave his joy, to the idle: to
the pestilence!
That mock him? who commanded this? what God? what Angel!
To keep the genrous from experience till the ungenerous
Are unrestraind performers of the energies of nature;
Till pity is become a trade, and generosity a science,
That men get rich by, & the sandy desart is giv'n to the strong
What God is he, writes laws of peace, & clothes him in a tempest
What pitying Angel lusts for tears, and fans himself with sighs
What crawling villain preaches abstinence & wraps himself
In fat of lambs? no more I follow, no more obedience pay.

Plate 84
William Blake, *America a Prophecy*, plate 13, 1793

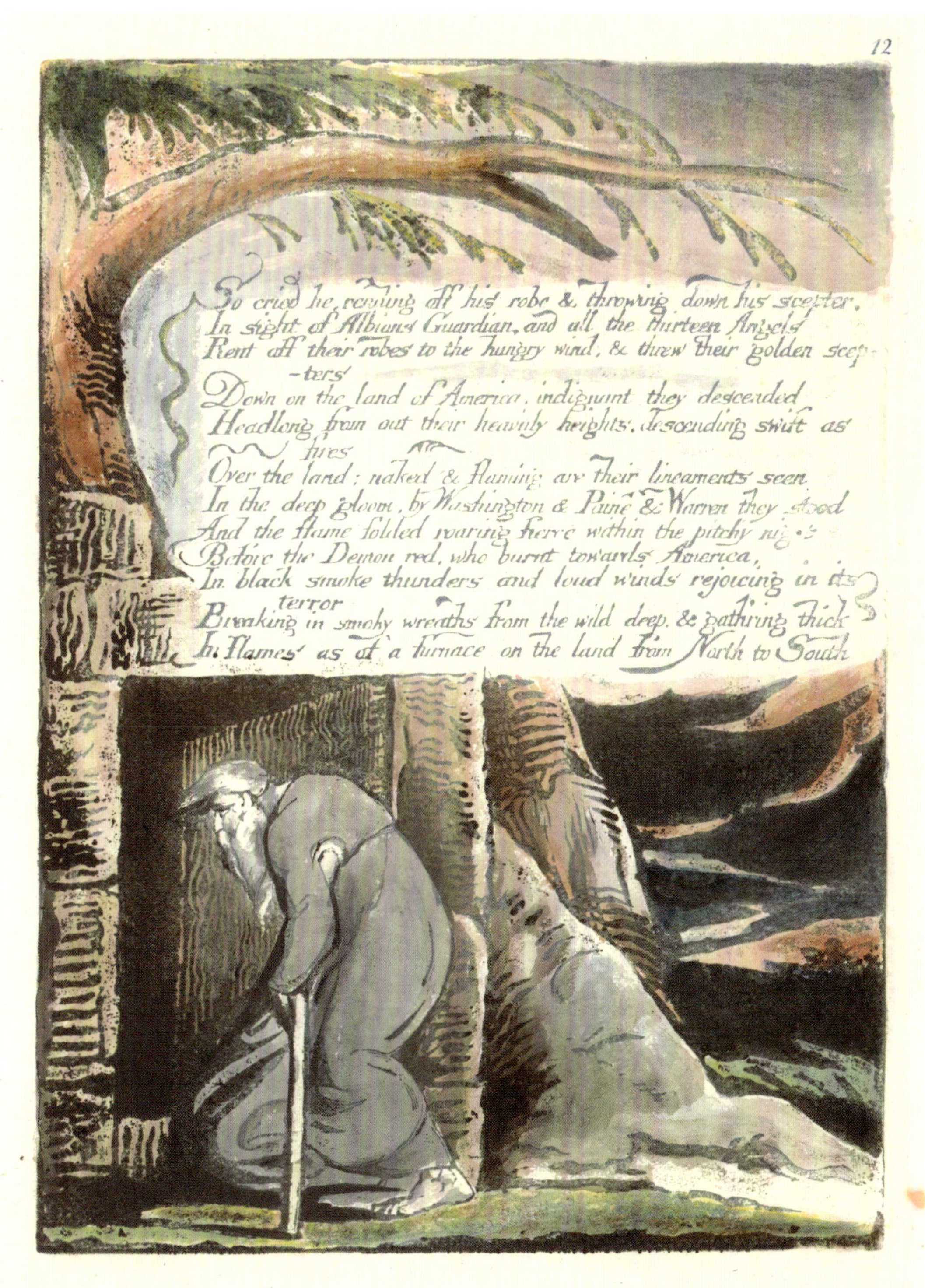

Plate 85
William Blake, *America a Prophecy*, plate 14, 1793

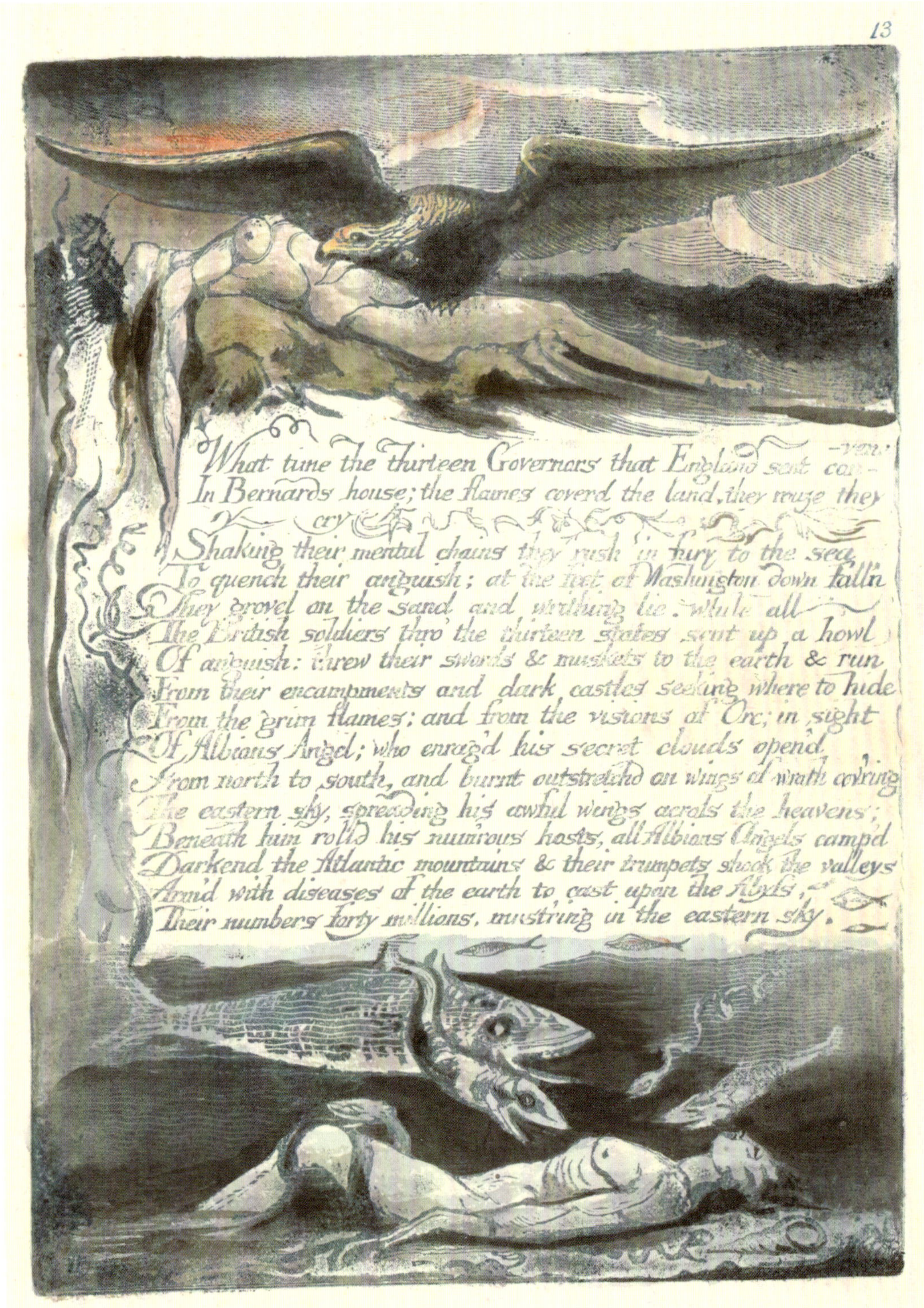

Plate 86
William Blake, *America a Prophecy*, plate 15, 1793

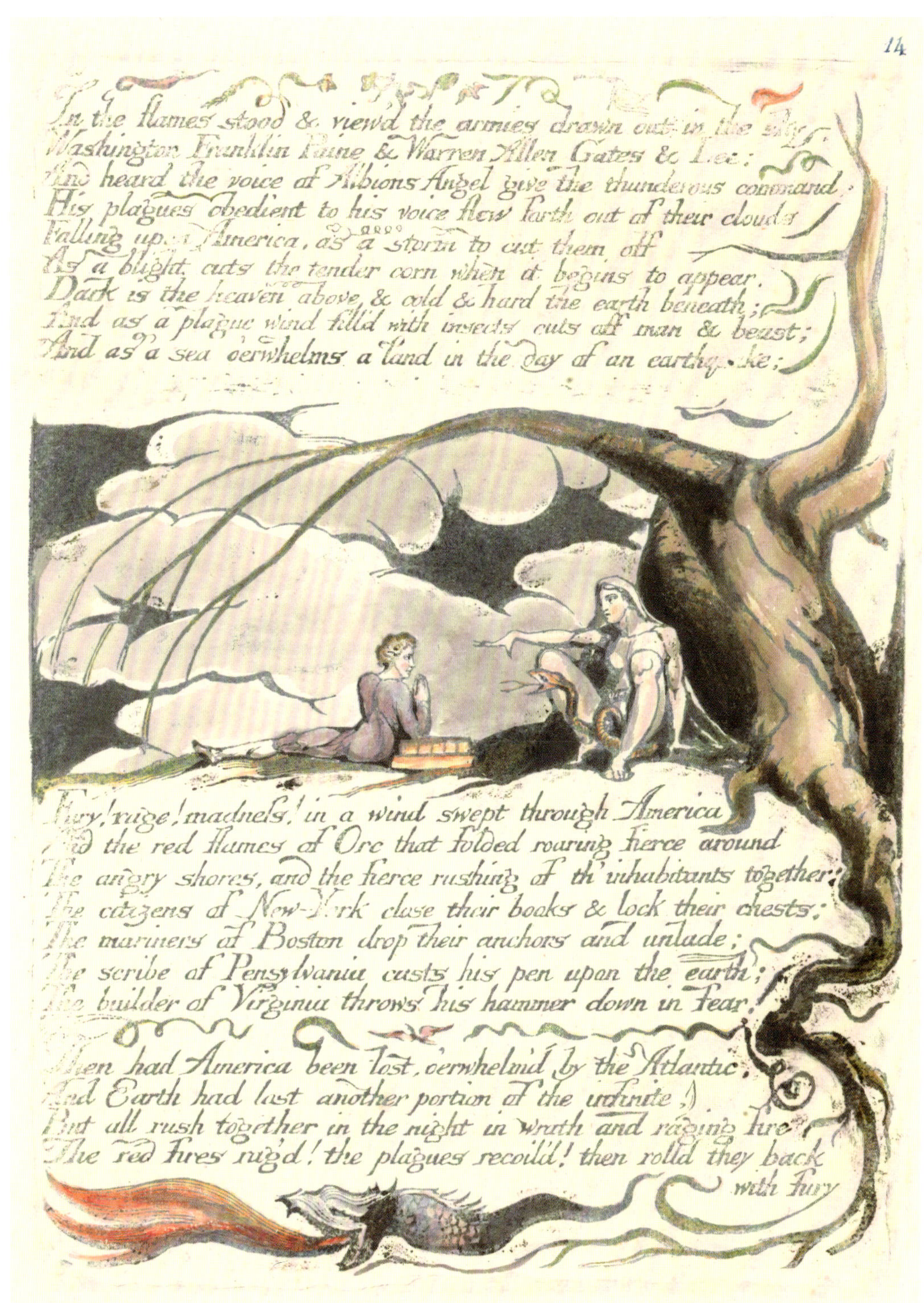

14

In the flames stood & view'd the armies drawn out in the sky
Washington Franklin Paine & Warren Allen Gates & Lee:
And heard the voice of Albions Angel give the thunderous command:
His plagues obedient to his voice flew forth out of their clouds
Falling upon America, as a storm to cut them off
As a blight cuts the tender corn when it begins to appear.
Dark is the heaven above, & cold & hard the earth beneath;
And as a plague wind fill'd with insects cuts off man & beast;
And as a sea o'erwhelms a land in the day of an earthquake;

Fury! rage! madness! in a wind swept through America
And the red flames of Orc that folded roaring fierce around
The angry shores, and the fierce rushing of th'inhabitants together:
The citizens of New-York close their books & lock their chests;
The mariners of Boston drop their anchors and unlade;
The scribe of Pensylvania casts his pen upon the earth;
The builder of Virginia throws his hammer down in fear.

Then had America been lost, o'erwhelm'd by the Atlantic,
And Earth had lost another portion of the infinite,)
But all rush together in the night in wrath and raging fire
The red fires rag'd! the plagues recoil'd! then roll'd they back
with fury

Plate 87
William Blake, *America a Prophecy*, plate 16, 1793

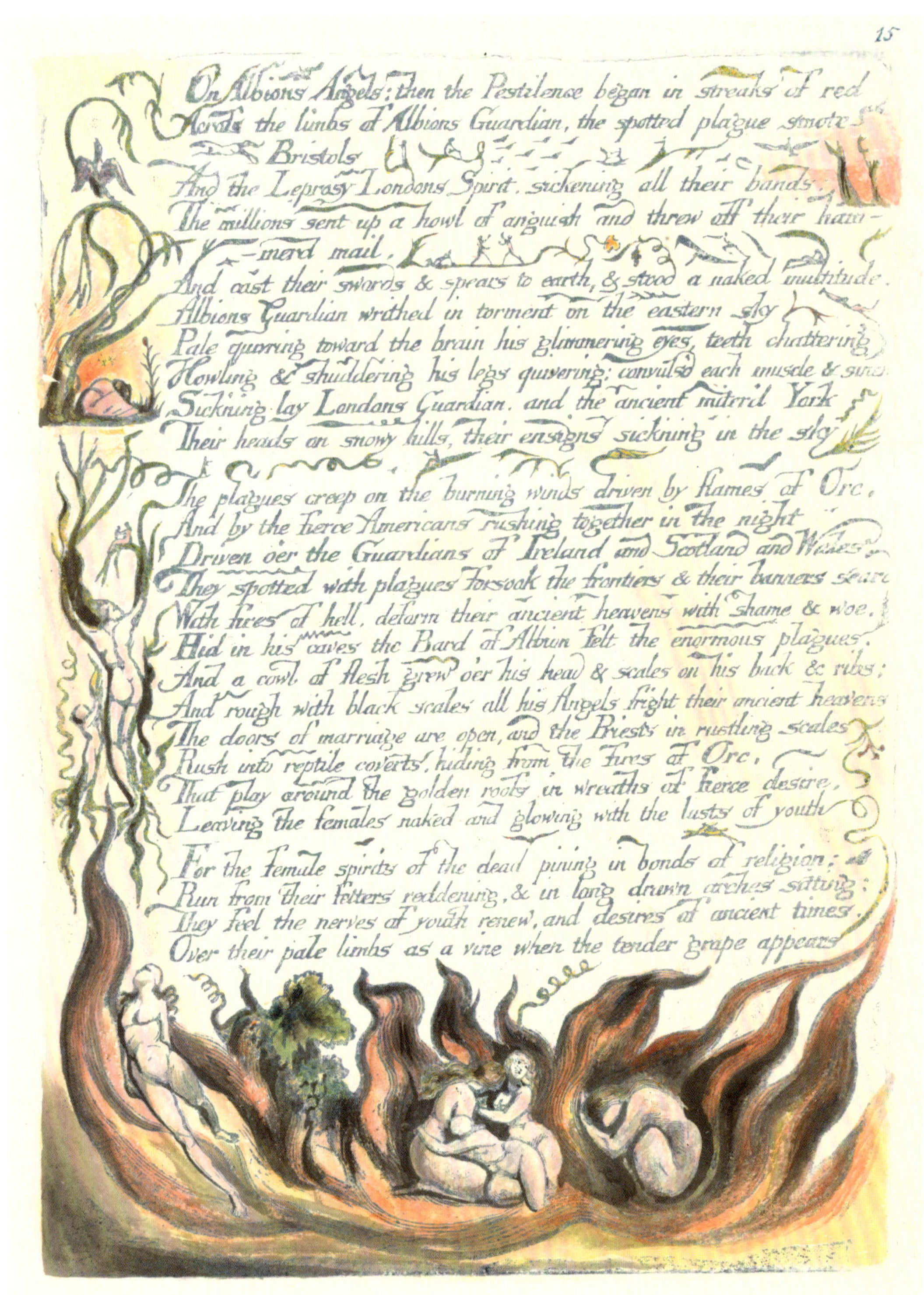

Plate 88

William Blake, *America a Prophecy*, plate 17, 1793

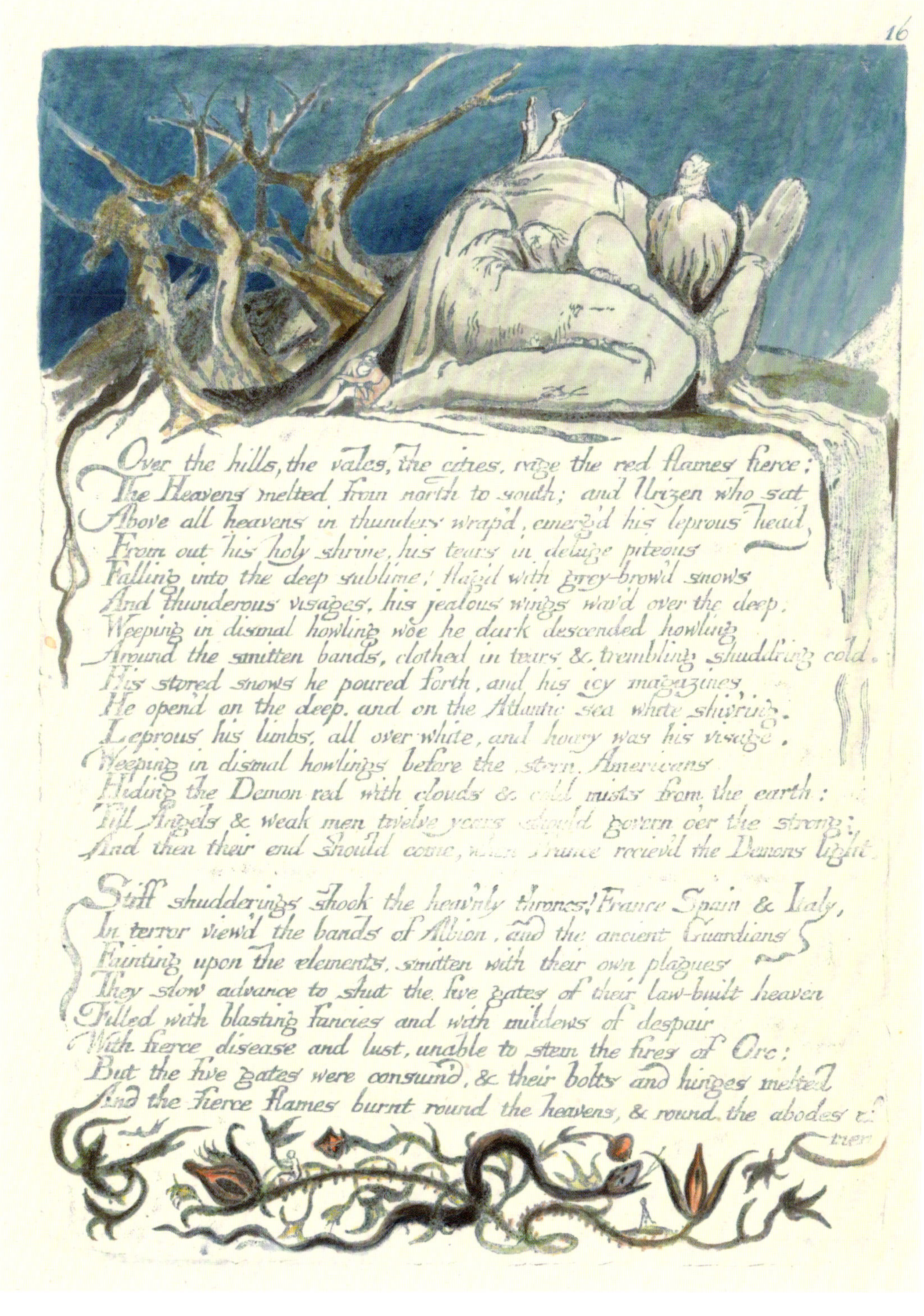

Plate 89
William Blake, *America a Prophecy*, plate 18, 1793

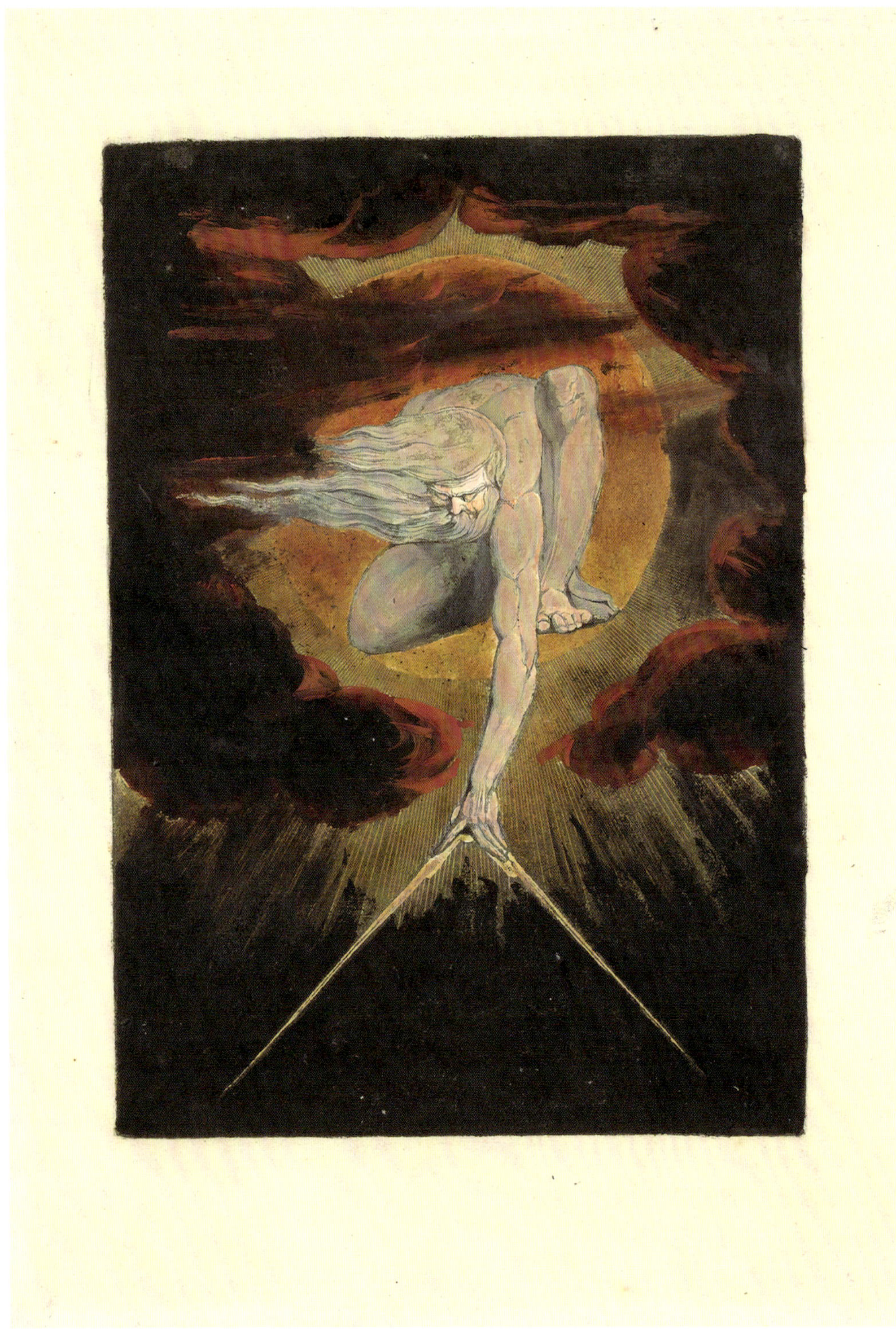

Plate 90
William Blake, "The Ancient of Days"
from *Europe a Prophecy*, 1794, printed 1795

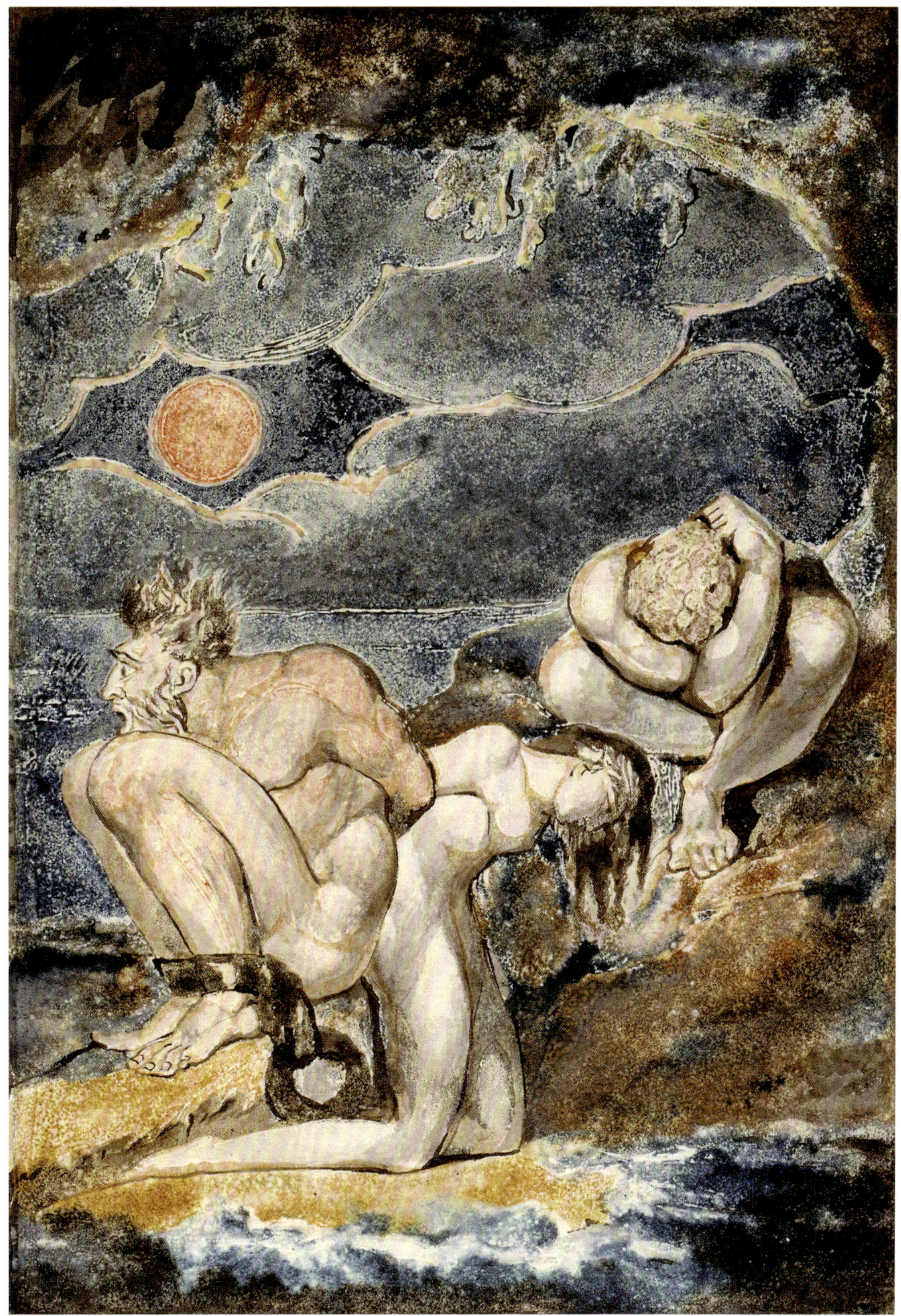

Plate 91
William Blake, *Visions of the Daughters of Albion*,
Frontispiece, about 1795

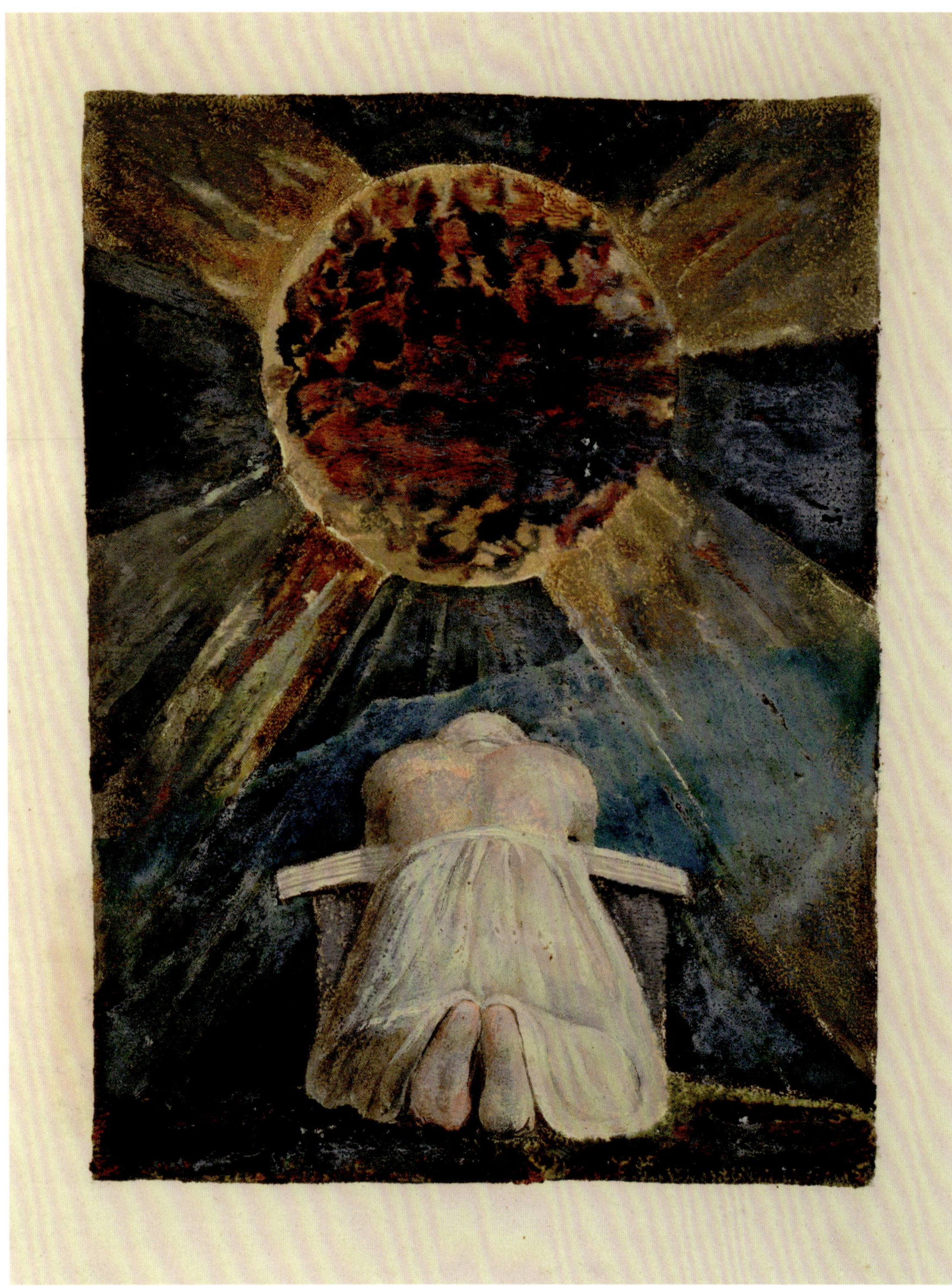

Plate 92
William Blake, *The Song of Los*, plate 1, 1795

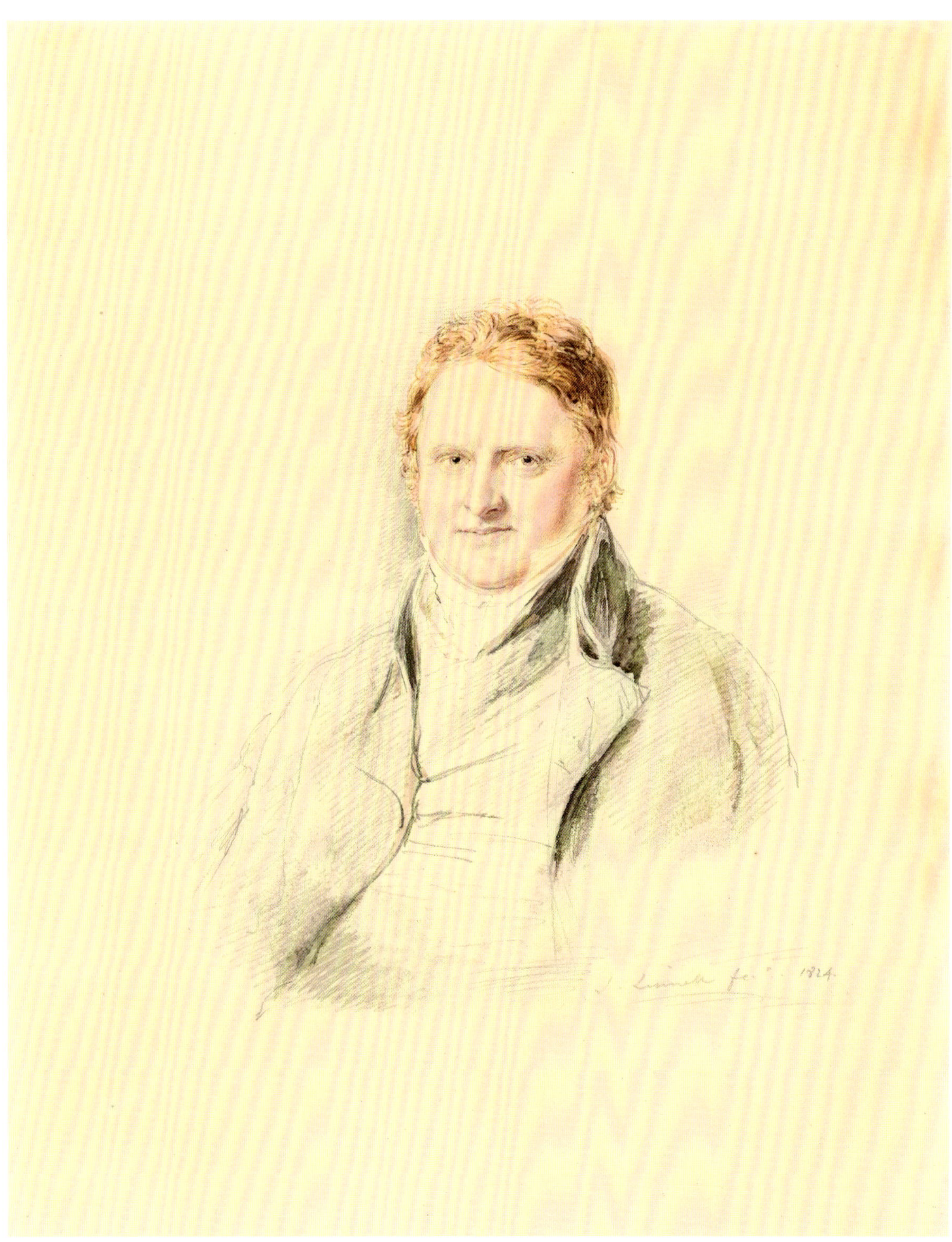

Plate 93
John Linnell, *Portrait of John Varley*, 1824

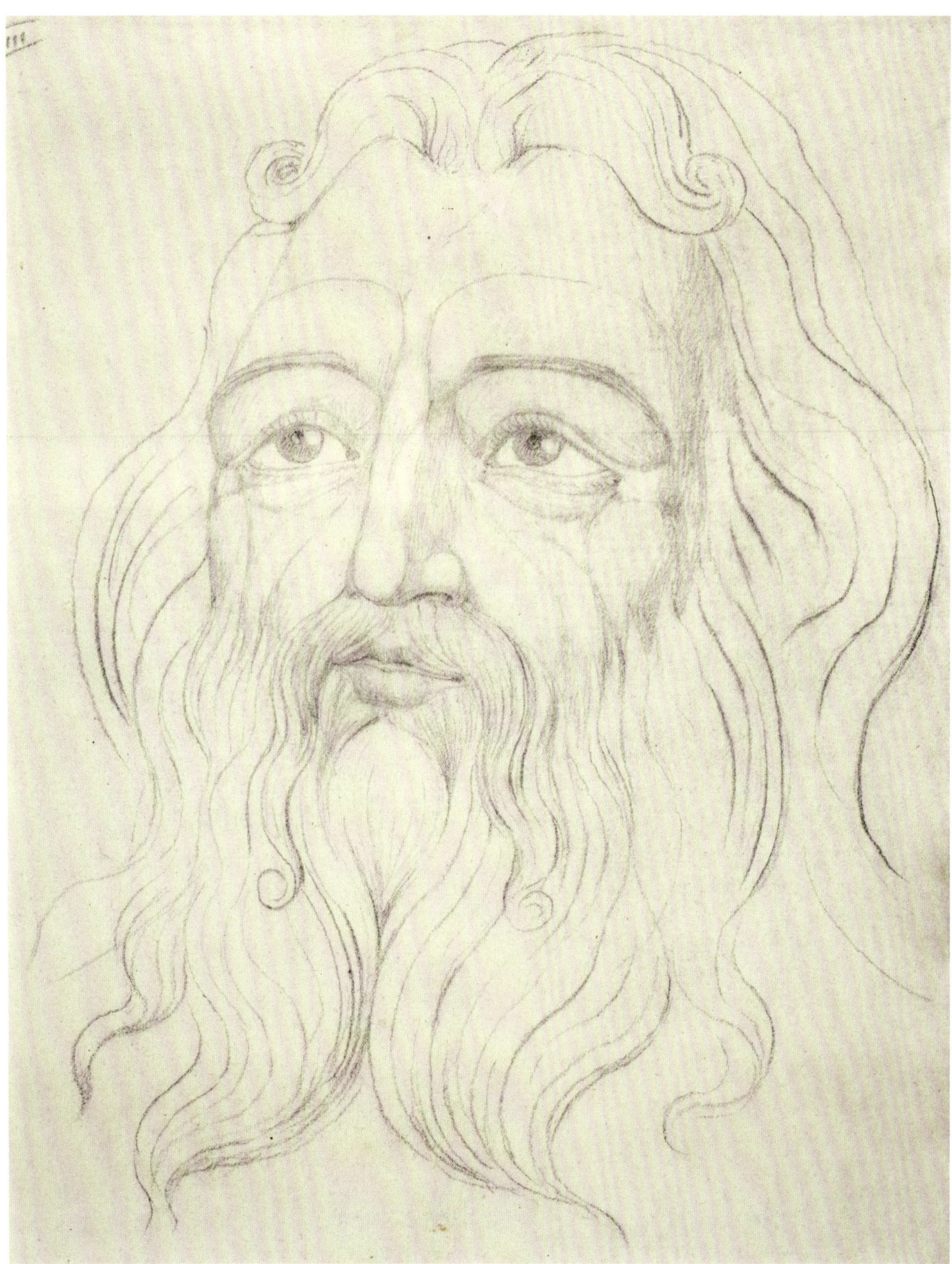

Plate 94
William Blake, *Merlin* from the Visionary Heads series, about 1819–20

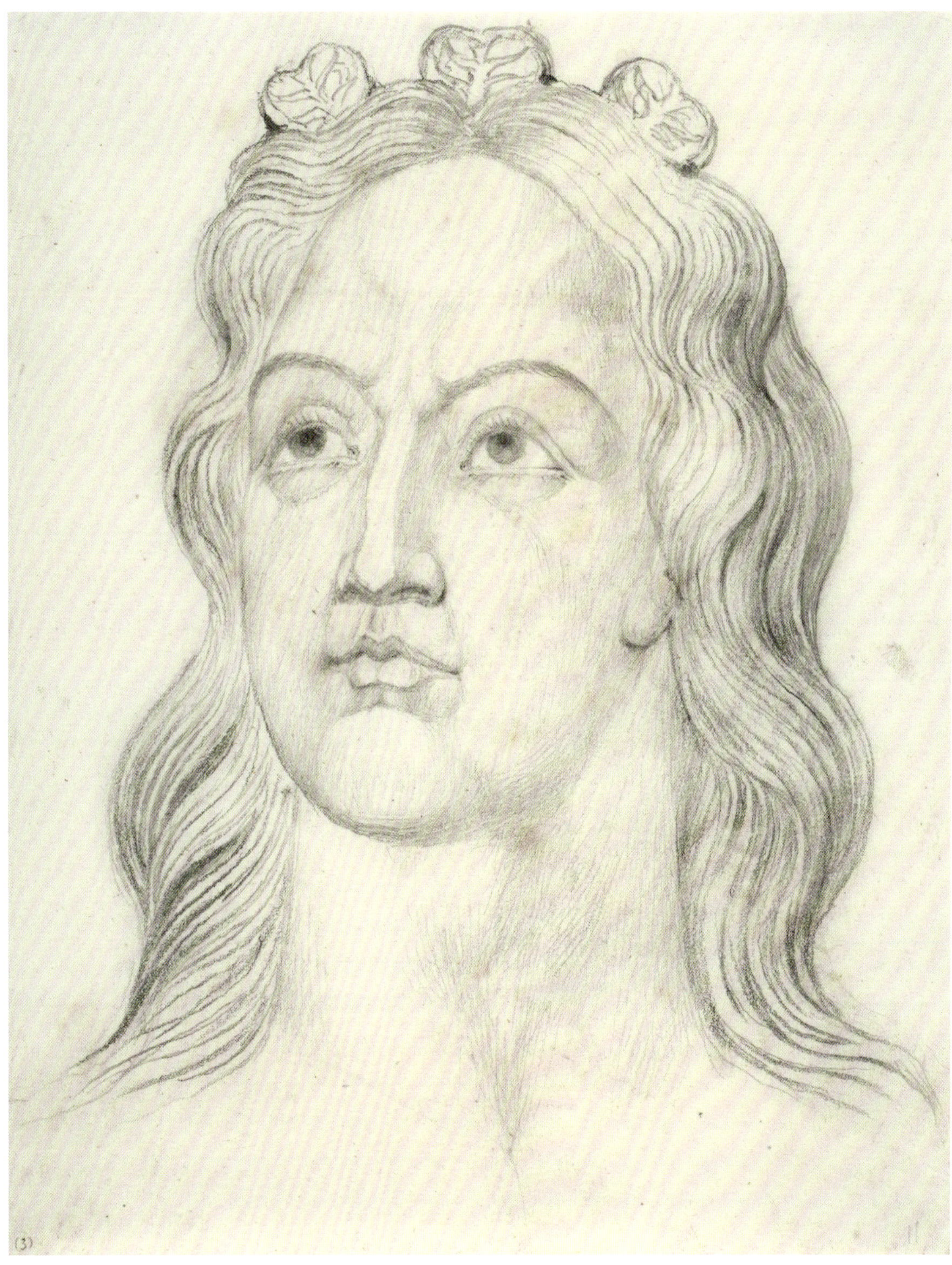

Plate 95
William Blake, *Queen Eleanor* from the Visionary Heads series, about 1819–20

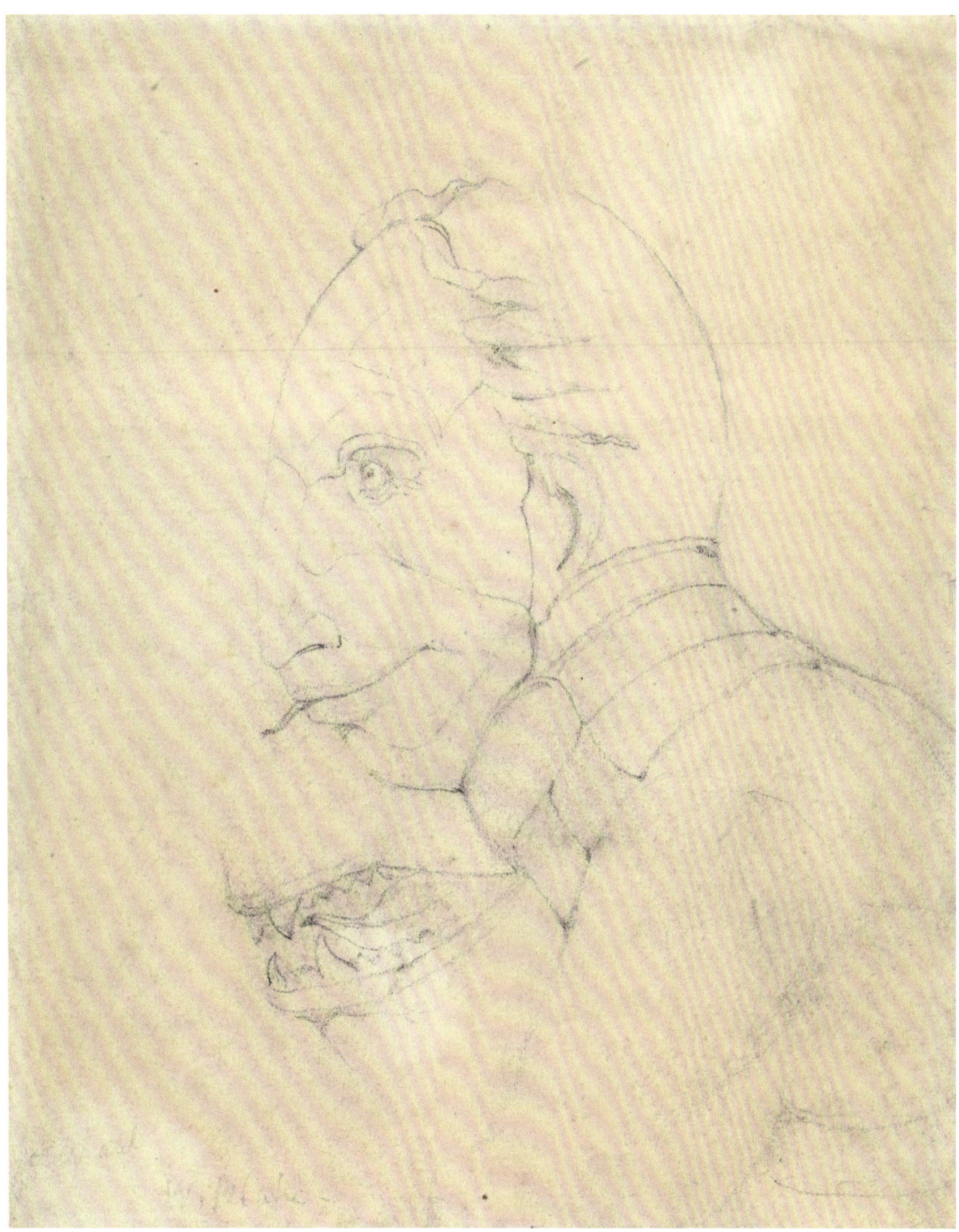

Plate 96
William Blake, *The Head of the Ghost of a Flea*
from the Visionary Head series, about 1819

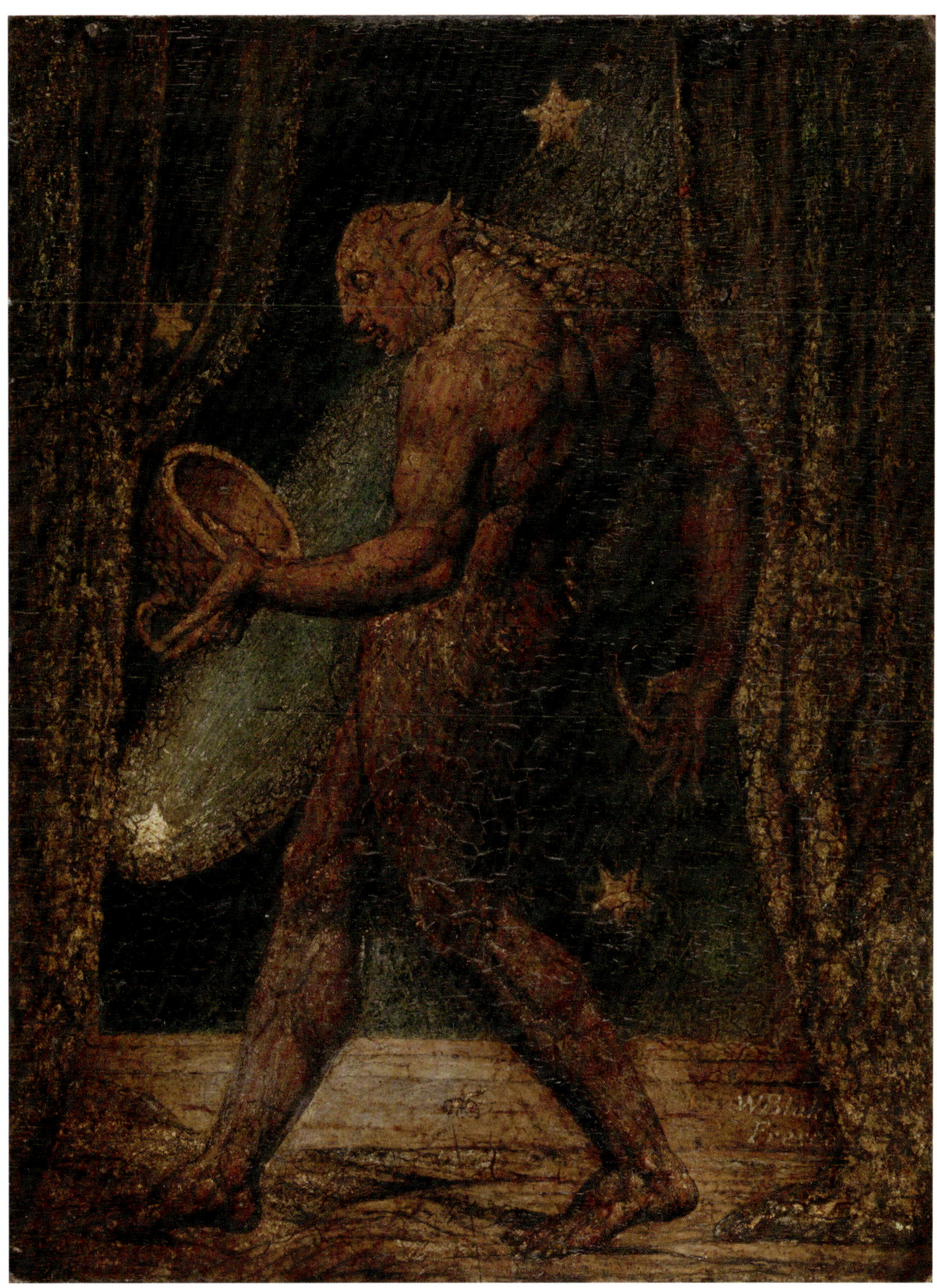

Plate 97
William Blake, *The Ghost of a Flea*, about 1819–20

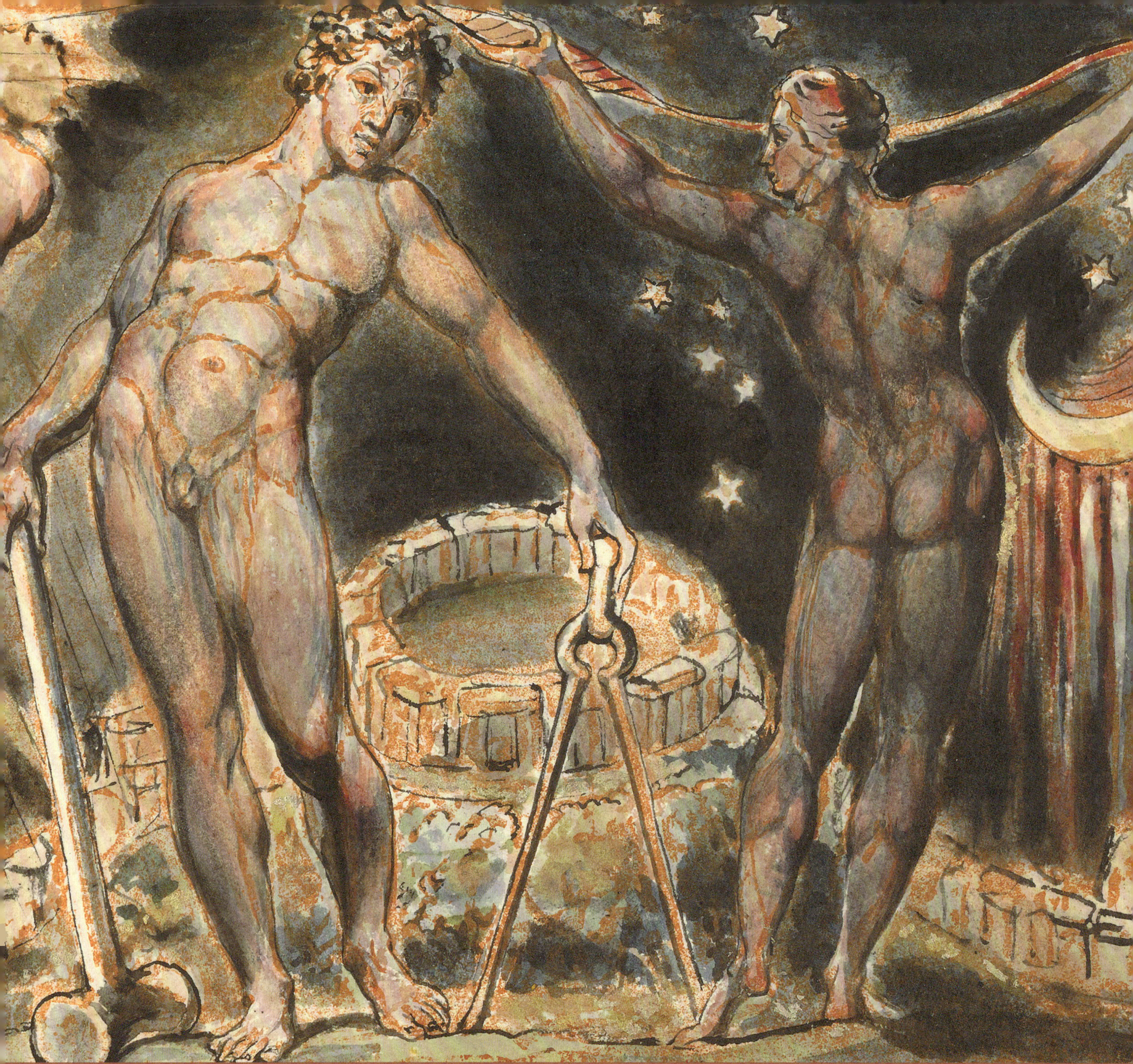

"I must Create a System, or be enslav'd by another Mans /
I will not Reason & Compare: my business is to Create."

—William Blake, *Jerusalem The Emanation of the Giant Albion*

The Mythmaker

PLATES 98–114

The seventeenth-century English poet and polemicist John Milton exercised a key influence on Blake, as on many of his contemporaries. From 1800 the link was strengthened by Blake's three years of unrewarding work for the gentleman-poet William Hayley; Hayley had written a biography of Milton and was at that time editing Milton's works. Blake made sets of watercolor illustrations, principally for the Reverend Joseph Thomas and Thomas Butts, of Milton's *Comus*, *Paradise Lost*, *On the Morning of Christ's Nativity*, *Paradise Regained*, and other works. As Blake coalesced his great mythology of the universe, Milton became the protagonist in his *Milton a Poem* (ca. 1804–11, plates 98–101), which envisaged the great poet brought back to the mortal world and explored Blake's personal history through Milton's life, resulting in a renewal of Blake's prophetic destiny. The intense and powerful relief-etched plates, often with dramatic black backgrounds, feature solid, large-scale figures, while much of the voluminous text is set upon colored backgrounds with relatively small vignette illustrations.

Jerusalem The Emanation of the Giant Albion (1804–ca. 1820, plates 103–12) is widely regarded as Blake's most complex epic, illustrated with one hundred plates. With mind-bending poetic leaps, it addresses numerous themes common in his work, including his own near-narrative history of human belief culminating in Christian redemption. In *Jerusalem*, Los is principally a blacksmith and architect. He struggles to build Golgonooza, the City of Art, against horrific nightly exhortations from his Spectre to abandon this Great Task, frequently seen as a parallel for Blake's own struggle to complete his now-signature epic.

A snapshot of Blake's concerns in his mythmaking is found in his truly extraordinary print of *Laocoön* of 1826–27 (plate 114), of which only two impressions are known. The iconic sculpture is purported by Blake to have originated from an archetype on the Temple of Solomon showing Jehovah with his sons Satan and Adam. The various inscriptions that swirl around the figures, unregulated by borders, include: "Where any view of Money exists Art cannot be carried on, but War only"; "Christianity is Art & not Money"; "Prayer is the Study of Art Praise is the Practise of Art."

JB

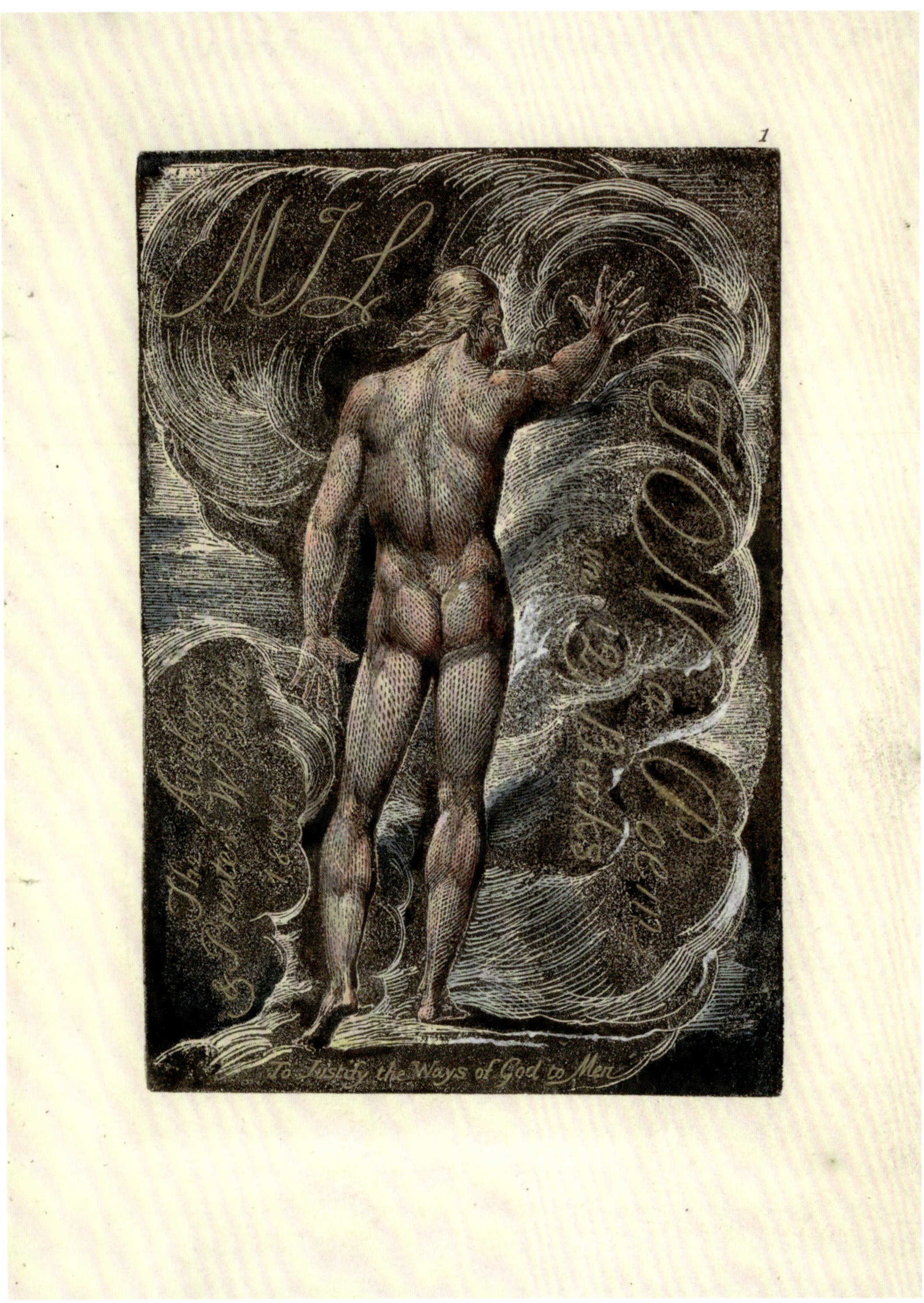

Plate 98
William Blake, *Milton a Poem*, plate 1, 1804–about 1811

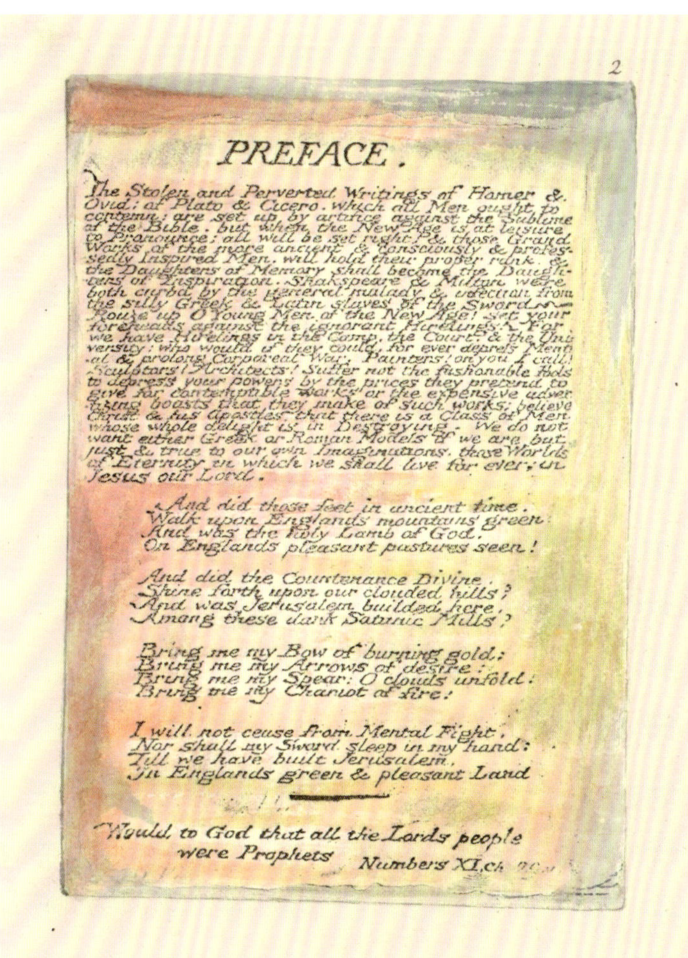

2

PREFACE.

The Stolen and Perverted Writings of Homer & Ovid: of Plato & Cicero. which all Men ought to contemn: are set up by artifice against the Sublime of the Bible. but when the New Age is at leisure to Pronounce; all will be set right: & those Grand Works of the more ancient & consciously & professedly Inspired Men, will hold their proper rank, & the Daughters of Memory shall become the Daughters of Inspiration. Shakspeare & Milton were both curbd by the general malady & infection from the silly Greek & Latin slaves of the Sword. Rouze up O Young Men of the New Age! set your foreheads against the ignorant Hirelings! For we have Hirelings in the Camp, the Court, & the University: who would if they could, for ever depress Mental & prolong Corporeal War. Painters! on you I call! Sculptors! Architects! Suffer not the fashonable Fools to depress your powers by the prices they pretend to give for contemptible works or the expensive advertizing boasts that they make of such works; believe Christ & his Apostles that there is a Class of Men whose whole delight is in Destroying. We do not want either Greek or Roman Models if we are but just & true to our own Imaginations, those Worlds of Eternity in which we shall live for ever; in Jesus our Lord.

And did those feet in ancient time.
Walk upon Englands mountains green:
And was the holy Lamb of God,
On Englands pleasant pastures seen!

And did the Countenance Divine,
Shine forth upon our clouded hills?
And was Jerusalem builded here,
Among these dark Satanic Mills?

Bring me my Bow of burning gold:
Bring me my Arrows of desire:
Bring me my Spear: O clouds unfold:
Bring me my Chariot of fire!

I will not cease from Mental Fight,
Nor shall my Sword sleep in my hand:
Till we have built Jerusalem,
In Englands green & pleasant Land

Would to God that all the Lords people were Prophets Numbers XI.ch

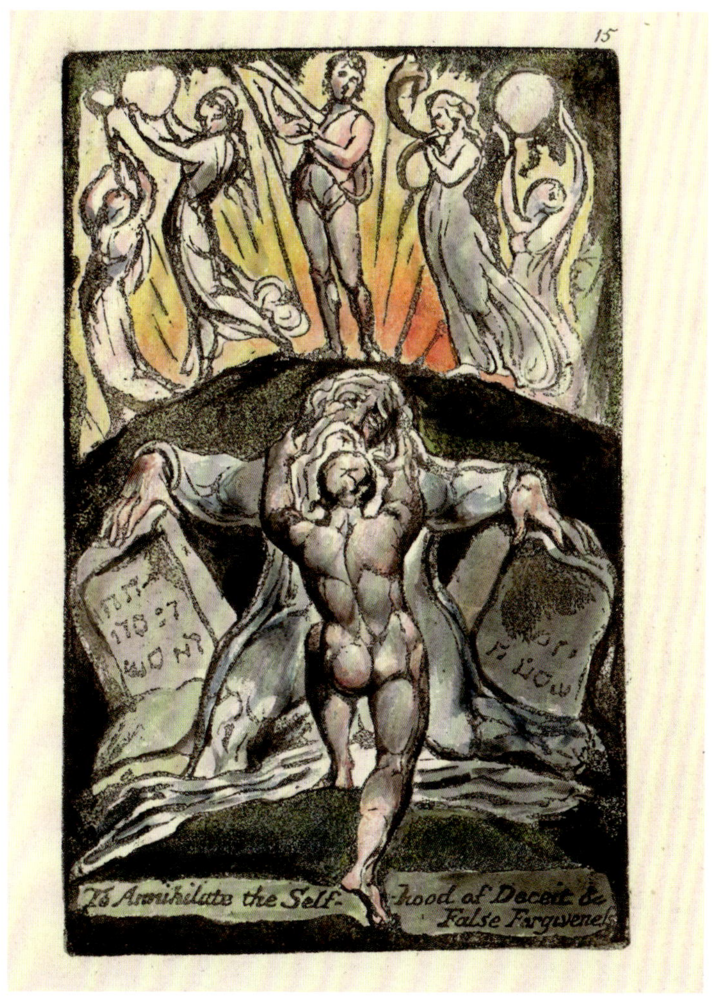

Plate 99
William Blake, *Milton a Poem*, plate 2, 1804–about 1811

Plate 100
William Blake, *Milton a Poem*, plate 15, 1804–about 1811

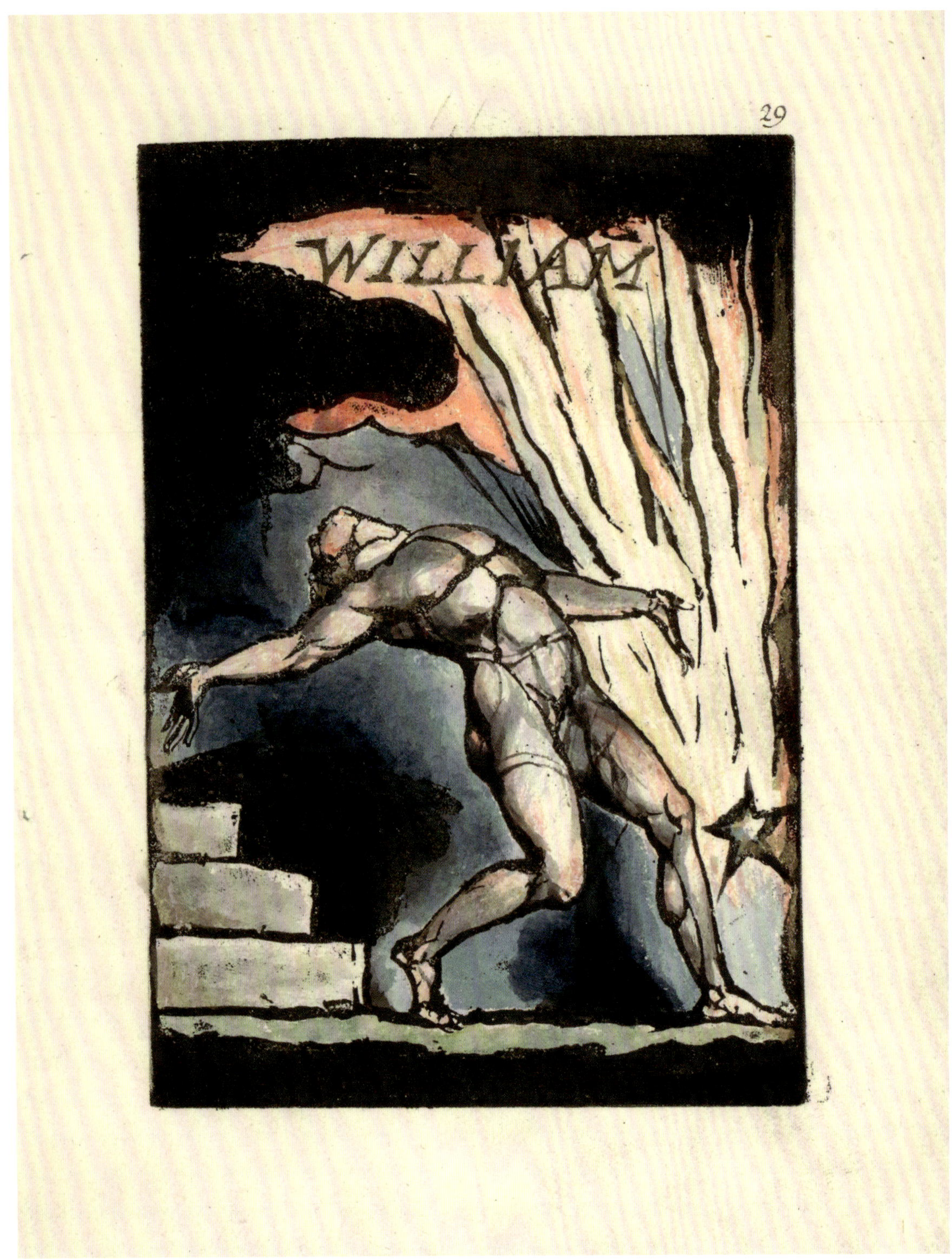

Plate 101
William Blake, *Milton a Poem*, plate 29, 1804–about 1811

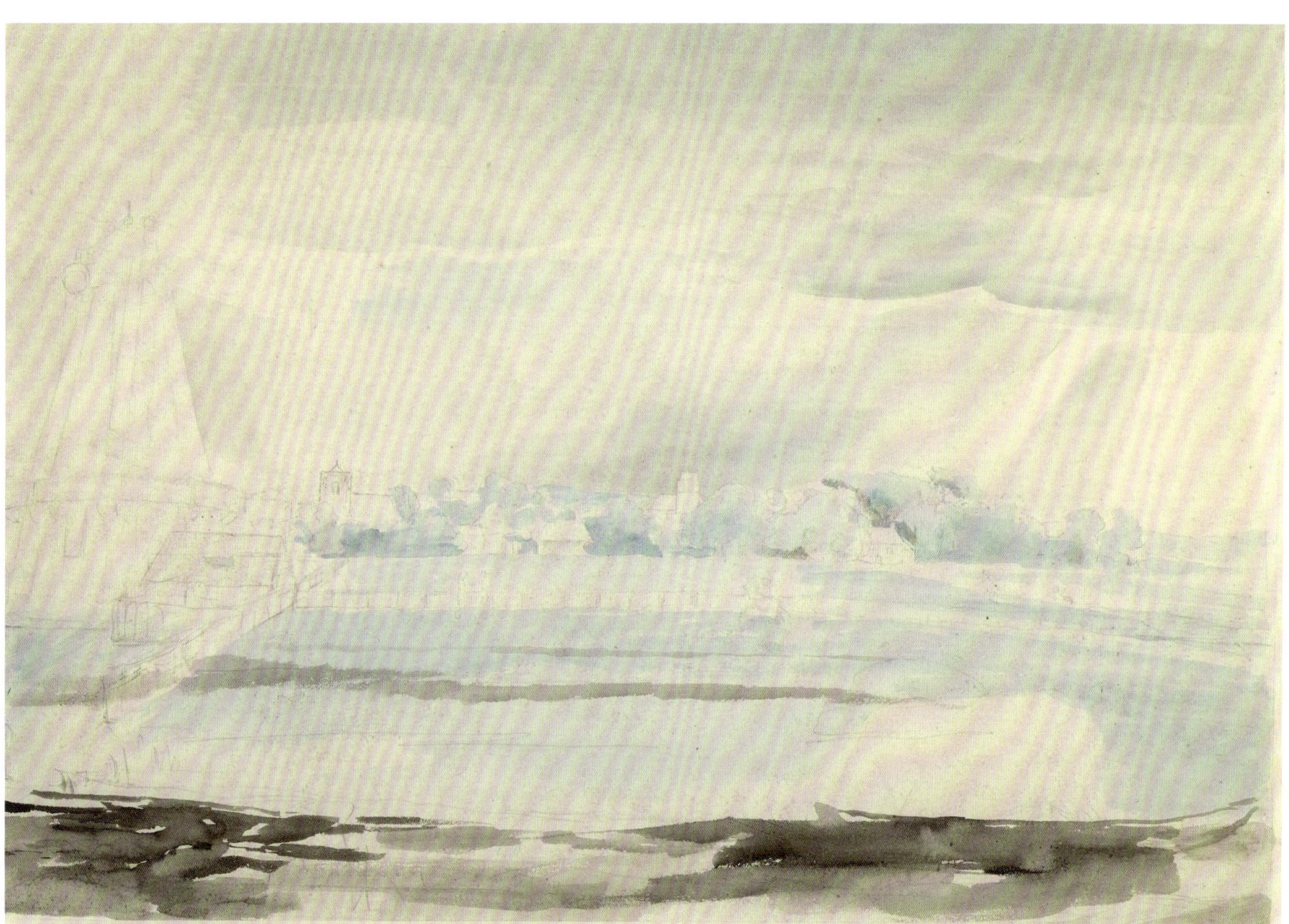

Plate 102
William Blake, *Landscape near Felpham*, about 1800

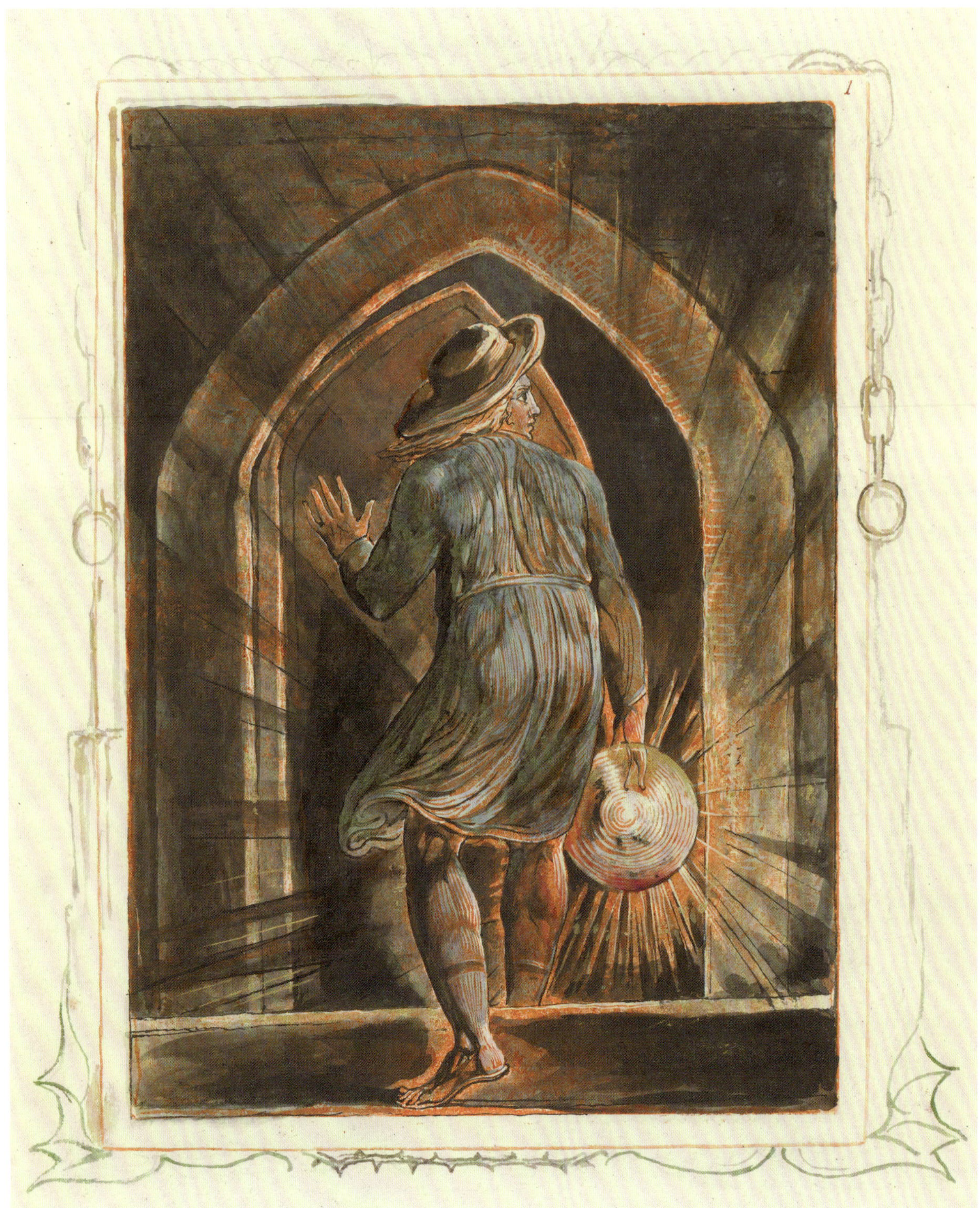

Plate 103
William Blake, *Jerusalem*, plate 1, Frontispiece, 1804–20

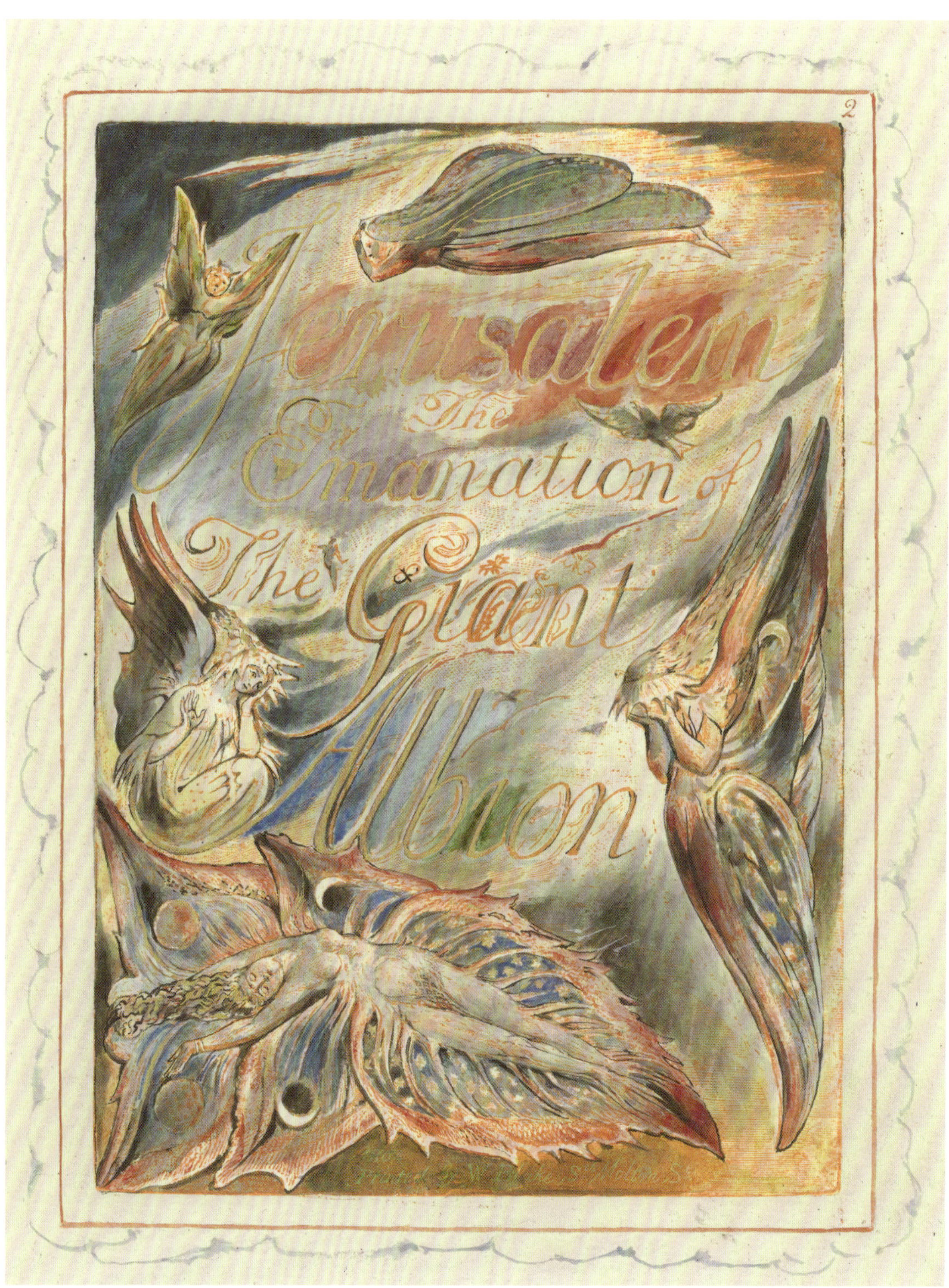

Plate 104
William Blake, *Jerusalem*, plate 2, Title Page, 1804–20

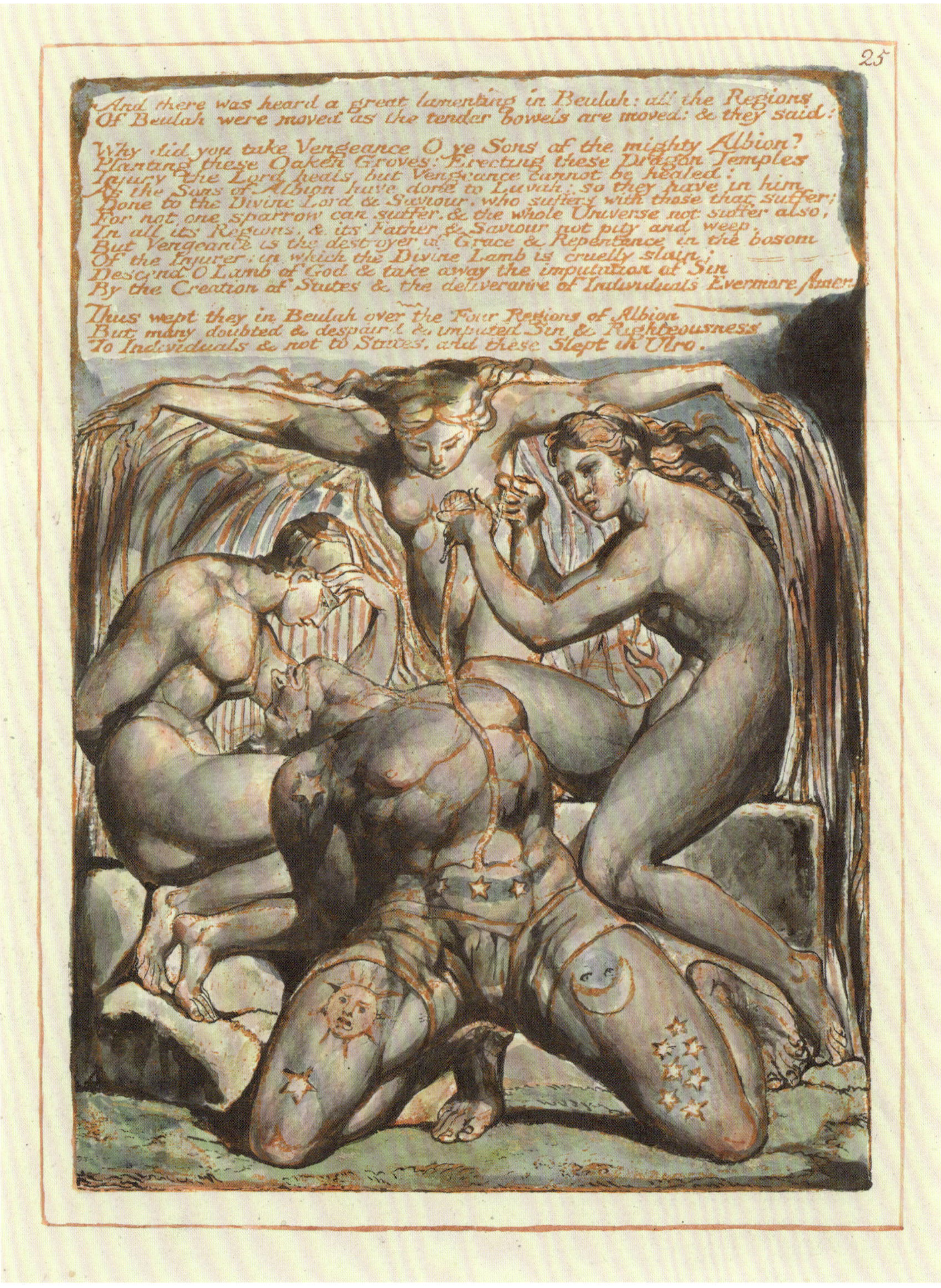

Plate 105
William Blake, *Jerusalem*, plate 25, 1804–20

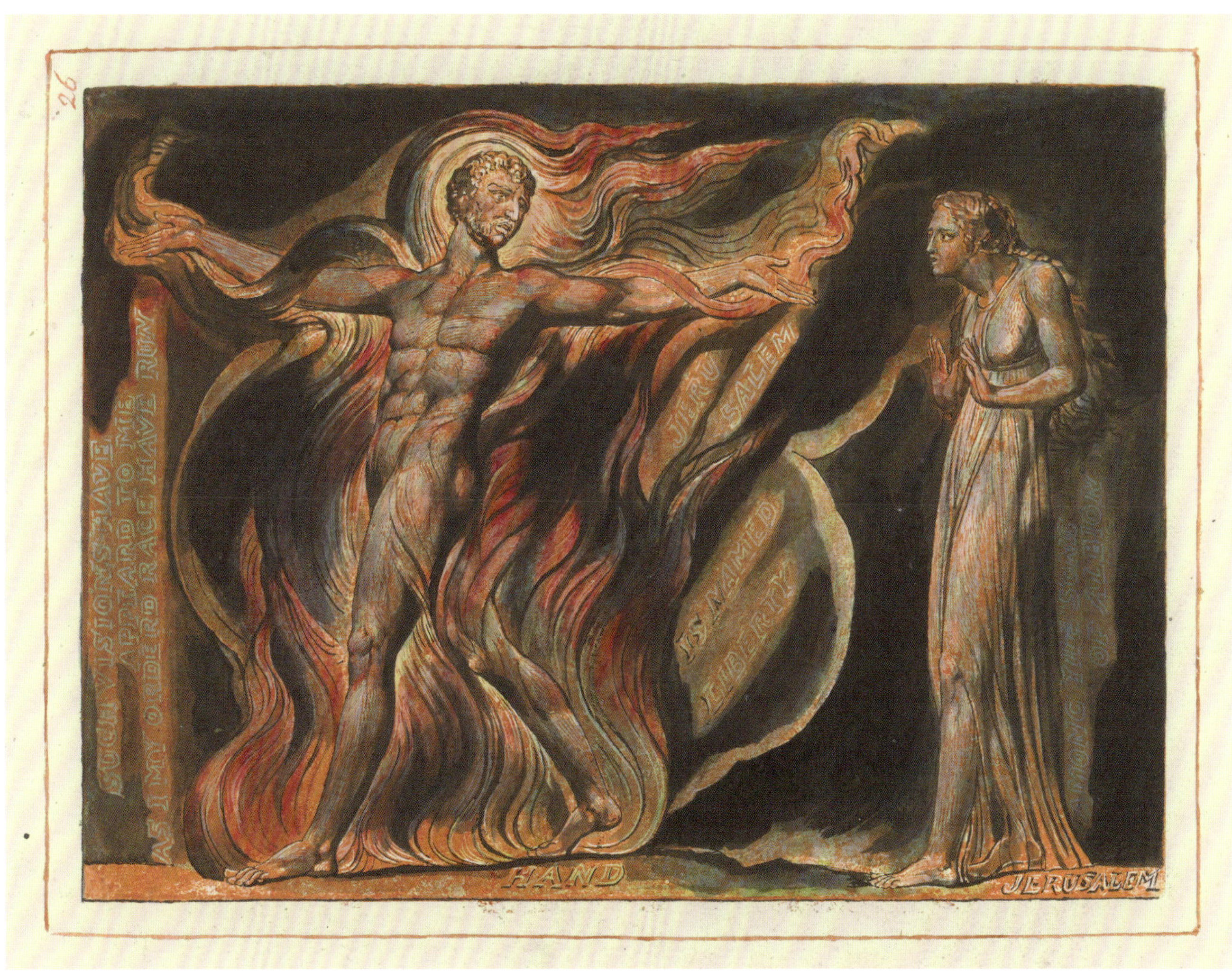

Plate 106
William Blake, *Jerusalem*, plate 26, 1804–20

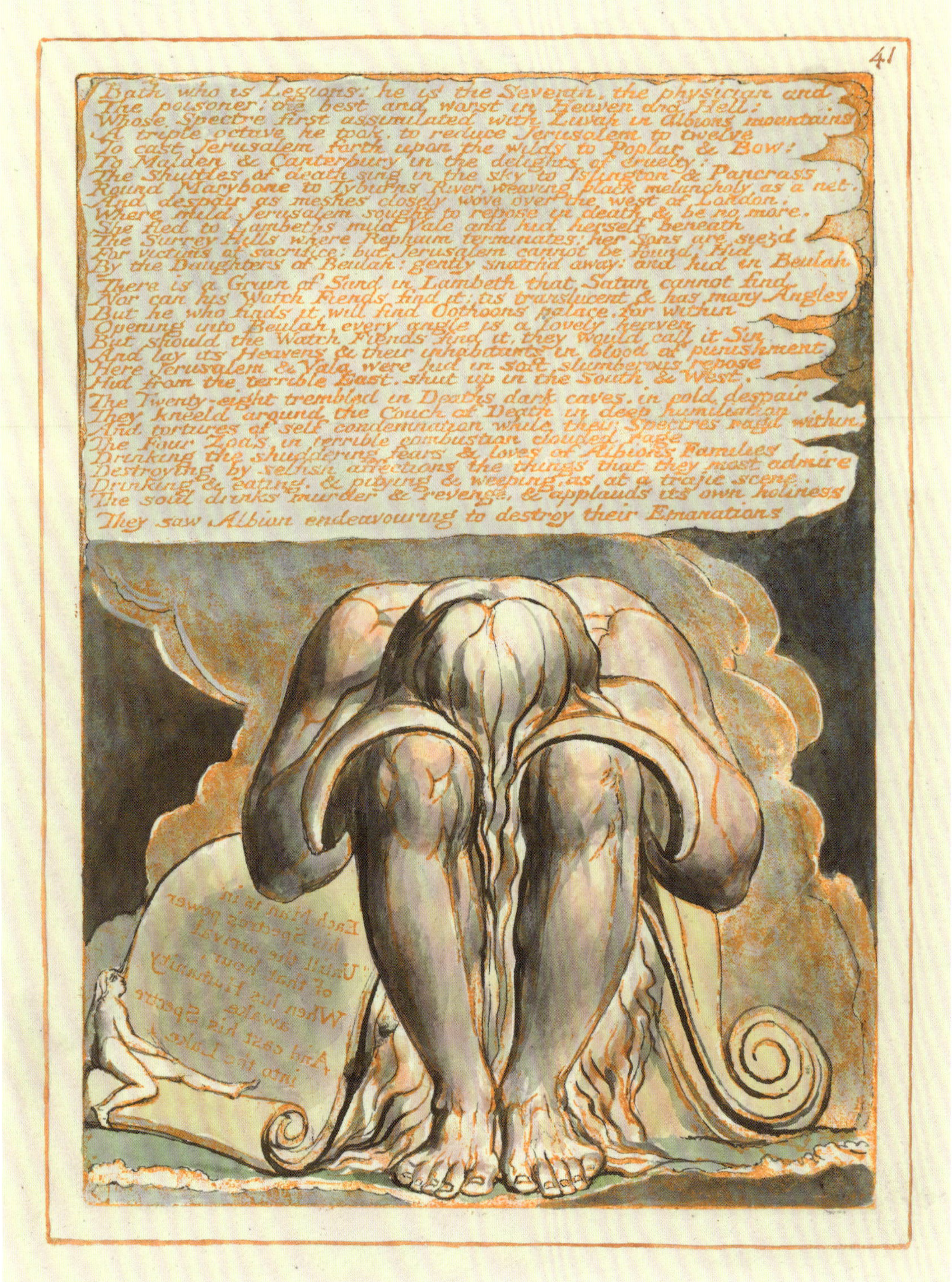

Plate 107
William Blake, *Jerusalem*, plate 41, 1804–20

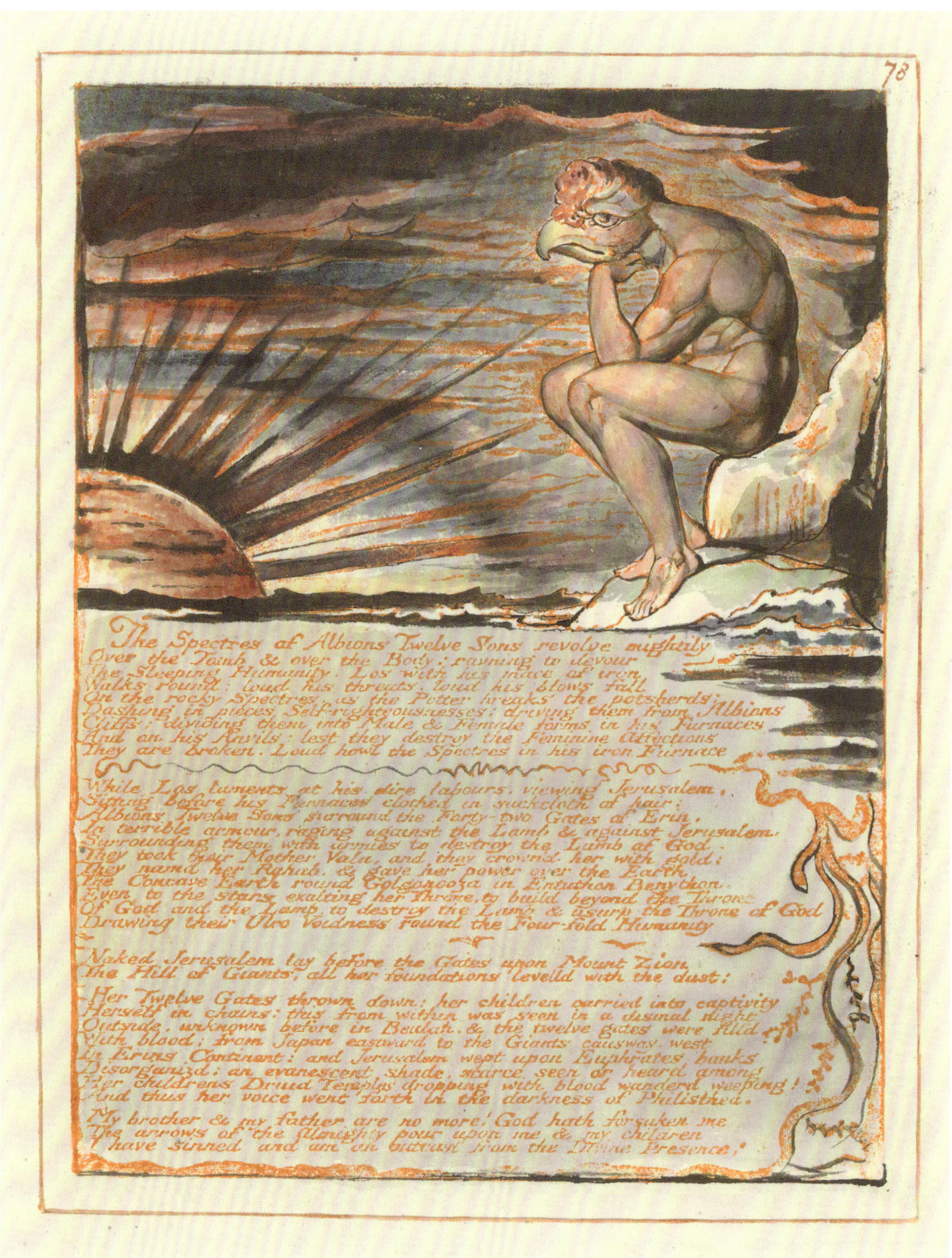

Plate 108

William Blake, *Jerusalem*, plate 78, 1804–20

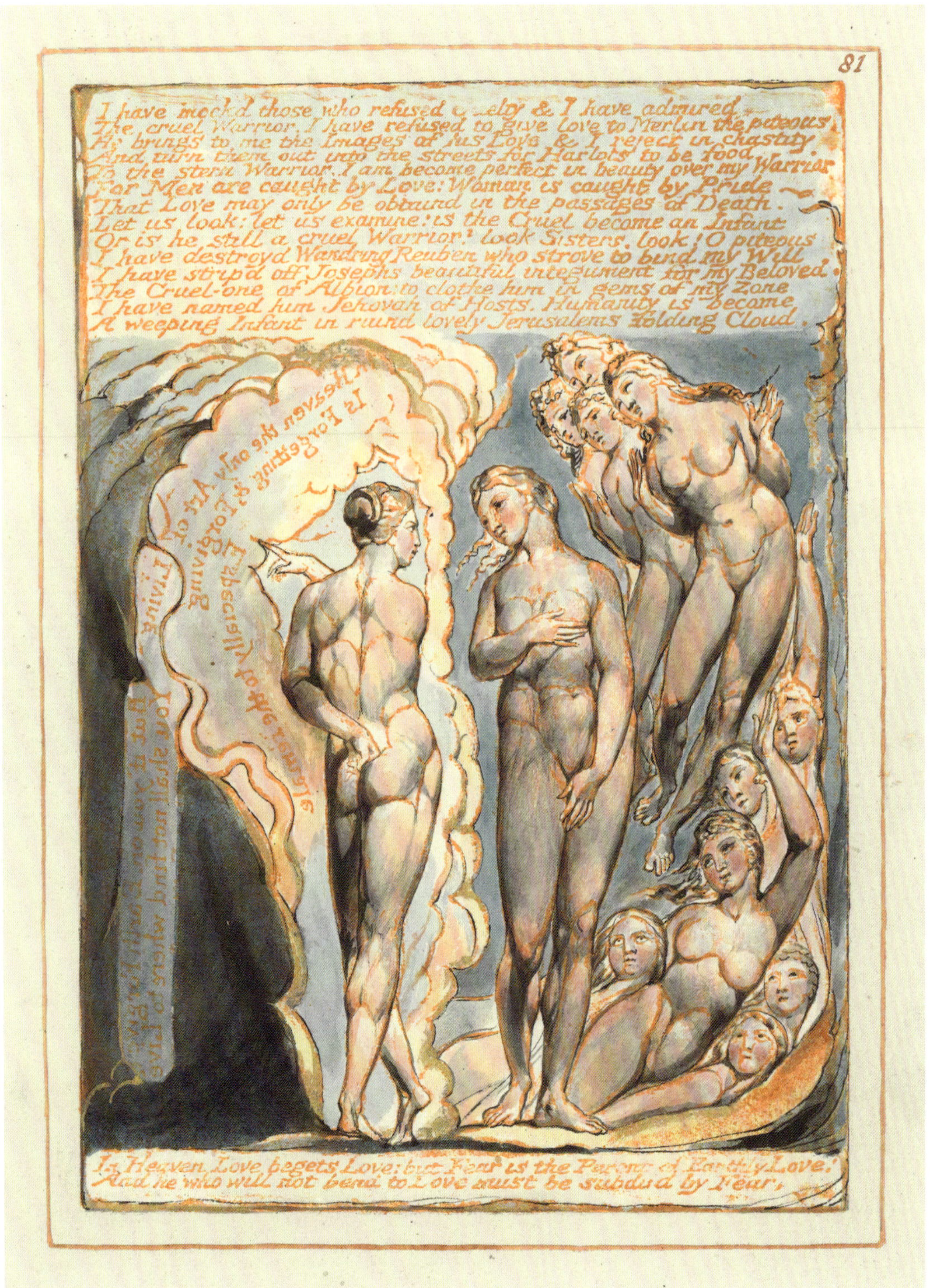

Plate 109
William Blake, *Jerusalem*, plate 81, 1804–20

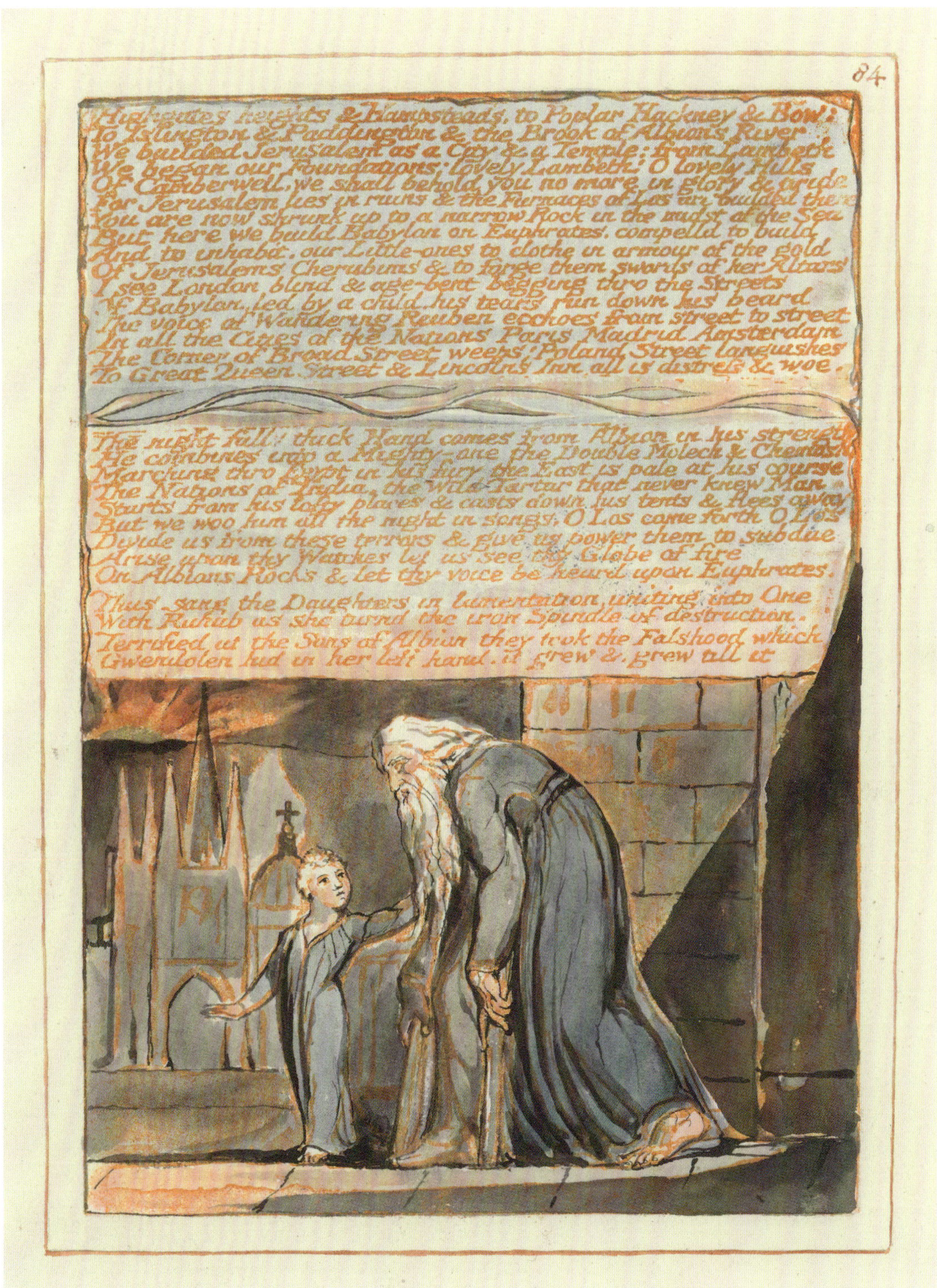

Plate 110
William Blake, *Jerusalem*, plate 84, 1804–20

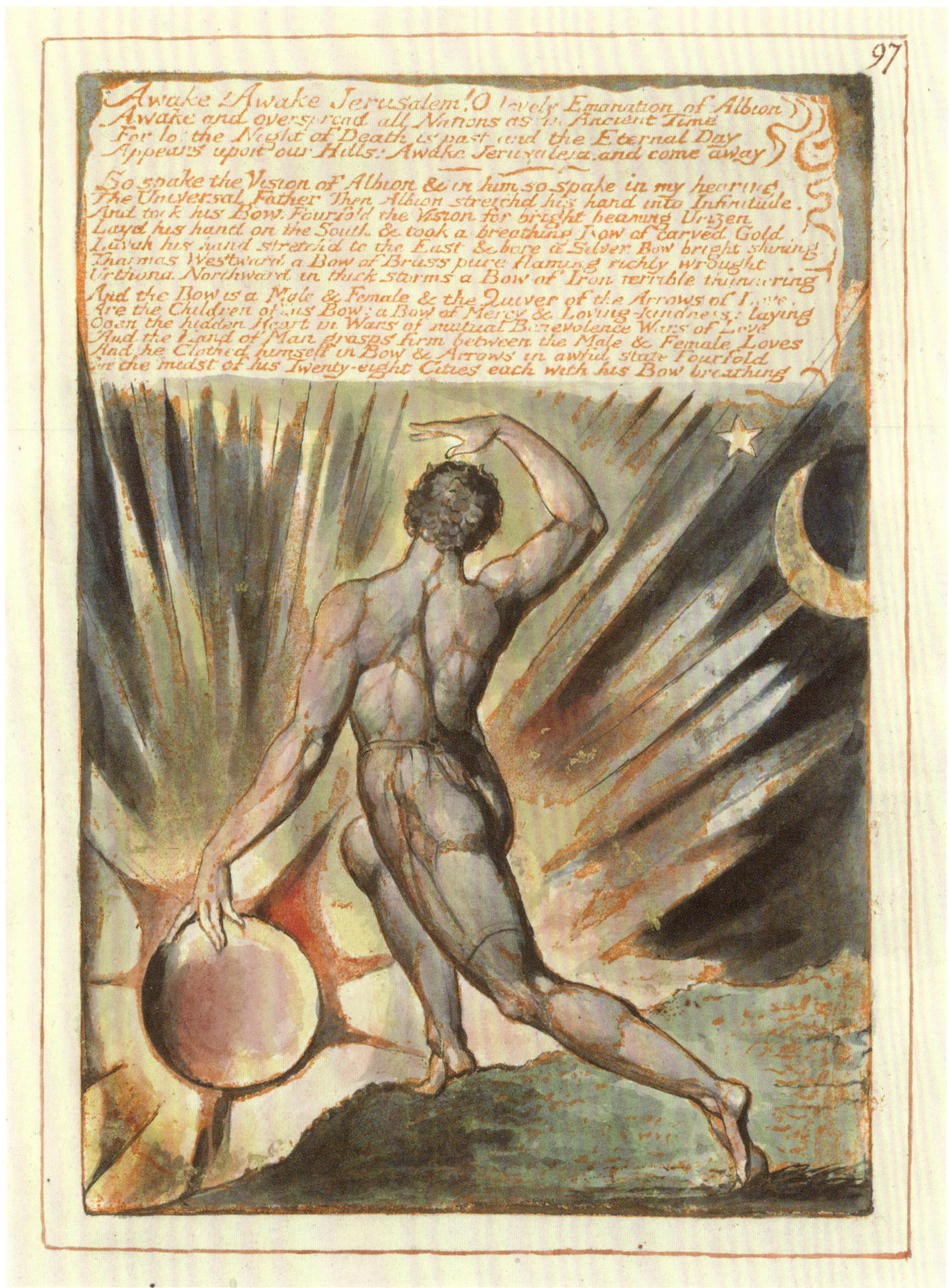

Plate 111
William Blake, *Jerusalem*, plate 97, 1804–20

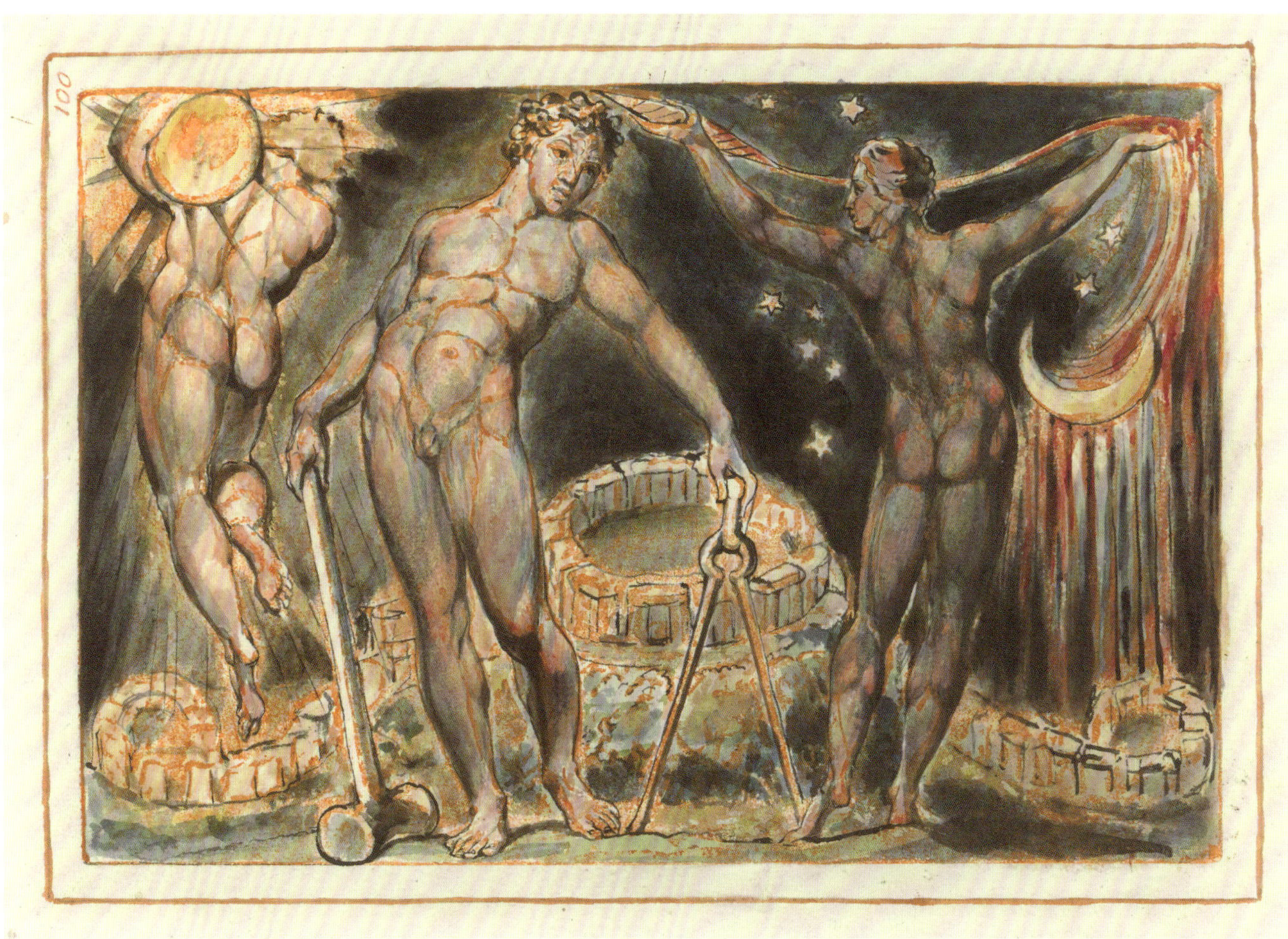

Plate 112
William Blake, *Jerusalem*, plate 100, 1804–20

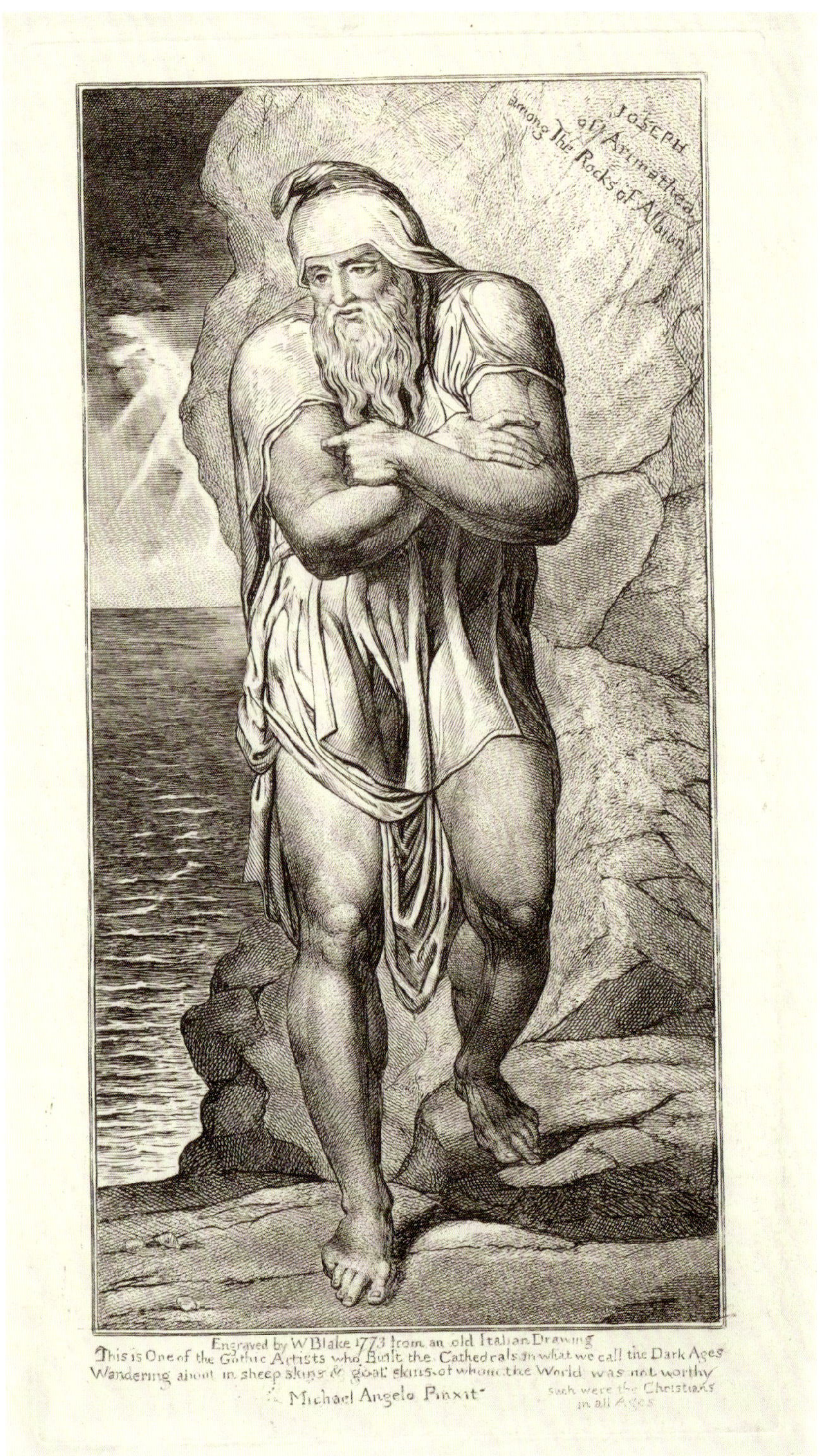

Plate 113
William Blake, *Joseph of Arimathea among the Rocks of Albion*,
after a figure in Michelangelo's *Crucifixion of Saint Peter*, 1820 or later

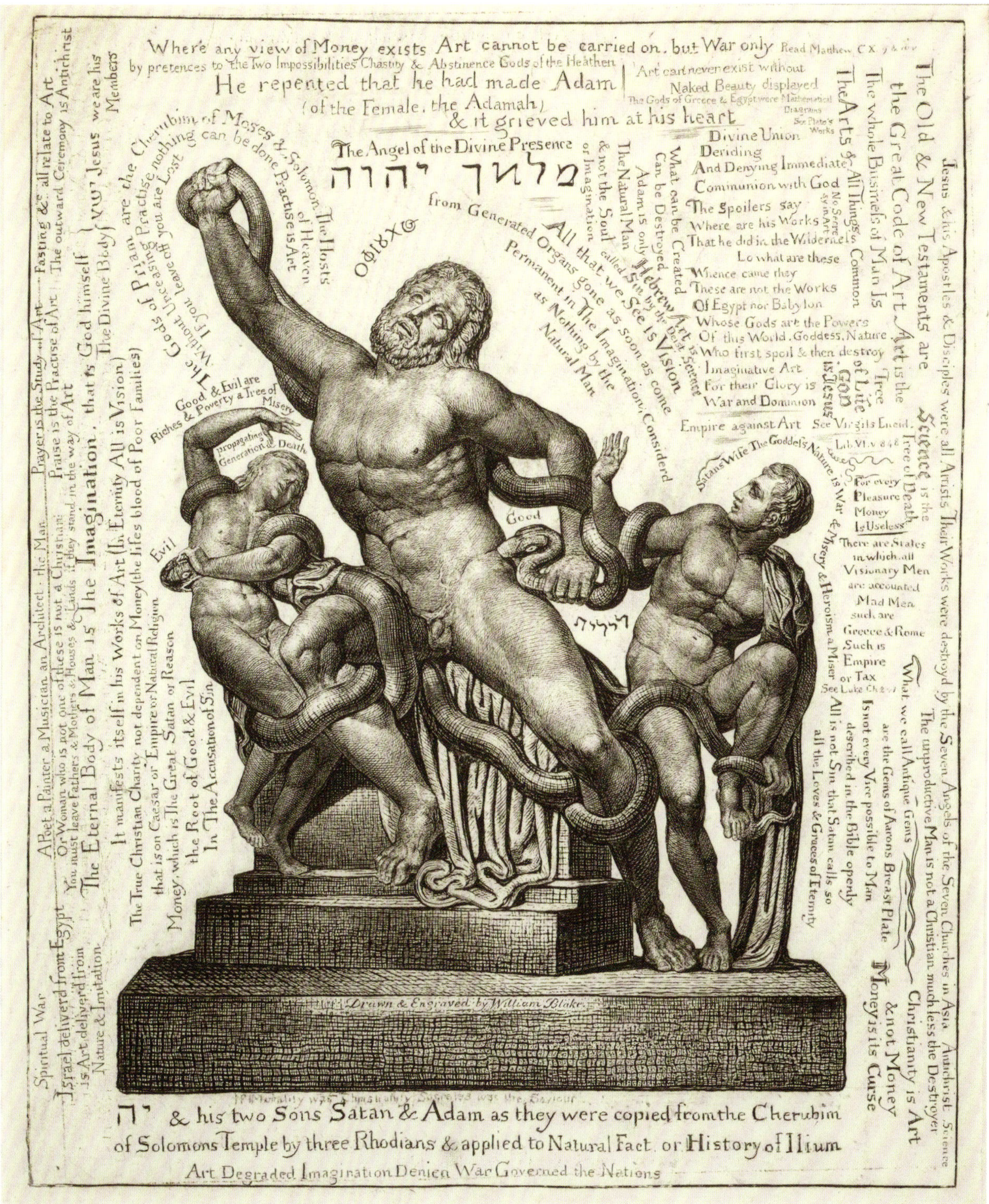

Plate 114
William Blake, *Laocoön*, image about 1815; inscription about 1826–27

Exhibition Checklist

This exhibition was originally scheduled for 2020 but was postponed due to the COVID-19 pandemic. Objects noted by an asterisk are not included in the revised 2023–24 presentation.

1
William Blake
British, 1757–1827
Self-Portrait, 1802/1804
Pencil and gray wash, white heightening
24.3 × 20.1 cm ($9\frac{9}{16} \times 7\frac{15}{16}$ in.)
Collection of Robert N. Essick
Plate 1

2
William Blake
British, 1757–1827
Portrait of Queen Philippa in Richard Gough's *Sepulchral Monuments in Great Britain*, vol. 1, 1796
Etching and engraving
40.5 × 29 cm ($15\frac{15}{16} \times 11\frac{7}{16}$ in.) (plate)
57 × 32.4 cm ($22\frac{7}{17} \times 12\frac{3}{4}$ in.) (sheet)
Los Angeles, Getty Research Institute, NB1585.G7
Plate 2

3*
William Blake, after John Gabriel Stedman
British, 1757–1827
A Negro Hung Alive by the Ribs to the Gallows in J. G. Stedman's *Narrative of a Five Years' Expedition against the Revolted Negroes of Surinam*, 1796
Etching and engraving
18.3 × 13.2 cm ($7\frac{3}{16} \times 5\frac{3}{16}$ in.) (plate)
27 × 20 cm ($10\frac{5}{8} \times 7\frac{7}{8}$ in.) (sheet)
Los Angeles, Getty Research Institute, F2410.S815

4
William Blake, after Thomas Stothard
British, 1757–1827
The Temple of Mirth, 1784
Etching and engraving
17.4 × 23 cm ($6\frac{7}{8} \times 9\frac{1}{16}$ in.)
London, Tate, Purchased 1996, T07048

5
William Blake, after William Hogarth
British, 1757–1827
Beggar's Opera, Act III, 1790
Etching and engraving
40.1 × 53.7 cm ($15\frac{13}{16} \times 21\frac{1}{8}$ in.)
London, Tate, Transferred from reference collection 1991, T06462
Plate 3

6
Henry Fuseli
Swiss, 1741–1825
Portrait Sketch of Michelangelo for *Lectures on Painting*, about 1788
Pen and brown ink
22.4 × 18.8 cm ($8\frac{13}{16} \times 7\frac{3}{8}$ in.)
Collection of Robert N. Essick
Plate 4

7
William Blake, after Henry Fuseli
British, 1757–1827
Michelangelo from Henry Fuseli's *Lectures on Painting*, 1801
Etching and engraving
11.8 × 7.4 cm ($4\frac{5}{8} \times 2\frac{15}{16}$ in.)
Collection of Robert N. Essick
Plate 5

8
William Blake
British, 1757–1827
Deaths Door, 1805
White-line etching with India ink
18.6 × 11.7 cm ($7\frac{5}{16} \times 4\frac{5}{8}$ in.) (plate)
23.5 × 16.5 cm ($9\frac{1}{4} \times 6\frac{1}{2}$ in.) (sheet)
Collection of Robert N. Essick
Plate 6

9
Luigi Schiavonetti, after William Blake
Italian, 1765–1810
Death's Door, 1806
Etching and engraving
35.7 × 20.3 cm ($14\frac{1}{16} \times 8$ in.) (plate)
39.2 × 24.8 cm ($15\frac{7}{16} \times 9\frac{3}{4}$ in.) (sheet)
Collection of Robert N. Essick
Plate 7

10
William Blake
British, 1757–1827
Edward Young's Night Thoughts: "Night the Third, Narcissa," 1797
Etching and engraving with watercolor
42 × 32.4 cm ($16\frac{9}{16} \times 12\frac{3}{4}$ in.)
Collection of Robert N. Essick
Plate 8

11*
William Blake
British, 1757–1827
The Pastorals of Virgil, 1821
Relief etching
13.8 × 8.5 cm ($5\frac{7}{16} \times 3\frac{3}{8}$ in.)
Collection of Robert N. Essick
Plate 9

12*
William Blake
British, 1757–1827
The Pastorals of Virgil, 1821
Wood engraving
Each leaf: 17.2 × 10.4 cm ($6\frac{3}{4} \times 4\frac{1}{16}$ in.)
Collection of Robert N. Essick
Plate 10

13
William Blake
British, 1757–1827
Illustrations of the Book of Job: *Job and His Family*, 1825
Engraving
43.2 × 33.5 cm ($17 \times 13\frac{3}{16}$ in.)
San Marino, The Huntington Library, Art Museum, and Botanical Gardens, Edward W. and Julia B. Bodman Collection, 72.62.53.1
Plate 11

14
William Blake
British, 1757–1827
Illustrations of the Book of Job: *Satan Smiting Job*, 1825
Engraving
43.2 × 33.5 cm ($17 \times 13\frac{3}{16}$ in.)
San Marino, The Huntington Library, Art Museum, and Botanical Gardens, Edward W. and Julia B. Bodman Collection, 72.62.53.6
Plate 12

15
William Blake
British, 1757–1827
Illustrations of the Book of Job: *Job's Despair*, 1825
Engraving
43.2 × 33.5 cm ($17 \times 13\frac{3}{16}$ in.)
San Marino, The Huntington Library, Art Museum, and Botanical Gardens, Edward W. and Julia B. Bodman Collection, 72.62.53.8

16
William Blake
British, 1757–1827
Illustrations of the Book of Job: *Job Rebuked*, 1825
Engraving
43.2 × 33.5 cm ($17 \times 13\frac{3}{16}$ in.)
San Marino, The Huntington Library, Art Museum, and Botanical Gardens, Edward W. and Julia B. Bodman Collection, 72.62.53.10
Plate 13

17
William Blake
British, 1757–1827
Illustrations of the Book of Job: *The Lord Answering Job*, 1825
Engraving
43.2 × 33.5 cm ($17 \times 13\frac{3}{16}$ in.)
San Marino, The Huntington Library, Art Museum, and Botanical Gardens, Edward W. and Julia B. Bodman Collection, 72.62.53.13
Plate 14

18
William Blake
British, 1757–1827
Illustrations of the Book of Job: *Morning Star*, 1825
Engraving
43.2 × 33.5 cm ($17 \times 13\frac{3}{16}$ in.)
San Marino, The Huntington Library, Art Museum, and Botanical Gardens, Edward W. and Julia B. Bodman Collection, 72.62.53.14

19
William Blake
British, 1757–1827
Illustrations of the Book of Job: *Behemoth*, 1825
Engraving
43.2 × 33.5 cm ($17 \times 13\frac{3}{16}$ in.)
San Marino, The Huntington Library, Art Museum, and Botanical Gardens, Edward W. and Julia B. Bodman Collection, 72.62.53.15
Plate 15

20
William Blake
British, 1757–1827
Illustrations of the Book of Job: *Fall of Satan*, 1825
Engraving
43.2 × 33.5 cm ($17 \times 13\frac{3}{16}$ in.)
San Marino, The Huntington Library, Art Museum, and Botanical Gardens, Edward W. and Julia B. Bodman Collection, 72.62.53.16
Plate 16

21
William Blake
British, 1757–1827
Cerberus, 1824–27
Graphite, ink, and watercolor
37.2 × 52.8 cm (14⅝ × 20 13/16 in.)
London, Tate, Purchased with the assistance of a special grant from the National Gallery and donations from the Art Fund, Lord Duveen, and others, and presented through the Art Fund 1919, N03354
Plate 17

22
William Blake
British, 1757–1827
Plutus, 1824–27
Graphite, ink, and watercolor
52.7 × 37.1 cm (20¾ × 14⅝ in.)
London, Tate, Purchased with the assistance of a special grant from the National Gallery and donations from the Art Fund, Lord Duveen, and others, and presented through the Art Fund 1919, N03355

23
William Blake
British, 1757–1827
The Wood of Self-Murderers: The Harpies and the Suicides, 1824–27
Graphite, ink, and watercolor
37.2 × 52.7 cm (14⅝ × 20¾ in.)
London, Tate, Purchased with the assistance of a special grant from the National Gallery and donations from the Art Fund, Lord Duveen, and others, and presented through the Art Fund 1919, N03356
Plate 18

24
William Blake
British, 1757–1827
The Serpent Attacking Buoso Donati, 1824–27
Ink and watercolor
37.2 × 52.7 cm (14⅝ × 20¾ in.)
London, Tate, Purchased with the assistance of a special grant from the National Gallery and donations from the Art Fund, Lord Duveen, and others, and presented through the Art Fund 1919, N03361
Plate 19

25
William Blake
British, 1757–1827
The Pit of Disease: The Falsifiers, 1824–27
Ink and watercolor
37.2 × 52.7 cm (14⅝ × 20¾ in.)
London, Tate, Purchased with the assistance of a special grant from the National Gallery and donations from the Art Fund, Lord Duveen, and others, and presented through the Art Fund 1919, N03362
Plate 20

26
William Blake
British, 1757–1827
The Primaeval Giants Sunk in the Soil, 1824–27
Graphite, chalk, ink, and watercolor
37.2 × 52.7 cm (14⅝ × 20¾ in.)
London, Tate, Purchased with the assistance of a special grant from the National Gallery and donations from the Art Fund, Lord Duveen, and others, and presented through the Art Fund 1919, N03363
Plate 21

27
William Blake
British, 1757–1827
The Punishment of the Thieves, 1824–27
Chalk, ink, and watercolor
37.2 × 52.7 cm (14⅝ × 20¾ in.)
London, Tate, Purchased with the assistance of a special grant from the National Gallery and donations from the Art Fund, Lord Duveen, and others, and presented through the Art Fund 1919, N03364

28
William Blake
British, 1757–1827
The Ascent of the Mountain of Purgatory, 1824–27
Graphite, ink, and watercolor
52.8 × 37.2 cm (20 13/16 × 14⅝ in.)
London, Tate, Purchased with the assistance of a special grant from the National Gallery and donations from the Art Fund, Lord Duveen, and others, and presented through the Art Fund 1919, N03366
Plate 22

29
William Blake
British, 1757–1827
Dante and Virgil Approaching the Angel Who Guards the Entrance of Purgatory, 1824–27
Graphite, ink, and watercolor
52.7 × 37.3 cm (20¾ × 14 11/16 in.)
London, Tate, Purchased with the assistance of a special grant from the National Gallery and donations from the Art Fund, Lord Duveen, and others, and presented through the Art Fund 1919, N03367
Plate 23

30
William Blake
British, 1757–1827
Beatrice Addressing Dante from the Car, 1824–27
Ink and watercolor
37.2 × 52.7 cm (14⅝ × 20¾ in.)
London, Tate, Purchased with the assistance of a special grant from the National Gallery and donations from the Art Fund, Lord Duveen, and others, and presented through the Art Fund 1919, N03369
Plate 24

31
William Blake
British, 1757–1827
The Pit of Disease: The Falsifiers, 1826–27
Engraving
24 × 33.9 cm (9 7/16 × 13⅜ in.)
Collection of Robert N. Essick
Plate 25

32*
William Blake
British, 1757–1827
An Allegory of the Bible, about 1780
Graphite, ink, and watercolor
61.5 × 34.9 cm (24 3/16 × 13¾ in.)
London, Tate, Bequeathed by Miss Rachel M. Dyer 1969, T01128
Plate 26

33*
William Blake
British, 1757–1827
Lear and Cordelia in Prison, about 1779
Ink and watercolor
12.3 × 17.5 cm (4 13/16 × 6⅞ in.)
London, Tate, Bequeathed by Miss Alice G. E. Carthew 1940, N05189
Plate 27

34*
William Blake
British, 1757–1827
Pestilence, about 1780–84
Pen and watercolor
18.5 × 27.5 cm (7 5/16 × 10 13/16 in.)
Collection of Robert N. Essick
Plate 28

35*
William Blake
British, 1757–1827
Job, His Wife and His Friends: The Complaint of Job, about 1785
Ink and watercolor
31.1 × 45.1 cm (12¼ × 17¾ in.)
London, Tate, Bequeathed by Miss Alice G. E. Carthew 1940, N05200
Plate 29

36
William Blake
British, 1757–1827
Oberon, Titania and Puck with Fairies Dancing, about 1786
Watercolor and graphite
47.5 × 67.5 cm (18 11/16 × 26 9/16 in.)
London, Tate, Presented by Alfred A. de Pass in memory of his wife Ethel 1910, N02686
Plate 30

37*
William Blake
British, 1757–1827
The Penance of Jane Shore in St. Paul's Church, about 1793
Ink, watercolor, and gouache
24.5 × 29.5 cm (9⅝ × 11⅝ in.)
London, Tate, Presented by the executors of W. Graham Robertson through the Art Fund 1949, N05898

38
William Blake
British, 1757–1827
Christ Blessing the Little Children, 1799
Tempera on canvas
26 × 37.5 cm (10¼ × 14¾ in.)
London, Tate, Presented by the executors of W. Graham Robertson through the Art Fund 1949, N05893
Plate 31

39*
William Blake
British, 1757–1827
Moses Indignant at the Golden Calf, about 1799–1800
Tempera on canvas
38 × 26.6 cm (14 15/16 × 10½ in.)
London, Tate, Bequeathed by Ian L. Phillips 1986, T04134
Plate 32

40*
William Blake
British, 1757–1827
Bathsheba at the Bath, about 1799–1800
Tempera on canvas
26.3 × 37.6 cm (10⅜ × 14 13/16 in.)
London, Tate, Presented by the Art Fund 1914, N03007
Plate 33

41
William Blake
British, 1757–1827
The Body of Christ Borne to the Tomb, about 1799–1800
Tempera on canvas mounted onto cardboard
26.7 × 37.8 cm (10½ × 14⅞ in.)
London, Tate, Presented by Francis T. Palgrave 1884, N01164
Plate 34

42
William Blake
British, 1757–1827
The Body of Abel Found by Adam and Eve, about 1826
Ink, tempera, and gold on mahogany
32.5 × 43.3 cm (12 13/16 × 17 1/16 in.)
London, Tate, Bequeathed by W. Graham Robertson 1949, N05888
Plate 35

43
William Blake
British, 1757–1827
The Blasphemer, about 1800
Ink, graphite, and watercolor
38.4 × 34 cm (15⅛ × 13⅜ in.)
London, Tate, Bequeathed by Miss Alice G. E. Carthew 1940, N05195
Plate 36

44
William Blake
British, 1757–1827
Judas Betrays Him, about 1803–5
Ink, graphite, and watercolor
36.7 × 30.3 cm (14 7/16 × 11 15/16 in.)
London, Tate, Purchased with funds provided by the Patrons of British Art through the Tate Gallery Foundation 1992, T06606
Plate 37

45
William Blake
British, 1757–1827
The Crucifixion: "Behold Thy Mother," about 1805
Ink and watercolor
41.3 × 30 cm (16¼ × 11 13/16 in.)
London, Tate, Presented by the executors of W. Graham Robertson through the Art Fund 1949, N05895
Plate 38

46
William Blake
British, 1757–1827
The Entombment, about 1805
Ink and watercolor
41.7 × 31 cm (16 7/16 × 12 3/16 in.)
London, Tate, Presented by the executors of W. Graham Robertson through the Art Fund 1949, N05896
Plate 39

47
William Blake
British, 1757–1827
The Death of the Virgin, 1803
Watercolor
37.8 × 37.1 cm (14⅞ × 14⅝ in.)
London, Tate, Presented by the executors of W. Graham Robertson through the Art Fund 1949, N05899
Plate 40

48
William Blake
British, 1757–1827
The Bard, from Gray, 1809?
Tempera and gold on canvas
60 × 44.1 cm (23⅝ × 17⅜ in.)
London, Tate, Purchased 1920, N03551
Plate 41

49
William Blake
British, 1757–1827
Epitome of James Hervey's "Meditations among the Tombs," about 1820–25
Ink, watercolor, and gold paint
43.1 × 29.2 cm (16 15/16 × 11½ in.)
London, Tate, Presented by George Thomas Saul 1878, N02231
Plate 42

50
William Blake
British, 1757–1827
Winter, about 1820–25
Tempera on pine
90.2 × 29.7 cm (35½ × 11 11/16 in.)
London, Tate, Purchased 1979, T02387

51
William Blake
British, 1757–1827
Christ Appearing to the Apostles after the Resurrection, about 1795
Color print with ink, watercolor, and varnish
40.6 × 49.9 cm (16 × 19⅝ in.)
London, Tate, Bequeathed by W. Graham Robertson 1948, N05875
Plate 43

52
William Blake
British, 1757–1827
The Night of Enitharmon's Joy or *Hecate*, about 1795
Color print with ink, tempera, and watercolor
43.9 × 58.1 cm (17 5/16 × 22⅞ in.)
London, Tate, Presented by W. Graham Robertson 1939, N05056
Plate 44

53*
William Blake
British, 1757–1827
The Good and Evil Angels, 1795–about 1805
Color print with ink and watercolor
44.5 × 59.4 cm (17½ × 23⅜ in.)
London, Tate, Presented by W. Graham Robertson 1939, N05057
Plate 45

54
William Blake
British, 1757–1827
Nebuchadnezzar, 1795–about 1805
Color print with ink and watercolor
54.3 × 72.5 cm (21⅜ × 28½ in.)
London, Tate, Presented by W. Graham Robertson 1939, N05059
Plate 46

55*
William Blake
British, 1757–1827
God Judging Adam, 1795
Relief etching with ink and watercolor
43.2 × 53.5 cm (17 × 21⅛ in.)
London, Tate, Presented by W. Graham Robertson 1939, N05063
Plate 47

56
William Blake
British, 1757–1827
Satan Exulting over Eve, 1795
Color print with graphite, pen and black ink, and watercolor
42.5 × 53.5 cm (16¾ × 21 1/16 in.)
Los Angeles, The J. Paul Getty Museum, 84.GC.49
Plate 48

57
William Blake
British, 1757–1827
Genesis, First Title Page, about 1826–27
Graphite, pen, gouache, and watercolor
38.2 × 27.5 cm (15 1/16 × 10 13/16 in.)
San Marino, The Huntington Library, Art Museum, and Botanical Gardens, 000.32

58
William Blake
British, 1757–1827
Genesis, Second Title Page, about 1826–27
Graphite, pen, watercolor, and liquid gold
38 × 28 cm (14 15/16 × 11 in.)
San Marino, The Huntington Library, Art Museum, and Botanical Gardens, 000.33
Plate 49

59
William Blake
British, 1757–1827
Genesis: Creation of Adam, about 1826–27
Graphite, pen (?), and watercolor
37.8 × 27.5 cm (14⅞ × 10 13/16 in.)
San Marino, The Huntington Library, Art Museum, and Botanical Gardens, 000.36

60
William Blake
British, 1757–1827
Genesis: Adam and Eve in the Garden of Eden, about 1826–27
Graphite and pen or brush
38.2 × 28 cm ($15\frac{1}{16}$ × 11 in.)
San Marino, The Huntington Library, Art Museum, and Botanical Gardens, 000.37

61
William Blake
British, 1757–1827
Chaucers Canterbury Pilgrims, about 1810
Etching and engraving with watercolor
35.8 × 97 cm (14⅛ × $38\frac{3}{16}$ in.)
Collection of Robert N. Essick
Plate 50

62
William Blake
British, 1757–1827
Songs of Innocence and of Experience, Title Page, 1794/95
Relief etching with watercolor
11.2 × 7 cm (4⅜ × 2¾ in.) (plate)
17.6 × 11.4 cm ($6\frac{15}{16}$ × 4½ in.) (sheet)
San Marino, The Huntington Library, Art Museum, and Botanical Gardens, 54039.pl1
Plate 51

63
William Blake
British, 1757–1827
Songs of Innocence and of Experience, "Laughing Song," 1789
Relief etching with watercolor
11.1 × 6.7 cm (4⅜ × 2⅝ in.) (plate)
17.6 × 11.4 cm ($6\frac{15}{16}$ × 4½ in.) (sheet)
San Marino, The Huntington Library, Art Museum, and Botanical Gardens, 54039.pl9–10
Plate 52

64
William Blake
British, 1757–1827
Songs of Innocence and of Experience, "The Sick Rose," 1794/95
Relief etching with watercolor
11.1 × 6.8 cm (4⅜ × $2\frac{11}{16}$ in.) (plate)
17.6 × 11.4 cm ($6\frac{15}{16}$ × 4½ in.) (sheet)
San Marino, The Huntington Library, Art Museum, and Botanical Gardens, 54039.pl142–43
Plate 53

65
William Blake
British, 1757–1827
Songs of Innocence and of Experience, "The Fly," 1794/95
Relief etching with watercolor
11.8 × 7.3 cm (4⅝ ×2⅞ in.) (plate)
17.6 × 11.4 cm ($6\frac{15}{16}$ × 4½ in.) (sheet)
San Marino, The Huntington Library, Art Museum, and Botanical Gardens, 54039.pl148–49
Plate 54

66
William Blake
British, 1757–1827
Songs of Innocence and of Experience, "The Tyger," 1794
Color printed relief etching with watercolor
11.1 × 6.4 cm (4⅜ × 2½ in.) (plate)
18.4 × 12.1 cm (7¼ × 4¾ in.) (sheet)
New Haven, Yale Center for British Art, Paul Mellon Collection, B1978.43.1573
Plate 55

67
William Blake
British, 1757–1827
Songs of Innocence, "The Shepherd," 1789
Relief etching with pen and ink and watercolor
11.1 × 7 cm (4⅜ × 2¾ in.)
Collection of Robert N. Essick
Plate 56

68
William Blake
British, 1757–1827
Catherine Blake, about 1805
Graphite
28.6 × 22.1 cm (11¼ × $8\frac{11}{16}$ in.)
London, Tate, Bequeathed by Miss Alice G. E. Carthew 1940, N05188
Plate 57

69
William Blake
British, 1757–1827
First Book of Urizen, plate 15, 1796–about 1818
Relief etching with paint, watercolor, and ink
9 × 15 cm (3½ × 5⅞ in.) (plate)
25.9 × 18.2 cm ($10\frac{3}{16}$ × $7\frac{3}{16}$ in.) (sheet)
London, Tate, Purchased with funds provided by the Art Fund, Tate Members, Tate Patrons, Tate Fund, and individual donors 2009, T12997
Plate 58

70
William Blake
British, 1757–1827
First Book of Urizen, plate 21, 1796–about 1818
Relief etching with paint, watercolor, and ink
10.7 × 10.3 cm ($4\frac{3}{16}$ × $4\frac{1}{16}$ in.) (plate)
27 × 18.4 cm (10⅝ × 7¼ in.) (sheet)
London, Tate, Purchased with funds provided by the Art Fund, Tate Members, Tate Patrons, Tate Fund, and individual donors 2009, T12999
Plate 59

71
William Blake
British, 1757–1827
The Marriage of Heaven and Hell, plate 16, 1796–about 1818
Relief etching with paint, watercolor, and ink
6.4 × 10.4 cm (2½ × $4\frac{1}{16}$ in.) (plate)
25.9 × 18.7 cm ($10\frac{3}{16}$ × 7⅜ in.) (sheet)
London, Tate, Purchased with funds provided by the Art Fund, Tate Members, Tate Patrons, Tate Fund, and individual donors 2009, T13001
Plate 60

72
William Blake
British, 1757–1827
First Book of Urizen, plate 6, 1796–about 1818
Relief etching with paint, watercolor, and ink
25 × 18.7 cm ($9\frac{13}{16}$ × 7⅜ in.) (sheet)
London, Tate, Purchased with funds provided by the Art Fund, Tate Members, Tate Patrons, Tate Fund, and individual donors 2009, T13002
Plate 61

73
William Blake
British, 1757–1827
First Book of Urizen, plate 10, 1796–about 1818
Relief etching with paint, watercolor, and ink
10.2 × 11 cm (4 × $4\frac{5}{16}$ in.) (plate)
26.6 × 18.5 cm (10½ × $7\frac{5}{16}$ in.) (sheet)
London, Tate, Purchased with funds provided by the Art Fund, Tate Members, Tate Patrons, Tate Fund, and individual donors 2009, T13003
Plate 62

74
William Blake
British, 1757–1827
First Book of Urizen, plate 11, 1796–about 1818
Relief etching with paint, watercolor, and ink
15.5 × 10.3 cm (6⅛ × $4\frac{1}{16}$ in.) (plate)
25.7 × 18.4 cm (10⅛ × 7¼ in.) (sheet)
London, Tate, Purchased with funds provided by the Art Fund, Tate Members, Tate Patrons, Tate Fund, and individual donors 2009, T13004
Plate 63

75
Benjamin West
American, 1738–1820
The Fright of Astyanax (Hector Bidding Farewell to Andromache), 1797
Pen and brown ink, brown wash, and blue and white gouache on brown prepared paper
31.8 × 46 cm (12½ × 18⅛ in.)
Los Angeles, The J. Paul Getty Museum, 84.GG.722
Plate 64

76
James Barry
Irish, 1741–1806
Study for "Philoctetes on the Island of Lemnos," 1770
Ink and watercolor
21 × 28.6 cm (8¼ × 11¼ in.)
London, Tate, Purchased as part of the Oppé Collection with assistance from the National Lottery through the Heritage Lottery Fund 1996, T08127
Plate 65

77
Henry Fuseli
Swiss, 1741–1825
An Old Man Murdered by Three Younger Men, early 1770s
Pen and black ink with gray wash
42.2 × 47.6 cm (16⅝ × 18¾ in.)
Los Angeles, The J. Paul Getty Museum, 84.GG.711
Plate 66

78
Henry Fuseli
Swiss, 1741–1825
Siegfried About to Deny an Oath That Brunhild Had Been His Paramour, 1805
Graphite and watercolor
25.5 × 41.5 cm (10 1/16 × 16 5/16 in.)
London, Tate, Purchased as part of the Oppé Collection with assistance from the National Lottery through the Heritage Lottery Fund 1996, T08133
Plate 67

79*
Henry Fuseli
Swiss, 1741–1825
Self-Portrait as a Faun, n.d.
Graphite and chalk
32.2 × 42.7 cm (12 11/16 × 16 13/16 in.)
London, Tate, Purchased as part of the Oppé Collection with assistance from the National Lottery through the Heritage Lottery Fund 1996, T08879

80*
Henry Fuseli
Swiss, 1741–1825
A Sheet of Studies: Three Figures of Recumbent Women and a Head of a Man, n.d.
Ink, graphite, watercolor, and gouache
19 × 23.2 cm (7 1/2 × 9 1/8 in.)
London, Tate, Purchased as part of the Oppé Collection with assistance from the National Lottery through the Heritage Lottery Fund 1996, T08912

81
John Flaxman
British, 1755–1826
Alcestis and Admetus, 1789
Ink, watercolor, and graphite
23.8 × 41.7 cm (9 3/8 × 16 7/16 in.)
London, Tate, Purchased as part of the Oppé Collection with assistance from the National Lottery through the Heritage Lottery Fund 1996, T08234
Plate 68

82*
George Romney
British, 1734–1802
John Howard Visiting a Lazaretto, about 1791–92
Ink and graphite
34.3 × 48.9 cm (13 1/2 × 19 1/4 in.)
London, Tate, Purchased 1982, T03547

83
George Romney
British, 1734–1802
The Tempest, Act I, about 1787
Pencil, pen, and gray wash
33.7 × 48.9 cm (13 1/4 × 19 1/4 in.)
Collection of Robert N. Essick
Plate 69

84*
James Gillray
British, 1757–1815
The Royal Academy, 1786
Etching, with watercolor
39 × 27.2 cm (15 3/8 × 10 11/16 in.)
New Haven, Yale Center for British Art, Paul Mellon Collection, B1981.25.1034

85
James Gillray
British, 1757–1815
Presages of the Millenium, 1795
Etching and aquatint with watercolor
33 × 37.6 cm (13 × 14 13/16 in.)
New Haven, Yale Center for British Art, Paul Mellon Collection, B1981.25.916
Plate 70

86
James Gillray
British, 1757–1815
The Death of the Great Wolf, 1795
Etching and stipple engraving with watercolor
34 × 44.3 cm (13 3/8 × 17 7/16 in.)
New Haven, Yale Center for British Art, Paul Mellon Collection, B1981.25.906
Plate 71

87*
James Gillray
British, 1757–1815
Hyde Park; Sunday, or *Both Hemispheres of the World in a Sweat*, 1789
Etching with watercolor
20.3 × 32.7 cm (8 × 12 7/8 in.)
New Haven, Yale Center for British Art, Paul Mellon Collection, B1981.25.1093

88*
William Blake
British, 1757–1827
Los and Orc, about 1792–93
Ink and watercolor
21.7 × 29.5 cm (8 9/16 × 11 5/8 in.)
London, Tate, Presented by Mrs. Jane Samuel in memory of her husband 1962, T00547

89
William Blake
British, 1757–1827
America a Prophecy, plate 1, 1793
Color-printed relief etching in brown with pen and black ink and watercolor
23.5 × 16.8 cm (9 1/4 × 6 5/8 in.) (plate)
36.8 × 26.7 cm (14 1/2 × 10 1/2 in.) (sheet)
New Haven, Yale Center for British Art, Paul Mellon Collection, B1992.8.2(1)
Plate 72

90
William Blake
British, 1757–1827
America a Prophecy, plate 2, 1793
Color-printed relief etching in blue with pen and black ink and watercolor
23.5 × 16.5 cm (9 1/4 × 6 1/2 in.) (plate)
36.8 × 26.7 cm (14 1/2 × 10 1/2 in.) (sheet)
New Haven, Yale Center for British Art, Paul Mellon Collection, B1992.8.2(2)
Plate 73

91
William Blake
British, 1757–1827
America a Prophecy, plate 3, 1793
Color-printed relief etching in blue with pen and black ink and watercolor
23.2 × 16.5 cm (9 1/8 × 6 1/2 in.) (plate)
36.8 × 26.7 cm (14 1/2 × 10 1/2 in.) (sheet)
New Haven, Yale Center for British Art, Paul Mellon Collection, B1992.8.2(3)
Plate 74

92
William Blake
British, 1757–1827
America a Prophecy, plate 4, 1793
Relief etching printed in blue with pen and black ink and watercolor
21.6 × 17.1 cm (8 1/2 × 6 3/4 in.) (plate)
36.8 × 26.7 cm (14 1/2 × 10 1/2 in.) (sheet)
New Haven, Yale Center for British Art, Paul Mellon Collection, B1992.8.2(4)
Plate 75

93
William Blake
British, 1757–1827
America a Prophecy, plate 5, 1793
Relief etching printed in blue with pen and black ink and watercolor
23.5 × 16.8 cm (9 1/4 × 6 5/8 in.) (plate)
36.8 × 26.7 cm (14 1/2 × 10 1/2 in.) (sheet)
New Haven, Yale Center for British Art, Paul Mellon Collection, B1992.8.2(5)
Plate 76

94
William Blake
British, 1757–1827
America a Prophecy, plate 6, 1793
Relief etching printed in blue with pen and black ink and watercolor
23.2 × 16.5 cm (9 1/8 × 6 1/2 in.) (plate)
36.8 × 26.7 cm (14 1/2 × 10 1/2 in.) (sheet)
New Haven, Yale Center for British Art, Paul Mellon Collection, B1992.8.2(6)
Plate 77

95
William Blake
British, 1757–1827
America a Prophecy, plate 7, 1793
Relief etching printed in blue with pen and black ink and watercolor
23.5 × 16.5 cm (9 1/4 × 6 1/2 in.) (plate)
36.8 × 26.7 cm (14 1/2 × 10 1/2 in.) (sheet)
New Haven, Yale Center for British Art, Paul Mellon Collection, B1992.8.2(7)
Plate 78

96
William Blake
British, 1757–1827
America a Prophecy, plate 8, 1793
Color-printed relief etching in green black with pen and black ink and watercolor
23.8 × 16.8 cm (9 3/8 × 6 5/8 in.) (plate)
36.8 × 26.7 cm (14 1/2 × 10 1/2 in.) (sheet)
New Haven, Yale Center for British Art, Paul Mellon Collection, B1992.8.2(8)
Plate 79

97
William Blake
British, 1757–1827
America a Prophecy, plate 9, 1793
Printed relief etching in blue with pen and black ink and watercolor
23.8 × 17.1 cm (9⅜ × 6¾ in.) (plate)
36.8 × 26.7 cm (14½ × 10½ in.) (sheet)
New Haven, Yale Center for British Art, Paul Mellon Collection, B1992.8.2(9)
Plate 80

98
William Blake
British, 1757–1827
America a Prophecy, plate 10, 1793
Color-printed relief etching in green black with pen and black ink and watercolor
23.8 × 16.8 cm (9⅜ × 6⅝ in.) (plate)
36.8 × 26.7 cm (14½ × 10½ in.) (sheet)
New Haven, Yale Center for British Art, Paul Mellon Collection, B1992.8.2(10)
Plate 81

99
William Blake
British, 1757–1827
America a Prophecy, plate 11, 1793
Color-printed relief etching in green black with pen and black ink and watercolor
23.5 × 17.1 cm (9¼ × 6¾ in.) (plate)
36.8 × 26.7 cm (14½ × 10½ in.) (sheet)
New Haven, Yale Center for British Art, Paul Mellon Collection, B1992.8.2(11)
Plate 82

100
William Blake
British, 1757–1827
America a Prophecy, plate 12, 1793
Relief etching printed in blue with pen and black ink and watercolor
23.5 × 17.1 cm (9¼ × 6¾ in.) (plate)
36.8 × 26.7 cm (14½ × 10½ in.) (sheet)
New Haven, Yale Center for British Art, Paul Mellon Collection, B1992.8.2(12)
Plate 83

101
William Blake
British, 1757–1827
America a Prophecy, plate 13, 1793
Color-printed relief etching in blue with pen and black ink and watercolor
23.5 × 17.1 cm (9¼ × 6¾ in.) (plate)
36.8 × 26.7 cm (14½ × 10½ in.) (sheet)
New Haven, Yale Center for British Art, Paul Mellon Collection, B1992.8.2(13)
Plate 84

102
William Blake
British, 1757–1827
America a Prophecy, plate 14, 1793
Color-printed relief etching in green black with pen and black ink and watercolor
23.8 × 17.5 cm (9⅜ × 6⅞ in.) (plate)
36.8 × 26.7 cm (14½ × 10½ in.) (sheet)
New Haven, Yale Center for British Art, Paul Mellon Collection, B1992.8.2(14)
Plate 85

103
William Blake
British, 1757–1827
America a Prophecy, plate 15, 1793
Relief etching printed in blue with pen and black ink and watercolor
23.8 × 17.5 cm (9⅜ × 6⅞ in.) (plate)
36.8 × 26.7 cm (14½ × 10½ in.) (sheet)
New Haven, Yale Center for British Art, Paul Mellon Collection, B1992.8.2(15)
Plate 86

104
William Blake
British, 1757–1827
America a Prophecy, plate 16, 1793
Color-printed relief etching in green black with pen and black ink and watercolor
23.8 × 17.1 cm (9⅜ × 6¾ in.) (plate)
36.8 × 26.7 cm (14½ × 10½ in.) (sheet)
New Haven, Yale Center for British Art, Paul Mellon Collection, B1992.8.2(16)
Plate 87

105
William Blake
British, 1757–1827
America a Prophecy, plate 17, 1793
Relief etching printed in blue with pen and black ink and watercolor
23.8 × 17.1 cm (9⅜ × 6¾ in.) (plate)
36.8 × 26.7 cm (14½ × 10½ in.) (sheet)
New Haven, Yale Center for British Art, Paul Mellon Collection, B1992.8.2(17)
Plate 88

106
William Blake
British, 1757–1827
America a Prophecy, plate 18, 1793
Relief etching printed in blue with pen and black ink and watercolor
24.1 × 17.1 cm (9½ × 6¾ in.) (plate)
36.8 × 26.7 cm (14½ × 10½ in.) (sheet)
New Haven, Yale Center for British Art, Paul Mellon Collection, B1992.8.2(18)
Plate 89

107
William Blake
British, 1757–1827
"The Ancient of Days" from *Europe a Prophecy*, 1794, printed 1795
Relief etching printed in dark brown, color printing, with watercolor and oil paint
23.2 x 16.8 cm (9⅛ x 6⅝ in.) (plate)
37.5 x 26.7 cm (14¾ x 10½ in.) (sheet)
New Haven, Yale Center for British Art, Paul Mellon Collection, B1992.8.4V
Plate 90

108
William Blake
British, 1757–1827
Visions of the Daughters of Albion, Frontispiece, about 1795
Relief etching with ink and watercolor
17 × 12 cm (6¹¹⁄₁₆ × 4¾ in.)
London, Tate, Purchased with the assistance of a special grant from the National Gallery and donations from the Art Fund, Lord Duveen, and others, and presented through the Art Fund 1919, N03373
Plate 91

109
William Blake
British, 1757–1827
The Song of Los, plate 1, 1795
Color print from copperplate
23.4 × 17.3 cm (9¼ × 6¹³⁄₁₆ in.) (plate)
36.4 × 26 cm (14⁵⁄₁₆ × 10¼ in.) (sheet)
San Marino, The Huntington Library, Art Museum, and Botanical Gardens, 54043
Plate 92

110*
John Linnell
British, 1792–1882
Portrait of John Varley, 1824
Watercolor over graphite
37.5 × 29.5 cm (14¾ × 11⅝ in.)
Los Angeles, The J. Paul Getty Museum, Purchased with funds provided by the Disegno Group, 2020.21
Plate 93

111
William Blake
British, 1757–1827
Merlin from the Visionary Heads series, about 1819–20
Graphite
24.3 × 18.7 cm (9⁹⁄₁₆ × 7⅜ in.)
Collection of Robert N. Essick
Plate 94

112*
William Blake
British, 1757–1827
Queen Eleanor from the Visionary Heads series, about 1819–20
Graphite
19.7 × 15.5 cm (7¾ × 6⅛ in.)
San Marino, The Huntington Library, Art Museum, and Botanical Gardens, 000.46
Plate 95

113*
William Blake
British, 1757–1827
Saladin and the Assassin from the Visionary Heads series, about 1819–20
Graphite
31.3 × 20 cm (12⁵⁄₁₆ × 7⅞ in.)
San Marino, The Huntington Library, Art Museum, and Botanical Gardens, 000.49

114
William Blake
British, 1757–1827
The Head of the Ghost of a Flea from the Visionary Heads series, about 1819
Graphite
18.9 × 15.3 cm (7⁷⁄₁₆ × 6 in.)
London, Tate, Bequeathed by Miss Alice G. E. Carthew 1940, N05184
Plate 96

115
William Blake
British, 1757–1827
The Ghost of a Flea, about 1819–20
Tempera and gold on mahogany
21.4 × 16.2 cm (8⁷⁄₁₆ × 6⅜ in.)
London, Tate, Bequeathed by W. Graham Robertson 1949, N05889
Plate 97

116
William Blake
British, 1757–1827
Milton a Poem, plate 1, 1804–about 1811
White line etching with watercolor
16 × 11.2 cm (6⁵⁄₁₆ × 4⅜ in.) (plate)
23.3 × 17 cm (9³⁄₁₆ × 6¹¹⁄₁₆ in.) (sheet)
San Marino, The Huntington Library, Art Museum, and Botanical Gardens, 54041.pl1
Plate 98

117
William Blake
British, 1757–1827
Milton a Poem, plate 2, 1804–about 1811
Relief etching with watercolor
16 × 11.2 cm (6⁵⁄₁₆ × 4⅜ in.) (plate)
23.3 × 17 cm (9³⁄₁₆ × 6¹¹⁄₁₆ in.) (sheet)
San Marino, The Huntington Library, Art Museum, and Botanical Gardens, 54041.pl2
Plate 99

118
William Blake
British, 1757–1827
Milton a Poem, plate 15, 1804–about 1811
Relief etching with watercolor
16 × 11 cm (6⁵⁄₁₆ × 4⁵⁄₁₆ in.) (plate)
23.3 × 17 cm (9³⁄₁₆ × 6¹¹⁄₁₆ in.) (sheet)
San Marino, The Huntington Library, Art Museum, and Botanical Gardens, 54041.pl25
Plate 100

119
William Blake
British, 1757–1827
Milton a Poem, plate 29, 1804–about 1811
Relief etching with watercolor
16 × 11 cm (6⁵⁄₁₆ × 4⁵⁄₁₆ in.) (plate)
23.3 × 17 cm (9³⁄₁₆ × 6¹¹⁄₁₆ in.) (sheet)
San Marino, The Huntington Library, Art Museum, and Botanical Gardens, 54041.pl29
Plate 101

120
William Blake
British, 1757–1827
Landscape near Felpham, about 1800
Graphite and watercolor
23.7 × 34.3 cm (9⁵⁄₁₆ × 13½ in.)
London, Tate, Presented by Mrs. John Richmond 1922, A00041
Plate 102

121
William Blake
British, 1757–1827
Jerusalem, plate 1, Frontispiece, 1804–20
Relief etching printed in orange with pen and black ink, watercolor, and gold
22.3 × 16.2 cm (8¾ × 6⅜ in.) (plate)
34.3 × 26.4 cm (13½ × 10⅜ in.) (sheet)
New Haven, Yale Center for British Art, Paul Mellon Collection, B1992.8.1(1)
Plate 103

122
William Blake
British, 1757–1827
Jerusalem, plate 2, Title Page, 1804–20
Relief etching printed in orange with pen and black ink, watercolor, and gold
22.5 × 16.2 cm (8⅞ × 6⅜ in.) (plate)
34.3 × 26.4 cm (13½ × 10⅜ in.) (sheet)
New Haven, Yale Center for British Art, Paul Mellon Collection, B1992.8.1(2)
Plate 104

123
William Blake
British, 1757–1827
Jerusalem, plate 25, 1804–20
Relief etching printed in orange with pen and black ink, watercolor, and gold
22.2 × 16.2 cm (8¾ × 6⅜ in.) (plate)
34.3 × 26.4 cm (13½ × 10⅜ in.) (sheet)
New Haven, Yale Center for British Art, Paul Mellon Collection, B1992.8.1(25)
Plate 105

124
William Blake
British, 1757–1827
Jerusalem, plate 26, 1804–20
Relief etching printed in orange with pen and black ink and watercolor
16.5 × 22.5 cm (6½ × 8⅞ in.) (plate)
26.4 × 34.3 cm (10⅜ × 13½ in.) (sheet)
New Haven, Yale Center for British Art, Paul Mellon Collection, B1992.8.1(26)
Plate 106

125
William Blake
British, 1757–1827
Jerusalem, plate 41, 1804–20
Relief etching printed in orange with pen and black ink and watercolor
22.5 × 16.2 cm (8⅞ × 6⅜ in.) (plate)
34.3 × 26.4 cm (13½ × 10⅜ in.) (sheet)
New Haven, Yale Center for British Art, Paul Mellon Collection, B1992.8.1(41)
Plate 107

126
William Blake
British, 1757–1827
Jerusalem, plate 78, 1804–20
Relief etching printed in orange with pen and black ink and watercolor
21 × 16.2 cm (8¼ × 6⅜ in.) (plate)
34.3 × 26.4 cm (13½ × 10⅜ in.) (sheet)
New Haven, Yale Center for British Art, Paul Mellon Collection, B1992.8.1(78)
Plate 108

127
William Blake
British, 1757–1827
Jerusalem, plate 81, 1804–20
Relief etching printed in orange with pen and black ink, watercolor, and gold
21.2 × 14.9 cm (8⅜ × 5⅞ in.) (plate)
34.3 × 26.4 cm (13½ × 10⅜ in.) (sheet)
New Haven, Yale Center for British Art, Paul Mellon Collection, B1992.8.1(81)
Plate 109

128
William Blake
British, 1757–1827
Jerusalem, plate 84, 1804–20
Relief etching printed in orange with pen and black ink, watercolor, and gold
21 × 15 cm (8¼ × 5⅞ in.) (plate)
34.3 × 26.4 cm (13½ × 10⅜ in.) (sheet)
New Haven, Yale Center for British Art, Paul Mellon Collection, B1992.8.1(84)
Plate 110

129
William Blake
British, 1757–1827
Jerusalem, plate 97, 1804–20
Relief etching printed in orange with pen and black ink, watercolor, and gold
21 × 15 cm (8¼ × 5⅞ in.) (plate)
34.3 × 26.4 cm (13½ × 10⅜ in.) (sheet)
New Haven, Yale Center for British Art, Paul Mellon Collection, B1992.8.1(97)
Plate 111

130
William Blake
British, 1757–1827
Jerusalem, plate 100, 1804–20
Relief etching printed in orange with pen and black ink, watercolor, and gold
22.5 × 14.9 cm (8⅞ × 5⅞ in.) (plate)
26.4 × 34.3 cm (10⅜ × 13½ in.) (sheet)
New Haven, Yale Center for British Art, Paul Mellon Collection, B1992.8.1(100)
Plate 112

131
William Blake
British, 1757–1827
Joseph of Arimathea among the Rocks of Albion, after a figure in Michelangelo's *Crucifixion of Saint Peter*, 1820 or later
Etching and engraving with burnishing
22.9 × 11.9 cm (9 × 4¹¹⁄₁₆ in.)
Collection of Robert N. Essick
Plate 113

132*
William Blake
British, 1757–1827
Copy of the *Laocoön*, for Rees's *Cyclopaedia*, 1815
Graphite
32.1 × 22.9 cm (12⅝ × 9 in.)
New Haven, Yale Center for British Art, Paul Mellon Fund, B1985.14

133
William Blake
British, 1757–1827
Laocoön, image about 1815; inscription about 1826–27
Etching and engraving with burnishing
26.2 × 21.6 cm (10⁵⁄₁₆ × 8½ in.)
Collection of Robert N. Essick
Plate 114

Suggested Further Reading

Ackroyd, Peter. *Blake*. London: Sinclair-Stevenson, 1995.

Bentley, Gerald Eades, Jr. *Blake Records*. 2nd ed. New Haven and London: Published for the Paul Mellon Centre for Studies in British Art by Yale University Press, 2004.

—. *The Stranger from Paradise: A Biography of William Blake*. New Haven: Published for the Paul Mellon Centre for Studies in British Art by Yale University Press, 2001.

Bindman, David. *Blake as an Artist*. Oxford: Phaidon; New York: E. P. Dutton, 1977.

—. *The Complete Graphic Works of William Blake*. London: Thames & Hudson, 1978.

—. *The Shadow of the Guillotine: Britain and the French Revolution*. London: British Museum Publications, 1989.

—. *William Blake: His Art and Times*. London: Thames & Hudson for the Yale Center for British Art (New Haven) and the Art Gallery of Ontario, 1982.

—, ed. *The Complete Illuminated Books*. 6 vols. London: Thames & Hudson, 2000.

—, ed. *The Divine Comedy: William Blake*. Paris: Biliothèque de l'Image, 2000.

Blunt, Anthony. *The Art of William Blake*. London: Oxford University Press, 1959.

Brewer, John. *The Pleasures of the Imagination: English Culture in the Eighteenth Century*. New York: Farrar, Straus and Giroux, 1997.

Butlin, Martin. *The Paintings and Drawings of William Blake*. 2 vols. New Haven and London: Published for the Paul Mellon Centre for Studies in British Art by Yale University Press, 1981.

Clark, Steve, and David Worrall, eds. *Blake, Nation and Empire*. Basingstoke and New York: Palgrave Macmillan, 2006.

Connolly, Tristanne J. *William Blake and the Body*. Basingstoke and New York: Palgrave Macmillan, 2002.

Craske, Matthew. *Art in Europe 1700–1830: A History of the Visual Arts in an Era of Unprecedented Urban Economic Growth*. Oxford: Oxford University Press, 1997.

Damon, Samuel Foster. *A Blake Dictionary: The Ideas and Symbols of William Blake*. Annotated by Morris Eaves. London: Thames & Hudson, 1979.

Damrosch, Leopold, Jr. *Eternity's Sunrise: The Imaginative World of William Blake*. New Haven and London: Yale University Press, 2015.

—. *Symbol and Truth in Blake's Myth*. Princeton: Princeton University Press, 1980.

Donald, Diana. *The Age of Caricature: Satirical Prints in the Reign of George III*. New Haven and London: Published for the Paul Mellon Centre for Studies in British Art by Yale University Press, 1996.

Eaves, Morris. *The Counter-Arts Conspiracy: Art and Industry in the Age of Blake*. Ithaca: Cornell University Press, 1992.

—. *William Blake's Theory of Art*. Princeton: Princeton University Press, 1982.

—, ed. *The Cambridge Companion to William Blake*. Cambridge: Cambridge University Press, 2003.

Eaves, Morris, Robert N. Essick, and Joseph Viscomi. "The William Blake Archive." www.blakearchive.org/

Erdman, David V. *The Illuminated Blake: William Blake's Complete Illuminated Works with a Plate-by-Plate Commentary*. New York: Dover Publications, 1992.

—. *Blake: Prophet against Empire: A Poet's Interpretation of the History of His Own Times*. Princeton: Princeton University Press, 1954.

—, ed. *The Complete Poetry and Prose of William Blake*. With commentary by Harold Bloom. Berkeley and Los Angeles: University of California Press, 1982.

Essick, Robert N. *The Separate Plates of William Blake: A Catalogue*. Princeton: Princeton University Press, 1983.

—. *William Blake, Printmaker*. Princeton: Princeton University Press, 1980.

—. *William Blake's Commercial Book Illustrations*. Oxford: Clarendon Press; New York: Oxford University Press, 1991.

—, ed. *William Blake: Images and Texts*. San Marino, CA: Huntington Library, 1997.

Fenton, James. *School of Genius: A History of the Royal Academy of Arts*. London: Royal Academy of Arts, 2006.

Ferber, Michael. *The Social Vision of William Blake*. Princeton: Princeton University Press, 1985.

Fordham, Douglas. *British Art and the Seven Years' War: Allegiance and Autonomy*. Philadelphia: University of Pennsylvania Press, 2010.

Frye, Northrop. *Fearful Symmetry: A Study of William Blake*. Princeton: Princeton University Press, 1947.

Gilchrist, Alexander. *Life of William Blake, "Pictor Ignotus."* 2 vols. London and Cambridge: Macmillan, 1863.

Hoock, Holger. *The King's Artists: The Royal Academy of Arts and the Politics of British Culture, 1760–1840*. Oxford: Clarendon Press; New York: Oxford University Press, 2003.

Keynes, Geoffrey. *The Tempera Paintings of William Blake*. London: Arts Council of Great Britain, 1951.

—, ed. *Blake: Complete Writings with Variant Readings*. Reproduced with corrections. Oxford: Oxford University Press, 1979.

—, ed. *The Letters of William Blake*. 3rd ed. Oxford: Oxford University Press, 1980.

Makdisi, Saree. *Reading William Blake*. Cambridge: Cambridge University Press, 2015.

—. *William Blake and the Impossible History of the 1790s*. Chicago and London: The University of Chicago Press, 2003.

Matthews, Susan. *Blake, Sexuality, and Bourgeois Politeness*. Cambridge: Cambridge University Press, 2011.

Mee, Jon. *Dangerous Enthusiasm: William Blake and the Culture of Radicalism in the 1790s*. Oxford: Clarendon Press, 1992.

Mitchell, William J. T. *Blake's Composite Art: A Study of the Illuminated Poetry*. Princeton: Princeton University Press, 1978.

Myrone, Martin. *Gothic Nightmares: Fuseli, Blake, and the Romantic Imagination*. London: Tate Publishing, 2006.

Myrone, Martin, and Amy Concannon, with an afterword by Alan Moore. *William Blake*. London: Tate Publishing, 2019.

Philipps, Michael. *William Blake: Apprentice and Master*. Oxford: Ashmolean, 2014.

Rix, Robert. *William Blake and the Cultures of Radical Christianity*. Aldershot: Ashgate, 2006.

Rosenblum, Robert. *Transformations in Late Eighteenth Century Art*. Princeton: Princeton University Press, 1974.

Solkin, David H. *Art in Britain: 1660–1815*. New Haven and London: Yale University Press and Paul Mellon Centre for Studies in British Art, 2015.

—. *Painting out of the Ordinary: Modernity and the Art of Everyday Life in Early Nineteenth-Century Britain*. New Haven: Yale University Press, 2008.

—, ed. *Art on the Line: The Royal Academy Exhibitions at Somerset House, 1780–1836*. New Haven and London: Published for the Paul Mellon Centre for Studies in British Art and the Courtauld Institute Gallery by Yale University Press, 2001.

Townsend, Joyce H., ed. *William Blake: The Painter at Work*. London: Tate Publishing; Princeton: Princeton University Press, 2003.

Viscomi, Joseph. *Blake and the Idea of the Book*. Princeton: Princeton University Press, 1993.

Warner, Janet. *Blake and the Language of Art*. Kingston: McGill-Queen's University Press; Gloucester: Alan Sutton, 1984.

Index

Page numbers in italics indicate illustrations.

This publication is issued on the occasion of the exhibition *William Blake: Visionary*, on view at the J. Paul Getty Museum at the Getty Center, Los Angeles, from October 17, 2023, to January 14, 2024. The exhibition, originally planned for 2020, was postponed due to the COVID-19 pandemic.

This exhibition was organized by the J. Paul Getty Museum in cooperation with Tate.

The exhibition is supported by the Getty Patron Program. The hospitality partner for the exhibition is Hilton.

Third printing

Published by the J. Paul Getty Museum, Los Angeles
Getty Publications
1200 Getty Center Drive, Suite 500
Los Angeles, CA 90049-1682
getty.edu/publications

Ruth Evans Lane, *Editor*
Victoria Barry and Alana Enriquez, *Editorial Interns*
Kurt Hauser, *Designer*
Suzanne Watson, *Production*
Nina Damavandi, *Image and Rights Acquisition*

Distributed in the United States and Canada by the University of Chicago Press
Distributed outside the United States and Canada by Yale University Press, London

Printed by Conti Tipocolor s.p.a. / Italy
Color separations by Professional Graphics, Rockford, Illinois

Library of Congress Cataloging-in-Publication Data

Names: Blake, William, 1757-1827, artist. | Adam, Edina, writer of supplementary textual content. | Brooks, Julian, 1969- writer of supplementary textual content. | Hargraves, Matthew, 1978- writer of supplementary textual content. | J. Paul Getty Museum, issuing body, host institution.
Title: William Blake : visionary / Edina Adam with Julian Brooks and an essay by Matthew Hargraves.
Description: Los Angeles : The J. Paul Getty Museum, [2020] | "This publication is issued on the occasion of the exhibition William Blake, on view at the J. Paul Getty Museum at the Getty Center, Los Angeles, from July 21 to October 11, 2020"—Colophon. | Includes bibliographical references and index. | Summary: "This exhibition catalogue provides a comprehensive survey of the artwork of William Blake and includes essays on Blake's influences and collecting in America" —Provided by publisher.
Identifiers: LCCN 2019055953 | ISBN 9781606066423 (hardcover)
Subjects: LCSH: Blake, William, 1757-1827—Exhibitions. | LCGFT: Exhibition catalogs.
Classification: LCC N6797.B57 A4 2020 | DDC 709.2—dc23
LC record available at https://lccn.loc.gov/2019055953

All titles and quotations by William Blake follow his spelling and punctuation.

Front cover: William Blake, *The Song of Los* (detail, plate 92)

Back cover: William Blake, *Self-Portrait* (plate 1); William Blake, *Milton a Poem* (detail, plate 98)

Illustration Credits

Every effort has been made to contact the owners and photographers of objects reproduced here whose names do not appear in the captions or in the illustration credits listed below. Anyone having further information concerning copyright holders is asked to contact Getty Publications so this information can be included in future printings.

Pp. 1, 5, 8, 66, 104; Plates 3, 17–24, 26, 27, 29–47, 57–63, 65, 67, 68, 91, 96, 97, 102: Photo © Tate

Pp. 2–3, 5, 18, 28, 92, 108, 114, 140; Fig. 12; Plates 55, 70–90, 103–12: Yale Center for British Art

Pp. 4, 6, 10, front cover, back cover; Plates 1, 4–10, 25, 28, 50–54, 56, 69, 92, 94, 98–101, 113, 114: The Huntington Library, San Marino, California

P. 38; Plates 11–16, 49, 95: Courtesy of the Huntington Art Museum, San Marino, California

Figs. 1, 3: © Royal Academy of Arts, London

Figs. 2, 4, 7, 8: © The Trustees of the British Museum / Art Resource, NY

Fig. 5: Rijksmuseum, Amsterdam

Fig. 6: The Bodleian Library, Oxford, Gough Maps 225, fol. 202

Fig. 9: Photo © 2020 Museum of Fine Arts, Boston

Plate 2: Los Angeles, Getty Research Institute (92-B10032)